THE JERVIS EFFECT

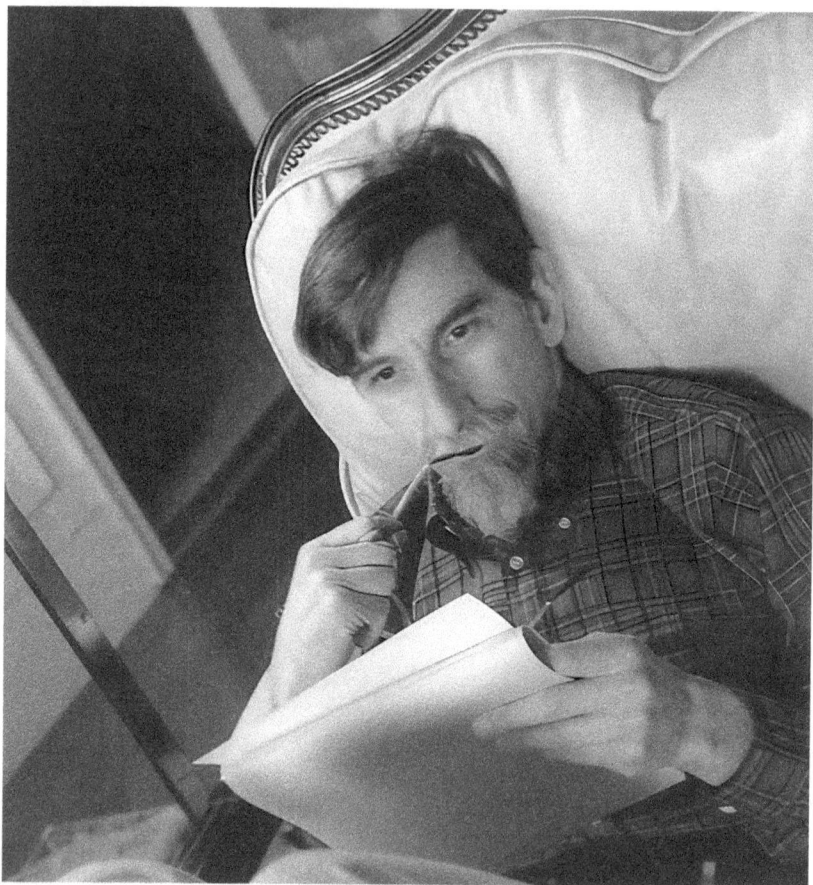

Robert Jervis reading at home in New York in the 1980s. He had no desk at home because he dictated his work while pacing.

Permission granted by Kathe Jervis.

THE JERVIS EFFECT

THE SCHOLARSHIP AND LEGACY
OF ROBERT JERVIS

EDITED BY
RICHARD H. IMMERMAN,
STACIE E. GODDARD,
AND DIANE N. LABROSSE

Columbia University Press
New York

Columbia University Press is grateful for the support of the Arnold A. Saltzman
Institute of War and Peace Studies, the School of International and Public Affairs,
and the Department of Political Science at Columbia University.

Columbia University Press
Publishers Since 1893
New York   Chichester, West Sussex
cup.columbia.edu

Library of Congress Cataloging-in-Publication Data
Names: Immerman, Richard H. editor
Title: The Jervis effect : the scholarship and legacy of Robert Jervis / edited by
Richard H Immerman, Stacie E. Goddard, and Diane N. Labrosse.
Description: New York : Columbia University Press, 2025. | Includes index.
Identifiers: LCCN 2025024326 | ISBN 9780231221542 hardback |
ISBN 9780231221559 trade paperback | ISBN 9780231563796 ebook
Subjects: LCSH: Jervis, Robert, 1940–2021—Influence | International relations
Classification: LCC JZ1242 .J468 2025
LC record available at https://lccn.loc.gov/2025024326

Cover design: Julia Kushnirsky

GPSR Authorized Representative: Easy Access System Europe, Mustamäe tee 50,
10621 Tallinn, Estonia, gpsr.requests@easproject.com

THIS VOLUME IS DEDICATED TO KATHE,
ALEXA, AND LISA JERVIS, AS WELL AS ALL
OF BOB JERVIS'S STUDENTS, COLLEAGUES,
AND FRIENDS

CONTENTS

V. ROBERT JERVIS AS PUBLIC INTELLECTUAL

VI. ROBERT JERVIS AS COLLEAGUE, MENTOR, AND FRIEND

THE JERVIS EFFECT

Bob Jervis giving one of his captivating classes in the seminar room in the Arnold A. Saltzman Institute of War and Peace Studies at Columbia University in 2006. His handwriting was notoriously bad; his lectures were brilliant.

Permission granted by Kathe Jervis.

INTRODUCTION

A League of His Own: The Sui Generis Scholarship of Robert Jervis

PAUL K. MACDONALD

I t is almost impossible to summarize Robert Jervis's scholarship in a short introduction, let alone in a single edited volume. There are a number of reasons why Jervis's work defies easy characterization. First, Jervis wrote on an astonishingly wide range of topics. These included how states signal to each another,[1] how states perceive (and misperceive) the world around them,[2] rational deterrence theory,[3] cooperation under anarchy,[4] international institutions and security regimes,[5] the impact of nuclear weapons,[6] the logic (and illogic) of US nuclear strategy,[7] systemic theories of international politics,[8] the politics of intelligence and intelligence failures,[9] the origins and dynamics of the Cold War,[10] the causes of war and great-power peace,[11] the evolution of US foreign policy in the post–Cold War period,[12] not to mention (with his daughter Alexa Jervis) the bargaining strategies employed by contestants on the hit CBS reality television series *Survivor*.[13] "Discerning a system in Jervis's approach," Joseph Parent observes, is complicated by "its open-endedness."[14]

Second, Jervis employed an astonishingly wide range of theories and methods to make sense of these topics. He was steeped in international relations theory, primarily the realist theories of scholars such as Hans Morgenthau and Kenneth Waltz.[15] He was also profoundly interdisciplinary, drawing from economists such as Thomas Schelling[16]; sociologists such as Erving Goffman, Charles Perrow, and Charles Tilly[17]; social psychologists such as Amos Tversky and Daniel Kahneman[18]; and diplomatic historians such as Paul Schroeder and Paul Kennedy.[19] Deborah Welch Larson describes Jervis as "an intellectual magpie," a scholar who was "remarkably open to new information, theories, and approaches."[20] Jervis was also, as Jack S. Levy emphasizes, a "sophisticated methodologist."[21] His first peer-reviewed article assessed the strengths and weaknesses of quantitative methods in the study of world politics, a theme he would return to throughout his career.[22] His own publications employed a wide range of methodologies drawn from political psychology,[23] foreign policy analysis,[24] counterfactual reasoning,[25] comparative historical analysis,[26] policy postmortems,[27] and policy analysis and advocacy.[28] Richard K. Betts rightly concludes that Jervis's work was "a model of theoretical innovation, intellectual breadth, and erudition" and that Jervis himself was a genuine "intellectual pluralist."[29]

Yet for all the diversity in topic and method, Jervis's work was strikingly distinctive and original, if not entirely sui generis. You always knew when you were reading a Robert Jervis piece (although misperceptions remained possible, as Thomas J. Christensen's hilarious anecdote about an unfortunate peer review illustrates).[30] First, Jervis's writing was "incredibly rich, bristling with insight," as Lawrence Freedman emphasizes.[31] To read a page of Jervis was to be treated to a carefully constructed argument, presented with various caveats and illustrated with clever historical examples. So many of the core concepts that we use in international relations—whether the "security dilemma," the "offense-defense balance," the "spiral model," "misperceptions," or the "nuclear revolution"—stem from Jervis's writings, even if he did not originate all of them. When I was searching for a dissertation topic as a young PhD student at Columbia University, one of the pieces of advice I received from my peers was simple: "pick up anything Jervis has written. There's a dissertation topic on every page."[32]

Second, and relatedly, there was a distinctive style and approach to Jervis's scholarship. For Doug Macdonald, a key trait of Jervis was his "ecumenical attitude toward ideas if they showed promise."[33] A Jervis piece would often unfold like a good-natured interrogation, both of the unsatisfactory ideas of others and the crippling weaknesses of his own. Jervis's scholarship likewise displayed "an appreciation for the ambiguity, uncertainty, and contingency of life," as James W. Davis emphasizes.[34] When he was passing judgment on policymakers for their misperceptions or intelligence organizations for their failures, he would somehow manage to do so without being judgmental, "without pathologizing the various processes under examination," as Rose McDermott stresses.[35] Both in person and on the page, Jervis's thinking often unspooled "like a jazz musician riffing on a theme," as Randall L. Schweller relates.[36] Although the core arguments were clearly presented, much of the joy in a Jervis performance was the unexpected improvisation, watching how he would take a claim and bend it in new and unexpected directions.

Reading through the contributions in this book, it becomes clear that many of the authors have their own favorite piece of Jervis's scholarship. Often it is something that they encountered early in their careers that helped spark their intellectual journeys. Michael Doyle praises the way in which Jervis's "Cooperation Under the Security Dilemma" (by far his most cited article) helped ground and reenergize realist theorizing in the late 1970s.[37] James D. Fearon describes how Jervis's discussion of the spiral and deterrence models in his book *Perception and Misperception in International Politics* (by far his most cited book) articulated the "underlying structural problem" of how states can signal their intentions to one another under anarchy, a topic game theorists would take up with renewed vigor in the 1980s and 1990s.[38] Stacie E. Goddard and Ronald R. Krebs describe how Jervis's first book, the "underappreciated classic" *The Logic of Images in International Relations*, anticipates many of the arguments constructivists would make in the 1990s and 2000s about how states form—and perform—collective identities.[39]

One of my own favorite overlooked pieces is Jervis's "Was the Cold War a Security Dilemma?," which appeared shortly after I arrived at Columbia for graduate school. The article is notable not only for the careful way in which it revisited traditional and revisionist arguments about the origins of the Cold War in light of new scholarship and evidence but also for its shocking conclusion. Jervis, who did so much to popularize the security dilemma as a concept, ultimately decided that the Cold War *was not* in fact a security dilemma but rather a "clash of social systems."[40] The article served as a model of how to use history not as a simplistic source of proof for one's own theories but rather as a rich tapestry to interrogate and refine them. Much like his writings on the First World War, which Volker R. Berghahn describes in detail, this article highlights Jervis's willingness to "wrestle with the problems that in his mind did not provide clear-cut answers."[41]

So how might one begin to characterize Jervis's work? One approach might be to situate him in his historical context. As Macdonald observers, Jervis "came to intellectual maturity in the political ferment of the 1950s and 1960s, affected strongly by McCarthyism, the nuclear weapons revolution, and the Vietnam War."[42] In the wake of the Cuban Missile Crisis and the calamitous decision to escalate in Vietnam, it made sense to focus on the psychological foibles of individual leaders to understand how they could have blundered into such dangerous confrontations.

One could also locate Jervis in his personal context, as someone who grew up in a left-leaning Jewish family in New York City and never lost his "Manhattanite provincialism."[43] Reading Jervis's personal reflections in his H-Diplo essay "How I Got Here," which is included as an appendix to this book, one gets a sense that his childhood instilled in him both a passion for politics in general and a respect for the moral weight of political decisions in particular.[44] Yet one of the striking things about Jervis's scholarship is that although it was informed by these political commitments, it was not beholden to them. Jervis could easily critique the Bush administration for embracing a grand strategy that he viewed as dangerous and unsustainable while simultaneously exonerating it for the failure to accurately assess Iraq's weapons of mass destruction program prior to the 2003 war.[45] It is ironic yet completely in character that someone who had passed out leaflets for Adlai Stevenson would go on to revitalize the field of security studies in the wake of the Vietnam War.

One could also acknowledge the various ways that Jervis's personal relationships informed his scholarly curiosities and contributions. Keren Yarhi-Milo describes Jervis as "a community builder and expert convener—he absolutely loved bringing people together."[46] Various contributors mention the infamous "Jervis lunches"—later "Jervis Zooms"—which helped foster ties across the Columbia community and beyond. Although he was most comfortable in academic settings, Jervis also built connections across the American national security bureaucracy. Michael Warner describes the varied efforts Jervis made as chair of the Central Intelligence Agency's (CIA) Historical Review Panel to "raise the productivity (and the stature) of its declassification effort."[47] As part of this endeavor, Melvyn P. Leffler recalls how Jervis "constantly prodded CIA officials to meet with and collaborate more with the State Department."[48] Richard H. Immerman concludes that "no scholar had the sources within the [intelligence community] that Jervis did because those sources within the [intelligence community] trusted him like no other scholar."[49] These chapters make it clear that although Jervis rarely coauthored works with others, he nevertheless viewed the production of knowledge as a collective and collaborative enterprise. Part of the reason why Jervis's scholarship is so distinctive and diverse is because he interacted with so many different people across academia and government.

An alternative approach, which is the primary one taken up in this volume, is to consider Jervis's contributions across different issue areas, whether international relations theory, literatures on psychology and bargaining, nuclear weapons and the practice of statecraft, intelligence studies, or international history. Even this approach has its limits, however. Consider the question of how we might place Jervis among the various paradigms and debates familiar to international relations theorists. Most contributors agree that Jervis was first and foremost a structural realist, albeit one who sought to "make structural realism realistic," as Doyle puts it.[50] Yet Jervis's understanding of structure was much different and less predictable than other realists, as Jack Snyder emphasizes. Rather than view structures as compelling states in a direct and linear fashion to engage in certain behaviors such as balancing, Jervis was much more concerned about "the unexpected, unintended, unwanted consequences" that could occur "when acting in a system."[51] Unlike many realists, Jervis's writings also cautioned against reducing the structure of the international system to the distribution of material capabilities. As Goddard and Krebs emphasize, Jervis did not assume that the actions that states might take during crises, such as dispersing one's bomber fleet, would necessarily send a clear and incontrovertible signal to an intended audience.[52] Jervis was a sort of structural realist but one who viewed the constituent elements of these structures in much more idiosyncratic terms.

Jervis's contributions to the vast literatures on psychology and bargaining are equally nuanced and sometimes contradictory. Stephen M. Walt is correct to note that "the common thread running through much of [Jervis's] scholarship was an effort to explain why it is so hard for states to understand each other."[53] At the same time, Charles L. Glaser is equally right to argue that "we should not overlook . . . Jervis's seminal contributions to rational theories, which are foundational to much of current international relations theory and national security policy."[54] There was often a compelling dialectic running through Jervis's analyses of strategic encounters between states. Different structural situations created rational incentives and trade-offs actors were compelled to confront, but it was precisely the creation of these uncomfortable decision points that encouraged psychological biases to creep in.[55] As Fearon nicely puts it, Jervis viewed misperceptions as "an underlying structural problem made worse by the dynamic application of a psychological bias layered on top of it."[56] Yet even if one could remove these *subjective* psychological biases, states could still fail to send clear and costly signals to one another. That is because, as Jonathan Mercer points out, Jervis's work suggests that "accurately assessing cost independent of beliefs is impossible."[57] Sometimes misperceptions result from an absence of *intersubjective* understanding. States are playing games based around entirely different understandings of cost using entirely different theories of victory.

Similar kinds of tensions are apparent in Jervis's discussions of statecraft, whether his focus was on the impact of nuclear weapons or the practice of intelligence assessment. Jervis famously argued that in a world with nuclear weapons, mutually assured destruction (MAD) should be considered "a fact, not a policy."[58] Yet as Cynthia Roberts notes, he "acknowledged that in practice actors have struggled to escape MAD more than he initially expected."[59] Jervis even wrote a book and multiple articles that were meant to convince American policymakers to abandon moves toward more counterforce-oriented strategies.[60] He might not have been "a technological determinist," as Robert F. Trager argues, yet at the same time, he strenuously denied the claim that nuclear revolution could ever be undone.[61] Similarly, in his analysis of intelligence assessments, Levy notes, Jervis concluded that "a major cause of intelligence failure is that intelligence analysts do not think like social scientists."[62] Yet as Janice Gross Stein highlights, Jervis was also sensitive to the fact that "inaccurate conclusions are not necessarily the result of flawed process."[63] Indeed, it is entirely possible that the use of *good* processes might make analysists *more* prone to reach faulty conclusions, especially if the adoption of "good social science" methods encouraged overconfidence. Even studying previous intelligence failures through postmortems, as Philip E. Tetlock points out, can introduce the possibility of error, if one self-assuredly assumes that understanding a previous failure makes one immune from future ones.[64] At times, it seems like statecraft is just a series of Jervisian pitfalls all the way down.

Jervis's relationship to international history is equally complex. Jervis had an encyclopedic knowledge of historical events, which as Marc Trachtenberg notes, "helped keep the theorizing down to earth and in touch with political reality."[65] For Larson, Jervis's "widespread reading and knowledge of history gave [him] an intuitive sense for what theories are likely to be correct and a commonsense view of what leaders do."[66] At the same time, as the historian Vladislav Zubok notes, "one of the lessons that Jervis drew from his studies of international history is the danger of 'overlearning' from the past."[67] History can simultaneously provide a check on one's own biases yet also be cherry-picked from to prove one's own points. More broadly, as Levy highlights, Jervis was a consummate social scientist and would often go to great lengths to point out the "different methodological approaches of the two disciplines."[68] Indeed, when I was a young assistant professor, Jervis delivered a keynote address to a conference at Williams College designed to bring historians and political scientists together. In his characteristically amiable manner, he criticized the tendency of some international historians to eschew theory and to adopt overly normative language in their writings.[69] As James McAllister recalls, "it would have been easy for Jervis to minimize or obscure" the differences between political science and history, yet "his concluding message was that the border between the two disciplines could not and *should not* be expected to dissolve."[70] Despite these seemingly irreconcilable differences, Diane N. Labrosse describes how Jervis founded an online discussion list in 2009, in a partnership with H-Diplo, to create space for interdisciplinary conversations among historians and international relations theorists.[71]

In the end, it does not matter whether we characterize Robert Jervis as an ambivalent realist, a rationalist who sees psychological failings everywhere, a policy analyst who appreciates the futility of policy, or a social science methodologist with a passion for international history. What ultimately sets Jervis's scholarship apart to me is its tone, its distinctive combination of "self-awareness and modesty," as Dipali Mukhopadhyay aptly describes it.[72] Echoing the comments by James Goldgeier and Elizabeth N. Saunders, I would suggest that Jervis's biggest intellectual legacy is the question many of us ask every time we encounter something puzzling or unexpected in world politics: "What would Jervis say about this?"[73] And the answer that we give to this question is necessarily incomplete and hesitant because to be a student of Jervis, as Freedman emphasizes, is to appreciate how "we can become too invested in our theories and policy predispositions . . . asserting them with more confidence than warranted and playing down awkward trade-offs."[74]

In a forgotten book chapter that Jervis wrote early in his career, he made the fascinating point that the accumulation of knowledge in a field is "not identical with increased understanding."[75] To illustrate this general principle, he used the story of Winnie-the-Pooh and the hunt for the mythical Woozle. In this story, Pooh sees a pair of tracks in the snow, which he assumes are the Woozle's. Pooh then calls for his friends to help him follow the creature, and soon the lone Woozle track has multiplied into a whole herd of Woozle tracks. Pooh and his friends are delighted and believe that they are on the verge of a great discovery, when in reality, the tracks are their own and they are simply walking in circles.

Over the course of his almost fifty-year career, Robert Jervis inspired many people to join him on his hunt to understand world politics. We have all collectively spent a lot of time wandering in circles, staring at tracks, hoping to find something meaningful. And anytime we think we may have stumbled on something profound, somewhere in the back of our heads, we can hear Bob's friendly but mischievous voice: Are you sure? How would you know?[76] What if you are wrong?

NOTES

1. See, for example, Robert Jervis, *The Logic of Images in International Relations* (Princeton University Press, 1970); Jervis, "Understanding Beliefs," *Political Psychology* 27, no. 5 (2006): 641–63; Jervis, "Signaling and Perception," in *Political Psychology*, ed. Kristen Monroe (Erlbaum, 2001), 293–312; Jervis, *How Statesmen Think: The Political Psychology of International Relations* (Princeton University Press, 2017); and Jervis, Keren Yarhi-Milo, and Don Casler, "Redefining the Debate Over Reputation and Credibility in International Security: Promises and Limits of New Scholarship," *World Politics* 73, no. 1 (2021): 167–203.

2. See, for example, Robert Jervis, "Hypotheses on Misperception," *World Politics* 20, no. 3 (1968): 454–79; Jervis, *Perception and Misperception in International Politics* (Princeton University Press, 1976); Jervis, "Foreign Policy Decision-Making: Recent Contributions," *Political Psychology* 2, no. 2 (1980), 86–101; and Jervis, "War and Misperception," *Journal of Interdisciplinary History* 18, no. 4 (1988): 675–700.

3. See, for example, Robert Jervis, "Deterrence Theory Revisited," *World Politics* 31, no. 2 (1979): 289–324; Jervis, "Deterrence and Perception," *International Security* 7, no. 3

(1982/1983): 3–30; Jervis, Richard Ned Lebow, and Janice Gross Stein, *Psychology and Deterrence* (Johns Hopkins University Press, 1985); Jervis, "Rational Deterrence: Theory and Evidence," *World Politics* 41, no. 2 (1989): 183–207; and Jervis, "The Confrontation Between the U.S. and Iraq: Implications for the Theory and Practice of Deterrence," *European Journal of International Relations* 9, no. 2 (2003): 315–37.

4. See, for example, Robert Jervis, "Cooperation Under the Security Dilemma," *World Politics* 30, no. 2 (1978): 167–214; Jervis, "Realism, Game Theory, and Cooperation," *World Politics* 40, no. 3 (1988): 316–49; Jervis, "Realism, Neoliberalism, and Cooperation: Understanding the Debate," *International Security* 24, no. 1 (1999): 42–63; and Jervis, "Dilemmas About Security Dilemmas," *Security Studies* 20, no. 3 (2011): 416–23.

5. See, for example, Robert Jervis, "Security Regimes," *International Organization* 36, no. 2 (1982): 357–78; Jervis, "From Balance to Concert: A Study in International Security Cooperation," *World Politics* 38, no. 1 (1985): 58–79; and Jervis, "A Political Science Perspective on the Balance of Power and the Concert," *American Historical Review* 97, no. 3 (1992): 716–24.

6. See, for example, Robert Jervis, "The Nuclear Revolution and the Common Defense," *Political Science Quarterly* 101, no. 5 (1986): 689–703; Jervis, "The Political Effects of Nuclear Weapons: A Comment," *International Security* 13, no. 2 (1988): 80–90; and Jervis, *The Meaning of the Nuclear Revolution* (Cornell University Press, 1989).

7. See, for example, Robert Jervis, "Why Nuclear Superiority Doesn't Matter," *Political Science Quarterly* 94, no. 4 (1979/1980): 617–33; and Jervis, *The Illogic of American Nuclear Strategy* (Cornell University Press, 1984).

8. See, for example, Robert Jervis, "Systems Theories and Diplomatic History," in *Diplomatic History: New Approaches*, ed. Paul Gordon Lauren (Free Press, 1979), 212–44; Jervis, *Systems Effects: Complexity in Political and Social Life* (Princeton University Press, 1997); and Jervis, "Complexity and the Analysis of Social and Political Life," *Political Science Quarterly* 112, no. 4 (1997/1998): 569–93.

9. See, for example, Robert Jervis, "Intelligence and Foreign Policy: A Review Essay," *International Security* 11, no. 3 (1986/1987): 141–61; Jervis, "Reports, Politics, and Intelligence Failures: The Case of Iraq," *Journal of Strategic Studies* 29, no. 1 (2006): 3–52; Jervis, "War, Intelligence, and Honesty: A Review Essay," *Political Science Quarterly* 123, no. 4 (2008/2009): 645–75; Jervis, *Why Intelligence Fails: Lessons from the Iranian Revolution and the Iraq War* (Cornell University Press, 2010); and Jervis, "Why Intelligence and Policymakers Clash," *Political Science Quarterly* 125, no. 2 (2010): 185–204.

10. See, for example, Robert Jervis, "The Impact of the Korean War on the Cold War," *Journal of Conflict Resolution* 24, no. 4 (1980): 563–92; Jervis, "The Military History of the Cold War," *Diplomatic History* 15, no. 1 (1991): 91–113; Jervis, "Was the Cold War a Security Dilemma?," *Journal of Cold War Studies* 3, no. 1 (2001): 36–60; and Jervis, "The Many Faces of SALT," *Journal of Cold War Studies* 24, no. 4 (2022): 198–214.

11. See, for example, Robert Jervis, "Variation, Change, and Transitions in International Politics," *Review of International Studies* 27 (2001): 281–95; Jervis, "Theories of War in an Era of Leading Power Peace," *American Political Science Review* 96, no. 1 (2002): 1–14; and Jervis, "Fighting for Standing or Standing to Fight?" *Security Studies* 21, no. 2 (2012): 336–44.

12.   See, for example, Robert Jervis, "The Future of World Politics: Will It Resemble the Past?," *International Security* 16, no. 3 (1991/1992): 39–73; Jervis, "A Useable Past for the Future," *Diplomatic History* 16, no. 1 (1992): 76–84; Jervis, "International Primacy: Is the Game Worth the Candle?" *International Security* 17, no. 4 (1993): 52–67; Jervis, "America and the Twentieth Century: Continuity and Change," *Diplomatic History* 23, no. 2 (1999): 219–38; Jervis, "Understanding the Bush Doctrine," *Political Science Quarterly* 118, no. 3 (2003): 365–88; Jervis, "Why the Bush Doctrine Cannot Be Sustained," *Political Science Quarterly* 120, no. 3 (2005): 351–77; Jervis, *American Foreign Policy in a New Era* (Routledge, 2005); Jervis, "Unipolarity: A Structural Perspective," *World Politics* 61, no. 1 (2009): 188–213; Jervis, "Liberalism, the Blob, and American Foreign Policy: Evidence and Methodology," *Security Studies* 29, no. 3 (2020): 434–56; and Jervis, "American Grand Strategies: Untangling the Debates," in *Oxford Handbook of Grand Strategy*, ed. Thierry Balzacq and Ronald R. Krebs (Oxford University Press, 2021), 441–56.

13.   Robert Jervis and Alexa Jervis, "Naked Ambition," *The Sciences* 40, no. 6 (2000): 38–42.

14.   See Joseph M. Parent's essay in this volume.

15.   See, for example, Robert Jervis, "The Contributions of APSA President Kenneth Waltz," *PS* 20, no. 4 (1987): 856–61; Jervis, "Hans Morgenthau, Realism, and the Scientific Study of International Politics," *Social Research* 61, no. 4 (1994): 853–76; and Jervis, "Realism and the Study of World Politics," *International Organization* 52, no. 4 (1998): 971–91.

16.   In particular, Thomas C. Schelling, *The Strategy of Conflict* (Harvard University Press, 1960); and Schelling, *Arms and Influence* (Yale University Press, 1966).

17.   In particular, Erving Goffman, *The Presentation of Self in Everyday Life* (Anchor, 1959); Charles Perrow, *Normal Accidents: Living with High-Risk Technologies* (Basic, 1984); and Charles Tilly, *Coercion, Capital, and European States, AD 990–1992* (Wiley-Blackwell, 1992).

18.   In particular, Amos Tversky and Daniel Kahneman, "Judgement Under Uncertainty: Heuristics and Biases," *Science* 185, no. 4157 (1974): 1124–31; Kahneman and Tversky, "Prospect Theory: An Analysis of Decision Under Risk," *Econometrica* 47, no. 2 (1979): 263–92; and Tversky and Kahneman, "The Framing of Decisions and the Psychology of Choice," *Science* 211, no. 4481 (1981): 453–58.

19.   In particular, Paul W. Schroeder, "World War I as Galloping Gertie: A Reply to Joachim Remak," *Journal of Modern History* 44, no. 3 (1972): 319–345; Schroeder, *The Transformation of European Politics, 1763–1848* (Oxford University Press, 1994); Paul Kennedy, *The Rise and Fall of British Naval Mastery* (Scribner, 1976); and Kennedy, *The Rise and Fall of the Great Powers* (Random House, 1987).

20.   See Deborah Welch Larson's essay in this volume.

21.   See Jack S. Levy's essay in this volume.

22.   Robert Jervis, "The Costs of the Scientific Study of Politics: An Examination of the Stanford Content Analysis Studies," *International Studies Quarterly* 11, no. 4 (1967): 366–93. See also Jervis, "Pluralistic Rigor: A Comment on Bueno de Mesquita," *International Studies Quarterly* 29, no. 2 (1985): 145–49; and Jervis, "Perestroika, Politics, and the Profession: Targets and Tolerance," in *Perestroika! The Raucous Rebellion in Political Science*, ed. Kristen Monroe (Yale University Press, 2005).

23.   See, for example, Robert Jervis, "Political Psychology: Challenges and Opportunities," *Political Psychology* 10, no. 3 (1989): 481–93; Jervis, "The Political Implications of Loss Aversion," *Political Psychology* 13, no. 2 (1992): 187–204; and Jervis, "The Implications of Prospect Theory for Human Nature and Values," *Political Psychology* 25, no. 2 (2004): 163–76.

24.   Robert Jervis, "Do Leaders Matter and How Would We Know?" *Security Studies* 22, no. 2 (2013): 153–79.

25.   See Robert Jervis, "Counterfactuals, Causation, and Complexity," in *Counterfactual Thought Experiments in World Politics: Logical, Methodological, and Psychological Perspectives*, ed. Philip E. Tetlock and Aaron Belkin (Princeton University Press, 1996).

26.   See, for example, Robert Jervis, "Containment Strategies in Perspective: A Review Essay," *Journal of Cold War Studies* 8, no. 4 (2006): 92–97; and Jervis, "The Politics of Troop Withdrawal," *Diplomatic History* 34, no. 3 (2010): 507–16.

27.   See Robert Jervis, "The Mother of All Post-Mortems," *Journal of Strategic Studies* 40, no. 1/2 (2017): 287–94; and Jervis, "Why Post-Mortems Fail," *Proceedings of the National Academy of Sciences* 24, no. 2 (2022). See also Richard Immerman's essay in this volume.

28.   See, for example, Robert Jervis, "Can the United States Get Iran to Yes? The Challenges of Coercive Diplomacy," *Foreign Affairs* 92, no. 1 (2013): 105–15; Jervis, "The Torture Blame Game: The Botched Senate Report on the CIA's Misdeeds," *Foreign Affairs* 94, no. 3 (2015): 120–27; and Jervis and Mira Rapp-Hooper, "Perception and Misperception on the Korean Peninsula," *Foreign Affairs* 97, no. 3 (2018): 103–17.

29.   See Richard K. Betts's essay in this volume.

30.   See Thomas J. Christensen's essay in this volume.

31.   See Lawrence Freedman's essay in this volume.

32.   See Randall L. Schweller's essay in this volume

33.   See Doug Macdonald's essay in this volume.

34.   See James W. Davis's essay in this volume.

35.   See Rose McDermott's essay in this volume.

36.   See Schweller's essay in this volume.

37.   See Michael Doyle's essay in this volume.

38.   See James D. Fearon's essay in this volume.

39.   See Stacie E. Goddard and Ronald R. Krebs's essay in this volume.

40.   Jervis "Was the Cold War a Security Dilemma?," 58.

41.   See Volker Berghahn's essay in this volume.

42.   See Macdonald's essay in this volume.

43.   See Richard K. Betts's essay in this volume.

44.   Robert Jervis, "How I Got Here," H-Diplo Essay 198, https://networks.h-net.org/node/28443 /discussions/5920317/h-diplo-essay-198-robert-jervis-learning-scholars-craft.

45.   Compare Jervis, "Understanding the Bush Doctrine," and Jervis, "Why the Bush Doctrine Cannot Be Sustained," with Jervis "Reports, Politics, and Intelligence Failures," and Jervis, *Why Intelligence Fails*, chap. 3. See also Janice Gross Stein's essay in this volume.

46.   See Keren Yarhi-Milo's essay in this volume.

47.   See Michael Warner's essay in this volume.

48. See Melvyn P. Leffler's essay in this volume.
49. See Richard H. Immerman's essay in this volume.
50. See Doyle's essay in this volume.
51. See Jack Snyder's essay in this volume.
52. See Goddard and Krebs's essay in this volume.
53. See Stephen M. Walt's essay in this volume.
54. See Charles L. Glaser's essay in this volume.
55. See, in particular, Jervis, "Realism, Game Theory, and Cooperation."
56. See James Fearon's essay in this volume.
57. See Jonathan Mercer's essay in this volume.
58. Jervis, *Meaning of the Nuclear Revolution*, 74.
59. See Cynthia Roberts's essay in this volume.
60. See, in particular, Jervis, "Why Nuclear Superiority Doesn't Matter"; Jervis, *Illogic of American Nuclear Strategy*; Jervis, "Strategic Theory: What's New and What's True," *Journal of Strategic Studies* 9, no. 4 (1986): 135–62; and Jervis, "The Nuclear Revolution and the Common Defense," *Political Science Quarterly* 101, no. 5 (1986): 689–703.
61. See Robert F. Trager's essay in this volume.
62. See Levy's essay in this volume.
63. See Janice Gross Stein's essay in this volume.
64. See Tetlock's essay in this volume.
65. See Marc Trachtenberg's essay in this volume.
66. See Deborah Welch Larson's essay in this volume.
67. See Vladislav Zubok's essay in this volume.
68. See Levy's essay in this volume.
69. See Robert Jervis, "International Politics and Diplomatic History: Fruitful Differences," H-Diplo/ISSF Essays, no. 1, March 12, 2010, https://issforum.org/essays/essay-1-jervis-inagural. These points echoed those found in Jervis, "Diplomatic History and International Relations: Why Are They Studied so Differently?," in *Bridges and Boundaries: Historians, Political Scientists, and the Study of International Relations*, ed. Miriam Fendius Elman and Colin Elman (MIT Press, 2001).
70. See James McAllister's essay in this volume, emphasis added.
71. See Diane N, Labrosse's essay in this volume.
72. See Dipali Mukhopadhyay's essay in this volume.
73. See James Goldgeier and Elizabeth N. Saunders's essay in this volume.
74. See Lawrence Freedman's essay in this volume.
75. Robert Jervis, "Cumulation, Correlations, and Woozles," in *In Search of Global Patterns*, ed. James Rosenau (Free Press, 1976).
76. See Joshua Rovner, "Bob Jervis on Hard Problems," in *H-Diplo|ISSF Tribute to the Life, Scholarship, and Legacy of Robert Jervis: Part II*, ed. Richard Immerman, Diane Labrosse, and Marc Trachtenberg, August 25, 2022, https://issforum.org/to/JervisTribute-2.

I

ROBERT JERVIS AND INTERNATIONAL RELATIONS THEORY

❖

1

ACTING IN WHICH SYSTEM?

JACK SNYDER

obert Jervis said that *System Effects* was his favorite among his books, and many scholars consider it his masterpiece. No doubt this wide-ranging, multidisciplinary book weighed heavily in his election to the National Academy of Science, a rare achievement in our field of international relations. Nonetheless, some feel that its gems of insight remain underexploited compared to the more thorough attention given to his other classics. This may partly reflect the fact that *System Effects* is something of a capstone work, integrating themes from earlier works on the systemic logic of the balance of power, the security dilemma in anarchy, and the perceived feedback processes that fuel conflict spirals and beliefs in falling dominoes.[1]

Jervis's reframing and extending of these insights from the viewpoint of general theories of complex systems open up new perspectives that warrant a fresh look. These new perspectives include paths thoroughly vetted in the book as well as some tantalizing bits that are less explored. Jervis's systems perspective is highly relevant to contemporary issues in a precariously changing international system that is fraught with shifting balances of power, more tightly connected global networks, heightened dilemmas of deterrence and containment, and systemic challenges to the "liberal international order." Who knew that a stalled-out Russian invasion of Ukraine would exacerbate inflation in the United States, roil global markets, and put large swaths of Africa on the brink of starvation?

Jervis began with the observation that complex systems are everywhere around us. He dissected examples from ecological systems, economic markets, industrial engineering, safety regulation, and more. Almost every scientific discipline has organized part of its intellectual enterprise around finding patterns in the complex interconnections of systems and their component parts.[2] And yet people tend not to be good systemic thinkers, inclined instead to expect linear effects. Jervis's mission was to warn against the unexpected, unintended, unwanted consequences that follow from this myopic view.[3]

Although he paid plenty of attention to the specific structural features that shape interactions and outcomes in systems, Jervis told the reader not to expect him to produce a new systemic theory of international politics or of anything else. Mostly he used theories off the shelf, such as Kenneth Waltz's systemic theory for applications to international relations, because Jervis said they were well suited to his "own concerns." This method launched his exploration of the central topic of *System Effects*, that is, "Acting in a System," as he entitled the concluding chapter. Across many different systems, Jervis's goal was to find recurrent decisional conundrums, patterns of perplexing behavior, and unintended outcomes set up by systemic complexity. These pitfalls prominently include underestimating the ripple of indirect effects across tightly interconnected systems, failing to anticipate "side effects" and delayed effects, overlooking the "emergent properties" of systems that differ from the characteristics of their parts, failing to see how the consequences of one's strategy depend on the strategies of others, and misjudging positive or negative feedback effects.[4]

ACTING IN ATOMIZED, ANARCHICAL, MECHANICAL SYSTEMS

In this setup, Jervis made a number of conceptual choices that prioritize some ways of thinking about systems over others. Always alert to different ways of looking at the world, he drew upon a wide range of ideas and examples, but nonetheless, his approach proceeded in a particular direction. He highlighted specific types of system and systemic patterns. He especially featured systems with prominent differences between the characteristics of the parts and the whole, systems with loose or no equilibria, systems that are atomistic in their interactions rather than organically integrated (notwithstanding his interest in ecology), and systems in which negative feedback is stabilizing and positive feedback destabilizing.[5] He noted that his analysis was based mainly on what the international relations literature calls the "automatic" theory of the balance of power rather than the "manually operated" version.[6] He spent less time examining human-designed social systems with complementary, mutually supportive parts in which positive feedback is stabilizing. Both kinds of system are of urgent concern for contemporary students of international relations, and the field is wide open for new work, especially on the better integrated, organic systems. Acting effectively in a system depends above all on knowing what kind of system you are acting in.

The atomized, anarchical, mechanical systems especially interested Jervis because they allow considerable room for actors' agency within the system's structure. Such systems, however, place heavy demands on the actors' understanding of the system's dynamics. In international politics, they require actors to develop skills of insight at the level of the Prussian chancellor Otto von Bismarck to understand how the system works. Alas, so few of the actors are Bismarcks who can figure out, for example, how to expand their sphere of influence without triggering destructive resistance and then consolidate the peace with a Reinsurance Treaty.[7] The Joe Bidens, Vladimir Putins, and Xi Jinpings of our own era are not playing at this level for reasons that Jervis's own theories anticipated. They inhabit systems that are too complex, interconnected, indeterminate, and unpredictable to master. Cognitive limitations and biases make their devilishly hard tasks even more impossible. In contrast, the central point of highly institutionalized social systems in which all vectors converge on an equilibrium is to constrain freedom of action in a way that makes everyone's choices more predictable.

Jervis's overall solution was to remember that acting in a system may require acting indirectly or doing two things at once—perhaps a direct action toward your goal but also a secondary action that anticipates and blocks systemic backlash that would otherwise subvert the primary action.[8] This prescription dovetails with the closing dictum of his classic *Perception and Misperception in International Politics*: As you are acting, keep an open mind. Be aware of the common tendency to see what you expect to see.

Remember that information that seems loosely consistent with your prior beliefs may also be consistent with contrary interpretations.[9] Monitor the results of your actions and adjust accordingly.

But the prescription of *System Effects* set an even more daunting standard. As Jervis put it, the actor can "never do only one thing."[10] Although Jervis featured the problem of delayed system effects, often the secondary countervailing move needs to be made at the same time as the primary initiative. "Wait and see" may come too late. The unanticipated reaction may have already gathered momentum in a tightly coupled system. By the time Putin finds out that his blitzkrieg has failed to seize the Kyiv airport and his army is incompetent at maneuver warfare, his credibility may already be irrevocably tied to the goal of dominating Ukraine. By the time Biden realizes that sanctions against Russia have accelerated inflation in the West, price increases may have already become self-reinforcing. The Black Sea might be irrevocably closed to grain shipments before anyone starts paying attention to the dire consequences for African food security. Sometimes not knowing which two things to do can be an insurmountable problem.

DESIGNING SYSTEMS THAT ARE LESS CONFOUNDING

When this is the case, as it will often be in the kind of system that Jervis described, the reader may conclude that the solution is not so much to do two things at once but to design a better system before systemic Galloping Gertie escapes from the stable.[11] Jervis could be masterful on this point. His field-creating article on the security dilemma prescribed verifiable nuclear arms control agreements to shift away from offensive first-strike weapons toward second-strike weapons that are distinguishable as serving only deterrent purposes.[12] Later critics who have complained that many actually existing weapons are indistinguishable between offensive and defensive types often miss the insight that weapons can be made distinguishable by agreement.[13] Jervis's point was that you need to redesign the system to be more stable, not tightly coupled like the proverbial scorpions in the bottle, the metaphor used by J. Robert Oppenheimer when warning at the dawn of the nuclear age about the dangers mankind confronted.[14]

Today, those who argue for cyber deterrence based on "defending forward" through "persistent engagement" take destabilizing features of cyber systems for granted instead of working to redesign them to be less tightly coupled.[15]

＊＊＊

Jervis discussed systems design issues at various points in *System Effects*. One of his favorite examples was Charles Perrow's diagnosis of "normal" industrial accidents, which was later applied by Scott Sagan to nuclear accidents. These occur in systems where all of the components are safe and reliable separately but are vulnerable to "common mode failures" when a system and its backup are vulnerable to an unanticipated disturbance that knocks out both at once.[16]

One might think that when such flaws are identified, tinkering can fix the problem, but Jervis warned that system effects bedevil the tinkerers. Several of his marquee examples depicted regulatory efforts perverted by system effects: seat belt laws causing drivers to speed up and kill more pedestrians, restrictions on police coercion leading to increased use of deception, and alarms on parked cars leading to increased hijackings of cars stopped at traffic lights.[17] Although Jervis was not opposed to regulation, his main focus on unraveling the puzzles of acting in existing systems leaves many issues of system design and reform in need of follow-up.

SYSTEMS AND THEIR PARTS

Focusing more on systems design issues might require exploring types of systems that Jervis did not emphasize, starting with his definition of a system. Jervis said that "we are dealing with a system when (a) a set of units or elements is interconnected so that changes in some elements or their relations produce changes in other parts of the system, and (b) the entire system exhibits properties and behaviors that are different from those of the parts." The latter stipulation can be interpreted variously in ways that matter for the analysis. He started with the anodyne example that the characteristics of benzene cannot be predicted from the properties of carbon, oxygen, and hydrogen, which compose it. But then he quotes the *Federalist Papers* authors on needing to design a constitutional system that would be stable and orderly despite the expectation that the temperament of the people who act in it will be rowdy and disorderly. Later Jervis cast doubt on the reductionist argument that international systems that are composed of a homogeneous regime type will be peaceful, asking about a world of Nazi states, and he speculated that a world of all democracies might not be peaceful if the reason for the current "democratic peace" is their common opposition to the threat from autocracies. He also invoked Adam Smith's invisible-hand paradox, in which selfish actors' interactions in the marketplace produce the social benefit of efficient production.[18]

In these arguments, Jervis made his typical move of showing the power of his argument by going immediately to the hardest case—here the case where the attributes of the system invert the attributes of the parts. He also made this move in his security dilemma article, showing how insecurity in anarchy can cause war even between status quo states that have nothing else to fight about. Many readers make the mistake of reading this as saying that the security dilemma is a theory of the causes of war that assumes that states seek only the status quo. Not so: Jervis wrote explicitly about predatory aggressors' behavior but noted that even they faced security dilemmas when their potential victims ganged up against them.[19]

Similarly, the case in which the attributes of parts are opposite to the attributes of their system should be seen as a hard case that tests the rule, not a necessary part of the definition of a system. Emergent properties may simply be the benefits of smoother coordination of preferences in a well-designed system rather than the inversion of opposed desires. An "automatic" balance of power system may make for a fascinatingly paradoxical equilibrium among rival expansionists, if and when it works, but a "manually operated" balance of power system in a system of states with mixed predatory and defensive motives is also analytically interesting and might be more stable.

Indeed, many of Jervis's examples show how systems shape the attributes of their parts and how the behavior of the parts can create a more compatibly aligned system, such that the system and its parts become mutually reinforcing. In his discussion of structure and agency, Jervis noted that ecological systems are shaped by the behavior of the species that populate them: elephants create their own grasslands. Conversely, environments shape the characteristics of their inhabitants: Kenneth Waltz explained that anarchy socializes states, and Otto Hintze went even further, showing that Germany's garrison state was the product of its especially vulnerable position in the center of the European balance of power system.[20] Completing the causal circle, the German state's militarism and nationalism led to the hyperoffensive Schlieffen Plan, which put the decision for world war in 1914 on a hair trigger, thus reinforcing the Hobbesian character of Europe's anarchical system. Along the same lines, Jervis talked about the "circular effects" of Japan's need for military security and economic autarky requiring aggressive imperial expansion. This reinforced the militarism of its regime and led to the US embargo and war that brought Japan's downfall.[21] In these examples, system effects tend to produce feedback that leads to the alignment of the characteristics of the part with its position in the system. Note that this alignment does not necessarily make for a desirable outcome for the actors in the system. Alexander Wendt took a comparable idea of circular effects of systemic structure, actor attributes, and agency in positing his "three cultures of anarchy," the Hobbesian, Lockean, and Kantian. The first is nasty and brutish and the latter two more desirable.[22]

ORGANIC SOCIAL SYSTEMS AND THEIR PARTS

Systems theorists in many disciplines note the difference between "mechanical" and "organic" systems in how the whole is related to its parts.[23] Émile Durkheim, Talcott Parsons, and the structural-functionalists assumed that mutually supportive institutions, a complementary division of labor, and normative solidarity are necessary for a social system to fulfill core functions of social integration, adaptation, goal attainment, and pattern maintenance.[24] In modern society, the division of labor meant that the parts of the system were not identical, Durkheim argued, but together these diverse parts would need to constitute an organic whole if the system were to function and endure. Contemporary historical sociologists avoid positing cohesive functionalism as an assumption, but many construct their theories of structure and change around the momentum of a system with somewhat coherently aligned principles and parts.[25]

In contrast, Charles Tilly advanced opposite assumptions about the social order in a slash-and-burn essay entitled "Useless Durkheim."[26] He argued that the state, the nation, and the demand for democratic participation in governance emerged as a consequence of international war and domestic "contentious politics." Democracy could emerge, he argued, only when the populace was able to break the stranglehold of entitled elites.

Karl Marx might be seen as having anticipated both of these kinds of assumptions. On one hand, he assumed that feudalism and capitalism each had its own coherent organizing principle that was sustained not only by a given mode of economic production but also by an integrated set of mutually supportive institutions, social roles, and norms governing social relations. On the other hand, each of these social orders gestated a revolutionary, oppositional class within the womb of its otherwise integrated, functional system—a class that emerged because of its role in the existing order but came to have an existential conflict of interest with that system and amassed the power to overturn it. As extended in the Bolshevik leader Vladimir Lenin's *Imperialism: The Highest Stage of Capitalism*, this was also an influential systemic theory of international relations (never mind that Waltz calls it reductionist).[27] History disappointed the predictions of this theory, but it is nonetheless a system theory with a well-specified mechanism of endogenous change.

Organic systems of various kinds get mentioned in passing in *System Effects*, but nowhere is the idea of an organic, functionally integrated system examined systematically. Even when discussing ecology and the animal kingdom, Jervis was mostly writing about atomistic, "mechanical" systems in which individual actors are competing for survival or maneuvering for advantage in the face of systemic incentives and constraints, not inhabiting socially defined roles or following institutionalized norms. This matters in today's context because many important systemic, equilibrium, and feedback effects pertain to the components of the "liberal international order," including its highly interconnected global economy, the suddenly infamous global supply chain, the diffusion of illiberal techniques used by demagogues in backsliding democracies, and the self-destruction of the free marketplace of ideas on global social media.

But are liberal orders organic in the Durkheimian sense, and do they work differently enough as systems to matter for the kind of analysis that

Jervis highlighted in the book? The answer to this may depend on the type of liberal system under discussion. The libertarian version that features atomized competitors operating in a minimally regulated marketplace would seem to fit easily into the kinds of atomistic system that Jervis featured. Analyzing the more heavily institutionalized, socially regulated version that international relations scholars call "embedded liberalism" might require some additional tools.[28] When Jervis commented on regulation, he mainly treated it in an atomistic way in which individuals game the system and confound the intentions of the regulators—a very good point but perhaps not the main point about this kind of system.[29]

SELF-REINFORCING VERSUS SELF-UNDERMINING SYSTEMS

Abraham Newman and Henry Farrell have explicitly theorized the liberal international information system as a self-undermining institution whose invisible-hand principles of free-speech absolutism have interacted with the rise of new media platforms, their libertarian business model, and the populist political moment to turn a pillar of liberal democracy into its nemesis.[30] This is a system effect but one dealing with an institutionalized dimension of the international order that affords a prominent role for norms and where dynamics of hierarchy and anarchy are both in play.[31] In my view, this example shows that it is possible to analyze free speech and media systems as atomized systems but only because they have been disastrously structured by libertarian technology platforms that enable an unregulated worldwide race to the bottom. The last time the United States had a reasonably well-functioning marketplace of ideas was during the high tide of embedded liberalism in the later 1950s with the Federal Communications Commission's Fairness Doctrine in place and the news delivered by professional journalists. That, too, produced a powerful system effect, according to an American Political Science Association prize-winning study: the absence of ideological and partisan polarization.[32] Let's invent a system theory that will help us figure out how to do that again.

This raises the more general question of whether the component parts of the liberal international order—not only free speech but also market capitalism, the rule of law, and democratic self-determination—are self-reinforcing and mutually reinforcing or whether they have become self-undermining and misaligned. Traditionally these components have been thought to be mutually reinforcing insofar as they are anchored in common principles, such as individual liberty, freedom of contracting, and the right to self-government. In international relations, scholars have argued that the success of liberal international regimes created a coherent, powerful support coalition anchored in those who benefit from the system at the domestic and international levels.[33] They also argue that having compatible institutional practices and rules facilitates cooperation, whether the issue is democracies routinely managing minor frictions, sovereign states crowding out heterogeneous forms of authority, or democratic regimes' contrasting attitudes toward democratic and undemocratic rising powers.[34] Even the Soviet leader Joseph Stalin thought that "everyone imposes his own system as far as his army can reach. It cannot be otherwise."[35] Empirically, greater systemic coherence may account for the finding that liberal democracies and pure autocracies are both more durable than mixed regimes.[36] The more it can be shown empirically that the system's parts do hang together, the more plausible it is to analyze them as a tightly interconnected system with self-reinforcing feedback.

Empirical studies of international regimes can help diagnose system effects that may have become self-undermining. A robust literature in social philosophy and history argues that the structural-functionalists are simply wrong in depicting a harmonious uniformity across the productive, regulatory, and legitimating institutions of most societies. This literature argues that a major engine of endogenous social change is the mismatch and friction between the principles and organizational features of the various components that make up a society.[37] In liberalism, the classic example is the tension between the political equality required by democratic rule and the economic inequality bred by free markets.[38]

"QUASI-EQUILIBRIUM"

Although not all systems tend toward equilibrium, systems theories in many disciplines and fields of application employ equilibrium as a central organizing concept. Balance of power theory in international relations has a complicated relationship to this concept, and so does Jervis's *System Effects*. After a good but inconclusive discussion that focuses on the systemic level, Jervis retreated to a more action-centered analysis of the negative and positive feedback that treats equilibrium as a directional tendency, not a point prediction of an outcome. This is a consequential choice because systems with very strong equilibrium tendencies, like markets in perfect competition, are easier to understand and act within than ones with very weak equilibrium tendencies, like oligopolistic markets.

In its most straightforward usage, a system is in equilibrium when all forces acting on it are in balance. A homeostatic system, like a thermostat or pendulum, returns to its equilibrium state after it is subjected to a disturbing force through the operation of some automatic adjustment based on negative feedback. Equilibrium does not necessarily imply a static system. It can also refer to change along a predictable "equilibrium path" in response to predictable incentives and causal forces, as in path dependence resulting from first-mover advantages and increasing returns to scale, or predictable strategic choices, as in a Nash equilibrium in game theory that leaves all players with outcomes that they cannot unilaterally improve upon.[39] Finally, an exogenous shock can disrupt a system and move it to a new equilibrium—a "punctuated equilibrium." Jervis noted, though, that sometimes what looks like a sudden collapse can be caused by a straw that breaks the camel's back after the accumulation of unobserved stresses and strains that come from within the system.

The concept of equilibrium has been at the core of the "old chestnut" question of whether the balance of power tends to produce "stability" in the international system as states form alliances to defend themselves against powerful aggressors.[40] Jervis quoted the kitchen-sink definition of Karl Deutsch and David Singer that stability means "the probability that the system retains all of its essential characteristics; that no single nation becomes dominant; that most of its members continue to survive; and that large-scale war does not occur."[41] Given the track record of the multipolar twentieth century, it is difficult to claim that the balance of power came anywhere near meeting that criterion. More insightful is the purportedly correct answer to an old Yale history department PhD exam question, "When in history did the balance of power work most effectively?" No, not during the Concert of Europe, but on July 31, 1914.

Early in his career, Kenneth Waltz was enamored with the concept of a competitive equilibrium leading to peace. His 1962 article quoted the claim of Immanuel Kant's *Perpetual Peace* that a "law of equilibrium . . . for the regulation of the really wholesome antagonism of contiguous States as it springs up out of their freedom . . . is constituted, whereby there is introduced a universal condition of public security among the nations."[42] Waltz concluded that Kant's "system of voluntary universal law rests upon an equilibrium of forces."[43] An evolved version of this idea stuck with Waltz years later in his capstone theoretical work, *Theory of International Politics*: "Balance-of-power theory is microtheory in precisely the economist's sense. The system, like a market in economics, is made by the actions and interactions of its units, and the theory is based on assumptions about their behavior."[44] But in that book, Waltz analogized not to firms in perfect competition, which by theory produces an equilibrium of supply and demand at a given price, but to oligopolistic competition—a better match for competition among the great powers—which by theory and empirical observation produces no unique, stable equilibrium. Prudently declining to put too much weight on the equilibrium analogy, Waltz's theory of the balance of power limits itself to the less ambitious argument that states get socialized to the logic of self-help in international anarchy or else they "fall by the wayside."[45]

Jervis offered many empirical objections even to these pared down claims: states don't learn efficiently, and even so, few of them get selected out of the system through the survival of the fittest.[46] Besides, because committing to a balancing alliance is frequently not the best move, learning what to do in an anarchical system is hard.[47] Jervis did due diligence based on the "formulation used in most of the literature" that a system is "unstable" if it is prone to changes, "especially wars," that alter "the number, arrangement, and goals of the states that in turn affect many patterns of behavior."[48] His conclusion from this exercise featured not equilibrium but "quasi-equilibrium," which keeps the idea of feedbacks but is wary about claiming that the outcome of competitive interaction in anarchy is stability.

More in line with Jervis's approach is the systemic effect of delayed feedback in producing disequilibrium. Delayed effects long played an important role in Jervis's thinking. A crucial point in his security dilemma article is that the benign intentions of a rising power can

change once it achieves a hegemonic position, making credible commitments impossible.[49] If anyone doubts Jervis's inclination to ironic
pessimism, his discussion of delayed system effects noted that the mass
extinction of predators can open the field for a new cohort of even
more deadly ones.[50] Delayed effects in a system, though often of great
consequence, are particularly difficult to foresee and gauge precisely.
"Declinists" predicted in the late 1980s that Japan would soon rival the
United States for hegemony, whereas "engagers" predicted that admitting China to the World Trade Organization in 2001 would consolidate
its "peaceful rise."[51]

Jervis offered the cobweb theorem, also known as the corn-hog cycle,
as an example of the uncertainty and misperception created by delayed
effects.[52] Economists have long noted that rising prices for scarce feed
corn lead pig farmers to cut back on future production, while those same
high prices can induce corn growers to expand production for the next
year of the cycle. This outcome, which produced lots of corn for fewer
hogs, resulted in falling demand and low prices for feed, inducing corn
growers to cut back for the following year just as pig farmers were preparing to ramp up production to take advantage of the lower corn prices.
This cycle of overshooting and undershooting demand could sometimes
last for years. Deductive economic theory predicts that whether the
cobweb-shaped supply-and-demand graph converges toward equilibrium
or diverges toward disequilibrium should depend on the price elasticity of
supply and demand for the commodities, which is affected by such factors
as the gestational period of the animals (a delayed response effect) and the
size of the markets for the goods. Empirical studies found that small farmers used to be very bad at predicting future prices, generally assuming a
linear projection of current prices, and they were unaware of the cycle
effect (heightened uncertainty as a result of the time delay). Such cycles
are far less prevalent nowadays because of larger, more efficient farms
and bigger export markets.[53] Jervis speculatively applied the theory to the
production of PhD students.[54]

In short, creatively theorizing how to understand and act in perverse
systems with disorderly or no equilibria is tremendously valuable, especially if it can be used to devise, implement, and regulate better systems
that have stronger equilibrium properties that make the effective strategy
more self-evident.

POSITIVE AND NEGATIVE FEEDBACKS
AS SYSTEMIC OR RHETORICAL

In the fourth chapter of *System Effects*, Jervis discussed negative and positive feedback in interconnected systems.[55] Neither is inherently desirable or undesirable, and neither has a monopoly on equilibrium effects. Negative feedback produces equilibrium in a thermostat, whereas positive feedback can produce movement along a predicted equilibrium path of change. Negative feedback against shaming can lead to backlash against human rights promotion, whereas positive feedback from wind vectors can cause a suspension bridge to swing wildly and collapse. An arms race can be seen as a system in which rivals impose stabilizing negative feedback on each other (if it ends in a peaceful stalemate), but it can also be seen as a positive feedback conflict spiral (if it ends in war by convincing both sides that war is inevitable and creating fleeting opportunities for a preventive attack). Jervis permitted himself the side comment that without negative feedback there would not be enough stability to sustain organized society, whereas without positive feedback there would be no change and growth.[56]

Normally we think of negative feedback as stabilizing international politics by pushing back against aggression and other disruptions that threaten the status quo. In Waltz's memorable phrase, this means that "in international politics, winning leads to losing." In contrast, positive feedback implies that changes are cumulative, success leads to success, conquest facilitates additional conquest, and outcomes snowball, perhaps accelerating as they roll downhill. Jervis analyzed three of the key mechanisms of positive feedback that concern strategists: the interdependence of commitments through their effect on reputation for resolve and signaling, bandwagon alignments with the stronger or rising power, and defeats that cumulate like falling dominoes as a result of their effect on morale or resources.[57]

These positive feedback mechanisms assume that the parts of the system are tightly interconnected. In such a system, peace and security are indivisible. The negative feedback mechanisms are more ambiguous. If winning leads to losing because every nation is highly motivated to defend its own homeland, and if logistics and terrain give huge advantages to the defenders, that is a negative feedback world that is resistant to conquest and not tightly coupled. But if winning leads to losing, if and only if a powerful global policeman of the status quo is constantly patrolling the turbulent frontier of empire (as per the National Security Council [NSC] 68 global containment doctrine), then negative feedback stabilizes the system only because crucial actors realize that the world is tightly coupled and dominoes could fall. Indeed, this is Jervis's distinctive insight, which he called the "Never Again" domino paradox.[58] Dominoes don't fall but perhaps only because the collapse of the first sounds the alarm and action is taken that falsifies the theory.

An important question is whether statements about the interdependence of reputational commitments and about the interconnected fate of potential dominoes should be understood as beliefs about the nature of the international system or as rhetorical claims to justify a preferred policy. The historian Frank Ninkovich writes in *Modernity and Power: A History of the Domino Theory in the Twentieth Century* (a book that Jervis owned, marked up, and cited) that the domino theory served as a metaphor for "the absence of a homeostatic, self-regulating system" and "lack of a self-equilibrating balance of power" in a "world organized as a tightly linked system . . . whose main feature is open-ended and uncontrollable escalation." And "least obviously, if the chain reaction cannot stop itself, it must be checked by a force capable of analyzing the domino process and subverting its dynamics."[59]

Thus, said Ninkovich, the "metaphor" of the domino theory served an "ideological" function for "interventionist rationales offered up in the late 1930s and during the cold war," in which "the symbol . . . became mightier than the reality." Secretary of State Dean Acheson argued at the Blair House meeting on intervention in Korea that "it was important for us to do something even if the effort were not successful" despite the fact that, or perhaps because, as Defense Secretary Louis Johnson told the Blair House group, "Korea is just a symbol. . . . It isn't important."[60] For Ninkovich, the underlying motivation for this narrative, beginning already with Woodrow Wilson, was to mobilize American public support for a globalist foreign policy that would "make the world safe for democracy."[61]

Jervis offered only "tentative" conclusions about the validity of the understudied domino theory but called it "oversimplified and misleading." Still, he noted that domino effects are more likely to occur when offense has advantages over the defense, when key states seek spoils rather than just security, and "when patterns of behavior and conceptions of interest are in flux." In particular, he said, "the aftermath of most large wars may similarly bring uncertainty which permits several kinds of positive feedback, including the possibility of falling dominoes."[62]

My own view is that the domino theory is one of the rhetorical myths of empire that expansionists use to justify policies that serve their parochial, political, and ideological interests in terms of the public interest in national security.[63] A question that needs more research is when and why the public and other audiences buy domino myths. This also raises the broader issue of the relationship between system effects and subjective perceptions of system dynamics, which may become self-fulfilling prophecies.

"ACTION-AROUSING GLOOMY VISION"

The domino theory paradox is not just a clever side point. This mechanism, which together with the similar "Lijphart effect" leads off the concluding chapter of *System Effects*, is the central take-home point of Jervis's book. Jervis approvingly quoted Albert Hirschman's concept of "action-arousing gloomy vision" in characterizing both the Lijphart effect and the domino paradox.[64]

Arendt Lijphart, a Dutch-born political scientist, is famous for his theory of power sharing among deeply divided identity groups, which he based on the Dutch system of bargaining among the leaders of the Catholic, Protestant, and labor "pillars." His conceptual nemesis, Donald Horowitz, argued optimistically that conflicts in ethnically divided societies could be mitigated by institutions that would encourage crosscutting cleavages or break up problematic identity blocs into smaller units. But Lijphart contended pessimistically that it was pointless to try to convince entrenched groups to resist the inevitable politicization of culture. It is better, he argued, to accept that identity politics is locked in, organize politics in a way that allows people to elect their own ethnic representatives, and then give the chosen group leaders vetoes to require decision making among them by consensus.[65]

Both the domino theory and the Lijphart effect illustrate Jervis's general strategy of accepting the hard realities of system-created conflicts but then using deftly tailored combinations of resistance and accommodation to achieve a tolerable outcome. Jervis's conclusion followed this up with the more general concept of quasi-homeostasis, whereby rivals dish out "negative feedback" in a way that "reduces the amount of change that occurs as actors respond to each other." If states push back too hard and "overshoot," they will "try to defuse the situation by concessions" to sustain "the desired level of risk" needed to "bring pressure to bear in a crisis."[66] The "quasi" indicates that this interaction with negative feedbacks does not necessarily produce a stable equilibrium. Rather it suggests calibrated resistance in the hope of moving roughly in the direction of a tolerable equilibrium. This resonates with the choices being faced by the United States and Russia during the Ukraine War.

Jervis concluded by stressing that the quasi-equilibrium and uncertainty of consequences in complex systems leave considerable "room for judgment."[67] Agency looms large in this concept of structure, and Jervis was a masterful guide to the subtle considerations that should inform its use. The problem, however, is that judgment will be exercised not only by the Bismarcks and the Martin Luther Kings but also by the Putins and the Trumps. Uncertainty in complex systems allows latitude not only for creative problem solving but also, as Jervis stressed, for unintended consequences. It also widens the door for perceptual bias and the construction of ideological narratives.

The possibility of reaching a stable outcome in situations of quasi-equilibrium depends not only on the agency of prudent leaders but also on the kind of incentives that are inherent in the system. Applying Jervis's security dilemma notion to international economic competition, Dale Copeland claims that there is a "trade security dilemma" when scale economies of production are so great that sustaining competitiveness is impossible without access to fully global markets, resources, and investment opportunities in leading economic sectors with implications for military security. When that is the case, great powers cannot be satisfied with a self-contained regional hegemony; they need to poach on each other's spheres of influence, causing mutual insecurity.[68] William Fellner's theory of oligopoly, from which Waltz derived parts of his system theory, included the similar notion of the "frontier market," in which the most aggressive first movers would lock in market dominance through scale economies.[69]

As for the future research agenda, I think the wide-open conceptual terrain lies in the area of the effects of systems that are designed to reduce internal contradictions, not just manage them, and to foster organic complementarities among the system's parts.[70] But in the meantime, we need to keep our powder dry and use Bob Jervis's books as guides for how to do that wisely.

NOTES

1. Robert Jervis, "Systems Theories and Diplomatic History," in *Diplomacy: New Approaches in History, Theory, and Policy*, ed. Paul Gordon Lauren (Free Press, 1979); Jervis, *Perception and Misperception in International Politics* (Princeton University Press, 1976); Jervis, "Cooperation Under the Security Dilemma," *World Politics* 30, no. 2 (1978): 167–214; Jervis, "Domino Beliefs and Strategic Behavior," in *Dominoes and Bandwagons: Strategic Beliefs and Superpower Competition in the Eurasian Rimland*, ed. Jervis and Jack Snyder (Oxford University Press, 1991).

2. George P. Richardson, *Feedback Thought in Social Science and Systems Theory* (University of Pennsylvania Press, 1991); Cynthia Eagle Russett, *The Concept of Equilibrium in American Social Thought* (Yale University Press, 1966).

3. Robert Jervis, *System Effects: Complexity in Political and Social Life* (Princeton University Press, 1997), 4.

4. Jervis, *System Effects*, 4, 92, 12–17.

5. Jervis, *System Effects*, 12–21, 44–48, 125–37.

6. Jervis, *System Effects*, 131.

7. Jervis, *System Effects*, 198; Stacie E. Goddard, "When Right Makes Might: How Prussia Overturned the European Balance of Power," *International Security* 33 (2008–2009): 110–42.

8. Jervis, *System Effects*, 271–75, 282–95.

9. Jervis, *Perception and Misperception*, 409–24.

10. Jervis, *System Effects*, 10–12.

11. Paul Schroeder, "World War I as a Galloping Gertie," in *The Outbreak of World War I*, ed. Holger Herwig (Houghton Mifflin, 1997), 142–51.

12. Jervis, "Cooperation Under the Security Dilemma."

13. Charles L. Glaser and Chaim Kaufmann, "What Is the Offense-Defense Balance and Can We Measure It?," *International Security* 22, no. 4 (1998): 44–82. See also Glaser's article in this volume.

14. J. Robert Oppenheimer, "Atomic Weapons and American Foreign Policy," *Foreign Affairs* 31 (1953): 525–35, 529.

15. Jervis's preliminary thoughts on the systemic risks of cyber escalation can be found in Jason Healey and Robert Jervis, "The Escalation Inversion and Other Oddities of Situational Cyber Stability," *Texas National Security Review* 3, no. 4 (2020): 30–53. On loose and tight coupling, Jervis, *System Effects*, 19; Charles Perrow, *Normal Accidents: Living with High-Risk Technologies* (Basic, 1984), 89–96. For an explicit application to nuclear command and control, see Paul Bracken, *The Command and Control of Nuclear Forces* (Yale University Press, 1983).

16. Jervis, *System Effects*, 41; Scott Sagan, *The Limits of Safety: Organizations, Accidents, and Nuclear Weapons* (Princeton University Press, 1995).

17. Jervis, *System Effects*, 68–73.

18. Jervis, *System Effects*, 6, 14–15, 35–36, 99, 66, 132.

19. Robert Jervis and Jack Snyder, "Civil War and the Security Dilemma," in *Civil Wars, Insecurity, and Intervention*, ed. Barbara Walter and Jack Snyder (Columbia University Press, 1999): 15–37.

20. Jervis, *System Effects*, 103–5; Kenneth Waltz, *Theory of International Politics* (Waveland, 2010); Otto Hintze, *The Historical Essays of Otto Hintze* (Oxford University Press, 1975).

21. Jervis, *System Effects*, 60.

22. Alexander Wendt, "Three Cultures of Anarchy," in *Social Theory of International Politics* (Cambridge University Press, 1999).

23. Russett, *The Concept of Equilibrium*, chap. 2.

24. Émile Durkheim, *The Division of Labor in Society* (Free Press, 1984); Talcott Parsons, "The Present Status of 'Structural-Functional' Theory in Sociology," in *Social Systems and the Evolution of Action Theory*, ed. Talcott Parsons (Free Press, 1977).

25. For various balanced views on this, see William Sewell, *Logics of History: Social Theory and Social Transformation* (University of Chicago Press, 2005), and Wolfgang Streeck and Kathleen Thelen, eds., *Beyond Continuity: Institutional Change in Advanced Political Economies* (Oxford University Press, 2005).

26. The essay is in Charles Tilly, *Big Structures, Large Processes, Huge Comparisons* (Russell Sage, 1989).

27. Vladimir I. Lenin, "Imperialism: The Highest Stage of Capitalism" [1917], in *The Lenin Anthology*, ed. Richard Tucker (Norton, 1975); G. A. Cohen, *Karl Marx's Theory of History: A Defence* (Princeton University Press, 1978).

28. John Gerard Ruggie, "International Regimes, Transactions, and Change: Embedded Liberalism in the Postwar Economic Order," *International Organization* 36, no. 2 (1982): 379–415.

29. Jervis, *System Effects*, 68, 70–73.

30. Abraham Newman and Henry Farrell, "The Janus Face of the Liberal International Information Order: When Global Institutions Are Self-Undermining," *International Organization* 75, no. 2 (2021), special issue on "Challenges to the Liberal International Order," 333–58. An earlier conceptual model for this kind of analysis in political science was the study by Avner Greif and David Laitin, "A Theory of Endogenous Institutional Change," *American Political Science Review* 98, no. 4 (2004): 633–52, comparing the self-undermining governance system of the Genoese podesta with the self-reinforcing system of

the Venetian empire. A possible problem is that Greif and Laitin's analysis loads the dice in favor of stability in the Venetian system by positing more cooperative actors in Venice from the outset, even before self-reinforcing dynamics kick in.

31. Jervis, *System Effects*, 10, 58, 136–37, does discuss system effects in norm-based international regimes, drawing on Jervis's articles on the Concert of Europe, so the application to this subject is not out of his study's scope conditions.

32. Markus Prior, *Post-Broadcast Democracy: How Media Choice Increases Inequality in Political Involvement and Polarizes Elections* (Cambridge University Press, 2007).

33. Robert Keohane, "The Demand for International Regimes," *International Organization* 36, no. 2 (1982): 325–55.

34. Bruce Russett, *Triangulating Peace* (Norton, 2001); Hendrik Spruyt, *The Sovereign State and Its Competitors* (Princeton University Press, 1994); Jack S. Levy, "Power Transition Theory and the Rise of China," in *China's Ascent: Power, Security, and the Future of International Politics*, ed. Robert S. Ross and Zhu Feng (Cornell University Press, 2008), 11–33.

35. Milovan Djilas, *Conversations with Stalin* (Harcourt Brace Jovanovich, 1963), 114.

36. Jack Snyder, *Human Rights for Pragmatists: Social Power in Modern Times* (Princeton University Press, 2022), 40–41.

37. For example, see Michael Mann, *The Sources of Social Power* (Cambridge University Press, 1986), vol. 1.

38. Karl Polanyi, *The Great Transformation* (Farrar, 1944).

39. Paul Pierson, *Politics in Time* (Princeton University Press, 2004); David M. Kreps, *Game Theory and Economic Modelling* (Oxford University Press, 1990).

40. Jervis, *System Effects*, 99, citing works by Raymond Aron and Stanley Hoffmann.

41. Jervis, *System Effects*, 95, citing Karl Deutsch and J. David Singer, "Multipolar Systems and International Stability," *World Politics* 16 (1964): 390–406.

42. Kenneth Waltz, "Kant, Liberalism, and War," *American Political Science Review* 56, no. 2 (1962): 336; see discussion in Paul R. Viotti, *Kenneth Waltz: An Intellectual Biography* (Columbia University Press, 2023).

43. Waltz, "Kant," 338.

44. Waltz, *Theory of International Politics*, 118.

45. Jervis, *System Effects*, 105, citing Waltz.

46. Jervis, *System Effects*, 104–5.

47. Jervis, *System Effects*, 195–96; John Mearsheimer, *The Tragedy of the Great Power Politics* (Norton, 2001).

48. Jervis, *System Effects*, 98, 136, 139, 143.

49. Jervis, "Cooperation Under the Security Dilemma," 168.

50. Jervis, *System Effects*, 29.

51. Samuel P. Huntington, "The U.S.: Decline or Renewal?," *Foreign Affairs* 67, no. 2 (1988): 76–96.

52. Jervis, *System Effects*, 259.

53. Donald Albert, "Swine Producers' Price Expectations and the Hog Cycle," West Economics Research Report No. 10, Department of Economics, North Carolina State University, October 1969, file:///Users/jacksnyder/Downloads/magr-northcarolinastate-147.pdf; Jim

Mintert, "What Happened to the Traditional Hog Cycle?," *Farm Progress*, August 6, 2021, https://www.farmprogress.com/hog/what-happened-traditional-hog-cycle.

54. Jervis, *System Effects*, 259.

55. Jervis, *System Effects*, 125–76.

56. Jervis, *System Effects*, 125

57. Jervis, *System Effects*, 166–68.

58. Jervis, "Domino Beliefs and Strategic Behavior."

59. Jervis, *System Effects*, 54; Frank Ninkovich, *Modernity and Power: A History of the Domino Theory in the Twentieth Century* (University of Chicago, 1994), xvi.

60. Ninkovich, *Modernity and Power*, xvi–xvii, 191–95.

61. Frank Ninkovich, *The Wilsonian Century: U.S. Foreign Policy Since 1900* (University of Chicago Press, 1999); Jack Snyder, "Dueling Security Stories: Wilson and Lodge Talk Strategy," *Security Studies* 24, no. 1 (2015): 171–97; Jack Snyder, *Myths of Empire* (Cornell University Press, 1991), 255–304.

62. Jervis, *System Effects*, 168–69, 173.

63. Snyder, *Myths of Empire*, 3–4.

64. Jervis, *System Effects*, 264, quoting Albert Hirschman, *A Bias for Hope: Essays on Development in Latin America* (Yale University Press, 1971), 284, 350–53.

65. Arend Lijphart, *Democracies: Patterns of Majoritarian and Consensus Government in Twenty-One Countries* (Yale University Press, 1984); Donald L. Horowitz, *A Democratic South Africa?: Constitutional Engineering in a Divided Society* (University of California Press, 1991).

66. Jervis, *System Effects*, 280–81.

67. Jervis, *System Effects*, 204.

68. Dale Copeland, *Making the World Safe for Commerce* (Princeton University Press, 2023).

69. William Fellner, *Competition Among the Few: Oligopoly and Similar Market Structures* (Knopf, 1949).

70. Antoine Bousquet and Simon Curtis, "Beyond Models and Metaphors: Complexity Theory, Systems Thinking and International Relations," *Cambridge Review of International Affairs* 24, no. 1 (2011): 43–62, doi:10.1080/09557571.2011.558054.

2

REALISM AND MISPERCEPTIONS

LAWRENCE FREEDMAN

As the crisis developed over the buildup of Russian forces around Ukraine, leading to the invasion that began on February 24, 2022, students of international relations struggled to make sense of what was going on. Because the decision to go to war was Russian president Vladimir Putin's, considerable effort was put into trying to discern his motives and objectives. Large theoretical debates about the relevance of realism as a guiding philosophy in the field appear to depend on whether his decisions could best be understood as a response to NATO's post-1991 enlargement, which was aggravated by the alliance's refusal to rule out Ukraine's eventual membership (even though this was unlikely to happen), or whether they reflected something more visceral—Moscow's refusal to accept the idea of an independent Ukraine that would follow its own distinctive path separate from that of the Russian Federation.[1] This became the strongest argument among those—largely the elders of realism—who found Putin's actions at least explicable and believed that the war could be ended through negotiations that addressed his security concerns.[2]

Once the war began, debates continued about the extent to which the United States and its allies should support Ukrainian resistance and counterattacks. At what point might this support create risks of major war between NATO and Russia, with all the dangers of escalation that implied? Was it also encouraging Ukraine to fight on in ways that were most likely to end in a painful disappointment, with the country left dismembered?

Alternatively, if Ukraine appeared to be succeeding, could this lead to a situation in which Putin faced humiliation and so might resort to nuclear weapons as a desperate measure?

The consensus view was that the Russian action was so egregious, conducted with such brutality, that NATO countries were bound to back Ukraine—at least once it demonstrated its determination and ability to fight. Once made, the commitment was one from which the United States and its allies dared not resile. It was vital that Russia emerge from the war chastened rather than emboldened. It also soon became apparent that there was no easy deal to be done with Moscow to conclude the war with a minimum of pain and lasting damage. Putin was an unreliable negotiating partner. More seriously, his demands were not simply about security arrangements between great powers, or even the management of a localized civil war in the Donbas, but about the continued existence of Ukraine. Because it was Ukraine's security that was at stake and Ukraine saw concessions to Moscow leading only to demands for further concessions, how could external parties engineer some optimum outcome?

There might be a bargaining element to all wars, but that does not mean that all wars end with compromise. In these distressing and tense circumstances, what actually was the "realistic" policy to adopt?

As scholars and policymakers try to navigate their way around these issues, one voice is missing. Scholars commonly lament that this is a time when we need Robert Jervis to help us find a way through these complex issues of practical policy and high principle. Jervis would have challenged everyone, remaining skeptical in the face of certainty, probing confident assertions, questioning how key concepts were being used, and being prepared to consider historical parallels if only to note their limited value. Most of all, he would have remained aware that the issues under discussion really matter, that we are not just considering theoretical constructs but real lives being lost and disrupted and terms being set for the security debates of the coming years. Along with the rest of us, he would have been enthralled and appalled by the war at the same time. It is an opportunity to test and refine our theories—but at what cost!

In this chapter, I make no attempt to answer the question of what Robert Jervis would have thought about the war in Ukraine. That would be presumptuous. Through a somewhat circuitous route, which I shall soon explain, I sought some general guidance from Jervis via his scholarship on how to understand this conflict, concentrating on the problem of Putin's perceptions of the world—and our perceptions of Putin's perceptions. Those familiar with Jervis's work will know this was one area where his contribution to the field was enormous. He was pioneer in the application of cognitive psychology to international affairs.[3] If we insist that theories of international relations depend for their validity on their ability to predict how individuals will make their choices, we may never be satisfied. This is especially so when dealing with autocrats. Therefore, the purpose of this exercise is to illuminate not only some of the specific aspects of this case but also the general problem of what can be assessed as misperceived and irrational in decision making and what can also be the potential source of distortion in our own analyses.

My original intention—from before this war began—was to look back at three seminal articles Jervis wrote about deterrence theory from 1979 to 1989 and to consider them as examples of his distinctive approach to the scholar's craft: "Deterrence Theory Revisited" (1977), "Deterrence and Perceptions" (1982–1983), and "Rational Deterrence: Theory and Evidence" (1989).[4] These articles were written during a period of great creativity and address the same theme from slightly different directions. Jervis's writing was incredibly rich, bristling with insight. We often have quite vague recollections of what was written decades ago, even in some of the classic pieces in our field, and rarely reread these writings because of the need to keep up to date with the latest literature. Yet old thoughts can still appear remarkably fresh and surprise us with their contemporary relevance. This became apparent once I had reread Jervis's articles. As the war was now underway, I decided to use them to explore some of the issues raised by the war. This unavoidably meant that I was going to be largely writing about the importance of misperception as an aggravating factor at times of crisis. These pieces were written just after the publication of Jervis's foundational work, *Perception and Misperception in International Politics*, which influenced all of them.[5]

Jervis wrote a lot and was writing until the end, so other pieces would also be instructive about aspects of the current crisis. But there was continuity in his thinking. We can have some confidence that the mature Jervis agreed with the young Jervis on the sources and impact of misperception because of the helpful preface he wrote for the 2017 republication of *Perception and Misperception*, in which he confirmed that he was content with his central thesis.

A NOTE ON STYLE AND METHOD

In terms of my original intention to explore this scholar's craft, I will make five brief points. First, Jervis's intellectual curiosity pushed aside any concern with disciplinary purity. In the preface to *Perception and Misperception*, he explains how he spent a year exploring the psychological literature to inform his analysis and also how much diplomatic history he had to pick up at the same time, all in the service of a research project that was at first framed as a problem in political science.

Second, I am not sure that any of these pieces would pass muster through a modern dissertation committee. In the first, and most important, piece on deterrence theory, "Deterrence Theory Revisited," he largely assumed a degree of familiarity with the work of the "second-wave" theorists that he was assessing.[6] The footnotes generally are few and far between, at least compared to, say, articles now appearing in *International Security*. There are no statistics and no hypotheses presented as propositions to be tested, as if these were matters that might be subjects to "proofs" and that might help us predict events rather than simply explain them in retrospect. He was bothered by the cause-effect issue without being able to resolve it. What he shows is the value of concepts in helping us to organize our thoughts and suggesting factors that need to be considered when looking at past events and those currently unfolding.

Third, he used concepts to explain the sources of error in policymaking and also in our understanding of the policymaking. He advised on things to look out for, and he did so in the form of a sustained argument—often it seems with himself as well as with the engaged reader. Interesting insights are left in the article bracketed as matters worth examining in more detail when time permits.[7] At times, you can feel Jervis resisting going off on an intriguing tangent. At one point, while making an apparently convoluted point, he asked the reader to stick with him as he realized that this was a bit of a stretch: "I admit that this argument is strained, and indeed I doubt that observers would follow the train of reasoning I have presented."[8]

Fourth, Jervis employed cases as illustrations to show that the phenomena being described had occurred in the past. He did not go through the rigorous process of searching for all possible cases across space and time to analyze their incidence. The big events of crisis and war are not that frequent, so in the end, it is enough to show that there is a possibility that one of these events might take a particular form, in the right conditions, not that it will happen often or even at all. Jervis stressed contingency throughout, warning against decontextualizing decisions and events. The method here alerts us to possibilities and enlightens us about the sources of our own errors as well as those of government.

Fifth, and this is relevant to current debates, Jervis was sensitive to the tension between the need of theory to treat states as similar sorts of beasts, so what works with one will work with another, and the fact that in practice these beasts are different, with their own internal drivers, predispositions, and sense of vital interests.

THE PROBLEMS WITH REALISM

In his preface to *Perception and Misperception*, Jervis explained that he came to research and write the book through his engagement with the revisionist critique of deterrence theory.[9] This critique warned of a self-fulfilling prophecy: actions based on a misperceived US view of the Soviet Union as aggressive led Moscow to treat the United States as a grave threat requiring a buildup of forces that confirmed the starting assumption in the United States. This "spiral model" was a classic security dilemma as "each side's efforts to make itself more secure had the unintended effect of making the other less secure, compounded if not caused by each side's misperception of the other."[10] By addressing an exaggerated menace, the US policy of deterrence increased rather than reduced the risk of a nuclear catastrophe.

Jervis did not agree that that there was no real conflict with the Soviet Union, but he took seriously the charge that deterrence theorists and policymakers had assumed rather than demonstrated Soviet hostility. At the very least, they should have thought about "the possibility that their policies were depending on and if not creating dangers to the country and the world."[11] Because he could not then get the materials to investigate whether the perceptions of the Soviet threat were accurate, he instead decided to explore the more general problem of how states perceive each other, noting that despite an apparent consensus that the causes of both world wars could be traced, at least in part, to misperceptions of different sorts, this question of perception was one that had not received much attention from the international relations community.

This line of inquiry was geared to great-power wars and the possibility that they could be caused by a tragic misunderstanding rather than a genuine conflict of interests. This distressing prospect still animates much international relations thought and explains the persistent interest in the security dilemma as a core problem in the field. At one level, it is unexceptional to observe how the perceptions of the acts of one side by the other can aggravate crises. It is, however, more of a challenge to argue that without such misperceptions there would be no crisis at all. Nonetheless, this focus encouraged a debate about the dangers of provocative acts, along with inappropriate and incredible commitments, and how it can be important to exercise restraint even when there are reasons to be concerned about a developing threat.

Although *Perception and Misperception* was prompted by this debate over deterrence theory and the Cold War, it went much further. It served as the foundation for much of Jervis's work over the subsequent decade. In his 1977 article on deterrence theory, he reviewed Alexander George and Richard Smoke's *Deterrence in American Foreign Policy: Theory and Practice*.[12] Jervis saw the book as an important contribution to what he called the "third wave" of deterrence theory, which provided an empirical check on the claims of the second wave.

⨯⨯⨯

During the first wave, which began as analysts contemplated the sudden introduction of atomic bombs in 1945, the logic of the nuclear age began to be appreciated. The work of these analysts achieved little prominence because they were not addressing the prime concerns of policymakers. It took some time before the work of theorists such as Bernard Brodie came to be appreciated.[13] This was not the problem with the second wave, which began in the mid-1950s and led to a period of remarkable conceptual innovation and a lasting influence on the way we think about nuclear weapons. Rather than discuss in detail the individual second-wave theorists, Jervis described their work as "so well known that little summary is needed." For his main source, he refers to James King's excellent but, potentially frustratingly for readers, unpublished manuscript on the New Strategists.[14]

Jervis placed the game of chicken at the heart of second-wave theorizing. The game imagined two juvenile delinquents driving cars toward each other, daring the other to swerve first. It was used as an analogy for an arms race or, indeed, any situations in which the first choice of both sides is to continue on a collision course but the second is to retreat and let the other side win rather than engage in a mutually disastrous confrontation. Each side decides whether to hold to its course by examining the payoffs and estimating the likelihood that the other will retreat. Those who grasped this model could see how it could lead to tactics that were contrary to common sense, such as severing communication links and feigning anger, irrationality, or a loss of control over militant factions in one's own organization. Jervis was skeptical and used the article to develop his own critique of these theories and also the realist tradition upon which they were based and which they had revived.

Before deterrence theory came along, he noted, realism suffered because "it was so vague as to accommodate almost all behavior and that it merely summarized what statesmen and even casual observers already knew. For all its attraction, Realism had provided few explanations for puzzling behavior and had produced few leads for further research. So, deterrence addressed this criticism and gave Realism a new impetus."[15]

But the old problems remained. The theory had little to say about how to change the other side's motives, how to transform hostile into peaceful relations, the role of rewards as well as punishments, and the origins of wars and courses of crises. At best it told "statesmen how to maintain a hostile and dangerous relationship. It does not tell them how this situation might be changed, nor can they be sure whether deterrence is appropriate. And applying deterrence tactics to a state that is not a menace is likely to create a great deal of unnecessary conflict."[16]

Because of the abstract quality of the theory, it treated states as being similar. Because it was still grounded in the experience, culture, and values of the West, it did not deal with questions of ethnocentrism. That is, do we see ourselves as being better than others, and how are we perceived? It was biased in favor of status quo powers, largely written from the standpoint of countries resisting change. The most familiar part of Jervis's criticism was that the theory overestimated the rationality of decision makers, especially under conditions of high stress.

When drawing attention to this feature, Jervis made a point that is still easily forgotten: critics tended to suggest that the dangers of irrationality lay in emotional impulsiveness, resulting in attacks being launched or other terribly risky actions, although irrationality can also lead to passive acquiescence even at a time when belligerence might be a rational approach. There is an understandable disposition (which I share) to assume that the resort to armed force is normally a bad idea, but that means that we may also miss circumstances where it makes sense.

Because the second-wave theory had been largely deductive, little effort had been made to search for supporting evidence to see whether decision makers behaved as deterrence theory predicted they should and whether their actions had the expected effects. This was where the third-wave scholars came in.[17] They identified difficulties that were not raised by earlier critics and encouraged a "general appreciation of how easy it is for things to go wrong" and "the innumerable points at which errors can occur."[18] They wondered whether there were any actual examples of the smart ploys discussed by second-wave theorists, such as the deliberate increase by leaders of the cost of retreating in order to convince others that they will stand firm or committing to a course of action because of the reputational stakes involved rather than the inherent value of that action.

We will consider what Jervis wrote about the sources of error, but it is important to keep in mind a point he made, almost in passing, about the circumstances in which these errors might matter most. "These disabilities and complications have less impact," he noted, "in relatively unambiguous situations, such as those involved in the deterrence of attacks to the superpowers' homelands."[19] This point deserves emphasis. Although few did more than Jervis to alert us to the risks of misperceptions, he also recognized that in some cases the essential features of a conflict can be seen in sharp relief, largely because of the importance of the interests engaged.

Jervis distinguished between intrinsic interests—"the inherent value the actor places on the object or issue at stake"—and strategic interests— "the degree to which a retreat would endanger the state's position on other issues."[20] This is relevant to the familiar claim, raised regularly whenever the United States backs away from a prior commitment (as in Syria in 2013) or withdraws despite a long intervention (as in Afghanistan in 2021), that one consequence will be the resultant fear of allies and partners that they might be abandoned in similar circumstances. Because a strategic interest might not flow naturally from an intrinsic interest, the deterrence literature is full of discussions about commitment—the ways in which a state might increase the costs to itself of retreating to improve its bargaining position.

The case studies used by the third-wave theorists demonstrated the importance of intrinsic interests. George and Smoke included the Berlin blockade, the outbreak of the Korean War and the later Chinese intervention, the 1956 Hungarian uprising, and the Cuban Missile Crisis.[21] The state with the greater intrinsic interest in an issue is likely to prevail because it will gain most by doing so and will lose most should it retreat. The degree of intrinsic interests shapes assessments of strategic interests and the incentives in any bargaining process. If such interest is lacking, any ploys, from making statements to moving troops, will still deprive any assertions of commitment of credibility, whereas if it is present, there is no need to attempt to create an artificial commitment. So Jervis was warning against overestimating the importance of commitments that are considered independently from intrinsic interests and making too much of the potential impact of the outcome of one conflict on another. The focus on intriguing and dramatic tactics in deterrence theory had come at the expense of attending to what really mattered to the parties involved—the "underlying balance of motivation."

He added that because states "generally place a greater value on keeping what they have than on making further gains,"[22] deterrence is usually easier than compellence. He could also have said that, for the same reason, defending territory is normally easier than occupying it. That does not mean that all the status quo is worth defending. It still depends on interests. Some changes are innocuous and others inevitable, and it is unwise to commit to preventing these. Of course there is a difference between what one might want to do with nuclear deterrence, threatening punishments for a major infringement of the status quo, and a conventional defense, where consideration must be given to the balance of forces as well as the balance of motivation. Nonetheless, this point is often forgotten in the analyses of the Russo-Ukrainian War, where there has been a focus from the start on the balance of military capabilities rather than motivation. Perhaps this is because motivation reflects emotion more than a dispassionate calculation of hard power. My view from the start of this war has been that the critical difference between the two sides is that

Ukrainians are fighting for their homeland and that the Russian home-land is not, to date, seriously threatened.

The final element of Jervis's critique of deterrence theory is its apolitical character. The theory did not ask about the origins of crises but picked them up once they were underway and assumed that both sides had high interests in their outcome. This led to a third proposition: "Most conflicts end in compromise; compromise is one of those things politics is all about. It is central to behavior even when important interests are engaged."[23] When one considers crises in which deterrence is in play, some political deal may well make sense as a means of avoiding war, as in Berlin from 1958 to 1962 or Cuba in 1962. Once a war has started, however, the intrinsic interests in the outcome of a conflict become even greater because lives have been lost and resources expended. Some intrinsic interests render compromise impossible. Another bias in the field of international relations that we might want to consider is whether a natural desire on the part of scholars to favor peaceful resolution of disputes through negotiations plays down the many reasons why such talks are apt to fail, especially when fighting is still underway.

This reflects a deeper bias in international relations scholarship and one that is also natural: to assume that good theory can advise on how crises can be kept in check and stop bad situations from getting worse. In the nuclear age, that naturally encourages proposals for compromise and restraint. So far, the Russo-Ukrainian War has reinforced the theories around nuclear deterrence because the theories have worked as might have been expected. Putin warned that direct interference by NATO countries risked the most severe response, and they have refrained from direct engagement while Russia has (thus far) refrained from attacking NATO countries. The critical feature of this conflict is that it is not a great-power war, and efforts have been made to stop it turning into one, but the conflict is one in which a nuclear state is trying to conquer all or part of a non-nuclear state that is being backed in its resistance by other states, some of which are nuclear. This is not unique. It was the position in which North Vietnam found itself in its fight against the United States. In the case of the war in Ukraine, it has kept many scholars, especially in the United States, preoccupied less with how to ensure that Ukraine survives against Russian aggression and more with how the conflict might turn, intentionally or inadvertently, into a full war between nuclear-armed states.

The concern about not being provocative produces arguments for restraint. Jervis was interested in the problem of self-deterrence. Anticipating what an opponent might do can create a situation when one state holds back out of fear of how the other might respond. Overstating the threat, paying far too much attention to fantastical assessments, encourages timidity. During the Cold War, Jervis observed that "a narrowed and distorted focus on implausible contingencies has led to an exaggeration of Soviet strength which could restrict U.S. freedom of action to a greater degree than Soviet deterrence policy does."[24] During the Russo-Ukrainian War, the Biden administration took no risks with escalation, eschewing measures that might trigger a disproportionate response from Moscow. Yet moves that would have been considered provocative prior to the war have been made without producing a reckless Russian response: Sweden and Finland joined NATO, and Ukraine's membership in the European Union (EU) was set in motion (this of course is the exact issue that triggered the crisis in relations with Russia in the summer of 2013). Despite some bluster, Russia let both developments pass. Once the NATO powers considered Ukraine's future security, alliance membership appeared as the obvious next step. Gradually, inhibitions in the United States, Germany, and elsewhere on the sort of weapons that could be supplied to Ukraine began to ease, although the debates have continued as if, for example, something fundamental might change in Russian behavior according to whether the weapons supplied would be more suitable for offensive than defensive operations or the range of artillery systems provided.

The backdrop to these debates in the West was the question of what exactly mattered to Moscow: Was the war really about the future of the European security order or a determination to bring Ukraine firmly into Russia' sphere of influence or even incorporate it into a greater Russian state, or was it the result of some complex combination of the two?

PERCEPTIONS

This brings us to the question of perceptions—both of Putin and his inner circle and of those who are trying to understand and anticipate Putin's decisions. Talk of misperception suggests the possibility of accurate perception, and Jervis was wary of such claims. He wrote about the inherent ambiguity of situations and how the available evidence might support several interpretations. This is related to the wide problem of why leaders fail to act rationally.

Jervis underscored that most individuals struggle with the two key attributes of a rational person: the ability to grasp the significance of new information and the ability to deal with probabilities. Thus "the images of the other" held by decision makers are "very resistant to change," and this will affect how they go about influencing their opponents' behavior. When it comes to probabilities, decision makers are prone to ignore them altogether and so act as though events are either certain or impossible, or else they estimate them carelessly, which is problematic when there is need to manipulate another's sense of risk. Nor are decision makers good at recognizing trade-offs. They tend to believe that the policy they favor is better than the alternatives on all value dimensions, even though those values are logically independent of each other. It can be hard to admit that the same policy can both provide better security and still raise the risk of an early war. Jervis concludes, "Thus, statesman often fail to weigh the costs of their decisions properly, continue to stand by an established policy even though it should be changed, and are unable to match and adjust their actions to the environment in a way that even bounded rationality requires."[25]

So in complex situations, strategies that require a detailed knowledge of the environment and precise calculations, and assume that this is the case with both sides, may misfire, although at this point Jervis introduced the qualification about the lesser impact these "disabilities and complications" have in relatively unambiguous situations.

If policy is to have the desired effect, it must be perceived as intended, yet an actor's perceptions are apt to diverge both from "objective reality" and from those of other actors. Jervis identified the frailties of cognition: how people consider their intentions to be sufficiently clear for there to be no concern about how they are perceived; how even in the mildest of international conflicts both sides rarely grasp the other's views; how decision makers assume that their opposite numbers see the world as they do and fail to check whether this is really the case; and how they have "much more confidence in their beliefs about the other's perceptions than the evidence warrants."[26]

Jervis listed four barriers to accurate perception. The first is overconfidence. People overestimate their cognitive abilities, see evidence as less ambiguous than it is, rely too much on analogies with the past as if they can provide independent confirmation of their established beliefs, treat opposing viewings cavalierly, and are overinfluenced by what will work in terms of recent successes and failures. The second barrier is that people do not appreciate trade-offs in values. Instead of weighing costs against benefits, they tend to assume that the benefits all go one way. This makes it difficult to recognize the choices that need to be made. As an example, Jervis cited President Jimmy Carter's desire to prevent proliferation and protect human rights, without recognizing that pushing states on one front might diminish the ability of the United States to push them on another, and once concessions were made on one of these goals in support of the other, there was a risk of appearing hypocritical. With Ukraine, the Biden administration initially presented this conflict, with some justification, as one of democracy versus autocracy, only then to appreciate that because other autocratic regimes must help Ukraine, this was not the best framing device.

The third barrier involves the assimilation of new information to preexisting beliefs. This is what we would now call confirmation bias. People pick out from the evidence what they expect to see. Jervis did not always see this as a big failing because of the ambiguity in situations. He noted that "statesmen who miss, misperceive, or disregard evidence are not necessarily protecting their egos, being blind to reality, or acting in a way that will lead to an ineffective policy."[27] Nonetheless, the implication of this tendency was that images of other states are difficult to alter. The fourth barrier is defensive avoidance. This is a form of denial—simply refusing to "perceive and understand extremely threatening stimuli." This, Jervis suggested, may be the result of domestic political needs that require that a potential threat be characterized in a particular way. The state may be too invested in one course of action to see the options available to the opponent.

These problems can manifest in how states view potential adversaries with whom they find it difficult to empathize. States often underestimate the desperation that their adversaries feel and incorrectly believe that the adversaries do not see them as a threat. Leaders act in accordance with theories to which they already subscribe and are more likely to be influenced by historical analogies with which their country has experience firsthand rather than by new data. They allow their view of their own situation to influence how they weigh the capabilities and intentions of others.

But sometimes the problem is not cognitive limitations so much as it suits leaders to believe certain things. There can be strong social and political pressures to stick with a view that is not well founded, for example, the holding together of a domestic coalition. When pushing for a policy, they will tend to minimize trade-offs. If the alternatives to their chosen policy are bleak, they may exaggerate the policy's chances of success and fail to gather the information or perform the analyses to check whether this is really the case. And when it comes down to implementation, especially when these prior errors lead to a poor strategy, the results are apt to be very different from those that were anticipated. As Jervis noted, much apparent misperception was motivated. It suited those advocating particular policies to promote a view of the adversary that supported those policies. This could include presenting the danger as being greater than is actually the case. Jervis provided as an example Britain's misreading of German strength prior to the Second World War. These "pessimistic assessments of German bombing were as much the product of policies as they were a cause of them."[28] This is a tendency that can affect academics as much as governments.

MISPERCEPTION AND PUTIN'S WAR

At the start of 2022, the Russian military buildup could be explained as either preparation for an invasion or a coercive bluff. It suited a number of countries, including Ukraine (because of the costs of mobilization), to play down the risks. Although it was evident that Russia could mount an invasion, it was far less clear what Russia could hope to achieve by doing so. Getting this assessment right depended on understanding how Putin viewed the world and accepting that this might lead him into a reckless and counterproductive decision. Thus, an accurate perception of the threat depended on the assumption that Putin had an inaccurate perception of the opportunities available to Russia.

Putin's inability to accept Ukraine as an entity that is truly independent of Russia probably goes back, as it does for many Russians, to the breakup of the Soviet Union in 1991. His concerns about popular movements that are hostile to Russia were shaped by the Orange Revolution of 2004–2005.[29] In 2013, he sought to prevent Ukraine from getting any closer to the West by coercing President Viktor Yanukovych to abandon an accession agreement with the EU. This triggered the Euromaidan movement (now known as the Revolution of Dignity). Once Yanukovych fled and Russia moved to destabilize Ukraine, the core themes of an artificial country, a putsch in Kyiv, and persecuted Russian-language speakers emerged, and they became staples of Putin's speeches and Kremlin propaganda. To what extent they were core beliefs or manufactured to provide pretexts for action remains a matter for debate.

Any assessment was complicated by Putin's belief in the possibility of a fabricated truth. The Kremlin provided many statements to explain its actions, but they were often inconsistent and contradictory, designed for political effect with no attempt at verisimilitude. Putin and his former Federal Security Service (FSB) colleagues were capable of manufacturing incidents for immediate political ends and making claims that their victims had responsibility for incidents in which they were hurt (such as attacks on residential buildings during the war).[30] That being said, most of the strategy that Putin followed in authorizing this war and in its conduct is only explicable if it is assumed that Putin believed what he wrote about the history of Ukraine and of Euromaidan and then became so invested in these beliefs that he ignored any discrepant evidence and authorized a war confident that they would prove to be correct. There is no evidence that any serious effort went into gathering information on Ukrainian political affairs and on whether Russian-language speakers would naturally hail an invading force as liberators. In an autocracy, few feel able to contradict the supreme leader. Once the war began and after it became apparent that the war had been launched on a deluded premise, there was no deviation for the official line. Only Putin could set a new one.

Western observers were unsure of what to make of Putin's expressed views and the warped historical narrative that appeared to underpin them. Could a casus belli be fashioned out of them? If one could, it pointed logically toward a war of conquest, at least of Ukrainian territory adjacent to Russia. Yet if this had motivated the military buildup, what was the point of all the demands for a new European security order that Russian diplomats had made weeks before the invasion? Despite Ukraine becoming the target of military pressure, no demands were made of Kyiv. This reflected Putin's narrative—that Ukraine's leaders were puppets of the United States and NATO—but it was still an odd way to conduct coercive diplomacy.

Some international relations scholars turned to the more familiar geopolitical ground of blaming NATO enlargement for the war. In general terms, this just did not work. However much Russia might not have liked its former allies joining NATO, the issue had been managed by other means, including the 1997 Founding Act, which was intended to regulate NATO-Russian relations.[31] Ukraine's membership had not been seriously on the agenda since the Bucharest Summit of 2008. From this perspective, the conflict was a version of the security dilemma, whereby Russia had been goaded into becoming more aggressive because of a growing security threat to its western borders. But this played down the impact of Putin's particular, and poorly founded, view of Ukraine. Moreover, even when Putin described why NATO membership would be a problem, fanciful stories were told about how Kyiv would drag NATO countries into a war intended to recover Crimea or get its own nuclear weapons—neither of which were likely and both of which could have been addressed diplomatically without any recourse to war.

Putin's behavior fit Jervis's conclusions: perceptions change slowly and can be maintained in face of discrepant information, and it is unwise to develop strategies that are too subtle and are fine tuned to get just the right amount of pressure. Even so, for Putin, the balance would have been different from that envisaged by Jervis, who wrote that these strategies should be "enough to show the other that the state is very serious but not enough to provoke desperate behavior."[32]

The Ukrainians always insisted that if war came they would fight. Did Putin take this seriously or simply assume that his forces would roll over any resistance? Jervis suggested that one of the reasons for the failure of deterrence prior to the Second World War was that the British and French failed to convince German leader Adolf Hitler not only that "they would fight if pushed too far, but also that they would continue to fight even after initial reverses." The key message, which was not been conveyed, was that once they were committed to the fight they would carry on until the bitter end.

Putin's failure to grasp that Ukraine was resilient and ready to defend itself flowed naturally from his delusional view of the character of the Ukrainian state. This created a crisis for him and the Russian military as the initial offensives faltered and then had to be abandoned in order to allow for a focus on the contested Donbas region. As noted, this situation does not appear in the classic international relations texts: the United States and its allies have backed a nonnuclear country in its war with a nuclear-armed country to the point where the latter might be defeated in a military campaign that was apparently undertaken in support of a vital interest.

At this stage, all the realist concerns about not provoking Russia rushed to the fore, as if Putin's failure to conquer was pushing him into a corner so that he might "lash out" in frustration, even though Russia was not being put under threat because of this failure. Therefore, according to this argument, the United States should push for early negotiations. When Russian forces regrouped and began to make limited advances in the Donbas, the argument was that Ukraine could not win and so the United States should push for early negotiations to create a deal to end the suffering. From both perspectives, those urging an imposed compromise were anticipating developments that had yet to occur, with either the Russians or the Ukrainians facing defeat, and were assuming that there was an alternative policy that could produce a better situation. The proposals for a deal always fell at the first hurdle—Ukraine ceding territory to Russia—something for which President Volodymyr Zelensky could not get a mandate and that would most likely lead to continuing instability in and around the ceded territories and chronic insecurity among NATO members bordering Russia. This is where the balance of motivation came in. Whatever the hardships, Ukraine was going to continue to fight. As a better policy, Ukrainian leaders urged the United States and its allies to continue to provide it the weapons with which to fight and to prevail. Meanwhile Putin, desperate to demonstrate that the war had not been futile and keen to avoid the reckoning that would come once the war ended without his objectives being met, preferred to keep fighting and insisted that the war would only end with the partition of the country, even demanding that Ukraine hand over territory that Russia had failed to occupy.

It is also worth noting an observation made in an essay by Jervis that he did not fully explore, that "incorrect explanations and predictions concerning other states' behavior are caused more often by misperceptions concerning their situations than by misperceptions about their predispositions."[33] Leaving aside the regular suggestions that Putin is stubborn and determined and his statements about his ability to achieve his objectives, it is always worth checking Putin's military options to see whether Russia is in a position to achieve what he wanted to achieve. In May 2023, during the course of a curious and short mutiny from which he escaped unscathed, Yevgeny Prigozhin, head of the Wagner Group, denounced Putin's senior commanders for their meat-grinder tactics and exposed the claims made by the Russian leader about increased Ukrainian activity against the Donbas enclaves as the reason for his "special military operation." By this time, he was seeking to keep Russia in the war, not because there was a chance he could win but because he dared not lose.[34]

INTERNATIONAL RELATIONS THEORY AND THE WAR

The Ukraine War is not yet over, and there is no doubt that more developments will come that may surprise and alarm us. My own view from the start was that it is important to support Ukraine and that many of the realist arguments against doing so, or at least to encourage negotiations that would be unavoidably disadvantageous to Kyiv, are in their own way unrealistic. But there is no point in engaging in elaborate postmortems about the quality of individual contributions, or even the field as a whole, when we are still in no position to come to definitive conclusions. Moreover, it is important that those who have contributions to make continue to do so, take some analytical risks, and accept that they might turn out to be wrong. There are large elements of ambiguity and uncertainty in the situation that can catch us all out. Even contributions that might make for embarrassing reading at a later date can still make the debate sharper and introduce considerations that might otherwise have been ignored.

But in making these contributions, a degree of humility is always required. Reading through Robert Jervis's work, the openness of his mind to new ideas and evidence is always apparent, along with his readiness to engage with positions with which he disagreed. His analysis of the sources of error in high-level decision making is relevant to the potential sources of error in our contributions. We can become too invested in our theories and policy predispositions and look for arguments and evidence to validate them, asserting them with more confidence than warranted and playing down awkward trade-offs. We forget to ask the difficult question, which Bob urged on policymakers, about what would be the evidence that might convince us to change or amend our views. It was a question he always asked of others and was prepared to answer for himself.

NOTES

1. For a useful survey of the range of views among international relations scholars on the importance of NATO enlargement, see "Was NATO Enlargement a Mistake?" *Foreign Affairs* Asks the Experts, April 19, 2022, https://www.foreignaffairs.com/ask-the-experts/2022-04-19/was-nato-enlargement-mistake.

2. The most prominent realist theorist who believed that the war was largely the West's fault was John Mearsheimer. Among many articles, see John J. Mearsheimer, "The Causes and Consequences of the Ukraine Crisis," *National Interest*, June 23, 2022. He took a similar position when the conflict first broke in 2014. John J. Mearsheimer, "Why the Ukraine Crisis Is the West's Fault. The Liberal Delusions That Provoked Putin," *Foreign Affairs* 93, no. 5 (2014): 77–89. For an interesting interview, see Isaac Chotiner, "Why John Mearsheimer Blames the U.S. for the Crisis in Ukraine," *New Yorker*, March 1, 2022; "Ezra Klein Interviews Emma Ashford," *New York Times*, March 18, 2022, https://www.nytimes.com/2022/03/18/podcasts/transcript-ezra-klein-interviews-emma-ashford.html; Stephen M. Walt, "The Realist Case for a Ukraine Peace Deal," *Foreign Policy*, March 29, 2022, https://foreignpolicy.com/2022/03/29/realist-case-ukraine-peace-deal/; John J. Mearsheimer, "The Causes and Consequences of the Ukraine Crisis," *National Interest*, June 23, 2022, https://nationalinterest.org/feature/causes-and-consequences-ukraine-crisis-203182; Barry R. Posen "Ukraine's Implausible Theories of Victory: The Fantasy of Russian Defeat and the Case for Diplomacy," *Foreign Affairs*, July 8, 2022, https://www.foreignaffairs.com/articles/ukraine/2022-07-08/ukraines-implausible-theories-victory. For a more moderate realist take, see "Transcript: Ezra Klein Interviews Emma Ashford," *New York Times*, March 18, 2022, and for an alternative view, see Fiona Hill and Angela Stent, "The World Putin Wants," *Foreign Affairs* 101, no. 5 (2022): 108–22.

3. Most notably, see Robert Jervis, *Perception and Misperception in International Politics*, 2nd ed. (Princeton University Press, 2017). First published in 1976.

4. Robert Jervis, "Deterrence Theory Revisited," *World Politics* 31, no. 2 (1977): 289–324; Jervis, "Deterrence and Perceptions," *International Security* 7, no. 3 (1982–1983): 3–30; Jervis, "Rational Deterrence: Theory and Evidence," *World Politics* 41, no. 2 (1989): 183–207. For reasons that will soon be apparent, I also looked at Jervis, "War and Misperception," *Journal of Interdisciplinary History* 18, no. 4 (1988): 675–700.

5. Jervis, preface to second edition of *Perception and Misperception*, xvi–xvii.

6. Including Thomas Schelling, whom Jervis mentioned often as a major influence on his thinking. Thomas Schelling, *Strategy of Conflict* (Harvard University Press, 1960).

7. For this attribute of Jervis's scholarship, see the essay by Randall Schweller in this volume.

8. Jervis, "Deterrence and Perceptions," 11.

9. For example, see Charles Osgood, *An Alternative to War or Surrender* (University of Illinois Press, 1962).

10. Jervis, preface to *Misperception*, xiii–xiv.

11. Jervis, preface to *Misperception*, xiii–xiv.

12. Alexander George and Richard Smoke, *Deterrence in American Foreign Policy: Theory and Practice* (Columbia University Press, 1974).

13. Bernard Brodie, *Strategy in the Missile Age* (Princeton University Press, 1959).

14. A number of copies were in circulation at the time, and I read it for the first edition of my *Evolution of Nuclear Strategy* (Macmillan, 1981). An electronic version is available at https://www.amazon.co.uk/Nuclear-Strategy-Jim-King-Manuscripts-ebook/dp/B005TUOEJY.

15. Jervis, "Deterrence Theory Revisited," 290.

16. Jervis, "Deterrence Theory Revisited," 293.

17. The focus of this particular essay is George and Smoke, *Deterrence in American Foreign Policy*. Many of the third-wave theorists appeared in a collection edited by Jervis, with Richard Ned Lebow and Janice Gross Stein, *Psychology and Deterrence* (John Hopkins University Press, 1985).

18. Jervis, "Deterrence Theory Revisited," 305.

19. Jervis, "Deterrence Theory Revisited," 311.

20. Jervis, "Deterrence Theory Revisited," 314

21. George and Smoke, *Deterrence in American Foreign Policy*.

22. Jervis, "Deterrence Theory Revisited," 317–18.

23. Jervis, "Deterrence Theory Revisited," 323.

24. Jervis, "Deterrence and Perception," 18–19.

25. Jervis, "Deterrence Theory Revisited," 311.

26. Jervis, "Deterrence and Perception," 4.

27. Jervis, "Deterrence and Perception," 25.

28. Jervis, "Deterrence and Perception," 16.

29. For background, see Lawrence Freedman, *Ukraine and the Art of Strategy* (Oxford University Press, 2019).

30. This practice goes back to the earlier stages of the conflict. Shaun Walker, "Russia Blames Kiev for Ukraine Violence After Mariupol Attack," *The Guardian*, January 25, 2015, https://www.theguardian.com/world/2015/jan/25/russia-kiev-ukraine-violence-mariupol.

31. North Atlantic Treaty Organization, "Founding Act on Mutual Relations, Cooperation and Security Between NATO and the Russian Federation, Signed in Paris, France," May 27, 1997, https://www.nato.int/cps/en/natohq/official_texts_25468.htm.

32. Jervis, "Deterrence and Perception," 26.

33. Jervis, "War and Misperception," 677.

34. Lawrence Freedman, "Putin Is Running Out of Options in Ukraine: Russia Edges Closer to a Reckoning," *Foreign Affairs*, July 25, 2023, https://www.foreignaffairs.com/ukraine/putin-running-out-options-ukraine?.

3

SEMINAL CONTRIBUTIONS TO RATIONAL THEORIES OF STATE BEHAVIOR

CHARLES L. GLASER

My first encounter with Robert Jervis's work was in 1980, when I was a graduate student at Harvard University's Kennedy School and beginning to learn about nuclear strategy. I had read a couple of articles by Paul Nitze—a prominent Cold War expert on nuclear strategy with influential government experience—that appeared to identify serious shortcomings in the US nuclear arsenal.[1] To my untrained eye, Nitze's arguments made little sense. Then I read Jervis's article "Why Nuclear Superiority Doesn't Matter"[2] and learned that these arguments also made no sense to this very insightful scholar. In one way or another, most of my work since then has been informed by, engaged with, or motivated by Jervis's work, as this chapter makes clear.

Before turning to substance, I want to comment on Jervis's contribution to the field. As I am sure many others will attest, his dedication to the field of security studies and international relations was enormous and likely unparalleled. Not only did he build some of the field's key institutions—for example, the Cornell Studies in Security Affairs book series—but he also provided tremendous support and insight to scholars of security studies and international relations theory. I observed him at dozens of research and book workshops over the years; he was always prepared with long lists of comments. He was a tough critic yet always enthusiastic and constructive. To his great credit, Jervis was fair and even-handed; he provided his insight and guidance not only to scholars with whom he agreed but also to those with whom he strongly disagreed.[3]

His sheer energy and commitment were remarkable. One anecdote captures this: A few years ago, Jervis took a five-hour bus trip to a junior scholar's book workshop, arriving just in time for the dinner. The day after the workshop, Bob got up before dawn to take the bus back to Manhattan. I wondered how he continued to find the energy and was awed that he still had the interest and enthusiasm.

To many scholars and students, Jervis is best known for his work on the role of individuals in states' decisions and the psychology biases that often undermine these individuals' decisions. This reputation is well deserved: his *Logic of Images in International Relations*[4] and *Perception and Misperception in International Politics*[5] broke new ground and launched a multidecade research agenda in and to which scores of scholars have participated and contributed.

However, we should not overlook Jervis's seminal contributions to rational theories of state behavior, which are foundational to much of current international relations theory and national security policy. These encompass many of the field's key concepts, including the security dilemma,[6] the spiral and deterrence models,[7] the offense-defense balance, and the nuclear revolution.[8] Jervis's writing on these concepts is theoretically rich, and his landmark publications put these arguments front and center in the international relations theory literature. Building on this foundation, continued research clarified and elaborated these arguments, and substantial debate ensued and continues.

The security dilemma exists when the policies that a state pursues in order to increase its security necessarily decrease its adversary's security (and in which the adversary's response would decrease the state's own security). Although Jervis was not the first to identify the security dilemma,[9] his formulation explained that the nature and intensity of the security dilemma could vary, which in turn influenced the extent of competition and the possibilities for cooperation.[10] The variation depends on two dimensions—the offense-defense balance and the offense-defense differentiability.[11] Competition will be more intense and war more likely as the advantage of offense over defense increases. Cooperation, specifically qualitative arms control, is possible when offense and defense are differentiable. The logic here is foreshadowed, in less general terms, by the modern theory of arms control, which identifies ballistic missile defense and missiles carrying multiple independently targeted reentry vehicles (MIRVs) as offensive types of systems that should be limited.[12] The security-dilemma framing extends the qualitative arms-control logic to other realms.

Jervis did not explicitly place the security dilemma in the context of structural realism, but his formulation enabled others to make this move. The security dilemma provides the logic by which states that are interested only in security end up engaging in competition. In turn, divergent understandings of the security dilemma play a decisive role in dividing the two key strands of structural realism. Defensive realism essentially accepts Jervis's argument that variation in the security dilemma should lead to variation in the intensity and forms of cooperation and competition.[13] Offensive realists, in contrast, hold that the security dilemma always drives states into competition, partly because they are driven to maximize their power and partly because states should assume the worst about their adversaries.[14]

Jervis's spiral model builds on and extends the role of the logic of the security dilemma. The security dilemma can be understood primarily in military terms, explaining arms races and the changes in military capabilities that they produce. A richer understanding also explains how the arming interaction that the security dilemma drives can also influence the political relations of states, that is, how they understand each other's motives. When the adversary's arming leads the state to believe the adversary is more hostile and dangerous, the state will in turn arm more intensively, which could convince its adversary that the state is more dangerous. The result is a negative political spiral in which negative beliefs about the opposing state's motives generate interactions that further worsen political relations. Jervis emphasized the role of misperception in generating spirals but also noted the possibility of spirals without misperceptions. If a state fails to appreciate that its adversary may be arming to increase its security (not to pursue nonsecurity or greedy goals), then the state will exaggerate the adversary's hostility and the danger it poses. This assessment is built on a misperception if the adversary's arming could be for either security or greed, which is often the case, but the state assumes incorrectly that the motive is greed. Others explained more fully how rational spirals are possible, even when a state understands that the opposing state faces a security dilemma that drives its actions.[15]

Jervis extracted the deterrence model from historical debates, including the Cold War debate over US policy toward the Soviet Union, and he highlighted the key theoretical issues that underpinned it. In contrast to the spiral model, the deterrence model essentially denies that the security dilemma matters because the adversary knows that the defender is a security seeker; consequently, the defender needs to worry little, if at all, about provoking the adversary or making it insecure. The deterrence model bundles together a variety of additional assumptions: the adversary is an expansionist/greedy state, the state's credibility is connected across issues, and the states have few shared interests. The deterrence-model argument that is built on this combination of assumptions calls for highly competitive policies, especially those that demonstrate the defender's resolve and the credibility of its threats. Jervis's work on the evolution of deterrence theory explained how alternative strands of thought supported or countered the deterrence model.[16]

Jervis's work also launched a flurry of research and debate about the offense-defense balance, including whether it could be measured and whether states could mold technology to meet their own goals instead of being constrained by it.[17] This debate has theoretical and policy implications. Much of the variation in competition that defensive realism claims to explain is possible only if states are able to measure and understand the offense-defense balance. On the policy side, current policies, as well as those during the Cold War, depend on measuring balance. For example, important analyses of China's anti-access/area denial posture, which is designed to keep US forces far from China's maritime periphery, provide an assessment of the offense-defense balance and, in turn, policy guidance for the US conventional force posture.[18] In addition, whether cyberattacks favor offense or defense has generated much discussion and analysis, as cyber has become an increasingly important dimension of modern warfare.[19]

The Meaning of the Nuclear Revolution is another of Jervis's major contributions. It provides the fullest statement of Cold War thinking on the implications of nuclear weapons. In addition to clarifying important misunderstandings—for example, mutual assured destruction (MAD) is not a strategy but a condition of mutual vulnerability—Jervis makes some bold predictions about the political implications of MAD: "peace [will prevail] between the superpowers, crisis will be rare, neither side will be eager to press bargaining advantages to the limit, the status quo will be relatively easy to maintain, and political outcomes will not be closely related to either the nuclear or the conventional balance."[20] Jervis's book provides the foundation for an emerging debate on the future of nuclear strategy and forces between states that are highly and comparably capable. Critics of the theory of the nuclear revolution are now challenging both whether MAD is immutable, as Jervis implies, and whether the predictions of the theory are correct.[21]

If we focus only on these tremendous scholarly contributions, we'd be overlooking an important dimension of Jervis's work. He was also dedicated to analyzing US policy and contributed substantially here as well. *The Illogic of American Nuclear Strategy*[22] provides a sustained, searing criticism of US nuclear strategy in the 1970s and early 1980s. We see Jervis's commitment to policy analysis on other topics as well, including the 2015 Iran nuclear deal[23] and the Bush Doctrine,[24] which provided the broad rationales for the 2003 US invasion of Iraq and for ambitious US foreign policies more generally. The desire to contribute to policy debates was not a passing interest for Jervis but instead a driving force behind much of his more scholarly and abstract research and his willingness to engage in the specifics of current policy debates.

Jervis was a true giant among scholars. He contributed tremendous energy to building and sustaining the fields of international relations theory and security studies. He made monumental contributions to the ideas and concepts that are at the heart of current theoretical debates. Robert Jervis will be missed and well-remembered; his scholarly legacy will live on by continuing to influence our understanding of the most important issues in international relations.

NOTES

1. Paul H. Nitze, "Assuring Strategic Stability in an Era of Détente," *Foreign Affairs* 54, no. 2 (1976): 207–32; and "Deterring Our Deterrent," *Foreign Policy*, no. 25 (1976–1977): 195–210.

2. Robert Jervis, "Why Nuclear Superiority Doesn't Matter," *Political Science Quarterly* 94, no. 4 (1979–1980): 17–633.

3. On this, see the essay by Austin Long as well as the online essays by Brendan Green, "The Philosopher King," H-Diplo, ISSF Tribute to the Life, Scholarship, and Legacy of Robert Jervis: Part I, ed. Richard H. Immerman, Diane N. Labrosse, and Marc Trachtenberg, February 4, 2022, https://issforum.org/to/JervisTribute-1, and Joshua Rovner, "Bob Jervis on Hard Problems," H-Diplo, ISSF Tribute to the Life, Scholarship, and Legacy of Robert Jervis: Part II, ed., Richard H. Immerman, Diane Labrosse, and Marc Trachtenberg, August 25, 2022, https://issforum.org/to/JervisTribute-2.

4. Robert Jervis, *The Logic of Images in International Relations* (Princeton University Press, 1970).

5. Robbert Jervis, *Perception and Misperception in International Politics* (Princeton University Press).

6. Robert Jervis, "Cooperation Under the Security Dilemma," *World Politics* 30, no. 2 (1978): 167–214.

7. Jervis, *Perception and Misperception in International Politics*, chap. 3.

8. Robert Jervis, *The Meaning of the Nuclear Revolution: Statecraft and the Prospect of Armageddon* (Cornell University Press, 1989); and Jervis, *The Illogic of American Nuclear Strategy* (Cornell University Press, 1984).

9. Credit for that belongs to John H. Herz, "Idealist Internationalism and the Security Dilemma," *World Politics* 2, no. 2 (1950): 157–80.

10. Jervis, *Perception and Misperception in International Politics*, chap. 3; and Jervis, "Cooperation Under the Security Dilemma."

11. Another early developer of offense-defense arguments was George H. Quester, *Offense and Defense in the International System* (Wiley, 1977).

12. Thomas C. Schelling and Morton H. Halperin, *Strategy and Arms Control* (Twentieth Century Fund, 1961).

13. Among others, see Barry R. Posen, *The Sources of Military Doctrine* (Cornell University Press, 1984); Charles L. Glaser, "Realists as Optimists: Cooperation as Self-Help," *International Security* 19, no. 3 (1994–1995): 50–90; Glaser, *Rational Theory of International Politics: The Logic of Competition and Cooperation* (Princeton University Press, 2010); and Stephen Van Evera, *Causes of War: Power and the Roots of Conflict* (Cornell University Press, 1999).

14. John J. Mearsheimer, *The Tragedy of Great Power Politics* (Norton, 2001).

15. Charles L. Glaser, "The Security Dilemma Revisited," *World Politics* 50, no. 1 (1997): 171–201; and Andrew H. Kydd, "Game Theory and the Spiral Model," *World Politics* 49, no. 3 (1997): 371–400.

16. Robert Jervis, "Deterrence Theory Revisited," *World Politics* 31, no. 2 (1979): 289–324.

17. Among others, see Charles L. Glaser and Chaim Kaufmann, "What Is the Offense-Defense Balance and Can We Measure It," *International Security* 22, no. 4 (1988): 44–82; Sean M. Lynn-Jones, "Offense-Defense Theory and Its Critics," *Security Studies* 4, no. 4 (Summer 1995): 660–91; and Keir A. Lieber, *War and the Engineers: The Primacy of Politics over Technology* (Cornell University Press, 2008).

18. Stephen Biddle and Ivan Oelrich, "Future Warfare in the Western Pacific: Chinese Anti-access/Area Denial, U.S. AirSea Battle, and Command of the Commons in East Asia,

International Security 41, no. 1 (2016): 7–48; and Eugene Gholz, Benjamin Friedman, and Enea Gjoza, "Defensive Defense: A Better Way to Protect Allies in Asia," *Washington Quarterly* 42, no. 4 (2019): 171–89.

19. For example, Rebecca Slayton, "What Is the Cyber Offense-Defense Balance? Conceptions, Causes, and Assessment," *International Security* 41, no. 3 (2016–2017): 72–109.

20. Jervis, *The Meaning of the Nuclear Revolution*, 45.

21. Austin Long and Brendan Rittenhouse Green, "Stalking the Secure Second Strike: Intelligence, Counterforce, and Nuclear Strategy," *Journal of Strategic Studies* 38, no. 1–2 (2015): 38–73; Keir A. Lieber and Daryl G. Press, *The Myth of the Nuclear Revolution: Power and Politics in the Atomic Age* (Cornell University Press, 2020); and Brendon Rittenhouse Green, *The Revolution That Failed: Nuclear Competition, Arms Control, and the Cold War* (Cambridge University Press, 2020).

22. Jervis, *The Illogic of American Nuclear Strategy*.

23. Robert Jervis, "Turn Down for What? The Iran Deal and What Will Follow," *Foreign Affairs*, July 15, 2015, https://www.foreignaffairs.com/articles/iran/2015-07-15/turn-down -what.

24. Robert Jervis, "Understanding the Bush Doctrine," *Political Science Quarterly* 118, no. 3 (2003): 365–88; and Jervis, "Why the Bush Doctrine Cannot Be Sustained," *Political Science Quarterly* 120, no. 23 (2005): 351–77.

4

THE JERVISIAN STYLE IN
INTERNATIONAL RELATIONS

JOSEPH M. PARENT

Jervisian:
| Jer'-vis-i-an | Jer'-vɪs-ðan | Jer'-vē-šən |

1. adj. relating to or characteristic of the political philosopher Robert Jervis.
2. n. a person who supports the views of political philosopher Robert Jervis.
3. n. of an intellectual style that adds consistency and complexity to perspectives lacking either.

Wonder isn't a good place to start; it's the best. One way or the other, the central theme of all writing on Robert Jervis is wonder. How did he do it? How did he do so much of it? How did he do it so well? Indisputably, Jervis was a wonderful person and scholar, and my experience as his student, which continues through the present, was miraculously similar to that of others.[1] Jervis was a complex person who studied complex things, and an impartial spectator would be right to stress this complexity squared. Yet alongside those images, I would like to offer an alternative.

Just because Jervis's reflection is hard to encompass in one mirror—psychologist, historian, political scientist, sociologist, international relations theorist . . . and all this before the introduction of hyphens—does not mean that we can consider him only in shards.[2] That would be some distortion; no one worked harder to integrate insights than Jervis. There is a powerful and systemic unity to his work that, in time, merits his inclusion in the pantheon of political philosophers. Jervis was a systems theorist of the first order, his ideas operate as a system, and his efforts unified knowledge without assaulting reality. Here, I make the case for Jervis as a political philosopher qualified for canonization (or whatever the secular equivalent is).

To develop the brief, I first discuss what constitutes the Jervisian style in international relations. Next, I explore a counterfactual of how the world would look without it. Then, I compare Jervis's outlook to that of other political philosophers. And last, I contrast the Jervisian style to the paranoid style in American politics and claim that the former fights the latter.

JERVISIAN STYLE

Discerning a system in Jervis's approach faces two disorienting obstacles: the obvious tensions in his thought and its open-endedness. First, let us consider the contradictions and ambivalences in his works, which he openly confessed. For example: "I was perhaps a premature rational choice theorist, which in part explains why my recent criticisms of this approach are, I hope, based on some understanding of and sympathy for it."[3] "I was always both attracted and repelled by parsimony." "Abstract theorizing is crucial," but "a deep commitment to empirical research" is essential.[4] Usually, he preferred reason to intuition, but sometimes the reverse.[5] His perspective was invariably interdisciplinary, and he had no qualms melding perspectives from different paradigms.[6]

Second, Jervis's corpus is resolutely open-ended, and it is hard to encapsulate the indefinite. As he remarked early on, the examples in his first book "in no sense constitute proof. Indeed they do not show that what I claim should occur given certain assumptions does in fact occur all, or even most, of the time."[7] Despite a lifetime of pioneering work, his observations remained cautious and modest: "We are headed for a difficult world, one that is not likely to fit any of our ideologies or simple theories."[8] His first book was about putting forth an image of oneself, the second was about how states perceive the images of others, but in his last book, although he would have liked to have been able to unite these images, "after forty-five years I can still make only limited steps in that direction."[9]

Yet there is a visible harmony for those who look. Jervis was a consistent systems theorist, and his theories mirror his subjects. The world is a shifting collection of overlapping systems: "Very little in social and political life makes sense except in the light of systemic processes." Systems have (1) a set of interconnected units so that changes in some elements or their relations produce changes in other parts of the system and (2) properties and behaviors of the whole that are different than those of the parts. Systems tend to be homeostatic, like thermostats or blood pH, and although inputs may vary widely, outputs tend to remain within a confined range. When people populate systems, however, there can be striking tipping points and unintended effects, although these tend to be exceptional.[10]

<hr />

The Jervisian style is fundamentally systemic; its answers are bands, not points. This can be frustrating at times—where is the concrete conclusion?—but it sidesteps the perils of false precision and hubris. What sometimes seem like quibbles, cavils, and technicalities are better depicted as honesty, prudence, and due process.

The approach is as social as the subject it studies. Jervis was little interested in coauthoring, but neither was he a reclusive genius. In fact, he was famous for reaching out to others, bringing them together, and brokering their exchange: "Sometimes it will be useful to ask who, if anyone, was right; but often it will be more fruitful to ask why people differed and how they came to see the world as they did."[11] The goal was not producing brilliant formulas in solitude but collective convergence on moving targets.

To Jervis, the problems and their remedies were as semistable as the world he watched. Generally, political actors tend to get into trouble with sloppy thinking: they fail to frame falsifiable hypotheses, examine crucial assumptions, ask what evidence would be present if their arguments were right or wrong, use the value of absent evidence, or employ the comparative method to isolate causal factors.[12] The best antidotes are better thinking habits: preventing premature mental closure, taking conflicting views seriously, maintaining openness to change, forcing people to confront trade-offs, and being wary of rhetoric trumping analysis.[13]

Similarly, Jervis thought the field functioned like the world. "If the discipline is functioning well, each school of thought enriches others as powerful research of one kind strengthens, not weakens, the alternatives." He went on: "Popular approaches inevitably are taken too far and call up opposing lines of argument; and if any important approach is ignored for too long, scholars will return to it as the picture of international politics becomes excessively imbalanced."[14] The logic is evolutionary, except the environment is social, not natural, and the equilibria is perspectival, not biological. The payoff could be consilience, where multiple independent lines of inquiry bundle together to strengthen conclusions each is too weak to reach on its own.

One of Jervis's most frequent references was *Rashomon,*[15] a movie about the same series of events from multiple perspectives. Each perspective is reliable enough to relay the basic facts of the story but not enough to avoid major divergences, ostensibly because each narrator had different self-serving biases. The film never reveals where the truth lays. It's tempting to greet this conclusion with a nihilistic shrug or a determined hope that, with the right set of eyes, the truth could be pinned like butterfly wings. Jervis succumbs to neither temptation. His work implied that the world is shared, and great things can happen when people overcome their biases and try to live in a common world.[16] But reality is restless, and only the consistent application of multiple approaches can close in on it.

IT'S A WONDERLESS LIFE

To isolate the impact of Jervis's scholarship, let us consider a different movie: *It's a Wonderful Life.* The plot is essentially a counterfactual about whether the world is better off with a particular individual in it, and Jervis was certainly fond of counterfactuals.[17] He would, of course, advise some agnosticism here; a world with only one thing different may not only be unlikely but also difficult to chart in all its consequent changes.[18] Still, he would find it productive and amusing, albeit not dispositive, to imagine a world he was not born in.

With some justice, counterfactuals are often unkind to individuals because, in large social systems, the influence of individuals is typically circumscribed. As the economist George Stigler once roasted his colleague Milton Friedman, "Milton, if you hadn't been born, it wouldn't have made any difference."[19] Jervis was certainly not the first systems theorist in international relations, nor the first to foreground interdisciplinary perspectives.[20] Yet it would be lunacy to suggest that Jervis's birth made no difference.

Exhibit A is the citation counts and surveys that put Jervis in the top ten of international relations scholars for the past few decades.[21] Exhibit B is the dizzying array of prominent thinkers who attest that Jervis changed their thinking. Thomas Schelling wrote, "*The Logic of Images in International Relations* has had more influence on me than anything else Bob has written. That's partly because the ideas were absolutely new to me. The analysis focused on something I hadn't thought about." John Mearsheimer testifies that "virtually all the international relations scholars in my cohort . . . were influenced in truly important ways by [Jervis's] scholarship." The list goes on.[22]

The influence these scholars describe is multifaceted: Jervis as a critic and convener, bringing people together, highlighting differences, noting inconsistencies, and fostering engagement.[23] Jervis embraced ambiguity and flux with multimethod, interdisciplinary approaches. Where some scholars take a lawyerly attitude toward their work, dutifully defending the unrepresented, and others take a chauvinistic attitude, dogmatically advocating for their sect, Jervis did neither. His role was closer to an arbitrator. He tried to get everyone in a room talking, get their stories straight, weigh and consider their briefs, and recommend a clement and appealable verdict. Nothing and no one could monopolize the truth, and being fair and inclusive provided more light and less heat. That judicious influence did not revolutionize the field, but it likely accelerated its development and expanded its appeal.

More to the point, he added wonder. Lawyers and chauvinists are tediously predictable; everyone knows what their conclusions will be—the only mystery is how they are going to get there. The reverse was true of Jervis. He put suspense in scholarship. Because he found the world so fascinatingly full of wonders, it was seldom clear where he would come out on an issue. And although one could rely on him to use ecumenical methods to get there, there were always strobe-light surprises along the way. Without his influence, surely the field would not be devoid of wonder, but it would surely be wonderless.

JERVIS AS POLITICAL PHILOSOPHER

What do you call someone so systematically absorbed by the wonder of politics? Historically, there is a clear answer: political philosopher.[24] What separates the great from the good is their judgment. But how to judge judgment? Here, too, there is something of a consensus. Those with sound judgment are spectators who overcome the limitations of their position by entering into innumerable perspectives and consistently considering issues impartially.[25] They bow to none and cannot be coerced by fame, fear, or fortune. The more widely they consult and consider, the more expert they judge. Hannah Arendt calls this common sense, not because everyone has it but because it is a sense that we cohabit a common world.[26]

Customarily, experts are equated with specialists, but the custom leads us astray in this case. Specialists sharpen the mind by narrowing it and hone it with routine. To be sure, sympathy and self-command are skills like any other, which require training and practice. But to take social systems in the round is anathema to narrowing or routinizing; it is to be a general specialist. The division of intellectual labor has been proceeding profitably for centuries, but a critical niche in that division is the generalists, who connect the parts into a working whole. International relations has a good claim to be a factory of general specialists, and Jervis had a good claim to be a lynchpin in international relations. He exemplified generalism as a calling.

Jervis was a political philosopher par excellence. He possessed the universal curiosity, impartial independence, sensible intellect, and systemic cast of mind that characterize the best of them. He never met a discipline, a paradigm, a theory, or a method that he could not learn from. He always said his favorite work was *System Effects*, and he embodied its arguments throughout his career. He had the power to hold a complicated subject in his palm and analyze it minutely and insightfully and then, with an impish turn, do it all over from different angle. The end result is political philosophy of the first order.

CONCLUSION

The Jervisian style in international politics makes a stark contrast with the paranoid style in American politics. Richard Hofstadter, himself a historian with a memorable writing style, coined the latter to pejoratively describe a tendency in US history for conspiratorial thinking, which was often partisan and pathological, projecting the deepest desires and fears of the right onto their opponents on the left.[27] Hofstadter got a number of things wrong about the paranoid style—it's less partisan and more political than he advertised it—but he was right to highlight its prevalence and perils.

The Jervisian style is the remedy to the paranoid style. It gently facilitates broad, rigorous, nonpartisan thought. It encourages all sides to slow down, cool off, and see things from other people's points of view. It sensitizes us to look out for what our perspective is missing and to remember that learning is a team effort. In an age when the paranoid style threatens to destabilize the institutions of truth, we urgently need the Jervisian style.

It is sometimes believed that knowledge will bring about a disenchanting of the world, that contempt will follow familiarity. Jervis thumbed his nose at those claims. He was a political philosopher with encyclopedic interests and profound insights who was just as spellbound by the world before his analysis as after. For the Jervisian style, the means and ends of all understanding are wonder.

NOTES

1.   My thanks to Paul MacDonald and Sebastian Rosato for comments. Kin claims to mine are made by James W. Davis and Brendan Rittenhouse Green. See Richard H. Immerman, Diane Labrosse, and Marc Trachtenberg, eds., "Tribute to the Life, Scholarship, and Legacy of Robert Jervis, Part I," *H-Diplo/ISSF*, February 4, 2022, https://issforum .org/admin/jervis-tribute-part-1.pdf; and Jacques E. C. Hymans, "Stanley Hoffman *Now*," *H-Diplo/ISSF*, Forum 33, April 8, 2022, https://networks.h-net.org/node/28443/discussions /10079634/h-diploissf-forum-33-2022-importance-scholarship-stanley.

2. I would be remiss, in the midst of an optical metaphor, not to note that the daughter of the Greek personification of wonder, Thaumas, is Iris, goddess of the rainbow and messenger between humanity and the gods.

3. Robert Jervis, *The Logic of Images in International Relations* (Columbia University Press, 1989), xiii.

4. Robert Jervis, *How Statesmen Think: The Psychology of International Politics* (Princeton University Press, 2017), 1, 5.

5. For instance, he preferred to analogize intelligence failures to batting averages rather than fielding percentages, despite the fact that no reliable method to collect such data existed, much less a comparable statistic. See Rober Jervis, *Why Intelligence Fails: Lessons from the Iranian Revolution and the Iraq War* (Cornell University Press, 2010), 178.

6. Robert Jervis, *American Foreign Policy in a New Era* (Routledge, 2005), chap. 1.

7. Jervis, *The Logic of Images in International Relations*, 17.

8. Jervis, *American Foreign Policy in a New Era*, 138.

9. Jervis, *How Statesmen Think*, 108.

10. Robert Jervis, *System Effects: Complexity in Political and Social Life* (Princeton University Press, 1997), 6, 12–13, 16, 295.

11. Robert Jervis, *Perception and Misperception in World Politics* (Princeton University Press, 1976), 29.

12. Jervis, *Why Intelligence Fails*, 3, 191.

13. See Jervis, *Why Intelligence Fails*, 3, 191; see also Jervis, *How Statesmen Think*, 135.

14. Robert Jervis, "Realism and the Study of World Politics," *International Organization* 52, no. 4 (1998): 971–72.

15. Jervis, *Why Intelligence Fails*, 175; Jervis, *How Statesmen Think*, 6, 269.

16. Jervis, *How Statesmen Think*, 280; Erving Goffman, *Strategic Interaction* (University of Pennsylvania Press, 1969), 3.

17. Perhaps also meta-counterfactuals. What if the plot had been real? Many argue that the upstate New York town in *It's a Wonderful Life* would have been better off without the film's protagonist. See Wendell Jamieson, "Wonderful? Sorry, George, It's a Pitiful, Dreadful Life," *New York Times*, December 18, 2008, https://www.nytimes.com/2008/12/19/movies/19wond.html; Dom Nero, "In *It's a Wonderful Life*, Pottersville Actually Looks Way More Fun Than Bedford Falls," *Esquire*, December 24, 2019, https://www.esquire.com/entertainment/movies/a30315437/its-a-wonderful-life-pottersville-better-than-bedford-falls/.

18. See Robert Jervis, "Counterfactuals, Causation, and Complexity," in Phillip Tetlock and Aaron Belkin, eds., *Counterfactual Thought Experiments in World Politics: Logical, Methodological, and Psychological Perspectives* (Princeton University Press, 1996), 309–16.

19. Quoted in Ian Ayres, "Making a Difference: The Contractual Contributions of Easterbrook and Fischel," *University of Chicago Law Review* 59, no. 1 (1992): 1391. This fits with Merton's multiples, the norm in science of simultaneous discovery. See Robert K. Merton, "Singletons and Multiples in Scientific Discovery: A Chapter in the Sociology of Science," *Proceedings of the American Philosophical Society* 105, no. 5 (1961): 470–86.

20. For systemic precursors, see Norbert Weiner, *Cybernetics: Control and Communication in the Animal and the Machine* (Wiley, 1948); Morton A. Kaplan, *System and Process in International Politics* (Wiley, 1957); Klaus Knorr and Sidney Verba, eds., *The International System: Theoretical Essays* (Princeton University Press, 1961); Eglė Rindzevičiūtė, *The Power of Systems: How Policy Sciences Opened Up the Cold War World* (Cornell University Press, 2016). For influential interdisciplinary precursors, see W. G. Sumner, *Folkways* (Dover, 2002 [1906]); Nicholas J. Spykman, *The Social Theory of Georg Simmel* (Atherton, 1966 [1925]); Edward Vose Gulick, *Europe's Classical Balance of Power: A Case History of the Theory and Practice of One of the Great Concepts of European Statecraft* (Norton, 1955); Quincy Wright, *A Study of War*, 2nd ed. (University of Chicago Press, 1965); and Irving L. Janis, *Victims of Groupthink: A Psychological Study of Foreign Policy Decisions and Fiascoes* (Houghton Mifflin, 1972).

21. Jervis is in the top three for international relations scholars in books. See https://books .google.com/ngrams/graph. For the latest Political Science 400 list, where Jervis places tenth for international relations scholars, see Hannah June Kim and Bernard Grofman, "The Political Science 400: With Citation Counts by Cohort, Gender, and Subfield," *PS: Political Science and Politics* 52, no. 2 (2019): 307. And for US surveys of the most influential international relations scholars, where Jervis has ranged from sixth to eighth since 2004, see https://trip.wm.edu/data/dashboard/faculty-survey.

22. Thomas Schelling, "Foreword," in James W. Davis, ed., *Psychology, Strategy and Conflict: Perceptions of Insecurity in International Relations* (Routledge, 2013), xi; John Mearsheimer, "Homage to Bob Jervis," in Immerman et al., eds., "Tribute to the Life, Scholarship, and Legacy of Robert Jervis, Part I," *H-Diplo/ISSF*, February 4, 2022, 84; Thomas Christensen and Keren Yarhi-Milo, "The Human Factor: How Robert Jervis Reshaped Our Understanding of International Politics," *Foreign Affairs*, January 7, 2022, https://www.foreignaffairs.com/articles/world/2022-01-07/human-factor.

23. See Robert Jervis, "Realism, Neoliberalism, and Cooperation: Understanding the Debate," *International Security* 24, no. 1 (1999): 42–63; Jervis, "Liberalism, the Blob, and American Foreign Policy," *Security Studies* 29, no. 3 (2020): 434–56.

24. See Plato, *Thaetetus* 155d; Aristotle, *Metaphysics* 982b; Adam Smith, "History of Astronomy," §§1–2; Dana Villa, *Arendt* (Routledge, 2021), 358.

25. See Cicero, *Tusculan Disputations*, I 39–40, V 9–10; Montaigne, *Essays*, I.27; Adam Smith, *Theory of Moral Sentiments*, I.iii.2.2–11, III.3.3–6, II.4.1–8; Immanuel Kant, *Critique of Judgment*, §40; J. G. Herder, "Whether We Need to Know the End of History in Order to Write History"; George H. Mead, *Mind, Self, and Society: From the Standpoint of a Social Behaviorist* (University of Chicago Press, 1967), 334; Mead, *On Social Psychology* (University of Chicago Press, 1977), 13, 18; Joshua Cherniss, *Liberalism in Dark Times: The Liberal Ethos in the Twentieth Century* (Princeton University Press, 2021), 158, 181, 195.

26. See Hannah Arendt, *Between Past and Future* (Penguin, 2006), 219.

27. See Richard Hofstadter, *The Paranoid Style in American Politics and Other Essays* (Vintage, 2008), chap. 1.

5

A NOT-SO-CLOSET CONSTRUCTIVIST?

STACIE E. GODDARD AND RONALD R. KREBS

Robert Jervis was an intellectual giant who refused to be categorized. His intellectual legacy will partly be defined by his contributions as a theorist of international relations whose writings on signaling, perception, and complexity were pathbreaking.[1] But Jervis was the rare political scientist whom historians spoke about with reverence, and his scholarship was unusually interdisciplinary. He cared deeply about the world beyond the ivory tower, and his analyses of intelligence failures and nuclear strategy had a particular impact on the US policy community.[2] Jervis was a liberal who had cut his teeth protesting the war in Vietnam and whose criticism of the US role in the nuclear arms race was unyielding and trenchant, but he also sought to create a space for conservative voices within an academy whose tendencies toward intellectual monoculture worried him.

As a scholar of international relations, Jervis was theoretically eclectic. As he reported, when students would ask if he was a realist, he would reply to "the annoyance of many of them . . . [that] there is no simple answer." Yes, Jervis was a realist insofar as he saw states as the core actors of international politics, maintained that leaders had to pursue power and interests under tremendous uncertainty, and averred that the "inability of states to bind themselves (and the knowledge that others cannot be bound) is a central feature of international relations."[3] He shared realism's proclivity to pessimism and its deep appreciation of power. But beyond these commitments, Jervis was theoretically ecumenical. He pulled liberally from social psychology, evolutionary theory, and sociology. He largely stood clear of the "paradigm wars" of the 1990s. From his perspective, "If the discipline is functioning well, each school of thought enriches others as powerful research of one kind strengthens, not weakens, the alternatives. No one approach consistently maintains a leading position: each of them catches important elements of international politics, and many of our arguments are about the relative importance of and the interrelationships among various factors."[4]

It is no accident that those of us who attended Columbia in the latter part of the 1990s and who had a constructivist bent but also sympathy for realism gravitated to Bob Jervis and found in him a supportive mentor.[5] This was not merely because Jervis was theoretically open-minded. It was also because his work intersected with, and in critical ways even anticipated, constructivist approaches to international politics. There were naturally limits to Jervis's constructivist inclinations, and he was skeptical of mainstream American constructivists' implicitly liberal normative commitments—what he viewed as their desire to "see world politics transformed by the spread of appropriate norms, identities, and concepts of world politics."[6] Yet, as card-carrying constructivists ourselves, we have always seen Bob's work as an inspiration. We became the scholars we are not despite Bob's interventions but because of them. Yes, any good dissertation advisor should think alongside their advisee's project. But Bob's probing questions of our projects revealed not only his intellectual generosity and depth, his ever-searching mind, and his encyclopedic knowledge but also how comfortable he was with critical aspects of the constructivist worldview.[7]

Our reflections on Bob Jervis's work extend beyond our personal experience. In our view, Jervis's writings—especially on signaling but also on psychology and systems dynamics—exhibited significant constructivist sensibilities. Although Jervis emphasized the centrality of strategic action, he understood that these interactions take place within, are enabled by, and are confined by existing systems of meaning and practice. He brought a distinctively social and relational framework to his research at the juncture of international relations and psychology. Jervis's writings on systems dynamics not only spoke to the agent-structure problem—the peculiar reality that agents' choices are confined by the structures within which they reside but that those structures are themselves produced and recon-figured by agents' choices—but also intersected with constructivists who question social scientists' ability to develop invariant causal laws and the-oretical statements.

At the same time, there were profound limits to Jervis's constructiv-ism. He remained indebted to individualist psychology, which inhibited his capacity to move beyond individual beliefs and perceptions and grasp collective phenomena like norms, social roles, and discourses. Although Jervis regularly referenced and invoked factors that are typically associ-ated with constructivist theorizing, he did not put these at the center of his analysis. When, on rare occasions, Jervis did train his analytical ener-gies on international norms, he could retreat into materialist foundations.

Nevertheless, we believe that Bob Jervis set out a stimulating intel-lectual agenda, and perhaps even a meeting ground, for constructivist, psychologist, rationalist, and realist scholars of international politics and history. If we collectively take up that agenda in the spirit of Jervis's searching and ecumenical mind, it will be a fitting tribute to this remark-able scholar, advisor, and human being.

JERVIS AS A CONSTRUCTIVIST FELLOW TRAVELER

Jervis never classified himself as a constructivist, although he often sug-gested that his work anticipated constructivist theorizing well before it would become part of the international relations mainstream.[8] We see three areas where Jervis's work complements and intersects productively with constructivist theorizing: his attention to intersubjective meaning and interpretation, his "strategic constructivist" commitments, and his sensitivity to contingency in social explanation.

THE IMPERATIVE OF INTERPRETATION

Realist in his inclinations, Jervis did not question the analytical value of starting with structural imperatives. Jervis's seminal analysis of the security dilemma—the difficulty states have in providing for their own security without thereby posing a threat to others and ultimately under-mining their own security—displayed the power of structural analysis,[9] but he also recognized that international structure, while offering an important starting point, rarely spoke clearly. Early in his career, in *The Logic of Images*, Jervis set out a basic belief about the world that shaped his scholarship to come: "A large number of interactions are ambiguous not only in terms of who won and lost, but also in terms of why the actors behaved as they did."[10] Even on the most fundamental questions—from threat perception to alliance politics to the consequences of inducements and threats (carrots and sticks)—Jervis declared that "structure . . . can rarely yield definitive answers." This was not just because "the external environment is rarely so compelling as to obviate the need for difficult judgments and choices," but because it typically allowed for deeply divergent "interpretations of behavior."[11]

Jervis came to this conclusion from his grounding in human psychology via critical reflection on the silences of game theory.[12] In his incisive take on the "neo-neo" debates of the 1980s, Jervis began by observing that game theory's power derives from the many factors that shape actors' calculations and are external to the game itself, being provided either by assumption or by empirical input.[13] This was hardly an original point, but many others focused on the characteristics of the actors—their exogenous preferences, beliefs, and so on. In contrast, Jervis turned to more social and processual elements. He focused on the ways in which streams of history were causally connected through the meaning actors imparted to those events. Those imputations, he averred, transformed the actors themselves and their interactions to the point that they were no longer playing the same game. As Jervis put it, "We often talk of repeated plays of a Prisoners' Dilemma. But this formulation is misleading when the preferences and beliefs of the actors, and the nature of the game itself, change as it is played. What is at stake and the nature of the issue is defined over time, as actors develop their positions, in part in response to the positions taken by others."[14] A self-declared social constructivist could not have put it any better. Events, in Jervis's view, did not speak for themselves. They required interpretation. And those interpretations had deep consequences, reshaping the reality that then confronted subsequent agents.

Human interpretation of the world lay at the center of Jervis's worldview, as it does for constructivists. Constructivists are attentive to the

ways in which situations are defined, seeing such definitions as both contingent and productive. How situations are defined affects who is considered a relevant party to the interaction, what identities are activated,
what courses of action the parties can envision, and thus what outcomes
will follow. In a similar vein, Jervis recognized that events had no inherent meaning, that they always had to be filtered through and interpreted
by human beings: "The interpretation of others' action is rarely self-
evident, but it is almost always important." He observed that "while the
standard PD [Prisoner's Dilemma] model points to four possible outcomes that need to be ranked, decision makers may define the situation differently—most frequently by ignoring the possibility of mutual
restraint." At times, he posited, "a lack of cooperation may be explained
in significant measure by the actors' inattention to the possibility of such
an outcome." It must be acknowledged that Jervis awkwardly discussed
this issue in the context of actors' preferences as if the "definition of the
situation" could be reduced simply to a preference ranking. But how situations are defined affects the very unit of analysis, and this, in turn,
Jervis pointed out, affects whether we see the actors as "cooperating" or
"defecting" and who we believe to have "won."[15] As Jervis once noted, Secretary of State Cyrus Vance thus indicated that the Carter administration
intentionally framed the invasion of the Shaba province in Zaire "as an
African—not an East-West problem."[16] Thomas Schelling had similarly
observed the importance of defining the Cuban Missile Crisis as either a
Caribbean Crisis, as the Soviet Union preferred, or as a superpower crisis,
as the United States insisted.[17]

SHAPING MEANING:
STRATEGY AND SOCIAL CONSTRUCTION

To place interpretation at the analytical center of global politics is thus to
recognize significant scope for the exercise of agency. Human beings do
not merely take the world as it is, but they remake it. For Jervis, whose
approach remained always grounded in psychology, this often took place
in the confines of the human mind, in individuals' first-order beliefs and
perceptions, in others' second-order beliefs and perceptions about others'
beliefs and perceptions, and in how human agents responded, often in

counterintuitive ways, to these first- and second-order beliefs and perceptions. But, on occasion, Jervis focused also on the mechanisms through
which actors in global politics imparted meaning, making and remaking
reality. Decades later, liberal constructivists would often treat the realm of
ideas as, in Hugh Heclo's terms, an arena for "puzzling," in which actors
might be persuaded by the "unforced force of the better argument," à la
Jürgen Habermas.[18] Decades earlier, Jervis started from more realist if
still constructivist premises. His actors engaged in meaning making as
a form of competition, of "powering." They understood that social categories have material consequences, and thus, they sought to bend those
categories to their will and interest. To paraphrase Karl Marx, however,
they made meaning but not just as they pleased and not under circumstances they chose. For Jervis, social construction was a deeply strategic
and power-laden process but one that could not be reduced to material
power alone.

Jervis paid most attention to the strategic construction of meaning in
his work on signaling, particularly in *The Logic of Images*. The problem
Jervis took up in this underappreciated classic is how actors convey their
intentions in global politics given the inherent problem of "cheap talk."
Rationalists offer a straightforward answer to this puzzle: senders select
their signals, and receivers interpret them, on the basis of cost, which,
above some cut point, constitutes a credible indicator of the actor's "type."
But Jervis advanced a different and far more constructivist argument.
Behavior, however "costly" it may be, does not seamlessly provide information, and verbal and symbolic communication is not mere "cheap talk."
In fact, Jervis observed that "while decision-makers rarely accept at face
value others' accounts of the motives, goals, calculations, and perceptions
that led to their decisions, this data is almost never ignored." In fact, he
contended, "the actor who quickly, confidently, and consistently defines
the situation in a given way can often convince the other that this picture
is an accurate representation of the interaction, or at least that this is the
situation as it appears to the actor, which is frequently all he needs to
accomplish."[19]

Signals, he further argued, "are not natural; they are conventional. That
is, they consist of statements and actions that the sender and receiver have
endowed with meaning in order to accomplish certain goals."[20] During
the Cold War, dispersing one's strategic bombers was interpreted as a

signal that one was moving up the escalatory ladder toward nuclear war. This action's power as a signal ironically derived from the fact that, as Jervis's former student Jon Mercer noted, it "has no military significance— that's why the United States has ICBMs [intercontinental ballistic missiles] and submarines."[21] As a signal whose meaning was "largely conventional," this action could be deprived of significance, and a new signal could be adopted and invested with meaning in its stead. Jervis maintained that "the United States could announce that whenever it raised a flag with a mushroom cloud pattern over a missile base this meant that it was taking an international event very seriously."[22]

Yet Jervis conceived of processes of social construction as always deeply strategic. In his view, which shaped our own conception of the social world (even when we were not entirely aware of it!), socially sensitive political actors were not "cultural dopes" who blindly obeyed some "logic of appropriateness" but rather were as a rule both culturally embedded and strategically sensitive.[23] For Jervis, investing and disinvesting particular signals with particular meanings, which he termed "coupling and decoupling," was not merely a coordination game, akin to driving on the left or right side of the road. The power to define the meanings associated with certain signals was the power to define the range of actions that were available in given circumstances and that could tilt the outcomes of a conflict. Because there were concrete interests at stake, Jervis argued, leaders would not only strategically select signals that they believed would most likely convey or, in some cases, conceal their intentions but also seek to alter the meanings bound up with particular signals. Jervis took an even harder constructivist turn in elucidating the efforts of actors in global politics to shape common interpretations of motives: the "coupling" and "decoupling" of "indices."[24]

Notwithstanding his tendency in *The Logic of Images* to emphasize agency, however, Jervis was sensitive to the limits of agentic social construction. He was allergic to the voluntaristic individualism of liberalism. His social constructivism recognized that meanings were sometimes deeply sedimented and "taken for granted," which impeded decoupling. He recognized the power of discursive formations that constituted the world within which individuals exercised agency. Thus he approvingly cited historians who attributed intense security competition early in the twentieth century to the prevalence of Social Darwinism, and he recognized that belief in the dominance of the military offense—the so-called "cult of the offensive"—was uniform and transnational.[25]

Another such discursive formation that served as an abiding preoccupation across Jervis's career is deterrence theory, specifically the interdependence of commitments and the need to uphold reputation.[26] A key axis of debate has been whether the underlying premise that states have stable dispositions, as resolute or irresolute "types," that guide their behavior across conflict zones has merit. Jervis was at times skeptical,[27] which followed from his openness to contingent processes of "decoupling," and his students' research placed his intuition on more solid analytical and empirical footing.[28] But he also acknowledged that "even if this view [that actors' have stable dispositions] is false . . . the actor must be guided by it if others believe it" and, by extension, even if they do not really believe it, if one believes that others really believe it. The result, as Jervis suggested, is to "require that a state's foreign policy have a kind of perceived unity."[29] Jervis always grasped the fact that leaders may seek to act strategically but that the existing "cultural toolkit," in Ann Swidler's influential later formulation, both enables and limits their capacity for strategic action.[30]

In *The Logic of Images*, Jervis thus set out an ambitious intellectual agenda on the politics of contested meaning in global politics. Unrestrained by the intellectual history of "constructivism," he gravitated toward a "strategic constructivism" that melded together two distinctive influences and disciplines—the rationalist economist Thomas Schelling and the sociologist Erving Goffman.[31] Constructivists took up this agenda only decades later, with little awareness or acknowledgment of Jervis's important contributions. It was also an intellectual agenda that Jervis himself regrettably did not avidly pursue over the coming decades, as his research swung between its more rationalist and its more psychological poles and as the influence of Goffman on his work waned. In his later publications, Jervis expressed his "hope to return to the unfinished task of bringing signaling and perception into closer alignment."[32]

Nor should we push Jervis's constructivism too far. Although Jervis appreciated the role of intersubjective meanings in underpinning strategic action, his work did not pursue how these meanings were constructed, how they were historically rooted, or how they might change over time. Never fully able to escape individualism, Jervis saw discursive formations as ideologies that exercised their impact by shaping individuals' preferences, rather than being more deeply constitutive.[33] For instance, belief in deterrence logic, as encapsulated within the rhetoric of the domino theory, did not simply reside within individuals as a belief. As a dominant discursive formation, it was not easily displaced even when the wars that were legitimated in its name, most notably the Vietnam War, proved disastrous. At times, moreover, Jervis suggested that there were inherent qualities of signals that made them more resonant; he did not see meanings as constructed "all of the way down." Nevertheless, Jervis was adamant that rationalist analysis needed to take intersubjective meanings seriously because it rested "on assumptions about each actor's expectations about how the other will behave—expectations that form socially."[34]

COMPLEXITY AND CONTINGENCY

Although Jervis styled himself a realist, he was not inclined to a structural-determinist theory of international politics. He did not think that such theorizing was either possible or productive, partly because human beings had to make sense of structural forces, partly because the international system's complexity generated unintended consequences, and partly because social interaction can reconfigure and even transform structures. Jervis was thus deeply attentive to agency and contingency in global politics. To appreciate the contingency of social phenomena is to recognize that the particular configuration that constitutes the analyst's object of interest could have been otherwise. Contingency similarly lies at the heart of the social constructivist worldview, which implies that social objects could have been constructed differently.[35] Of course, one may be sensitive to contingency without being a constructivist, but Jervis's reasons for doing so dovetailed nicely with constructivist sensibilities.

As Nuno Monteiro noted in a review of *System Effects*, Jervis's approach to the agent-structure problem mirrored social theoretic and international relations constructivist arguments about the mutual constitution of structures and agents.[36] Jervis was skeptical of liberal dreams of transcending anarchy, and he never went as far as to say, à la Alexander Wendt, that "anarchy is what states make of it."[37] He found realism's insight that to a significant degree the international system's anarchic structure made competition among states inevitable, too compelling. Yet

System Effects, which he described as the favorite of all his books, provides countless examples of agents' interactions transforming their environment, ranging from the natural world (the interaction between elephants and acacia trees) to individuals (how actions during "first contact" shape the emerging structure) to international relations. At times, Jervis limited the impact of interaction to characteristics of the agents themselves: "the capabilities, preferences, and beliefs of actors can also be changed by interaction." But the consequences could also blur into features of the structure. Jervis observed that Argentina's invasion of the Falklands transformed the definition of the situation: it "chang[ed] the issue for international audiences from the illegitimacy of colonialism to the illegitimacy of the use of force."[38]

Jervis even went so far as to question the very distinction between agents and structures. In his telling, the fact that agents' interactions could have such transformative effects means that "we can no longer fruitfully distinguish between actors and their environments, let alone say much about any element in isolation." In a characteristically lucid way, Jervis rendered this idea concrete by exploring the impact of nuclear weapons, and decision makers' response to them, on international anarchy. As he described, "We often refer to international situations as precarious, unstable, or dangerous. But, again, if statesmen perceive them as such and fear the consequences, they will act to reduce the danger—one reason why the Cuban Missile Crisis did not lead to war was that both sides felt this could be the outcome if they were not very careful. Nuclear weapons generally have this effect. Because statesmen dread all-out war, international politics is safer than it would otherwise be, and probably safer than if war were less destructive."[39]

Jervis also dismissed structural determinism because the international environment always works through human beings. Humans are not automatons, reacting predictably to shifts in their environment. They are reflective, social creatures. Unlike many other realists, Jervis therefore saw a meaningful albeit limited capacity for agency: "The failure to appreciate the fact that the behavior of the actors is in part responsible for the environment which later impinges on them," he wrote, "can lead observers—and actors as well—to underestimate actors' influence." Jervis's stance on the agent-structure problem was nuanced. His actors were never romantic heroes who rose effortlessly above their circumstances.

Their agency was always deeply embedded, simultaneously made possible and confined by the context of action. Jervis was appreciative of the contingency of systems' origins, believing that "many possible worlds are compatible with the basic laws of physics, chemistry, biology, and economics," but he was also attentive to dynamics of positive feedback that locked in initial contingent choices and produced "great stability after it has been operating for a time."[40]

Jervis's appreciation for both agency, albeit confined and channeled, and contingency had much in common with a constructivist sensibility. It also led him to emphasize the role of history and path dependence. "Problems arise in a context and out of a history," he observed. "When clear points of choice occur, they are often structured by the settings in which they arise." In his account, those settings could be the result of countless factors ranging from "industrial vagaries" to "unexpected events" to "the accidents of a change in relevant laws." A superficial reader of Jervis's oeuvre might find that surprising because Jervis's method often seemed to treat history as a grab-bag of disconnected examples with which to illustrate his theoretical points. Although this is a sin for which professional historians often lambaste international relations scholars, Jervis was never the target of this perennial charge. Historians rightly saw Jervis as an intellectual companion who appreciated that events took place within history. Jervis thus noted in his critique of game theory that "where the players are is strongly influenced by where they have been." As an example, he cited Britain's failure to cooperate with Germany and restrain Russia in 1914 with reference to its having done so in the immediately preceding crisis and the resulting fear that doing so again would have devastating consequences for the Triple Entente.[41] Put differently, like a good historian, Jervis was pointing out that many cases in international politics are not independent of each other. They occur within streams of events that are causally linked, and "earlier incidents [alter] actors' perceptions and calculations, and sometimes their basic preferences and values."[42] Although statistical databases would treat these crises as independent "cases," Jervis implied that this was an unsustainable position. The constructivist worldview similarly recognizes that seemingly sedimented and stable "social facts" are always the contingent product of past interactions. Imposing analytical order on events, as social science does, entails somewhat arbitrarily interrupting a stream of history.

Jervis's commitment to historical context and contingency ultimately led him to be skeptical, even more than some "mainstream constructivists" were, about predictive social science. Causation is certainly not absent from Jervis's accounts, and he argued that it was possible to have some degree of theoretical generalization. In *System Effects*, for example, he set out numerous abstract mechanisms that operate across diverse realms. But Jervis questioned whether "the discipline's desire to pin down causation by eliminating selection effects, reciprocal causation, and endogeneity . . . leads to a downplaying of the importance of these phenomena not—or not only—as threats to causal inference but as fundamental forces operating in the world."[43]

THE LIMITS OF JERVIS'S CONSTRUCTIVISM

However, as we have already suggested, Jervis was not a thoroughgoing constructivist. First, although Jervis was not a liberal voluntarist, who saw people as capable of making unencumbered choices, he often remained indebted to the liberal individualism of social psychology. True, he saw regulative, prescriptive norms as stabilizing features of international politics, and he put significant stock at times in morality. He grasped and acknowledged the significance of conventions not only in signaling but also in determining what constitutes "defection."[44] But very often Jervis sought to collapse collective phenomena back into individualist or at least aggregative ones. His very vocabulary—preferences, beliefs, perceptions—reflected his individualist ontology. Although Jervis appreciated how past social interactions could reshape these characteristics of individuals, he was rarely comfortable with a truly social ontology that attributed power to *collective* phenomena, from norms to discourses to dominant narratives. For Jervis the psychologist, these did not exist except insofar as individuals believed in them, expressed them, and adhered to them. His world was typically that of the subjective not the *inter*subjective.

Second, although Jervis, with his catholic mind, at times recognized the power of norms, conventions, narratives, discourses, and the like, they did not become a focus of his intellectual pursuits. *The Logic of Images* might have become a shortcut to constructivism if Jervis had centered his analytical energies on the "coupling" and "decoupling" of "signals" and "indices." Instead, he followed the path of cognitive psychology to understand how signals were interpreted by their receivers. As a result, he devoted little attention to how actors invested signals and symbols with new meanings and why particular efforts came to fruition while others fell short. He did not explore how such conscious strategic efforts became unquestioned "common sense" and how their deeply political origins became obscured. Jervis supported such work, as our work and that of his other students attests, but he did not, except on rare occasions and in offhand passing comments, contribute directly to such research himself.

ROBERT JERVIS AND
THE FUTURE OF CONSTRUCTIVISM

Jervis's wide-ranging insights into international relations continue to influence us. We think his insights should shape ongoing and future research grounded in social constructivist commitments. Constructivists would be well served to revisit, reengage, and build upon Jervis's strategic constructivist approach to contested meaning and communication in international politics. Jervis rightly noted that the literature on signaling devotes much more attention to the issuers of the signal, and their possible reasons for doing so, than to the signal recipients and how they interpret the signal. There is, Jervis observed, often a disconnect between the two, and how targets receive and make sense of signals is of equal, if not greater, importance.[45] Jervis similarly noted, in his seminal article on "security regimes," that such regimes are possible only if "actors . . . believe that others share the value they place on mutual security and cooperation," a condition that he deemed both necessary and "not trivial."[46] We have only to look at our own interactions with others to grasp how common miscommunication is and how often meanings are not shared. Meetings of the minds are all too rare, Jervis noted, because no two human beings have precisely the same experiences, occupy identical positions, and process information in precisely the same way. Divergent mental schemas underpin different motivated biases and perceptions.[47]

Constructivists often assert that "shared knowledge" and "social facts" constitute international politics. They commonly presume that the constellations of meaning associated with these intersubjective phenomena, from international norms to social roles, are widely shared. This, ironically, is not a far cry from the rationalist presumption that all actors naturally grasp the meaning of signals the same way. Just as Jervis cautioned against the latter presupposition and suggested that human psychology could explain the significant slippage between the intention of the signal's sender and the inference(s) made by the signal's observer(s), he would caution against the former. Constructivists would be well advised to heed his warning. Actors in global politics, from diplomats to officials at nongovernmental organizations (NGOs) to violent nonstate actors, differ in their positions and may well also differ in how they interpret and relate to intersubjective phenomena. Social objects do not act in the international arena; people do. The act of interpretation is the pathway that leads from social phenomena to individual action. Constructivists, in our view, too often treat the meaning of social objects as settled rather than contested. The contested practice of meaning making should lie at the heart of constructivist theorizing about international politics. Constructivists may be productively inspired by the psychological insights into the multiplicity of meanings that can be, and often are, attributed to social objects. Social life is composed of both common sense and contested realms. The scope of those realms varies across both space and time, and political actors have good reason to set the unquestioned common sense foundations of our world. Constructivist international relations should not proceed from the presumption of either settled shared meaning or ever-ongoing contestation. It should devote itself precisely to understanding how social objects move across realms, in part as the production of conscious, strategic political action; why social objects fall into one or the other of these realms at different times; how settled constellations of meaning produce social outcomes; and how common sense becomes destabilized.

Jervis's research should also inspire scholars to look more closely at process and interaction as sites of social construction and contestation. Constructivism in the United States gained attention as a critique of structuralism, particularly neorealism's emphasis on the determinative effects of anarchy.[48] Yet constructivists long struggled with the agent-structure problem as well, tacking between structure and agency with little idea of how to bring them together. Some focused on how structures—normative structures rather than material ones—shaped agents' behavior, principally through socialization into the dominant rules of the game. Others highlighted the central role of transnational actors, who often worked for NGOs, in introducing new norms into and thereby reweaving the social fabric of global politics. The first group offered a more social structural determinism, seemingly with little room for agency; the second group offered appreciation of radical agency, seemingly unencumbered by structure.

Jervis's work on international systems may provide a way out. It draws our attention not to the macro level (structure) or micro level (agents) but to the meso level of interaction, to "how action is situated within an interconnected and interactive system."[49] There are parallels here between Jervis's work and that of "relationalist" constructivists. Relationalists, like Jervis in *System Effects*, emphasize the "the theoretical and analytical significance of connections, ties, transactions and other kinds of relations among entities" that "give rise to both actors and the environments in which they find themselves."[50] Starting with interaction may offer a more productive path forward, allowing for a fuller, more vivid picture of the processes by which agents and structures constitute each other.

Moving to the meso level comes at some theoretical cost. Reflecting on *System Effects* fifteen years after it was published, Jervis found that his "book could be seen as anti-theoretical, not in the sense of abandoning abstractions, but rather in questioning the utility of a unified overarching theory."[51] For those who aspire to promulgate universal theories that apply over time and space, focusing on contingent interactions, developing general mechanisms that combine in unpredictable ways, and elucidating meso-level processes will be unsatisfying, even slippery. But Jervis's contributions stand as a reminder that one need not be a grand theorist or offer universal, invariant models of world politics to produce significant contributions to international relations theory.

Bob Jervis may not have been a card-carrying constructivist. Even so, his attention to strategic action amid contested social meaning and interpretation continues to inform our work and, we believe, sets out a productive research program for constructivists more generally. We hope that many will take up the charge and give Jervis, a constructivist fellow traveler, his due.

NOTES

1. Robert Jervis, *The Logic of Images in International Relations* (Columbia University Press, 1989 [1970]); Jervis, *Perception and Misperception in International Politics*, new ed. (Princeton University Press, 2017 [1976]); Jervis, *System Effects: Complexity in Political and Social Life* (Princeton University Press, 1997).

2. Robert Jervis, *The Illogic of American Nuclear Strategy* (Cornell University Press, 1984); Jervis, *The Meaning of the Nuclear Revolution: Statecraft and the Promise of Armageddon* (Cornell University Press, 1989); Jervis, *Why Intelligence Fails: Lessons from the Iranian Revolution and the Iraq War* (Cornell University Press, 2010).

3. Robert Jervis, "Politics and Political Science," *Annual Review of Political Science* 21 (2018): 8, 9.

4. Robert Jervis, "Realism in the Study of World Politics," *International Organization* 52, no. 4 (1998): 971–72.

5. Bob Jervis was the advisor to both authors, who received their PhD degrees from Columbia (Krebs in 2003 and Goddard in 2004).

6. Jervis, "Realism in the Study of World Politics," 974.

7. On constructivism, especially in the form Jervis appreciated it, see, among many others, Nicholas Onuf, "Constructivism: A User's Manual," in *International Relations in a Constructed World*, ed. Vendulka Kubalkova, Nicholas Onuf, and Paul Kowert (M.E. Sharpe, 1998), 58–78; Peter J. Katzenstein, ed., *The Culture of National Security: Norms and Identity in World Politics* (Columbia University Press, 1996); Ian Hurd, "Constructivism," in *The Oxford Handbook of International Relations*, ed. Christian Reus-Smit and Duncan Snidal (Oxford University Press, 2009), 298–316.

8. See, for instance, Jervis, "Politics and Political Science," 7.

9. Robert Jervis, "Cooperation Under the Security Dilemma," *World Politics* 30, no. 2 (1978): 167–214.

10. Jervis, *Logic of Images*, 175.

11. Jervis, *System Effects*, 204–9, at 209, 205; see also 226–30.

12. On the nature and purposes of game theory, see Thomas C. Schelling, "What Is Game Theory?" in his *Choice and Consequence* (Harvard University Press, 1984), chap. 10; and Duncan Snidal, "The Game Theory of International Politics," in *Cooperation under Anarchy*, ed. Kenneth A. Oye (Princeton University Press, 1986), 25–57.

13. Robert Jervis, "Realism, Game Theory, and Cooperation," *World Politics* 40, no. 3 (1988): 317–49.

14. Jervis, "Realism, Game Theory, and Cooperation," 321.

15. Jervis, "Realism, Game Theory, and Cooperation," 336, 323, 329–31.

16. Quoted in Jervis, *System Effects*, 24.

17. Thomas C. Schelling, *Arms and Influence* (Yale University Press, 2020 [1966]), 64.

18. Hugh Heclo, *Modern Social Politics in Britain and Sweden: From Relief to Income Maintenance* (Yale University Press, 1974); Thomas Risse, " 'Let's Argue!': Communicative Action in World Politics," *International Organization* 54, no. 1 (2000): 1–39.

19. Jervis, *Logic of Images*, 174–75.

20. Jervis, *Logic of Images*, 139.

21. Jonathan Mercer, "Rational Signaling Revisited," in *Psychology, Strategy, and Conflict: Perceptions of Insecurity and International Relations*, ed. James Davis (Routledge, 2013), 71.

22. Jervis, *Logic of Images*, 229.

23. That said, Jervis did appreciate the power of habitual action (see "Realism, Game Theory, and Coooperation," 320) and thus anticipated the turn to unreflective action embodied by the "practice turn" and the "logic of habit," represented respectively by the work of Vincent Pouliot and Ted Hopf (a former Jervis student). See Vincent Pouliot, *International Security in Practice: The Politics of NATO-Russia Diplomacy* (Cambridge University Press, 2010); Emanuel Adler and Vincent Pouliot, eds., *International Practices* (Cambridge University Press, 2011); and Ted Hopf, "The Logic of Habit in International Relations," *European Journal of International Relations* 16, no. 4 (2010): 539–61.

24. Jervis, *Logic of Images*, chaps. 6–7.

25. Jervis, "Realism, Game Theory, and Cooperation," 325–26.

26. Jervis would surely have acknowledged the impact of the Vietnam War in critically shaping his intellectual persona and passions; he touched on it in Jervis, "How I Got Here," Learning the Scholar's Craft Series, March 4, 2020, https://hdiplo.org/to/E198 and https://issforum.org/essays/PDF/E198.pdf.

27. See, for instance, Jervis, *System Effects*, 168–71. But on the whole, Jervis was fairly agnostic, and his views fluctuated. See, for instance, Jervis, "Domino Beliefs and Strategic Behavior," in *Dominoes and Bandwagons: Strategic Beliefs and Great Power Behavior in the European Rimland*, ed. Robert Jervis and Jack Snyder (Oxford University Press, 1991), 20–50; Jervis, *System Effects*, 171–73; and, most recently, Jervis, Keren Yarhi-Milo, and Don Casler, "Redefining the Debate Over Reputation and Credibility in International Security: Promises and Limits of New Scholarship," *World Politics* 73, no. 1 (2021): 167–203.

28. See especially Ted Hopf, *Peripheral Visions: Deterrence Theory and American Foreign Policy in the Third World, 1965–1990* (University of Michigan Press, 1994); and Jonathan Mercer, *Reputation and International Politics* (Cornell University Press, 1996).

29. Jervis, *System Effects*, 23; see also 168–71.

30. Ann Swidler, "Culture in Action: Symbols and Strategies," *American Sociological Review* 51, no. 2 (1986): 273–86.

31. As Jervis himself acknowledged decades later: Jervis, "Politics and Political Science," 7.

32. Jervis, "Politics and Political Science," 16.

33. See the discussion in Jervis, "Realism, Game Theory, and Cooperation," 325–26.

34. Jervis, "Realism in the Study of World Politics," 978.

35. On contingency and constructivism, see Ian Hacking, *The Social Construction of What?* (Harvard University Press, 2000).

36. Nuno Monteiro, "We Can Never Study Any One Thing: Reflections on Systems Thinking and IR," *Critical Review* 24, no. 3 (2012): 351–52.

37. Alexander Wendt, "Anarchy Is What States Make of It: The Social Construction of Power Politics," *International Organization* 46, no. 2 (1992): 391–425.

38. Jervis, *System Effects*, 59, 55.

39. Jervis, *System Effects*, 59.

40. Jervis, *System Effects*, 56, 155–161, at 156.

41. Jervis, "Realism, Game Theory, and Cooperation," 320, 321.

42. Robert Jervis "System Effects Revisited," *Critical Review* 24, no. 3 (2012): 403.

43. Jervis "System Effects Revisited," 395.

44. Jervis, "Realism, Game Theory, and Cooperation," 344–48, at 348; 331.

45. Robert Jervis, "Signaling and Perception: Drawing Inferences and Projecting Images," in *Political Psychology*, ed. Kristen R. Monroe (Lawrence Erlbaum, 2002), 293–309. See also Jervis, *How Statesmen Think: The Psychology of International Politics* (Princeton University Press, 2017), 107–24.

46. Robert Jervis, "Security Regimes," in *International Regimes*, ed. Stephen D. Krasner (Cornell University Press, 1983), 177.

47. See Jervis's extensive discussion of such matters in his *Perception and Misperception*.

48. See, most notably, John J. Mearsheimer, *The Tragedy of Great Power Politics* (Norton, 2001).

49. Jervis, "System Effects Revisited," 396.

50. Patrick Thaddeus Jackson and Daniel H. Nexon, "Reclaiming the Social: Relationalism in Anglophone International Studies," *Cambridge Review of International Affairs* 32, no. 5 (2019): 2.

51. Jervis, "System Effects Revisited," 396.

6

THE "FOURTH" ASSUMPTION FOR
THE OPERATION OF BALANCE
OF POWER SYSTEMS

RANDALL L. SCHWELLER

The definition of "insight" is the act or outcome of grasping the inward or hidden nature of things or of perceiving in an intuitive manner the true nature of a situation. I can think of no better way to describe the mind of Robert Jervis. Over the past six decades, no theorist of international relations has written as many sentences, paragraphs, and pages of indispensable theoretical insights, of complex logics lucidly and intelligently explained, of analytical brilliance packaged in pithy, quotable phrases as Jervis did. Driven by counterintuitive ideas and novel ways of perceiving complex problems, Jervis cast new light on matters we thought were familiar. All his writings follow the same pattern: one good idea after another. Sometimes he expounded on these ideas; more often he left them dangling like low-lying fruit for others to pick. And his food for thought was always worth the chewing. This, in my view, is the Jervis effect: leaving precious ideas, like hundred-dollar bills, on the ground for others to pick up and profit by, a point to which I will return.[1]

Consider his thoughts about the balance of power. Consistent with Kenneth Waltz's thinking, Jervis conceived of balances of power arising spontaneously and organically out of the conflicts of human beings organized as groups (states in the modern era) that seek self-preservation and dispute over the sharing of the world and its riches—all of which engender irreconcilable international differences. One of the most significant and unappreciated points that Jervis ever made was his "fourth" crucial assumption for the operation of a balance-of-power system: "war must be a legitimate instrument of statecraft."[2] So much confusion in the literature could have been avoided if everyone who has ever written about balance of power and the supposedly competing theory of power transition (or power preponderance) had been forced beforehand to read this line and fully grasp its implications.

Contrary to the standard claim that has become a staple of quantitative statistical studies generated by the peace-science wing of the field, balance-of-power and power transition theories do not make competing predictions regarding which distribution of power, an even or unbalanced one, best promotes peace. Balance-of-power theory is not about war or peace but rather the survival of great powers as politically autonomous actors. When this is understood, the two theories are entirely complementary. Power concentrated in the hands of one state makes peace *plentiful* while making the political autonomy and influence of everyone except the hegemon *scarce*. Because great powers seek to maximize their power and influence, peer competitors eventually rise to challenge the hegemon and its existing order. These dissatisfied rising challengers serve as catalysts for balancing behaviors (building arms and forming alliances) among rival camps. Balancing behaviors are preparations for war, not peace. If major-power war eventually breaks out, as it did in 1914 and 1939, there is no reason to conclude that the balance of power failed to operate properly. Quite the opposite: balance of power requires that war be a legitimate tool of statecraft, and so its presence does not refute but rather supports the theory.

As Harold Lasswell observed in 1935, the balancing of power rests on the expectation that states will settle their differences by fighting.[3] This expectation of violence exercises a profound influence on the types of behaviors exhibited by states and on the system as a whole. It was more than just the prospect of war that triggered the basic dynamics of past multipolar and bipolar systems, however. It was the anticipation that powerful states sought to, and would if given the right odds, embark on territorial conquests that shaped and shoved actors in ways that are consistent with the predictions of Waltzian balance-of-power theory. In other words, war in the preatomic age was seen not just as a remote option on the table, a so-called "last resort," but also as a very probable event. Thus, Nicholas Spykman commences his discussion of power politics and war:

"The international community is a world in which war is an instrument of national policy and the national domain is the military base from which the state fights and prepares for war during the temporary armistice called peace."[4] These conventional but mostly forgotten views of the balance of power faithfully follow the concept's initial appearance in the climactic episode of the Trojan War, where Zeus intercedes, lifting high his golden scales with death in either pan, as Achilles chases Hector around the walls of Troy. As Martin Wight explains, "Homer's use of the figure of the balance has no connection with international order. It is the symbol, not of stable peace, but of the culminating point of struggle."[5]

When war is unthinkable among the great powers, it is hard to see how polarity exerts the constraints predicted by structural balance-of-power theory. According to Jervis, this is precisely the world that exists today. His Presidential Address at the 2001 American Political Science Association meetings called attention to the unprecedented development of a security community among the leading states—the United States, Western Europe, and Japan (curiously from today's standpoint, China was left off the list)—as the defining feature of today's world politics, a "change of spectacular proportions, perhaps the single most striking discontinuity that the history of international politics has anywhere provided."[6] Among members of the community, war had become unthinkable, and bandwagoning and balancing would "not map on the classical form of the balance of power."[7] Of course, as Jervis observed, international politics can change rapidly. Even so, it is difficult to see how major-power war could become thinkable again given the threat of nuclear annihilation, the benefits of peace grounded in the perceived decoupling of territorial conquest from national prosperity, and the shared values and beliefs about how the world works among the major powers.

Next, consider Jervis's thoughts on misperception caused by structural uncertainty in the actor's external environment and how these thoughts undermine the bargaining model of international conflict and its resolution. For Jervis, a core problem with the formal bargaining literature is its central premise—that rational people with the same information cannot reach conflicting estimates of uncertain events. Such a claim is almost certainly wrong in the real world—wrong to the point where it becomes a dubious core assumption to construct "useful" theories of international relations.[8] It is no mystery, if one reads Jervis's work on information processing, why leaders with the same information might reach different estimates about the utility of war. Given the many difficulties in estimating the probable costs and benefits of war (e.g., the shortage of reliable data, the excess of "unknowable" information, the large number of decision points, leaders' different risk propensities), it would be truly puzzling if leaders tended to reach the same estimates about its utility. Yet, employing the "people with the same information will reach the same estimates of uncertain events" assumption, the bargaining model proposes that, ceteris paribus, as two sides reveal information about their capabilities and intentions, a bargaining space will open to permit a war-avoiding bargain.[9]

Jervis's work on signaling and misperception casts grave doubts on this proposition. It suggests, instead, that new information, though not entirely useless, may be ineffective in avoiding war. Specifically, the notion that "costly signaling" solves the problem of incomplete information ignores Jervis's considerable body of work on the difficulties states encounter in both sending and receiving signals. The link between actions and images is rarely firm and immutable. As Jervis put it, "Few actions are unambiguous. They rarely provide anything like proof of how the state plans to act in the future."[10] Both signals and indices can be manipulated by the sender for purposes of deception or, conversely, misperceived by the observer when they are meant to convey the truth.

Regarding the latter, cognitive theory has advanced many hypotheses about how motivated biases and the need for cognitive economy limit people's ability to process information in purely rational and efficient ways. We are all cognitive misers to some degree. Our perceptions of others' intentions, resolve, trustworthiness, and capabilities, therefore, often persevere in the face of credible evidence and costly signals to the contrary. Yet, the core assumption that drives most formal theories is that costly signaling, usually in the form of tied hands or sunk costs, eliminates uncertainty by separating the wheat (trustworthy) from the chaff (untrustworthy "cheap talkers"), turning pooling equilibria into separating ones.[11] For Jervis and those who appreciate his work on misperception, this straightforward, unproblematic approach to signaling is no way to run a railroad.

The links between misperception and conflict become even more compelling when we introduce complexities at the level of intrastate relations to those at the interstate level. As Alfred Vagts noted back in 1939:

> Again and again, military men have seen themselves hurled into war by the ambitions, passions, and blunders of civilian governments, almost wholly uninformed as to the limits of their military potentials and almost recklessly indifferent to the military requirements of the wars they let loose. Aware that they may again be thrown by civilians into an unforeseen conflict, perhaps with a foe they have not envisaged, these realistic military men find themselves unable to do anything save demand all the men, guns, and supplies they can possibly wring from the civilians, in the hope that they may be prepared or half prepared for whatever may befall them.[12]

Here we see how even "rational military men" are driven by the motivated biases of their civilian leaders to adopt practices and plans associated with militarism and arms racing, both of which make war more likely, to prepare for worst-case scenarios.

The key point is that international politics takes place within an uncertain environment riddled by structural uncertainty and misperceptions about others' signals, intentions, resolve, capabilities, strategies, and actions. Costly signaling alone cannot overcome all problems associated with information processing, whether driven by motivated or unmotivated cognitive biases. And because "historians and political scientists are drawn to the study of conflict more often than to the analysis of peaceful interactions," misperception is almost entirely associated with spiraling hostilities and war—those driven by imagined rather than real conflicts of interest. This is the "tragedy" of international politics under anarchy. But a corollary view of misperception is Jervis's orthogonal insight that misperception probably plays a major role in harmonious relationships as well as hostile ones. On this point, he suspects harmonious relationships "are the product of routinized and highly constrained patterns of interaction more often than the result of accurate perceptions."[13]

Here we have a shining example of the Jervis effect on the field. What appears to be a throw-away line in a Jervis article inspires a wonderful book on the subject: *Constructive Illusions: Misperceiving the Origins of International Cooperation* by Eric Grynaviski. Contrary to the conventional wisdom that international agreements are the products of mutual understanding, Grynaviski argues that international cooperation is more likely and more productive when states wrongly believe that they share a genuine understanding of each other's position. It was precisely these kinds of "constructive misunderstandings" that facilitated the superpower détente between 1972 and 1979. Indeed, "without false intersubjective beliefs, cooperation may have never begun."[14]

As his student, I was riveted by Jervis's lectures. He approached the materials in a semistructured manner, like a jazz musician riffing on a theme. You could see the wheels turning in his head as he set several thematic ideas in motion, partially expounding on one and then moving on to another with the promise to return to this or that idea later. When it was over, it all came together or not. But even when it didn't cohere into a tightly packaged whole, we left intellectually satisfied and more curious than when we entered the lecture hall.

Having never known the field without Jervis's large presence, I can only imagine how much poorer its development would have been if he had decided to do something else with his life. As one of the grateful salmon at Columbia that made it upstream, I am certain that my own scholarly development would have been immeasurably poorer if not for the great fortune of meeting Robert Jervis and having been mentored by him. More important, he was funny in a playful, good-natured way. There was no snark or nastiness to his jokes. He was old-school, Marx Brothers funny, which nicely segues into a story about the only time he seemed genuinely peeved at me.

One Sunday morning in the summer of 1989, I wanted to enter the locked International Affairs building (which was literally across the street from my apartment on the first floor). I didn't have a key, so I waited for someone (anyone) to come down the elevator and open the door. Finally, Robert Jervis of all people showed up. Rather than open the door, he asked me, "What's the magic word?" I responded, "Abracadabra?" He repeated, "What's the magic word?" I tried again: "Open sesame?" After several minutes of this, he finally broke down and opened the door, saying: "Swordfish! What's the matter with young people today? You don't watch Marx Brothers movies?" Now that I'm older than Jervis was back then, I find myself similarly frustrated about young people's ignorance of famous lines from Woody Allen movies. "What's the world coming to? What do they teach people these days?" The world will never see the likes of Robert Jervis again. It is a far poorer place without him.

NOTES

1. See also Randall Schweller, "Jervis's Realism," in *Psychology, Strategy and Conflict: Perceptions of Insecurity in International Relations*, ed. James W. Davis (Routledge, 2013), 25–46, which contains a few similar arguments.

2. Robert Jervis, "From Balance to Concert: A Study of International Security Cooperation," in *Cooperation Under Anarchy*, ed. Kenneth A. Oye (Princeton University Press, 1986), 60.

3. Harold D. Lasswell, *World Politics and Personal Insecurity* (Free Press, 1965 [1935]), chap. 3.

4. Nicholas John Spykman, *America's Strategy in World Politics: The United States and the Balance of Power* (Harcourt, Brace, 1943), 447.

5. Martin Wight, "The Balance of Power and International Order," in *The Bases of International Order: Essays in Honour of C. A. W. Manning*, ed. Alan James (Oxford University Press, 1973), 86.

6. Robert Jervis, "Theories of War in an Era of Leading-Power Peace," *American Political Science Review* 96, no. 1 (2002): 1–14, here 1.

7. Robert Jervis, *American Foreign Policy in a New Era* (Routledge, 2005), 31.

8. See Jonathan Kirshner, "Rationalist Explanations for War? *Security Studies* 10, no. 1 (2000): 143–50.

9. For exemplary works that employ the bargaining model, see James Fearon, "Rationalist Explanations for War," *International Organization* 49, no. 3 (1995): 379–414; Branislav L. Slantchev, "The Principle of Convergence in Wartime Negotiations," *American Political Science Review* 97, no. 4 (2003): 621–32; Dan Reiter, "Exploring the Bargaining Model of War," *Perspectives on Politics* 1, no. 1 (2003): 27–43; James D. Fearon, "Bargaining, Enforcement, and International Cooperation," *International Organization* 52, no. 2 (1998): 269–305; Robert L. Powell, "Bargaining Theory and International Conflict," *Annual Review of Political Science* 5, no. 1 (2002): 1–30.

10. Robert Jervis, *The Logic of Images in International Relations* (Columbia University Press, 1970), 9.

11. See Andrew H. Kydd, *Trust and Mistrust in International Relations* (Princeton University Press, 2005).

12. Alfred Vagts, *A History of Militarism: Civilian and Military*, rev. ed. (Meridian, 1959 [1937]), 33–34.

13. Robert Jervis, "War and Misperception," in *The Origin and Prevention of Major Wars*, ed. Robert I. Rotberg and Theodore K. Rabb (Cambridge University Press, 1989), 106.

14. Eric Grynaviski, *Constructive Illusions: Misperceiving the Origins of International Cooperation* (Cornell University Press, 2014), 44. Grynaviski is a former student of mine.

7

A LIBERAL REALIST

DOUG MACDONALD

The H-Diplo|RJISSF online tributes to Robert Jervis, many of which are included in this volume, were enlightening. It was a pleasure, but not an unanticipated one, to see the outpouring of sadness, admiration, and gratitude that accompanied the passing of one of the great international relations[1] scholars in the United States and, I would guess, in the world. It is somehow reassuring that so many talented people hold such similar views of Jervis as a scholar, a mentor, a teacher, a colleague, and a human being. Again, this was expected, but it is still impressive to see in the event.[2]

Jervis became my dissertation advisor and I his teaching assistant in 1980–1981, shortly after his arrival at Columbia University. The association continued for the next forty-one years, being especially reinvigorated with the general onset of the internet in the 1990s, which allowed the easy exchange of ideas and documents that was a mainstay of our intellectual and personal relationship. In one sense, we complemented each other in our research interests. He was a deductive theorist who largely avoided systematic primary research, whereas I am a middle-range historicist who enjoys archival research.[3] We met intellectually in our mutual interest in the ontological and epistemic questions that intersect between history and social science. He told me in 2022 that he actually considered me a military historian, while I demurred and claimed to be an intelligence-military historian who is interested in the politics of those two activities. We never followed this point up, which was fortunate for me as I do not really know what I meant by that. If we had had more time, I am sure he would not have let me get away with it without an explanation. We were not direct intellectual collaborators in our work in the sense he was with many other former students.

So, the fates smiled on me. I had the great fortune to have two great mentors at Columbia, Jervis and William T. R. Fox, one of the founders of the systematic study of international relations in the twentieth century in the United States.[4] Part of Jervis's and my mutual attraction was that we were both historically oriented political scientists.

Jervis had the wonderful trait of great teachers for empathetic critical encouragement. He supported my dissertation project, which was controversial with some at Columbia. I could not have written it without his support. Jervis shared the trait among great advisors and scholars: an ecumenical attitude toward ideas if they showed promise.

Following graduate school at Columbia, our relationship was a long-distance one but no less important for me because, as one who taught at a geographically isolated teaching college with no graduate students and heavier workloads, I was somewhat out of the loop, and I also had to deal with personal and family medical issues. Jervis understood the constraints and was characteristically supportive in his reactions. For example, in 2000, I had to decline his invitation to attend a formal event to celebrate his taking office as the president of the American Political Science Association (APSA). There were other such declines over the years, and he was unfailingly understanding. And he continued to extend invitations. Consequently, I had the opportunity to chair a tribute panel to him and his book *The Logic of Images in International Relations* at an International Studies Association meeting in the early 1990s and attend events in his honor at Columbia University.[5] The onset of the internet and email facilitated communications immensely.

The essay that follows—part remembrance, part analysis—is largely based on those experiences. It concentrates on Jervis's early years at Columbia within the context of great changes taking place at the university in the study of international relations more generally and as a generational shift among its leading practitioners. These changes included movement away from the "traditional" study of international relations toward a more "scientific" approach to the discipline. Both approaches centered around the notions of the parameters of sovereignty of the nation-state and the nature of anarchy in the international system. Regardless of one's theoretical, methodological, or political perspective, those twin concerns have been the sinews of international relations scholarship since the nineteenth century.[6] The rhetoric has shifted and definitions altered, but the basic arguments over subject matter have remained similar conceptually.

These were some of the major issues that were generally discussed and debated among the professors and graduate students in my graduate student era (1977–1985) and were an integral part of Jervis's midcareer role in the field and his influence on future developments. Indeed, at least according to graduate student rumors (hereafter, GSR), that semi-informed nether world inhabited by those learning their craft at a university, Jervis was hired at Columbia not only as one of the most promising young scholars in the United States (he was only forty and had an immensely influential book and article in hand, as well as significant government service in his CIA postmortem on the fall of the shah of Iran in 1979) but also to bring the changes occurring in the study of international relations to the university's future. It was an inspired choice.

⸗∞⸗

The formal subdiscipline of international relations in the discipline of political science does not have a particularly long history in the United States. Perhaps because of this, there has been a general lack of interest in the subdiscipline for much historiographical self-reflection until recently and that has been done mostly by intellectual historians from outside the United States. Perhaps, too, it is partly because international relations scholars fancy themselves as producing theories and concepts that are timeless, whose value crosses time and space in their relevance. If so, then concentrating on the intellectual context of their creation becomes less important. As Jervis wrote as recently as 1994, "political science is a very trendy discipline. Few books or articles are cited a decade, let alone a generation, after they are written. When scholars die, their ideas die with them, although they may be reinvented later and trumpeted as new."[7] This may have been still largely true in 1994, never mind in 1980 when Jervis arrived at Columbia, but certainly is no longer so. His ideas and other international relations scholars' contributions will long outlive all of us. It wasn't until the 1980s that the early historiographical arguments began and then in a very cursory manner. It is only in the twenty-first century that this literature has bloomed and ensured the lengthy shelf life of varying international relations approaches in historical context. A lack of historiographical self-reflection in international relations also obscures the changes that occur in scholarly discourse due to political developments.

In the United States, what historically have been called idealism and realism in international relations are better understood as two variants of a broader ideology of liberalism than autonomous intellectual constructs. Even the terms idealism and realism are somewhat deceptive, as when one looks at those who are given such labels in the pre–World War II period and after, they are in fact amorphous groups of scholars who often had much more in common than either side would admit. The polemical demands of contemporary political and intellectual contention created numerous oversimplifications that outlasted the specific issues involved. The questions of the normative parameters of sovereignty and the instrumental necessities of anarchy have been the mainstay of political and intellectual contention, but the debate, such as it is, is over a difference of degree not a difference of kind, and that binary is somewhat overdrawn conceptually, and especially politically, when applied to contemporary policies.[8] It is my contention that what were sometimes called idealists versus realists in the postwar milieu in fact were two different kinds of liberalism, and the contention is as much political and ideological as it is intellectual. I will replace the word *idealist* with *reformist* because not many of the prewar scholars still maintained many of the prewar liberal assumptions but did maintain a belief in what Fox called "pragmatic meliorism."[9] The liberal reformists and liberal realists of the post–World War II period adopted elements of realism not to abandon liberalism but to save it following the events of the 1930s and 1940s.[10]

Such ideological contradictions permeate the varieties of liberal thought in many areas across the spectrum. This was reflected in Jervis's approach to politics in general, something of which he was well aware. A strongly committed liberal in domestic politics, he was just as strongly a committed realist in foreign affairs. Recognizing this complexity in liberal ideology aids in understanding his essentially dialectical approach to knowledge.

In support of my claim, I begin with the assumption expressed by Jervis that realism, liberalism, and Marxism remain the primary modes of international relations inquiry and that the new kids on the block, such as constructivism, have a way to go before they can compete as modes of analysis. My main interest here is in what I see in historical political context as Jervis's liberal realism.[11] Approached from a biography of knowledge perspective, he was a strong political liberal ("card-carrying member of the ACLU," he used to say) and came to intellectual maturity in the political ferment of the 1950s and 1960s, affected strongly by McCarthyism, the nuclear weapons revolution, and the Vietnam War. He believed that nuclear weapons and bipolarity had fundamentally altered international relations, thus making much past liberal theorizing of security in international relations of limited usefulness. This led him to a realist orientation that was somewhat at odds with his more general political orientation in many respects. Reconciling the two helped shape his intellectual and scholarly interests.[12]

Jervis was primarily interested in security studies, which emphasizes conflict among nation-states, and he viewed international relations more as a separate academic discipline unto itself, as it had become during his education in the 1950s and 1960s. Those were also the years of the dominant "end of ideology" school of thought, and despite his intense interest in cognitive biases and psychological processes, Jervis never gave ideology much of his attention because he saw it mainly as rationalization for what were choices based on deeper beliefs and processes, at least until the Cold War was over.[13]

One of the fundamental differences between prewar theorists and Jervis and, by extension, between reformist and realist liberals is the nature of the international system itself. This is partly reflected in the confusion over the origins of international relations as an object of study. Scholars and other interested observers of the systematic study of international relations cannot even agree on a point of origin for the existence of international relations as a subject. Some appeal to early origins reaching back into ancient times, citing sages such as Thucydides (c. 460–400 BCE), Sun Tzu (c. 544–496 BCE), or Kautilya (c. 375–283 BCE) as early creators of analytical rather than heroic treatments of interpolity behavior.[14] Some would time the origins of international relations to the emergence of the modern nation-state during and after the French and American Revolutions.[15] Others argue that such posited continuities are somewhat forced and that the systematic study of international relations was a late nineteenth- or twentieth-century phenomenon, beginning just before or after World War I.[16] Still others argue that international relations is a post–World War II development, part of a political science "enlightenment" in a "heroic" vision of politics emerging from the defeat of the Axis powers.[17] What most scholars have in common is an essentialist view of the nature of the global political world as a society, as self-conscious interacting units.[18]

Although siding with the structural realists on the largely asocial nature of the international system, Jervis insightfully noted that although Hans Morgenthau was a strong realist, like the reformist liberals and other pre–World War II scholars, he also viewed the international realm as a society: "Thus, for Morgenthau a degree of moral consensus among nations is a prerequisite for a well-functioning international order. In contrast to more recent analysts like [Kenneth] Waltz (and myself), Morgenthau argues that the balance of power arose not only out of the clash of competing self-interests but out of a common culture, respect for other's rights, and agreement on basic moral principles."[19]

It was only when the "scientific" theorists and their systems approaches that became popular in the 1960s and after, and especially with structural realists, that the international order was portrayed as being literally made up of interactive "units" rather than nation-states that are ruled and peopled by real human beings with all the contradictions and analytical overlaps that includes. Structural realism is a brilliant theory as far as it goes in explaining mechanistic "unit" behavior and material processes. But according to the reformist liberal scholars, it does not sufficiently explain human behavior.[20] Intellectual parsimony has its place, but this is a step too far. Although he greatly admired Waltz's work, as a political psychologist, Jervis saw it as of only limited use.

I will not enter such debates here in any detail, although the origins of international relations are and were a matter of some importance, especially when contemplating the nature of change in the subdiscipline reflecting changes in world politics. But the variety is too immense to cover here. Suffice it to say that Jervis aligned with scholars like Waltz who saw the post–World War II system as fundamentally different from earlier variations,[21] at least during the Cold War.

───── ∞∞∞ ─────

As noted, in the period under consideration (1977–1985), the primary debate at Columbia was between those who largely dated the legitimate study of international relations to the postwar period (the liberal realists) and those who desired to salvage at least some of the rationalist Enlightenment political traditions of liberalism but with the harsh lessons of the 1930s and 1940s considered and learned (the liberal reformists). These concepts were quite prevalent in the 1950s and 1960s in the United States and the "free world" more generally. In politics, such liberal reformist theorizing led to the "tough liberals" of the Kennedy and Johnson eras.[22] According to this formulation, both normative and instrumental considerations should be maintained over time, while recognizing that in times of crisis instrumental policies in service to state survival must take precedence. This lesson was taken from the 1930s and 1940s.

Given that the United States had sacrificed liberal values at home to protect the broader security of the country before in the Civil War, World War I, and World War II, this value conflict was not unprecedented. The controversy involved how or whether to do so in a "cold war," without national survival in obvious immediate threat. Prior to World War II, there were many precursors in the United States and elsewhere of the normative-instrumental debate. The American reformist liberal scholars who created the conceptual hybrid in the 1940s and 1950s had already moved in that intellectual direction in the 1920s and 1930s. The "legal realism" movement among American legal scholars had a significant effect on the political scientists of that period.[23] Concentrating on the instrumental consequences of legal decisions rather than simply on their normative ones, the legal realists led a movement toward similar concepts in other areas, especially during the New Deal period. When liberalism collapsed on the European continent in 1940, there were in place intellectual concepts that facilitated a change in policies. Such arguments were not unknown to American political science scholars, although they were only vaguely viewed and seen as outdated. This lack of awareness affected the *kinds* of precedents for realist thinking that would be acceptable later to American thinkers and is typical of post–World War II international relations scholars in their rush to label the prewar period monolithically "utopian." Yet this attempt to salvage aspects of past theorizing was not some sort of nativism; reformist liberals were very cosmopolitan scholars. They believed that the earlier complexity of liberal theorizing prior to World War II, which was portrayed by early doctrinal Cold War realists as a group of lockstep "utopians," had largely been overlooked or, worse, inaccurately presented to post–World War II students and the public.[24]

This perceived need to synthesize normative and instrumental values long predated World War II in liberal social science and reaches back at least to Max Weber with his concept of ethical "substantive rationality."[25] According to this view, to produce useful guides for action in social life, long-term values must over time trump short-term material interests, although the latter might be necessary in the shorter term. In the long term, actions must be pursued and defended ("rationalized" in Weber's terms) by values rather than interests.[26] In liberal thought and politics, the process matters, and the ends do not justify the means except in extraordinary circumstances. The stuff of politics is deciding when those circumstances become extraordinary enough to forego "normal" ethics. Doctrinal realists may wish it would go away, but this is a recurring policy dilemma in American foreign policy because of the continued strength of liberal ideology. It continues to bedevil American leadership in foreign policy and will do so as long as the United States is a predominantly liberal country.[27]

Reformist liberals differed from liberal realists in that they were not willing to so easily forego normative concerns for security goals even while recognizing the inherent tension between the two values in the real world. They were opposed by the so-called "émigré realists," who were mostly European refugees from states that underwrote totalitarian ideologies, and their American converts, who eschewed liberal foreign policy goals in foreign policy to varying degrees and pressed the instrumentalist case.[28] In addition, the new realists were skeptical of public opinion inputs into foreign policy decision making, perhaps understandable in reaction to their recently "isolationist" new national home, something that rubbed against American liberal political norms. But the actual differences were matters of degree. Reformists were not without interest in machtpolitik.

Realists were not merely "anti-Whigs" out to get rid of liberalism in a project of various counter-Enlightenment strategies.[29] Much of American Cold War scholarship and politics were shaped by these competing conceptualizations of its role in the world, at least until the breakdown of the liberal Cold War synthesis into normative and instrumentalist factions largely over the Vietnam War and American policies in the developing world more generally.[30] Such arguments were the basis for the study of international relations, according to the reformists. Power analysis was necessary but more about means than long-term goals. Its simplifications did not tell us enough about human psychology and political possibilities, which are necessary to understand human behavior. As William Fox put it in his 1985 critique of the influential British realist E. H. Carr: "Finding one's way between the excessive voluntarism said to have been an American vice and the excessive involuntarism of those who believe in appeasement at any cost or those who believe in an unending struggle with the forces of darkness is difficult, but that is what gives the academic study of international relations its social utility." He offered a distinction between the "doctrinal" realist versus the "empirical" (that is, reformist) realist: "The doctrinal realist does not need to examine how nation-state actors really behave because he has already posited how they must behave by virtue of their nation-stateness in a multi-state world system. The empirical realist by contrast looks to see how they actually behave and perhaps beyond that to examining the possibilities for tolerable coexistence."[31]

Jervis was much closer to being an empirical realist than a doctrinal or "structural" realist such as John Mearsheimer and Kenneth Waltz, respectively, at least on some important questions such as the causes of the Cold War.[32] It is a subtle but important distinction. Hence his close attention to historical accuracy and epistemological questions often are put aside by international relations scholars in their "stylized history" or "potted" use of historical "evidence."[33] Put differently, although Jervis confined his primary research to the *Foreign Relations of the United States* series and other published documents, he dispassionately examined varying interpretations of what is available empirically about a particular form of behavior rather than cherry-pick information to support a particular argument.[34]

Jervis noted that his own use of historical examples was "couched in terms of propensities and tendencies" and relied upon "aspects of many cases to illustrate points and demonstrate the plausibility of arguments." Such usages were merely heuristic devices to demonstrate a point and stimulate thinking and future research, not historical analysis, although he forgivingly added "the heuristic use of crucial historical cases has proven so attractive as to overwhelm a more accurate portrait of the cases themselves."[35]

In sum, the differences between liberal reformists and liberal realists during the Cold War were real, even though they have been exaggerated by more doctrinal adherents on either side in order to "sell" favored American policies. From a scholarly perspective, the recent post–Cold War historiography of international relations, which is primarily done by history scholars outside the discipline, is in the process of correcting some of these exaggerations. This was something the reform liberals were calling for as early as the 1960s. Sovereignty and anarchy remained the primary issues for both groups, and the argument was primarily, as it has long been, over how to deal with them given differing policy preferences within the broad ideological category of liberalism.

⸺ ⁂ ⸺

One of the reasons for Jervis's widespread respect and influence among international relations scholars is that he tended to think dialectically, always tempering one argument with the possibility of being wrong and therefore the possible accuracy of other plausible explanations: "If the discipline is functioning well, each school of thought enriches others as powerful research of one kind strengthens, not weakens, the alternatives. No one approach consistently maintains a leading position: each of them catches important elements of international politics, and many of our arguments are about the relative importance of and the interrelationships among various factors."[36]

Even when he believed strongly in the inadequacy of an idea—for example, reformist institutionalism or international law—Jervis treated the idea with respect and explained why he believed that a generally realist approach to the idea was superior. He sometimes articulated concepts in clear binary terms, but he did not abandon them there.[37] But his ecumenical approach to ideas could lead him to take unusual positions at times and seemingly "waffle" at others. He was not afraid to change his mind or take a middle position if the evidence did not permit a clearer choice.[38] To many of us, that is a feature not a bug in his thinking.

One of the few criticisms I have heard about Jervis's work was based on this willingness to entertain virtually all contrarian ideas. According to this view, in effect, he never saw a clever idea he didn't like. This view is incorrect; over the years, Jervis not only promoted the unorthodox but also revisited such ideas over time to see if they had panned out. Sometimes they did, and sometimes they did not. In private discussions, he expressed this kind of disappointment in constructivism, an innovation that he had initially been enthusiastic about.[39] Over time, he argued and correctly in my view, these scholars were overlooking some of the basic insights that had already emerged in the political psychology field of which he was a leader. True to form, he did not reject constructivism but put it in his "we shall see" category. He also agreed that this is a consistent problem in an unreflective discipline such as international relations: you not only ignore thinking of high quality on the subject that came before but also claim something as "new" that is only partially so without even realizing it.

Waltz's many defenders, including Jervis, counter that Waltzian structuralism is only a theory that is meant to help us understand the international system, not an explanation of an international society whose complexity defies parsimonious, unified theorizing. Fair enough. But Waltz's structuralism not only eliminated ideology, historical memory, public opinion, and so on, within its parameters as a theory but also eliminated the role of elites to a large degree, which was something new. As Waltz argued in 1997, in answer to the historian Paul Schroeder's (and separately John Vasquez's) critique of neorealism and its version of a "system," "Schroeder rejects structural theory because it fails to account for the motives of statesmen. Yet, as William Graham Sumner wrote: 'Motives from which men act have nothing at all to do with the consequences of their action (1911).' I would say 'little' rather than 'nothing,' but the point is clear."[40]

What Schroeder had presented as evidence against such an approach Waltz labeled "a mélange of irrelevant diplomatic lore."[41] In answer to Vasquez's critique, Waltz argued that Morgenthau's type of realism "differs fundamentally from mine." For Morgenthau and, by extension, liberal realism more generally, "balances are intended and must be sought by the statesmen who produce them. For me, balances are produced whether or not [they are] intended." Again, international structure is produced independent of human volition, and humans, elite or masses, do not matter much. Even if this is "correct," many of us, and not only reformist liberals, are not interested in pursuing such a narrow understanding of world politics, which we see as a pluralistic, interconnected, and thoroughly human endeavor—as a society not a system. To describe the difference in Waltz's useful terms in *Man, the State, and War*, of three "images" or what J. David Singer called "levels of analysis" in a review of Waltz[42]—the human element, domestic regime type, and international system—reformist and realist liberals utilize all three, whereas after 1979, Waltz reduced anything important theoretically to image three alone.

Why Robert Jervis was such a defender of Waltz's approach even though he disagreed with it is an intriguing question that demonstrates his ecumenicism. After all, Jervis is the international relations scholar who made the study of individual psychological behavior a mainstream intellectual concern, one who could write as recently as 2015 that:

> Domestic politics is central to whether, how and when revolutionary states become socialized. Although socialization is supposed to operate most heavily on new actors, in fact revolutionary states often resist such processes, especially because they are hard to reassure. Domestic and international factors are likely to interact, as they did with [Mikhail] Gorbachev's USSR and probably are doing with contemporary Iran, and this points to the importance of domestic politics within the other states in the system as well. For the United States domestic politics enters in both directly and in the American perceptions of the other's domestic system because of its tradition of "second image" thinking, to use Waltz's term.[43]

In explaining this seeming paradox, I return to Jervis's open-mindedness, pluralism, and appreciation of an elegant and contrary idea or theory. He did not fully agree with Waltz's structural realist approach even though he was a realist himself. He possessed too curious and contrary an intellect to sit at one table. He agreed with Waltz that the international order was a system and was skeptical of the lasting effects of benign motives and general good faith that the word "society" can imply. Moreover, both the Axis powers and the Soviet Bloc rejected the norms and goals of reform liberalism, not to mention lesser potential threats such as Fidel Castro's Cuba or Mao Zedong's China (and apparently in China today as per its leaders' opposition to a "rules-based" international system) who objected to them even more strenuously. What answer did reformist liberalism have other than borrowing some of the basic conceptualizations, prescriptions, and cynicism of realism? Liberalism has survived as an ideology and a research agenda because of its flexibility and willingness to learn. No one personified that flexibility more than Robert Jervis, apparently to the consternation of some students who prefer less complex and more linear explanations of world politics.[44]

I left Columbia in 1985–1986 for an Olin postdoc research fellowship at the Center for International Affairs at Harvard University, followed by a one-year position at Wellesley College in 1986–1987. The next year, I passed over a tenure track offer from a large state university in favor of a two-year position at Colgate University. I stayed for the next twenty-seven years.

The relationship with Jervis became a long-distance one. I would call him occasionally, and when the internet became ubiquitous in the 1990s, I would send him documents or my opinion that I thought he might find interesting. He usually did. He would occasionally ask for my opinion on a subject. During this period, he established himself as a major academic nuclear strategist, an unusually broadly engaged social scientist, a colleague and collaborator with leading diplomatic historians, and one of the leading international relations scholars in the world. Like most of his friends, colleagues, and former students, I exulted in his success. I have never heard a word of criticism of this success, not a hint of "Why him?" His work was simply too prolific and too good to begrudge him his fame. He was not only a superb and prolific scholar but also a generous and decent person. And a lot of fun. These qualities are not always coterminous among academics.

I will not deal with his work in this period, as we were generally interested in different things. But it was during this period that the Cold War ended, which for the sake of convenience I'll date in 1989. Because it was foreseen by very few, it sent both historians and social scientists back to the drawing board to varying degrees.

In a recent academic biographical interview, Jervis mentioned the effects on his own work:

> Shortly after I published my second book on American nuclear strategy, the problem all but disappeared; after I co-edited a book on Soviet-American relations, the Union of Soviet Socialist Republics (U.S.S.R.) disappeared. Friends have suggested that I should now write about AIDS, racism, or poverty [and maybe they will disappear]. I don't think I'll push my luck. Instead, I'll try to understand the paradoxical and complex effects that characterize the workings of systems, especially those whose elements are people or states. This project is particularly enjoyable because almost everything I read supplies examples and stimulates my thinking.[45]

With the nuclear threat diminished and bipolarity no longer very useful in explaining the post–Cold War world, he went looking for new lessons to learn.

In a sense, the end of the Cold War freed him to explore other non-security subjects in which he had great interest. The leading example of this is *Systems Effects*, a book he was especially attached to in part because of the lack of interest in it prior to publication.[46] Though he characteristically kept his finger in many intellectual pies, this emphasis on "system effects" renewed his interest in cybernetics and brought him back to subsystem-level processes and to intelligence feedback mechanisms. The interest in intelligence remained a consistent background factor in our relationship, especially in the twenty-first century. With James Wirtz, we formed a small discussion group on the subject that involved many fruitful discussions and exchanges.

Systems Effects served two main purposes for other scholars. First, it offered an expansion on the idea that the international order is a system rather than a society (at least in the ways the reformists posed it). Though it included an impressive array of illustrations to bolster the point (the footnotes contain amazingly broad examples from the natural and social worlds), its international relations elements are a strong argument for Waltz's position that "units"/states interact dynamically among themselves and simultaneously with the structure of the system itself. Waltz theorized that the system does so, but Jervis theorized how and why it does so and how such interaction can confound even the most rational and informed policy choices. To put his innovation in Waltzian terms, Jervis borrowed from complexity theory the notion that "systems effects" occur, interact across levels of analysis, and have causal consequences, though of varying importance, at all three levels of analysis—the human, the domestic political, and the system.

He accomplished this without using what some see as the deterministic consequences of Waltz's theory. Yes, the system constrains "unit" behavior over time in identifiable patterns, but it is impossible to predict how it will do so. Those patterns only reveal themselves during the processes of interaction and are highly contingent on material and ideational factors in all actors and at all levels, naturally some more than others. Thus, Waltz's work is theoretically useful in identifying and focusing attention on the presence and influence of system patterns of constraint, but as powerful as those constraints may be, "unit"/state behavior remains contingent to a significant degree on the inputs from images one and two.

Jervis took a middle position between structure and agency, arguing that the processes involved are so complex that with the present state of knowledge we are theoretically just out of the starting gate. It might be remembered that in his subsequent publications Jervis returned to the psychological and domestic processes (e.g., intelligence/feedback) in some of his research, and his interest in what international relations scholars call "historians' questions"—Waltz's "mélange of irrelevant diplomatic lore"—grew precipitously.[47] I do not think it would have done so if *System Effects* had been meant merely as a defense of systems theory. Structuralism is a step forward theoretically but can only take us so far. As Jervis complimented Waltz's work, "Even when you disagree, he moves your thinking ahead."[48] With *Systems Effects*, in many ways Jervis left Waltz behind, at least on image two.

Second, *System Effects* is partially an answer to the recent works of the economist Albert O. Hirschman, a scholar that Jervis (and through him, I) admired greatly. Specifically, what peaked Bob's interest was his examination of patterns of argumentation against change in *The Rhetoric of Reaction: Perversity, Futility, Jeopardy*, a book Hirschman later admitted was a "tract" based on his own reaction to what he saw as the "neoconservative" political assault on the welfare state in the Reagan years.[49]

Though the book was an anticonservative "tract," Hirschman later acknowledged that it applied just as well to reformists who were defending a status quo. In my view, having discussed Hirschman with Jervis, a secondary and largely implicit purpose of his book was to answer the "reactionary" charge and explain how political liberals such as Waltz and himself were not against the desirability of change per se but, rather, were skeptical of the ability to pursue it in other societies. In doing so, the reformer might just make things worse, a favorite conservative and realist argument against reformist liberals. If the system itself confounds purposive directed change, especially from external inputs, it does not matter what the reformer desires. This is a very old argument that goes back at least to the French Revolution in modern liberal discourse. During the Cold War, the debate led to alternating periods of reformist intervention and cultural relativism in American foreign policy as both approaches appeared to fail.[50]

Herein lies a paradox for the liberal realist that Jervis became more interested in after the publication of *System Effects*. If directed change is futile because of the confounding processes of system effects abroad, why wouldn't this also be the case in domestic politics, as Jervis in fact abundantly demonstrates in the book? Why would one support reform in one realm and not the other if both are doomed to futility by system effects? Conservatives may be politically wrong or right, but they are more consistent ontologically than liberal realists by being skeptical of directed change in both spheres. This is also true of the reformist liberals. They advocate pragmatic meliorism in both domestic and foreign policies. They also may be wrong, but they are more consistent in their prescriptions than liberal realists. This is a paradox that *System Effects* never solved and in fact sharpened. Logical consistency can be overvalued, of course, but this paradox is grounded in competing empirical and theoretical claims with real-world policy implications.[51]

The debate will undoubtedly continue. Indeed, it may prove intractable because it is based on deeply held subjective values that may be mutually exclusive in important ways. It would not be the only seemingly unsolvable contradiction in liberalism.

———— ⚭ ————

So, for me, the early twenty-first century was a period of mutual exchange and occasional meetings with Jervis. We had dinner together at a Society for Historians of American Foreign Relations conference, that sort of thing. From 2005 to 2007, I was a visiting senior researcher at the United States Army War College's (USAWC) "think tank," the Institute of Strategic Studies, working on the topics of Islamist networks in Southeast Asia, insurgencies in the region, and piracy. During my stay there, Jervis had drawn up a list of actions that might be pursued to withdraw from Iraq and asked me to gather some opinions from my colleagues at the USAWC, which I did discretely. He was disappointed when some of the officers I consulted agreed with his analysis but were reluctant to say so publicly as it would be branded by some as "defeatism" and run against the "can do" attitudes that the military must maintain to do their dangerous work. When I asked about plans for political programs that might be tried so that the United States could pull out of Iraq, I was told by an officer who had served on Defense Secretary Donald Rumsfeld's staff that the secretary had not only forbidden his staff to draw up any such plans but threatened to "have your career" if he found anyone had done so.[52] The United States let the Iraq nation collapse without even trying to stop it in the early days of the occupation. This was apparently based on the anti-nation-building "lesson" that self-proclaimed realists drew from the American experience in Vietnam, a lesson that had been overlearned.[53]

My interests shifted after post–Cold War declassifications of American intelligence and a growth of translations and primary source–based histories emanating from Vietnam became available in the twenty-first century. With these developments, I began finding many anomalies and errors in the American intelligence effort there, even though the official Vietnamese and American histories are inconsistent and incomplete.[54] For example, many of the conclusions from intelligence sources in the so-called "Pentagon Papers," which remain the motherlode of primary sources for many nonspecialist scholars, are factually inaccurate and did not include some of the highly classified signals intelligence (SIGINT) material that called much of their analyses into question (especially during the end of their research period, 1967–1968). This raised the fundamental question of the nature of American understanding of the hybrid war, even at the highest levels.[55] Similarly, I found highly suggestive, though less compelling, evidence that the Communist side was apparently just as ignorant of actual relative conditions of the insurgency, as southern cadres consistently misinformed them. Jervis, James Wirtz, and I batted these numbers and documents around after about 2019 as I began working on a revision of the orthodox view of the Vietnam War. On October 6, 2021, Jervis emailed me: "I think very few people understand that the old numbers are simply wrong."[56] Both Jervis and Wirtz gave me important advice and read draft chapters. I had retired from teaching in 2014, partly because my hearing was failing, and gave the project my full attention.

Then the fates turned against us. In December 2020, Jervis was diagnosed with lung cancer. Then in the spring of 2021, I was diagnosed with pulmonary fibrosis, a lung disease that in my case is deteriorative and incurable. Jervis and I joked about the cruel coincidence. I reminded him that I smoked heavily back at Columbia, and he replied, "I should have smoked!" When we discussed the improbability of both of us getting fatal lung diseases, I told him he was carrying this mentor thing too far. Whistling past the graveyard, I suppose, but what else can one do? Poor James Wirtz had to put up with all this and descriptions of our respective therapies that could not have been fun to overhear. Bob rallied in the summer of 2021 as I faded. In the fall, I rallied and he faded. And then Bob was gone.

During the summer when he was doing well and I was not, I told Bob of my discouragement. The doctors said I could live for six weeks, six months, or six years. He emailed me that "the only thing you can do is to keep going and be glad you are alive another day."

A mentor to the end.

NOTES

1. This essay is adapted from a larger, forthcoming one for H-Diplo/RJISSF's "Learning the Scholar's Craft" series. For the purposes of this forum, I am using international relations interchangeably for the study and practices of world politics. The forthcoming essay will deal with Columbia University and developments in international relations more generally.

2. Richard H. Immerman, Diane N. Labrosse, and Marc Trachtenberg, eds., "Tribute to the Life, Scholarship, and Legacy of Robert Jervis, Part I," *H-Diplo/ISSF*, February 4, 2022, https://issforum.org/ISSF/PDF/ISSF-Jervis-Tribute-1.pdf; Immerman et al., eds., "Tribute to the Life, Scholarship, and Legacy of Robert Jervis, Part II," *H-Diplo/ISSF*, August 25, 2022, https://issforum.org/ISSF/PDF/ISSF-Jervis-Tribute-2.pdf.

3. I am using "historicist" in its "original sense" as posited by the late British historian Martin Wight as a "doctrine that all values are historically conditioned, that reality itself is a historical process, and that history can teach nothing except philosophical acceptance of change." This is in contrast to the later interpretation of the word as representing a "doctrine that history has a purpose and direction, that its movement is largely predictable,

and that it can (under proper interpretation) teach everything we need to know about life and prescribe our duties. In this new sense [the later version] it is a label for Hegel and Marx, Spengler and Toynbee." Martin Wight quoted in Andrew Ehrhardt, "Everyman His Own Philosopher of History: Notions of Process in the Study and Practice of Foreign Policy," *Texas National Security Review* 5, no. 3 (2022): fn. 78, at https://tnsr.org/2022/03 /everyman-his-own-philosopher-of-history-notions-of-historical-process-in-the-study -and-practice-of-foreign-policy/.

4. Nicolas Guilhot, ed., *The Invention of International Relations Theory: Realism, the Rockefeller Foundation, and the 1954 Conference on Theory* (Columbia University Press, 2011). Guilhot exaggerates wildly in his use of the word "invention" here, but his portrayal of Fox's influence in the 1940s–1950s is generally correct.

5. Robert Jervis, *The Logic of Images in International Relations* (Columbia University Press, 1989).

6. Brian C. Schmidt, *The Political Discourse of Anarchy: A Disciplinary History of International Relations* (State University of New York Press, 1998).

7. Robert Jervis, "Hans Morgenthau, Realism, and the Study of International Politics," *Social Research* 61, no. 4 (1994): 853–77, 853. I do not know why he would write such a thing. This article and many others demonstrate that Morgenthau and his ideas were quite alive long after his death.

8. See the excellent historiographic article on these issues in the 1930s in Peter Wilson, "The Myth of the 'First Great Debate,'" in *International Relations and the First Great Debate*, ed. Brian C. Schmidt (Routledge, 2012), 16–32.

9. For an excellent brief overview of Professor Fox's theoretical orientation and reformist liberalism, see Elizabeth C. Hanson, "William T. R. Fox and the Study of World Politics," in *The Evolution of Theory in International Relations: Essays in Honor of William T. R. Fox*, ed. Robert L. Rothstein (University of South Carolina Press, 1991), 1–20.

10. For a similar argument, see Michael C. Williams, "In the Beginning: The International Relations Enlightenment and the Ends of International Relations Theory," *European Journal of International Relations* 19, no. 3 (2013): 647–65. The "enlightenment" of which Williams writes is of an expansion of political science after World War II, not the European Enlightenments of the eighteenth and nineteenth centuries. On the oversimplification of the liberal approaches of the 1900s–1930s by postwar realists and other critics, see Jerome Weiss, "E.H. Carr, Norman Angell, and Reassessing the Realist–Utopian Debate," *The International History Review* 35, no. 5 (2013): 1156–84; see also the essays in Schmidt, *International Relations and the First Great Debate*.

11. I cannot deal here with the theoretical richness of the contending "schools" of the realist paradigm, for example, defensive versus offensive realists, structuralist versus neoclassical, and so on. For an interesting overview of how Jervis's work fits into the broader realist paradigm, see Randall Schweller, "Jervis's Realism," in *Psychology, Strategy, and Conflict: Perceptions of Insecurity in International Relations*, ed. James W. Davis (Routledge, 2013), 25–46.

12. See, for example, his framing of the issues in an H-Diplo roundtable he chaired on June 1, 2010, entitled "Politics and Scholarship," at https://issforum.org/ISSF/PDF/ISSF -Roundtable-1-2.pdf.

13. See his more ideological interpretation in Robert Jervis, "Was the Cold War a Security Dilemma?" *Journal of Cold War Studies* 3, no. 1 (2001): 36–60.

14. Robert Gilpin, *War and Change in World Politics* (Cambridge University Press, 1981).

15. Mlada Bukovansky, "The Altered State and the State of Nature: The French Revolution and International Politics," *Review of International Studies* 25, no. 2 (1999): 197–216.

16. Constantinow Koliopoulos, "International Relations and the Study of History," *Oxford Research Encyclopedia of International Studies*, December 22, 2017, https://oxfordre.com /internationalstudies/view/10.1093/acrefore/9780190846626.001.0001/acrefore -9780190846626-e-242.

17. Williams, "In the Beginning," 647–65; George Liska, "The Heroic Decade and After: International Relations as Events, Discipline, and Profession," *SAIS Review* 10, no. 4–5 (1966): 5–11.

18. One of the foundational postwar articulations of this traditionalist viewpoint and the "English School" is Hedley Bull, *The Anarchical Society: A Study in World Order* (Mac-Millan, 1977). I cannot go into the history of the English School here, but for my purposes, it is a part of reformist liberalism despite its sometimes self-declared "realism."

19. Jervis, "Hans Morgenthau, Realism, and the Study of International Politics," 14.

20. William T. R. Fox, "Review of Kenneth N. Waltz's *Theory of International Politics*," *American Political Science Review* 74, no. 2 (1980): 492–93.

21. Kenneth N. Waltz, *Theory of International Relations* (Columbia University Press, 1979).

22. For example, David Halberstam, *The Best and the Brightest* (Ballantine, 1993).

23. For an excellent treatment, see Olivier Zajee, translated and edited by Cadenza Academic Translations, "Legal Realism and International Realism in the United States during the Interwar Period," *Revue française de science politique* 65, nos. 5–6 (2015): 785–804.

24. The pejorative use of "utopian" applied to liberal institutional reformism in international relations theoretical discourse was popularized by British historian E. H. Carr, in *The Twenty Year Crisis: An Introduction to the Study of International Relations* (Harper Perennial, 1964). For the debates in the early postwar years, see K. J. Holsti, "Retreat from Utopia: International Relations Theory, 1945–1970," *Canadian Journal of Political Science/ Revue Canadienne de Science Politique* 4, no. 2 (1971): 165–77.

25. Weber defines "substantive rationality" as "the degree in which a given group of persons, no matter how it is delimited, is or could be adequately provided with goods by means of an economically oriented [that is, instrumental] course of social action. This course of action will be interpreted in terms of a given set of ultimate values no matter what they may be." Max Weber, *The Theory of Social and Economic Organization*, ed. Talcott Parsons (Oxford University Press, 1947), 185.

26. For a discussion, see Steven Kalberg, "Max Weber's Types of Rationality: Cornerstones for the Analysis of Rationalization Processes in History," *American Journal of Sociology* 85, no. 5 (1980): 1145–79.

27. See President Joe Biden's wrestling with the problem in relations with Saudi Arabia and other nations in 2022, even when American survival was not at stake, at https://www.msn .com/en-us/news/politics/biden-juggles-principles-pragmatism-in-stance-on-autocrats /ar-AAYlTZ2?rc=1&ocid=winp1taskbar&cvid=f5e0587f658e4bd19295aadb1467c505.

28.   Professors William T. R. Fox and Annette Baker Fox named the most prominent émigrés in 1961: John Herz, Hans Kelsen, Hans Morgenthau, Sigmund Neumann, Stefan Possony, Hans Speier, Nicholas Spykman, Robert Strausz-Hupe, and Arnold Wolfers. Fox and Fox, "The Teaching of International Relations in the United States," *World Politics* 13, no. 3 (1961), 339–59, 339, fn. 2.

29.   See the provocative article by Nicolas Guilhot, "Portrait of the Realist as a Historian: On Anti-Whiggism in the History of International Relations," *European Journal of International Relations* 2015, no. 1 (2015): 3–26.

30.   Ole R. Holsti and James N. Rosenau, *American Leadership in World Affairs: Vietnam and the Breakdown of Consensus* (Allen and Unwin, 1984).

31.   William T. R. Fox, "E.H. Carr and Political Realism: Vision and Revision," *Review of International Studies* 11 (1985): 6, 13.

32.   Jervis, "Was the Cold War a Security Dilemma?," 36–60.

33.   On the use of "stylized history" and "potted" history by political scientists, see Robert Jervis, "Models and Cases in the Study of International Conflict," in Rothstein, *The Evolution of Theory in International Relations*, 64–65. For the tendency of humans to reason in support of internally acceptable opinions rather than objective truth seeking, see Hugo Mercier and Dan Sperber, "Why Do Humans Reason? Arguments for an Argumentative Theory," *Behavioral and Brain Sciences* 34, no. 2 (2011): 57–74.

34.   On this, see the essay by Volker Berghahn in this volume.

35.   Jervis, "Models and Cases," 64–65.

36.   Robert Jervis, "Realism in the Study of World Politics," *International Organization* 52, no. 4 (1998): 971–91, 972.

37.   See Jack Snyder, "Both Fox and Hedgehog: The Art of Nesting Structural and Perceptual Perspectives," in *Psychology, Strategy, and Conflict: Perceptions of Insecurity in International Relations*, ed. James W. Davis (Routledge, 2013), 13–24.

38.   On this, see, for example, the essays by Jack S. Levy and Marc Trachtenberg in this volume.

39.   He later wrote about it: "The popularity of alternative approaches to international politics cannot be explained entirely by their scholarly virtues. Among the other factors at work are fashions and normative and political preferences. This in part explains the increasing role of rationalism and constructivism. Important as they are, these approaches are necessarily less complete than liberalism, Marxism, and realism. Indeed, they fit better with the latter than is often realized." "Abstract" in Jervis, "Realism in the Study of World Politics," 971.

40.   Kenneth N. Waltz, "Evaluating Theories," *American Political Science Review* 91, no. 4 (1997): 914. Waltz was specifically critiquing Paul Schroeder, "Historical Reality vs. Neo-Realist Theory," *International Security* 19 (1994):108–48, and John A. Vasquez, "The Realist Paradigm and Degenerative Versus Progressive Research Programs: An Appraisal of Neotraditional Research on Waltz's Balancing Proposition," *American Political Science Review* 91 (1997): 899–912.

41.   Waltz, "Evaluating Theories," 914.

42.   J. David Singer, "Review: International Conflict: Three Levels of Analysis, Reviewed Work: *Man, the State, and War: A Theoretical Analysis* by Waltz," *World Politics* 12, no. 3

(1960): 453–61; see also J. David Singer, "The Levels-of-Analysis Problem in International Relations," *World Politics* 14, no. 1 (1961): 77–92. Since that time, others have introduced additional levels that they deem important, for example, the bureaucracy, without much success. See Henrik Bliddal, "The Enduring Logic of the Three Images: Kenneth N. Waltz's *Man, the State, and War*," in *Classics of International Relations: Essays in Criticism and Appreciation*, ed. Henrik Bliddal, Casper Sylvest, and Peter Wilson (Routledge, 2013), 92–100.

43. Robert Jervis, "Socialization, Revolutionary States, and Domestic Politics," *International Politics* 52, no. 5 (2015): 609–16, 609. Randall Schweller argues that Bob's realism uses images one and three. Schweller, "Jervis's Realism," 25–26. This was true during the Cold War, but following its demise, he increasingly referred to image two causal factors, including for the Cold War itself. See also Jervis, "Was the Cold War a Security Dilemma?"

44. For some reactions from various students to Jervis's form of argumentation, see Stacie E. Goddard, "Review of James W. Davis, ed., *Psychology, Strategy, and Conflict: Perceptions of Insecurity in International Relations* (Routledge, 2012)," H-Diplo/ISSF, May 16, 2014, https://issforum.org/essays/23-psychology-strategy-conflict; Snyder, "Both Fox and Hedgehog."

45. "Jervis," *Gale Literature: Contemporary Authors* (Gale, 2022), n.p.

46. Robert Jervis, *System Effects: Complexity in Political and Social Life* (Princeton University Press, 1998.)

47. For example, Robert Jervis, *Why Intelligence Fails: Lessons from the Iranian Revolution and the Iraqi War* (Cornell University Press, 2011); Jervis, *How Statesmen Think: The Psychology of International Politics* (Princeton University Press, 2017); and numerous articles. James Wirtz maps out the new emphasis on intelligence studies later in Jervis's career in Wirtz, "Robert Jervis: Remembering the Dean of Intelligence Studies," *Intelligence and National Security* 37, no. 5 (2022): 732–40. In my own interactions with Bob, he displayed great interest in the new declassified information on intelligence emerging in the twenty-first century and especially from signals intelligence (SIGINT), one of the most closely held areas of intelligence.

48. Quoted in "Kenneth Waltz," at https://military-history.fandom.com/wiki/Kenneth_Waltz.

49. Albert O. Hirschman, *The Rhetoric of Reaction: Perversity, Futility, Jeopardy* (Harvard University Press, 1991). His admission of the "tract" is in Hirschman, "The Rhetoric of Reaction—Two Years Later," *Government and Opposition* 28, no. 3 (1993): 292–314.

50. Douglas J. Macdonald, *Adventures in Chaos: American Intervention for Reform in the Third World* (Harvard University Press, 1992).

51. For a discussion of *System Effects*, see the essay by Jack Snyder in this volume.

52. Confidential conversation, 2007.

53. Dominic Tierney, "Avoiding Nation-Building from Nixon to Trump," *Parameters* 48, no. 1 (2018): 25–36; Tierney, "The Backlash Against Nation-Building," *Prism* 5, no. 3 (2015): 12–27. As Tierney succinctly puts it elsewhere, Americans are "addicted to regime change and allergic to nation building." Tierney, "How We Fight: Crusades, Quagmires,

and the American Way of War," a talk given at Swarthmore College, https://www
.swarthmore.edu/news-events/how-we-fight-crusades-quagmires-and-american-way-war.

54. For some of the anomalies in the infiltration levels from North Vietnam into the South
that strongly suggest northern control of the insurgency and declining support for it in
South Vietnam long before 1968, see my contribution to the H-Diplo Roundtable on
Edwin E. Moise's *The Myths of TET: The Most Misunderstood Event of the Vietnam War*
(University Press of Kansas, 2017), ed. Diane Labrosse, July 16, 2018, https://networks
.h-net.org/node/28443/discussions/2050015/h-diplo-roundtable-xix-44-myths-tet-most
-misunderstood-event#_Toc519252002.

55. For a similar questioning of the orthodox view of the nature of the war, see Edward C.
O'Dowd, "What Kind of War Is This?" *Journal of Strategic Studies* 37, nos. 6–7, (2014):
1027–49.

56. Email, Jervis to Macdonald, October 6, 2021.

8

THE FIELD OF SECURITY STUDIES

STEPHEN M. WALT

Robert Jervis was a gentle giant of modern international relations theory and security studies. His analytical powers were exceptional, his knowledge of military and diplomatic history astounding, and his work ethic extraordinary. These talents were married to a level of generosity, cheerfulness, and all-around sanity that is rare among academics. I am sure there were moments when he was frustrated and perhaps even angry, but most people who knew him will find it hard to imagine him being anything but gracious, calm, and supportive, even toward those with whom he might disagree.

I was not a student of Jervis's and I never taught in the same department with him. Yet he influenced how I thought about international relations years before my own career got started. His article "Hypotheses on Misperception" was required reading for the introductory international relations class I took during my junior year in college, and I found it utterly fascinating.[1] Reading the book version—the classic *Perception and Misperception in International Politics* (1976)—the following year helped convince me to eschew law school and get a PhD instead.[2] Along with a few other works, these writings gave me the sense that international politics was a subject that could be analyzed systematically and that theory could help us understand behavior that might otherwise seem random, confusing, or tragic.

Jervis's writings have appeared on my course syllabi every year since I began teaching thirty-seven years ago. Why? Because they address central questions in our field, and the answers he provides are novel, interesting, sometimes profound, and always well-informed. How do states see each other? What actions will make them fearful, and under what conditions will they try to address that fear by using force? How do states try to signal intentions to each other, and what makes these signals credible? Why is it so hard for states to cooperate for mutual benefit, and what conditions or actions make it easier for them to do so? When is deterrence more likely to fail? How did the invention of nuclear weapons affect relations between states, and what policies does the "nuclear revolution" call for? Teaching international relations without including Jervis's work would be an act of educational malpractice.

The common thread running through much of Jervis's scholarship was an effort to explain why it is so hard for states to understand each other. That concern for signaling, communication, and perception informed his subsequent work on deterrence theory, nuclear strategy, security regimes, and intelligence. To do this, he drew primarily upon the vast literature in social and cognitive psychology but also on the work of the sociologist Erving Goffman.[3] Jervis's great contribution was to marry theoretical works from other disciplines with his own broad and deep knowledge of how states (and their leaders) acted in the real world of politics. Although he was not the first person to apply psychology or sociology to the study of foreign policy, none of his predecessors (and few, if any, of his successors) did so with the same level of insight.

Although he never constructed a grand macro theory of his own, he was still very much a theorist who developed general explanations for recurring phenomena and gave us new ways to see them. Think about his distinction between "signals" and "indices" in *The Logic of Images in International Relations* (an argument that anticipates later work by game theorists and evolutionary biologists on "costly signals"); his contrasting accounts of the "spiral model" and "deterrence model" in *Perception and Misperception*; his adroit application of attribution theory, cognitive dissonance, and other psychological concepts to elite decision making; his elegant explanation for how second-strike nuclear capabilities could mitigate the "security dilemma" and foster greater cooperation; or his subtle and closely reasoned exploration of how systems effects shaped outcomes in a wide variety of social settings.[4] In these works, he gave readers a tool or a roadmap to guide their thinking and to help make sense out of the dizzying complexity of social life.

I first met Jervis when I was a graduate student, shortly after he had left UCLA for Columbia. He came to Berkeley to give a talk at a moment when I was struggling to formulate a dissertation topic, and I somehow arranged to meet with him one on one and talk about some early ideas I had for a thesis on alliances. I don't remember what either of us said at that first encounter, but what I do remember was that he was friendly, unpretentious, encouraging, and above all willing to devote an hour of his day to a student he'd never laid eyes on before. I am sure there are countless other people who could tell a similar story.

Apart from various encounters at conferences and workshops, my main association with him began in the early 1990s, when he and Robert Art invited me to join them as a coeditor of the *Cornell Studies in Security Affairs*, the book series they founded in the early 1980s. The academic subfield of security studies was somewhat moribund during this period, and Art and Jervis understood that younger scholars needed a respected, peer-reviewed outlet for their early works if they were going to rise within academe and have a lengthy scholarly career. In addition to lending their own reputations to this enterprise, the two Bobs kept a keen eye out for rising talents and gave younger scholars invaluable advice on how to turn promising but flawed dissertations into first-rate books. The series they created helped launch dozens of successful careers, eventually spawned similar efforts at other presses, and played a major role in rebuilding the subfield. It reminds us that great scholars leave their mark not only in what they write but also by providing collective goods and field leadership.

For me, working with the two Bobs on the Cornell Series was both an honor and an education. As an editor, Jervis was tough but fair-minded and a fount of wisdom and common sense. His editorial instincts and encyclopedic knowledge of the scholarly literature saved countless authors from careless errors, and the easy working relationship among our editorial troika owed much to his and Robert Art's generosity of spirit, integrity, and absence of ego.

Robert Jervis made the rest of us smarter, and he left the field of security studies in better shape than he found it. No scholar could ask for a better legacy.

NOTES

1. Robert Jervis, "Hypotheses on Misperception," *World Politics* 20, no. 3 (1968): 454–79.
2. Robert Jervis, *Perception and Misperception in International Politics* (Princeton University Press, 1976; new edition, 2017).
3. Erving Goffman, *The Presentation of Self in Everyday Life* (Anchor, 1959).
4. Robert Jervis, *The Logic of Images in International Relations* (Columbia University Press, 1989); Jervis, *Perception and Misperception*; Jervis, "Cooperation Under the Security Dilemma," *World Politics* 30, no. 2 (1978):167–214; and Jervis, *Systems Effects: Complexity in Political and Social Life* (Princeton University Press, 1997).

II

ROBERT JERVIS, PSYCHOLOGY, AND BARGAINING

9

A LEADER AND A SUBVERSIVE

Robert Jervis's Contradictory Contributions
to International Relations Theory

THOMAS J. CHRISTENSEN

I am grateful to Richard Immerman, Stacie Goddard, and Diane Labrosse for asking me to contribute to this volume honoring my mentor, colleague, and friend, Robert Jervis. This chapter focuses on two of his books published in 2017: the new edition of his classic *Perception and Misperception in International Politics* and a collection of his essays under the very appropriate title *How Statesmen Think*, the question that motivated Jervis's work for six decades.[1] These books encapsulate Jervis's ability throughout his career to illuminate broad forces in international politics without losing sight of the role of individual decision makers who perceive and misperceive those broad forces in consequential ways that ultimately determine international outcomes.

Before I turn to his many professional contributions, however, I wanted to share a story that I believe partially captures Bob's generous, humble, and humorous personality. I told this story several years ago when I spoke at a session in his honor at the annual meeting of the American Political Science Association (APSA) and again in February 2023 at his memorial service. Here goes.

A HUMBLE, HUMOROUS, AND GENEROUS MENTOR

I was a graduate student at Columbia University in the late 1980s, and one year, I was lucky enough to secure an outside grant that provided funds for a small office in what is now the Saltzman Institute for War and Peace Studies. This placed me just a few doors from Professor Robert Jervis, who had taught two of my classes, was my boss when I was a teaching assistant, and had agreed to join my dissertation committee.

It was in this time period that Jervis received the Grawemeyer Award for his book *The Meaning of the Nuclear Revolution*, a prestigious honor that includes a substantial monetary prize.[2] In his generosity, he decided to share the wealth by providing an unlimited supply of gourmet ground coffee and a coffee machine in a public space in the institute. For a struggling graduate student, this meant a lot. No more trips to the local Greek diner to buy weak coffee in smallish blue paper cups decorated with the Parthenon. What was much more important than the coffee, however, is that the coffee machine provided a gathering place for me as a student to chat with Professor Jervis and other members of the very busy faculty (note, we never referred to him as "Bob" until we had successfully defended our dissertations).

On one such occasion, Professor Jervis approached me at the machine with an opened envelope and a letter. (This was before email!) He had a quizzical look on his face. He handed me the letter and said, "Tom, I do not know how I should feel about this letter. Is it an insult or a compliment?" The letter was from a refereed publication rejecting something he had submitted. He was asking me about how to react to one of the referee's comments, which read: "In this piece, the author is trying hard to be Bob Jervis. But this author is no Bob Jervis." I laughed very hard then and still laugh now as I write this. Professor Jervis was free of an inflated ego and full of humor, so he laughed along with me. When I composed myself, I told him that I found this to be a great compliment to him as a scholar, however insulting it was to the piece in question.

At the APSA meeting at which I presented this story, I hoped that the many young scholars in the audience would take heart in it. Even the great Robert Jervis, who was receiving a lifetime achievement award that day, could have his work be summarily rejected by an academic publisher and could still find that an occasion for laughter and affirmation.

I now turn to a discussion of Jervis's path-breaking scholarly work.

A GIANT AND A GADFLY IN
INTERNATIONAL RELATIONS THEORY

Robert Jervis was at the same time a giant and a gadfly, a leader and a subversive in the field of international relations. In his career, Jervis was often a theorist in the mainstream political science tradition. In some of his most famous works—including "Cooperation Under the Security Dilemma" and *The Meaning of the Nuclear Revolution*—Jervis has shown his skill at creating deductively derived theories about how states should respond to structural and technological changes in international security affairs.[3]

Those works are extraordinary and have made an enormous contribution to the literature. But Jervis also noted with frustration that actual policymakers often diverged from the expectations and prescriptions of his theories and those of other international relations scholars. He lamented that despite the inescapable background condition of mutual nuclear vulnerability, the two Cold War superpowers still developed destabilizing offensive nuclear weapons designed to target their enemies' arsenals, planned to fight "limited" nuclear wars of various levels of intensity, and obsessed about local conventional balances of power around the world. Jervis thought it would have been safer and less fiscally burdensome if Washington and Moscow had fully accepted the condition of mutually assured destruction and properly understood the stabilizing effects that condition should produce at all levels of potential military conflict.[4]

Jervis was much more than a mainstream international relations theorist. As the eminent historian Paul Kennedy pointed out in the online tribute to Jervis that preceded this volume, he was also an honorary diplomatic historian.[5] He published many works of analytic diplomatic history, including four articles and one book review in the field's leading refereed journal, *Diplomatic History*.[6] He was chair of the CIA's Historical Review Panel. He helped create and sustain the H-Diplo/ISSF website, and appropriately, it is now named after him. The APSA award for the best book in international history and politics is named after Jervis and the diplomatic historian Paul Schroeder.

Jervis's appreciation of diplomatic history was also evident in many of his most famous political science publications. Especially in books like *Perception and Misperception in International Politics* and *How Statesman Think*, he was interested in explaining how leaders actually behaved, rather than how they should have behaved according to a pure, context-free theoretical logic. His real rebellion against mainstream political science was his insistence that decision makers, at the end of the day, are human: they suffer from cognitive limitations, biases, and personality quirks.[7] Those individual characteristics often make them poor subjects for deductively derived, structural explanations, which rely on the assumptions of scholars about how rational actors *should* interact and how they *should* react to objective changes in the environment in which they operate. In other words, scholars ascribe motivation to actors that those actors do not always share and therefore believe that those actors will react to changes in their objective environment in predictable ways when they often do not. In the preface of the revised edition of *Perception and Misperception*, Jervis states that the book itself does not have a single clear theoretical take. This is true unless, of course, one considers intelligent and historically rooted skepticism about clear theoretical takes themselves to be a strong theoretical position.

How Statesman Think, an updated compilation of previously published works, continues in this tradition. In a very real sense, the book brings together Jervis's two skills as a deductively oriented social science theorist and an inductive diplomatic historian. Jervis was enamored of general theories of coercive diplomacy, like Thomas Schelling's Nobel Prize–winning game theories of conflict, and general theories of human psychology, like Amos Tversky and Daniel Kahneman's Nobel Prize–winning work on prospect theory.[8] But Jervis was a master at demonstrating that although the theories themselves may be general, it takes a tremendous amount of detective work to apply them to real-world cases. To illuminate the parsimonious power of the elegant theories, we need to get into the particular psychological makeup and perceptions of state leaders.

In Schelling's theoretical work on coercive diplomacy, a core concept is the perceived status quo that can either be preserved through deterrence or changed through compellence. Because Schelling deems compellence to be much more difficult to achieve than deterrence, the distinction could hardly be more important. So the need to understand leaders' varying perceptions of the status quo is built into the theory in a way that strongly privileges scholars like Jervis, who are steeped in diplomatic history, over the vast majority of game theorists in political science, who have focused almost exclusively on mathematics in their intellectual training and simply assume as given many things that in the real world vary wildly and consequentially across actors.

The same can be said for one of the most important lessons of Schelling's game theoretic work, which is repeated often in the essays in *How Statesmen Think*: successful deterrence requires credible threats of punishment if proscribed behavior is adopted, but it also requires credible assurances that the punishment will be withheld if the perceived status quo is preserved. Without such assurances, the target has no reason to comply with the demands attached to the threat. There is always tension between these two equally important missions in coercive diplomacy, and that tension is captured by the concept of the security dilemma: a country's individual efforts to secure itself through defense buildups and deterrence can be misread by another state as fundamentally hostile and aggressive, leading to a countering effort that could leave both sides less secure.

To understand successful and failed instances of deterrence (or compellence), we need to comprehend not only the threatening and reassuring signals sent but also how those signals are perceived by the target. In his qualitative research, Jervis was therefore careful and rigorous to show what leaders were actually thinking. Unfortunately, such care is rarely reflected in the coding of cases for large n databases in the mainstream security studies literature, which ironically prides itself on superior scientific rigor.

Just as Schelling's theories are broadly applicable but difficult to apply in every case, so is Amos Tversky and Daniel Kahneman's prospect theory. Because humans behave very differently when protecting what they have than when gaining new things, how issues are framed by individuals as being in the realm of gains or the realm of losses is all important. We need to know a lot about the psychology of individual actors in the political world to determine what they themselves would consider a gain from the perceived precrisis status quo and what they would consider a loss. This can only be accomplished through careful empirical research into leaders' psychology in each case, which sometimes requires not only reviews of secondary histories but also analysis of primary documents and memoirs. When teaching the field seminar in international relations theory at Columbia, Jervis had his graduate students analyze the Crowe Memorandum, a 1907 British government assessment of German aspirations and strategy in the years before the outbreak of the First World War.[9] As he did in his own publications, he wanted his students to explore critically the thinking and perceptions of actual government leaders, not just show whether or not their eventual behavior correlated positively with the expectations of a deductively derived theory.

Jervis applied these analytic skills not only as a scholar and teacher but also as a public servant. He served as an advisor to the intelligence community both to help officials there understand the causes of catastrophic intelligence failures and to decide what documents could be safely declassified and released to the general public. In my years interacting with people from that community, I have heard nothing but praise for Jervis both as a keen but fair critic and as a generous and empathetic fellow traveler. He understood well how difficult it is to draw accurate conclusions from a world of imperfect information and, sometimes, intentional deception by foreign governments.

Scholars who are also former foreign policy practitioners have praised Jervis's published work as a helpful tool in both policymaking and intelligence analysis.[10] As a former government official myself, I agree with them wholeheartedly. Jervis's theoretical toolbox is much more useful to policymakers than most mainstream theories in the international relations literature because contingency is built into Jervis's generalizable approaches. There is plenty of room to allow for consideration of what policymakers know from experience to be important: individual leaders matter; context matters; diplomatic signals need to be crafted carefully to demonstrate both resolve and restraint; and how the other side thinks about an international crisis or problem is as important and sometimes more important than how one's own side thinks about such issues.[11]

Jervis published *How Statesman Think* and a new edition of *Perception and Misperception in International Politics* in 2017, the same year that Richard Thaler won the Nobel Prize for his work in behavioral economics, which, like the works of Jervis and Tversky and Kahneman, treats economic actors as full humans rather than robotic utility maximizers.[12] It is also fitting that the books were published in the first year that President Donald J. Trump assumed office for the first time. Trump's election demonstrated the importance of the individual leader and his or her psychology in international politics in ways that Jervis's work captures so well.[13] And in an indirect and unintended way, Trump's presidency validated Jervis's subversive arguments about the need to consider such particularistic variables in social science. Many scholars who take a very different approach and suggest in their work that what really matters in domestic and international politics are broad structural pressures on political actors, not those actors' individual personalities, had their theoretical convictions tested by Trump's election. Many expressed uncharacteristic worry over this particular individual's presence in the Oval Office. And since Trump announced his candidacy for president again in 2023, can even adherents to the most abstract international theories and rational actor models seriously argue that the outcome of the 2024 presidential campaign will not be enormously consequential for US foreign policy and international politics more generally? Perhaps deep down these generalist international relations theory scholars think more like Robert Jervis than their published works might suggest.

NOTES

1. Robert Jervis, *Perception and Misperception in International Politics* (Harvard University Center for International Affairs, 2017); and Jervis, *How Statesman Think: The Psychology of International Politics* (Princeton University Press, 2017).

2. Robert Jervis, *The Meaning of the Nuclear Revolution: Statecraft and the Prospect of Armageddon* (Cornell University Press, 1989).

3. Robert Jervis, "Cooperation Under the Security Dilemma," *World Politics* 30, no. 2 (1978): 167–214; and Jervis, *The Meaning of the Nuclear Revolution.*

4. For Jervis's complaints about US military doctrine under conditions of mutually assured destructions, see Jervis, *The Meaning of the Nuclear Revolution*; and Robert Jervis, *The Illogic of American Nuclear Strategy* (Cornell University Press, 1984). In *How Statesmen Think*, Jervis recognizes that the Soviet leadership did not accept "security dilemma thinking" and therefore did not behave in accordance with it until Soviet leader Mikhail Gorbachev's rule, which did not begin until 1985, 186–187

5. Paul Kennedy, "Robert Jervis: My Diplomatic History Buddy," in "Tribute to the Life, Scholarship, and Legacy of Robert Jervis, Part I," ed. Richard H. Immerman, Diane Labrosse, and Marc Trachtenberg, *H-Diplo/ISSF*, February 4, 2022, https://issforum.org /ISSF/PDF/ISSF-Jervis-Tribute-1.pdf.

6. Robert Jervis, "The Military History of the Cold War," *Diplomatic History* 11, no. 1 (1991): 91–113; Jervis, "A Usable Past for the Future," *Diplomatic History* 16, no. 1 (1992): 76–84; Jervis, "America and the Twentieth Century: Continuity and Change," *Diplomatic History* 23, no. 2 (1999): 219–38; Jervis "The Politics of Troop Withdrawal: Salted Peanuts, the Commitment Trap, and Buying Time," *Diplomatic History* 34, no. 3 (2010): 507–16; and Jervis, "The End of the Cold War on the Cold War? A Review of Leffler's *A Preponderance*

of Power," *Diplomatic History* 17, no. 4 (1993): 651. Also see Jervis, "Systems Theories and Diplomatic History," in *Diplomatic History: New Approaches*, ed. Paul Lauren (Free Press, 1979); Jervis, "The Balance of Power and the Concert of Europe: Perspectives from Political Science," *American Historical Review* 97, no. 3 (1992): 716–24; Jervis, "Diplomatic History and International Relations: Why Are They Studied So Differently?," in *Bridges and Boundaries: Historians, Political Scientists, and the Study of International Relations*, ed. Miriam Fendius Elman and Colin Elman (MIT Press, 2001): 385–402; and Jervis, "Comments on Trachtenberg," *Historically Speaking* 8, no. 2 (2006): 17–18. Jervis also published multiple book reviews on the H-Diplo website.

7. On this aspect of Jervis's work, see Thomas J. Christensen and Keren Yarhi-Milo, "The Human Factor: How Robert Jervis Reshaped Our Understanding of International Politics," *Foreign Affairs*, January 7, 2022, https://www.foreignaffairs.com/articles/world/2022-01-07/human-factor.

8. Representative examples of their work include Thomas C. Schelling, *Strategy of Conflict* (Oxford University Press, 1963); Schelling, *Arms and Influence* (Yale University Press, 1967); and Amos Tversky and Daniel Kahneman. "Prospect Theory: An Analysis of Decision Under Risk," *Econometrica* 47, no. 2 (1979): 263–91.

9. Eyre Crowe, "Memorandum on the Present State of Relations with France and Germany," in *British Documents on the Origins of the War*, ed. G. P. Gooch and Harold Temperley (His Majesty's Stationary Office, 1928), 417. Eyre Crowe was a leading expert on Germany in the British Foreign Office and called for a more resolute stance against Germany and a tighter balancing alliance with France.

10. See, for example, the reviews by James B. Steinberg and Philip Zelikow in the H-Diplo|ISSF Roundtable Review of Robert Jervis's *Perception and Misperception in International Politics* and *How Statesmen Think: The Psychology of International Politics*, H-Diplo|ISSF Roundtable, Volume X, No. 4, December 8, 2017, http://issforum.org/ISSF/PDF/ISSF-Roundtable-10-4.pdf.

11. For an excellent recent critique of the neorealist and rational choice literature in international relations along these lines, see Jonathan Kirshner, *An Unwritten Future: Realism and Uncertainty in International Politics* (Princeton University Press, 2022). I think that the reader will find this book a fine companion to the two works by Robert Jervis that I discuss here. It is a pity that Jervis never had the chance to read this book.

12. For Thaler's pathbreaking work on "the endowment effect," in which people value more highly the same object if they already own it and are considering it for sale than if they are considering purchasing it, see Richard H. Thaler, "Toward a Positive Theory of Consumer Choice," *Journal of Economic Behavior and Organization* 1, no. 1 (1980): 39–60. For a retrospective on his own work in behavioral economics, see Thaler, *Misbehaving: The Making of Behavioral Economics* (Norton, 2015).

13. See Robert Jervis, "President Trump and International Relations Theory," in *Chaos in the Liberal Order: The Trump Presidency and International Politics in the Twenty-First Century*, ed. Jervis et al. (Columbia University Press, 2018): 3–7; and Jervis, "The Trump Experiment: An Assessment," in *Chaos Reconsidered: The Liberal Order and the Future of International Politics*, ed. Jervis et al. (Columbia University Press, 2023): 15–27.

10

UNDERSTANDING LIFE AND LIFE'S CHOICES

A Tribute

JAMES W. DAVIS

It is perfectly true, as the philosophers say, that life must be understood back-wards. But they forget the other proposition, that it must be lived forwards.
—SØREN KIERKEGAARD (*JOURNALEN* JJ:167, 1843)

R obert Jervis and I first discussed the Danish theologian's oft-cited journal entry after an undergraduate lecture class for which I was the teaching assistant. Bob had used the citation to make a point during a discussion of the diplomacy surrounding the fall of the Berlin Wall and what many referred to as the end of the Cold War, but he didn't remember its provenance. I took some satisfaction from the fact that I could remind him of the source.[1] As we discussed the quotation while walking back to the Institute of War and Peace Studies—it was not yet the Saltzman Institute—I began to understand just how profound he thought the statement to be. In subsequent years, I recognized how his own research and his approach to scholarly practice and collegiality were influenced by the manifold implications of Kierkegaard's observation. And only weeks before he died, we returned to Kierkegaard in an email exchange on the article Bob had just finished for the *Proceedings of the National Academy of Sciences*.[2] Commemorating his long overdue election to the National Academy of Sciences, the article would turn out to be his last.

In this brief tribute to my mentor and friend, I necessarily look backward: at the scholarly legacy of a giant in the field of international relations and the many doors he opened for me and others. Though modest, Bob was aware of his influence in the field. Yet I suspect he remained uncertain about his legacy, about whether anyone would choose to walk through the doors he opened and, if so, where they might end up. For in understanding that life must be lived forward, he was keenly aware of the ambiguity, uncertainty, and contingency such a predicament entails. Any effort to understand his scholarly legacy (and I suspect in many ways his private life) must recognize how he was not only guided but also motivated by this view of the human condition.

In what follows, I highlight how an appreciation for the ambiguity, uncertainty, and contingency of life can be seen in two themes running through Jervis's scholarship: knowing and judging. In doing so, I revisit some of the questions I explored in my contribution to the Festschrift published in honor of Jervis's seventieth birthday[3] and then conclude with a few personal experiences that confirm the importance of contingency in my own ongoing journey. Though I am uncertain as to where I will end up, looking back, all roads lead to Bob.

ON KNOWING

How do we know that we know something? The straightforward answer and one often provided by Jervis himself is: "It's complicated!" But although the answer to my question might be straightforward, it reveals little, and little that was of interest to Jervis was straightforward. Indeed, simply to ask an interesting question in international relations is to enter a world of complexity.

"Why did the Cold War stay cold?" Jervis posed this question to the undergraduates in a lecture only to deconstruct it. What do we mean by the term "war"? Sustained conflict involving organized armed forces producing a minimum of a thousand battle-related fatalities? Probably not. In what sense and for whom was the Cold War "cold"? Would our assessment of this period of international relations change if we were to refer to it as "the era of sustained superpower competition"? Calling this particular conflict the Cold War inevitably led to the search for winners and losers, an exercise that in turn might corrupt our efforts to understand its origins. The discussion was quite ironic given that in other classes, Jervis decried the influence of deconstructionism in the social sciences!

Jervis recognized that making sense of the social world presents particular challenges not only because perceptions of our environment are mediated by preexisting concepts and beliefs, some of which will be idiosyncratic, but also because we are usually trying to understand others with whom we are engaged in a strategic interaction and who simultaneously are trying to understand (and likely manipulate) us. In this regard, Jervis viewed the challenge confronting scholars and decision makers to be similar. The central theme of *Perception and Misperception in International Politics* is that decision makers tend to assimilate ambiguous information to preexisting belief structures, a process that often leads to misperceptions and flawed inferences.[4] Jervis feared that scholars, who are armed with theory and know how the story ended, are likewise primed to see some things while overlooking others that might lead to rather different conclusions. Although uncomfortable with language smacking of postmodernism, he recognized that theory and data are interrelated in significant ways. Hence, rather than starting with outcomes and trying to fit developments to our concepts and models—that is, trying to understand outcomes backward—it might be better to start with the problems that decision makers confront and then try to "see" the world through their own eyes.

Of course, the task is difficult. Often, we lack the necessary data. But even when available, the data are suspect, for not only are decision makers often trying to deceive their adversaries but also the wise among them understand their place in history and may be trying to deceive future scholars.[5] Jervis was particularly attuned to—and I believe ultimately impressed by—Henry Kissinger's efforts to influence future scholarship on his actions as national security advisor and secretary of state through careful attention to the documentary record and a clever framing of controversial issues in his memoirs. He took obvious pleasure in pointing to examples where Kissinger was caught at his game.[6]

Because the task of knowing is so complex, no single tool is adequate to the task. This observation goes a long way toward explaining why Jervis not only was open but also contributed to research from a variety of disciplines and theoretical perspectives, with seminal contributions to the fields of political psychology, structural realism, nuclear strategy, arms control, deterrence, regime theory, diplomatic history, intelligence analysis, and complexity theory.

For graduate students who were affiliated with Columbia University's Institute of War and Peace Studies, the example was at once inspiring and intimidating. Mastering the debates and methods of political science was daunting enough. But to study with Jervis meant engaging with a coterie of giants from cognate disciplines *in person*. Imagine the exhilaration and sense of inadequacy that comes with extended and intense discussions of work in progress with the likes of McGeorge Bundy, Paul Schroeder, and Marc Trachtenberg![7] Not only was there the challenge of absorbing the substance of their historical arguments, but also there was the need to come to terms with the historical method and what often was a not-so-subtle critique of the discipline to which many of us had just committed ourselves. For those who chose to walk through this particular door, however, the clash of academic cultures resulted in more creative sparks than intellectual fatalities. Bob was delighted when I suggested that Trachtenberg join my dissertation defense committee,[8] welcomed Marc's influence on James McAllister's important study of the postwar German question,[9] and took satisfaction in the substantive dialogue between political scientists and historians made possible by Colin Elman and Miriam Fendius Elman's edited volume *Bridges and Boundaries*.[10]

For those of us interested in political psychology, the model was similar. An invitation to join Bob's Political Psychology Workshop was an invitation to engage with the scholarship of Alexander George, Lucian Pye, Ned Lebow, Janice Stein,[11] Amos Tversky, and Daniel Kahneman (far before the latter two were socially acceptable in political science or economics). Regulars included established scholars, such as Jack Snyder and Jack Levy, but also fellow upstarts, including Barbara Farnham and Rose McDermott.[12] The workshop also provided a forum to discuss ongoing projects of younger scholars. I especially remember the discussions we had of Jonathan Mercer's pathbreaking dissertation on reputation, a project that Jervis supervised even as it critiqued some of the central arguments about deterrence that were developed by Thomas Schelling, a scholar Bob revered.[13]

Again, Jervis was opening doors, even if he could not be certain of the path any of us might take should we choose to pass through them. In my case, the journey led to an application of prospect theory to questions surrounding the use of rewards and assurances in deterrence, which in turn had me corresponding with George, Kahneman, Lebow, and Stein, the latter two becoming close friends and mentors.[14] In a study of President Franklin D. Roosevelt's wartime decision making, Farnham examined the effects of the domestic political context on leaders' efforts to cope with value conflicts in foreign policy decision making.[15] Meanwhile, McDermott moved beyond prospect theory to engage with a wider range of research in psychology, genetics, and the emerging field of neuroscience, eventually becoming a trail blazer in the development of the experimental method in international relations.[16]

The breadth of expertise reflected in the work of the generations of graduate students Jervis mentored is impressive enough. Truly remarkable were the innovative ways in which Jervis could apply tools derived from the disparate disciplines, theories, and methods to deliver novel insights that often contradicted his previous commitments. Randall Schweller, who is himself an accomplished theorist, compared Jervis's virtuosity to that of a jazz musician: "You could see the wheels turning in his head as he set several thematic ideas into motion, partially expounding on one and then moving on to another with the promise to return to this or that idea later."[17] Trachtenberg's observation is similar: "[Jervis] looks at a problem in a certain light and he makes certain points about it. The points are often quite striking, but after making a certain argument, you can practically hear him saying to himself: 'Now wait a minute, isn't there another way of looking at it?' The perspective shifts, and soon everything appears in a rather different light."[18]

Some might conclude that such an approach to scholarship reflects a lack of theoretical commitment or some deep-rooted indecisiveness. Precisely the opposite was the case. Because Bob was convinced that the world we study is highly complex and characterized by multiple connections among the various parts, he felt that unambiguous arguments based on isolating particular cause-and-effect relationships are likely to lead us to miss much of what is truly of interest.[19]

ON JUDGING

Understanding life backward implies beginning our analysis with the observable results of prior choices, a fact that tends to strongly influence if not determine our assignations of praise or blame. Jervis understood that the approach is often misleading. As realists have long argued, international outcomes do not necessarily follow from intentions; hence, we cannot infer the latter from the former. A simple example from what may be Jervis's most cited work will suffice to underscore the point.[20]

The lack of an international sovereign that could prevent the resort to violence leads to what John Herz termed the security dilemma: the fact that one state's efforts to enhance its security often are perceived to menace the security of others, provoking countermeasures such that each remains insecure.[21] Because of anarchy, Jervis argued that even two peacefully inclined leaders will find it difficult to signal benign intent and, through the operation of the security dilemma, can find themselves in a war neither desires.[22] The fact that outcomes need not reflect intentions complicates straightforward efforts to judge leaders' decisions.

Elsewhere, I have discussed at length how Jervis's approach to judging nevertheless fits into realism's preference for evaluating political decision makers based on the consequences of their choices (*Verantwortungsethik*) rather than the values that motived them (*Gesinnungsethik*).[23] At first glance, the affinity is not readily apparent. For in highlighting how cognitive limitations and the efforts of others to deceive routinely confound decision makers' abilities to accurately perceive their environments and in stressing the difficulties of predicting the full range of effects caused by acting in complex systems, Jervis's scholarship would seem to absolve leaders of responsibility for the negative outcomes of their decisions. Perhaps we can dispense with classical realism's view of political man as essentially evil and instead imagine a world of basically good, if fallible, people who are trying to cope with difficult situations?[24] Indeed, some have referred to his approach as the "no fault" school.[25]

Jervis recognized that his theoretical convictions complicated efforts to judge decision makers and decision making. But as both a scholar and a consultant to the US government, he spent decades analyzing foreign policy decision making in order to point out not only how things can go awry but also how to improve decision making given the limitations on our ability to know and control the social world. We try to learn from the past so that we might do better in the future. His own approach is exemplified by his conduct of and reflections on postmortems of intelligence failure,[26] and the affinity to Kierkegaard is clear.[27]

Most important is the need to separate our judgments about the process of decision making from our assessments of the quality of the decision itself as reflected in the results it produced. The task is complicated by the fact that postmortem analyses are conducted at a distance:

> The conditions under which people worked fade and become obscure even in their minds and can never be known by the reviewer. Such a person knows what the outcome of the events is, and he cannot fail to be influenced by that knowledge. Moreover, the material that he reads in order to determine what happened, what people knew, and what they wrote about it comes to him in a form much different from the way it comes to the intelligence analyst. The reviewer has the opportunity to read material through in a coherent order. For the analyst working on events as they happened, material or information must be absorbed as it comes in—sometimes in fragments, often not in a timely fashion.[28]

Yet empathy for the intelligence analyst does not imply absolution. As Jim Wirtz put it, "estimates written to meet the needs of the day have to withstand the test of time."[29] A focus on the process that led to conclusions alerts us to the fact that one can be right for the wrong reasons or wrong even though every effort was made to reach valid conclusions and guard against bias. But because we tend to focus our efforts on understanding "bad" results, we are likely to overlook the many positive outcomes that resulted from bad process. All too often we are selecting on the dependent variable.

For Jervis the remedy was better social science. The comparative method can help establish whether the putative errors in process are unique or perhaps are common and thus also present in cases where things turned out better. Counterfactual analysis allows us to explore the possibility that the outcome might have been the same even if the decision maker had behaved differently. And thinking in terms of alternative explanations helps us establish not only where inferential errors occurred but also whether there was a less ambiguous match between the evidence available and alternative views that were expressed at the time. To argue that one should have done a better job of connecting the dots is banal. The problem confronting foreign policy decision makers is that there usually are many ways to do so, especially in complex systems where

the relations among variables are multiple, nonlinear, and often characterized by complex feedback loops.

In his postmortem of the US intelligence community's (IC) erroneous
conclusion that Iraq's president Saddam Hussein had reconstituted his
program to develop weapons of mass destruction (WMD), empathy for
the challenges confronting analysts combined with good social science
method allowed Jervis both to refute popular claims that the IC had suc-
cumbed to political pressure and to locate important errors in process that
led to flawed inferences.[30] Nonetheless, Jervis concluded that even a good
process likely would have led to the assessment that Iraq had an active
and broadly based WMD program. The conclusion provoked intense discussions among many of Bob's former students as well as fellow scholars
of intelligence. Almost all of us had opposed the war, and many feared
that letting Bush administration officials off the hook for the decision to
launch it would only provide grist for the mills of those whose theories of
international relations and policy preferences were so obviously at odds
with Jervis's own.[31]

Such impulses were misguided. For if the IC was not guilty of telling
politicians what they wanted to hear, Jervis's findings made it difficult for
the political branches to absolve themselves of responsibility and scape-
goat the IC for the decision to go to war and its consequences. Jervis
recognized that the responsibility for the war lay with the Bush administration and an enabling Congress.[32] It was likely that hawks in the administration would have manipulated any assessment produced by the IC to
fit conclusions reached on other grounds if only to avoid the necessity
of acknowledging the value trade-offs implied by any significant foreign
policy decision. Although he recognized the psychological impulse to be
universal, Jervis nonetheless criticized failures of US leaders to acknowledge value conflicts and what Max Weber termed the "incidental" costs
involved in pursuing political objectives.[33] To quote Arnold Wolfers, Jervis's favorite international relations theorist: "The moral dilemmas with
which statesmen and their critics are constantly faced revolve around
the question of whether in a given instance the defense or satisfaction of
interests other than survival justify the costs in other values."[34] Although
he recognized the difficulty of predicting the ultimate effects of our
actions, Jervis was true to an ethic of consequences in demanding that
American decision makers confront their range of choice and weigh the

intended benefits of their actions against the potential costs to other values: "The temptation to believe that the environment is so extreme as to compel the most awful actions and the statesmen's hubris of thinking that their acts are beyond judging are terribly strong and must be constantly resisted. . . . Perhaps as shocking as the calculated violations of moral standards are the many cases in which statesmen do not even think of what their acts will costs in terms of innocent lives, deplorable precedents, and values sullied."[35]

And yet, Jervis recognized the virtues of confidence and perseverance for effective leadership once a decision is made. For if confidence depended on knowledge, political action would be debilitated altogether.[36] Life must be led forward.

ON COLLEGIALITY

The political mind—more specifically, how political actors think (or sometimes don't)—was a major focus of Jervis's scholarship. Yet, I suspect he found very few decision makers whose thought processes he coveted even on those occasions when he did approve of their choices or recognized the virtue of their self-confidence. After all, decision makers, by definition, eventually have to decide. And although he held strong beliefs, one of the most striking characteristics of Bob's approach to analysis was his reluctance to cast final judgement. As Trachtenberg recognized, Jervis's intellectual virtue was found in a driving need to ask whether a given question, problem, or puzzle could be viewed from yet another perspective, one that might lead to the identification of different causal processes and assessments of the effectiveness, reasonableness, or perhaps even wisdom of some decision maker's choice.[37] Whether in the classroom, the political psychology research seminar, workshops with historians, or his famous lunch groups[38] (which, as a result of COVID, were conducted via Zoom during his last year of life), Bob was always probing others in search of novel perspectives.

Suspending final judgment meant eschewing theoretical and methodological trench warfare, mistrust of assertions of authority, openness to new ideas and people, and above all, humility with respect to his own claims to knowledge. These intellectual and personal virtues were fundamental to the collegiality that defined Bob and to the collegial environment he cultivated at Columbia University.

Looking back, I now understand how these virtues facilitated my own journey in the discipline. I came to know Bob Jervis in a chance encounter in the mid-1980s. I was an editorial intern at *Foreign Affairs* and had the opportunity to serve as rapporteur for a Council on Foreign Relations study group that Michael Mandelbaum had convened on the Soviet approach to arms control. I was a nobody in a room of accomplished scholars and practitioners, but Bob nonetheless approached me during a break and asked about my plans for the future. I told him I was in the process of applying to graduate schools, having been encouraged to do so by Mandelbaum, but allowed that I probably did not have the undergraduate record to be accepted into the best programs. In an illegible script, he noted my name and told me to apply to Columbia. I followed his advice and have always suspected that something close to divine intervention played a role in my eventual admission.

Looking forward, I realize Bob's intellect will forever be beyond my reach. Yet in tribute to his legacy and in recognition of the many debts I owe, I can recommit myself to the many examples he set: as a responsible scholar, committed teacher, respectful colleague, and valued friend.

NOTES

1. After reading a draft of this essay, Bob's wife, Kathe, informed me that he was reading from a book by Kierkegaard on a tour of the Soviet Union during which they first met.
2. Robert Jervis, "Why Postmortems Fail," *Proceedings of the National Academy of Sciences* 119, no. 3 (2022): e2116638118.
3. James W. Davis, ed., *Psychology, Strategy and Conflict: Perceptions of Insecurity in International Relations* (Routledge, 2013).
4. Robert Jervis, *Perception and Misperception in International Politics* (Princeton University Press, 1976).
5. Jervis's interest in deception led to his distinguishing "signals" from "indices," a distinction that would play a role in Michael Spence's Nobel Prize–winning scholarship on costly signals. See Robert Jervis, *The Logic of Images in International Relations* (Princeton University Press, 1970); and A. Michael Spence, "Signaling in Retrospect and the Informational Structure of Markets," *American Economic Review* 92, no. 3 (2002): 434–59.
6. A favorite example was Kissinger's early efforts to deflect and mitigate blame for excluding multiple independently targetable reentry vehicles from Strategic Arms Limitation

Talks I. Evidence that these were disingenuous to say the least is provided by Raymond L. Garthoff, *Détente and Confrontation: American-Soviet Relations from Nixon to Reagan* (Brookings Institution, 1985), 141–150. For a brief overview of the issue, see Michael Krepon, "Retrospectives on MIRVing in the First Nuclear Age," *Arms Control Wonk*, blog, April 5, 2016, https://www.armscontrolwonk.com/archive/1201264/retrospectives -on-mirving-in-the-first-nuclear-age/.

7. The eventual publications included McGeorge Bundy, *Danger and Survival: Choices About the Bomb in the First Fifty Years* (Random House, 1988); Paul W. Schroeder, *The Transformation of European Politics 1763–1848* (Oxford University Press, 1994); and Marc Trachtenberg, *A Constructed Peace: The Making of the European Settlement, 1945–1963* (Princeton University Press, 1999). Fittingly, Trachtenberg was one of the editors of the ISSF online tribute to Jervis and is one of the contributors to this memorial volume.

8. I remember well the debate I had with Trachtenberg at my dissertation defense over my critique of Raymond Sontag's interpretation of the War-in-Sight Crisis, a critique I could engage in only because Trachtenberg had taught us the importance of examining for ourselves the primary documents on which historians were basing their claims. See James W. Davis, *Threats and Promises: The Pursuit of International Influence* (Johns Hopkins University Press, 2000), 81–93.

9. James McAllister, *No Exit: American and the German Problem, 1943–1954* (Cornell University Press, 2002). See too McAllister's contribution to this volume.

10. Colin Elman and Miriam Fendius Elman, eds., *Bridges and Boundaries: Historians, Political Scientists, and the Study of International Relations* (MIT Press, 2001).

11. See Janice Gross Stein's contribution to this volume.

12. Jack Levy, Rose McDermott, and Jack L. Snyder have all contributed essays to this memorial volume. Sadly, Barbara Reardon Farnham died in 2016.

13. Jonathan Mercer, *Reputation and International Politics* (Cornell University Press, 1996). Also see Mercer's contribution to this volume.

14. Davis, *Threats and Promises*. For the original articulation of prospect theory, see Daniel Kahneman and Amos Tversky, "Prospect Theory: An Analysis of Decision under Risk," *Econometrica* 47 (1979): 263–91.

15. Barbara Reardon Farnham, *Roosevelt and the Munich Crisis: A Study in Political Decision-Making* (Princeton University Press, 2000).

16. Rose McDermott, *Risk-Taking in International Politics: Prospect Theory in American Foreign Policy* (University of Michigan Press, 1998); and Rose McDermott, "Experimental Methodology in Political Science," *Political Analysis* 10, no. 4 (2002): 325–42.

17. Randall Schweller, "Jervis's Realism," in Davis, ed., *Psychology, Strategy and Conflict*, 41. Schweller returns to this theme in his contribution to this volume.

18. Marc Trachtenberg, "Robert Jervis and the Nuclear Question," in Davis, ed., *Psychology, Strategy and Conflict*, 115–16.

19. Robert Jervis, *System Effects: Complexity in Political and Social Life* (Princeton University Press, 1997), 73.

20. Robert Jervis, "Cooperation Under the Security Dilemma," *World Politics* 30, no. 2 (1978): 167–214.

21. John H. Herz, "Idealist Internationalism and the Security Dilemma," *World Politics* 2, no. 2 (1950): 157–80.

22. Jervis, "Cooperation Under the Security Dilemma," 182; Jervis, "The Political Effects of Nuclear Weapons: A Comment," *International Security* 13, no. 2 (1998), 90. Paradoxically, owing to system effects—the unintended consequences of actions in a complex system— competition among revisionist states often creates a stable balance of power that makes war between them less likely. See Jervis, *System Effects*, 131–46; Kenneth N. Waltz, *Theory of International Politics* (Addison Wesley, 1979).

23. James W. Davis, "The (Good) Person and the (Bad) Situation: Recovering Innocence at the Expense of Responsibility?," in Davis, ed., *Psychology, Strategy and Conflict*, 199–219.

24. For a statement of the classical realist position, see Hans J. Morgenthau, "The Evil of Politics and the Ethics of Evil," *Ethics* 56, no. 1 (1945): 1–18.

25. Eliot A. Cohen and John Gooch, *Military Misfortunes: The Anatomy of Failure in War* (Free Press, 1990), 40–43.

26. See Richard H. Immerman's essay, "The Art and Science of the Postmortem," in this volume.

27. See Robert Jervis, *Why Intelligence Fails: Lessons from the Iranian Revolution and the Iraq War* (Cornell University Press, 2010).

28. Robert Jervis and John P. Devlin, "Analysis of NFAC's Performance on Iran's Domestic Crisis, Mid-1977–November 1978," declassified as CIA-RDP86B00269R001100110003-4, as cited in James J. Wirtz, "The Art of the Intelligence Autopsy," in Davis, ed., *Psychology, Strategy and Conflict*, 182.

29. Wirtz, "The Art of the Intelligence Autopsy," 183.

30. Jervis, *Why Intelligence Fails*, 123–55.

31. At the time one of the editors of the *European Journal of International Relations*, I was thrilled when Jervis submitted a critique of the Bush administration's Iraq policy. See Jervis, "The Confrontation Between Iraq and the US: Implications for the Theory and Practice of Deterrence," *European Journal of International Relations* 9, no. 2 (2003): 315–37. See also Jervis, "Understanding the Bush Doctrine," *Political Science Quarterly* 118, no. 3 (2003): 365–88.

32. But see Eliot Cohen's defense of the policymaker's predicament in his contribution to the roundtable review of *Why Intelligence Fails*. H-Diplo XI, 32, July 9, 2019, 6–8, https://issforum.org/roundtables/PDF/Roundtable-XI-32.pdf

33. Max Weber, "'Objectivity' in Social Science and Social Policy," in *The Methodology of the Social Sciences*, ed. E. A. Shils and H. A. Finch (Free Press, 1949), 53.

34. Arnold Wolfers, "Statesmanship and Moral Choice," *World Politics* 1, no. 2 (1949): 189–90.

35. Robert Jervis, *The Meaning of the Nuclear Revolution: Statecraft and the Prospect of Armageddon* (Cornell University Press, 1989), 133–34.

36. Jervis, *Why Intelligence Fails*, 162–65.

37. Trachtenberg, "Robert Jervis and the Nuclear Question," 115–16.

38. On the Jervis lunches, see the essays by Helen Milner and Tonya Putnam in Richard H. Immerman, Diane Labrosse, and Marc Trachtenberg, eds., "Tribute to the Life, Scholarship, and Legacy of Robert Jervis, Part I," *H-Diplo/ISSF*, February 4, 2022, https://issforum.org/ISSF/PDF/ISSF-Jervis-Tribute-1.pdf.

11

ON "COOPERATION UNDER THE SECURITY DILEMMA"

MICHAEL DOYLE

I t is widely agreed in the field of international relations that Robert Jervis was a giant. But views on what made him so may differ among us. I think all can agree that he established the study of cognitive psychology as an integral part of foreign policy. But I do not plan to say anything more on that; others are in a better position to weigh in with authority.

I should mention at the outset of this appreciation that he and I differed intellectually more than we cohered. We were at different ends of the world politics "elephant." He focused on decisions and psychology; I, on domestic structural determinants and political philosophy. Which end of the elephant was which we can leave open.

What made him a giant to me were his practices as a student-focused teacher and as a colleague-focused departmental citizen and his insights into what could make structural realism realistic.

I first met Jervis almost fifty years ago when he and Stanley Hoffmann were recruited by the Harvard Government Department to teach an introductory course in international relations. Such a course for some reason had not previously been thought to be an integral part of the international relations curriculum. In his lectures, Hoffman invited the students to share the highest reaches of sophisticated global savoir faire. With beautifully crafted, truly inspiring rhetoric, he invited students to appreciate a world of primary, secondary, and tertiary forces shaping the changing dynamics of the Cold War and alliance politics. A few weeks into the semester,

Jervis gathered the bewildered "section persons" (teaching assistants, of whom I was one) who were attempting to keep up with Hoffman for a locker-room pep talk directed toward how we could fall back on teaching the reading list—because, after all, we were going to test the students on it at the end of the semester.

I observed these practical talents again in the vital role he played in the Columbia Political Science Department, which I joined in 2004. Jervis was our unofficial, academic shop steward. He built bridges and opened channels of communication and organized solidarity every week by assembling colleagues to go to lunch. When a community needs to communicate, nothing beats eating and talking. Jervis made sure that happened regularly across fields and with ever-changing combinations of colleagues. Mostly as a result, intellectual diversity became one of Columbia's academic strong suits.[1]

But my most significant engagement with Bob was through his scholarship. Year after year, I included Jervis's article "Cooperation Under the Security Dilemma" as essential reading for international relations students at Johns Hopkins and Princeton in the 1980s and 1990s.[2] The value, for me, of structural realism was established by the insights of Hobbesian anarchy and its "state of war." But I don't think we would have paid as much attention as we did were it not for Kenneth Waltz's extension explaining bipolar stability[3] and Jervis's explanation of how cooperation could vary while still operating under the core assumptions of the paradigm. Both were remarkably progressive advances in the paradigm not only for the powerful insights they offered but also for building so directly on the core assumptions of the paradigm: the number, relative power, and material circumstances of unitary states in systemic anarchy.

Jervis's exploration of cooperation theory stood out for the breadth of the examples it drew upon. They ranged from accounts of Austrian diplomat Klemens von Metternich's diplomacy to remarks from a nineteenth-century Philadelphia newspaper on the nondefensive character of knives and sword canes (which can be so easily used for surprise and are not much use in defense). It also reflected a true depth of analysis in discussions of the dilemmas of 1920s and 1930s naval and military strategy and the distinctive implications of intercontinental ballistic missiles and submarine-launched ballistic missiles.

He opened the article, fittingly, with the core, tragic insight of structural realist anarchy:

> The lack of an international sovereign not only permits wars to occur, but also makes it difficult for states that are satisfied with the status quo to arrive at goals that they recognize as being in their common interest. Because there are no institutions or authorities that can make and enforce international laws, the policies of cooperation that will bring mutual rewards if others cooperate may bring disaster if they do not. Because states are aware of this, anarchy encourages behavior that leaves all concerned worse off than they could be, even in the extreme case in which all states would like to freeze the status quo.[4]

The absence of an international sovereign then makes stag dilemmas effectively similar to prisoner's dilemmas. In the prisoner's dilemma, the felons have an incentive to defect from cooperation (DC) in their hope of cutting a favorable plea bargain with the court. When both do so, both suffer the full weight of conviction (DD) with the incrimination each provided for the other. Jean-Jacques Rousseau's stag dilemma parable is different. It assumes that the hunters can attain the mutually preferred share of the stag they can capture if all of them remain rationally steadfast in cooperation (CC). In Jervis's lucid interpretation of Rousseau's parable, the hunters may share a preference for an equal share of the stag, but if they cannot trust and be assured of the commitments of the other hunters, they will nonetheless succumb to the temptation of catching the (much less desirable) hare that each can catch on his own (DC). When all then dash for the hare, all wind up with nothing or a small share of the much less meaty hare (DD). Under these circumstances, the security dilemma arises when even efforts to cooperate (improve hunting skills) have the effects of making others less secure (when they are all seizing the hare).

Jervis acknowledged that he has drawn a "gloomy picture, [and] the obvious question is, why are we not all dead? Or, to put it less starkly, what kinds of variables ameliorate the impact of anarchy and the security dilemma?"[5] Rather than a static picture, he next shows how factors can alter the payoffs and thus make the outcomes less preordained. Increasing the value of cooperation (CD and CC) or reducing the value of defection

(DC) or communicating accurate intentions in the stag dilemma or iterating the prisoner's dilemma such that the prisoners learn to punish defection as a way to incentivize cooperation: all these can make a difference.

Moreover, understanding the variables that alter incentives becomes an essential determinant of changing the "games" that shape world politics. Jervis argued that "situations vary in the ease or difficulty with which all states can simultaneously achieve a high degree of security. . . . [They include] the impact of beliefs, geography, and commitments (many of which can be considered to be modifications of geography, since they bind states to defend areas outside their homelands)."[6] Before World War I, Germany was nearly forced to adopt something like the Schlieffen Plan (which presupposed preemption or at least a quick victory over one rival) because of its central position and the hostility it faced from Russia and France. Defending the empire in India embroiled Britain in defending Egypt or South Africa in order to maintain trade and communications. The two oceans spared the United States an extra-"continental commitment" until the Cold War made the security of Western Europe a vital interest.

He concluded with the two additional variables that made the article famous: "Two crucial variables are involved: whether defensive weapons and policies can be distinguished from offensive ones, and whether the offense or the defense has the advantage."[7]

Whether the offense or the defense has the advantage is a matter mostly of geography, technology, and cost. Some terrains are difficult to cross (e.g., mountains, thick forests, desserts), and cannons overcame castles in early modern Europe. When it is much more costly to buy the weapons to conquer than to defend against those weapons, defense predominates, and vice versa.

Distinguishing offense from defensive weapons and postures can be more difficult. Jervis acknowledges the issue raised by Salvador de Madariaga, the Spanish statesman active in the disarmament negotiations of the interwar years: "A weapon is either offensive or defensive according to which end of it you are looking at."[8] Yet, with cautions, distinctions can be drawn and are acted upon, although not always wisely. The statesman of 1914 anticipated a quick offensive-dominant war led by industrial mobilization and the railroad. Instead, they got the trenches and stalemate. Nuclear weapons overcome any defense, but stability comes from deterrence that is, ironically, most threatened by attempts at defense.

Jervis wrapped up the rich argument with a powerfully evocative two-by-two table. It contains a happy quadrant in which weapons are distinguishable and the defense is dominant and a "doubly dangerous" quadrant in which the weapons are not distinguishable and the offense predominates. Then there are two more ambiguous quadrants in which the defense predominates but weapons are not distinguishable leading to a security dilemma mitigated by the capacity to defend and incentives for arms control and then a quadrant in which the offense is superior but weapons are distinguishable, allowing for the identification of aggressors by the weapons they choose.

Altogether, the article is one of the stars in the firmament of international relations scholarship. It invented neither the security dilemma nor the offense-defense balance, but it combined them in a thoroughly coherent manner, explored their implications when combined, and demonstrated their powers of insight—and their limitations—across a truly impressive range of international history.

To say that we will miss Robert Jervis's qualities of teaching, citizenship, and scholarship is an understatement.

NOTES

1. One of my Columbia colleagues and a former student of Jervis's, Alexander Cooley, suggested to me that in addition to believing in diversity for its own sake, Jervis may have thought of its beneficial "systems effects."
2. Robert Jervis, "Cooperation Under the Security Dilemma," *World Politics* 30, no. 2 (1978): 167–214.
3. Kenneth N. Waltz, "The Stability of a Bipolar World," *Daedalus* 93, no. 3 (1964): 881–909.
4. Jervis, "Cooperation Under the Security Dilemma," 167.
5. Jervis, "Cooperation Under the Security Dilemma," 170.
6. Jervis, "Cooperation Under the Security Dilemma," 183.
7. Jervis, "Cooperation Under the Security Dilemma," 186.
8. Jervis, "Cooperation Under the Security Dilemma," 201.

12

PERSPECTIVES ON THE SECURITY DILEMMA

JAMES D. FEARON

R obert Jervis pioneered the application of research in cognitive and social psychology to the study of international politics. In the process, he developed a theoretical synthesis that continues to structure and drive a great deal of productive research on international cooperation and conflict. His analysis of the dynamics of the "security dilemma"—in which both rational and irrational factors lead to dangerous military escalation—is foundational and has spread to regular employment in foreign policy debates. In his work on how state leaders signal and fail to signal their intentions in international disputes, Jervis was one of the first to identify cost as a determinant of credibility and also to work out how specific psychological biases generate misperceptions of signals in particular conflict contexts.[1] He developed a theoretical framework in which state leaders' perceptions and misperceptions of other states' military intentions drive much of the high politics of national security decision making.[2] This framework has received considerable empirical support, informs policymaking, and is the basis for continuing empirical and theoretical research by international relations scholars from remarkably diverse research traditions. Finally, Jervis applied his approach to the analysis of nuclear deterrence, nuclear crises, and nuclear weapons policies, creating a body of work that, sad to say, remains highly relevant for the evaluation and critique of US defense policy.[3]

I met Professor Jervis for the first time when I was a graduate student at Berkeley. I think he was on a visiting committee, of a type that I now know tends to be fully booked. He took the time to sit down with me and listen to an incoherent rendition of early or midstream dissertation ideas. I don't remember specifics of the conversation, but I do remember his thoughtfulness, patience, and wry humor, traits to which the other authors in this volume attest.

We had only limited and occasional direct contact over the years, but Jervis's thinking about international politics has been a constant and hugely influential mental companion. *The Logic of Images in International Relations* was tremendously influential when I was writing my dissertation, and I am still puzzling over the idea of the security dilemma as he laid it out.[4]

Over the past two years I have been thinking about Jervis's ideas and arguments even more than usual. To what would have been the great surprise of my 2020 self, I found myself working in 2021 and 2022 as an advisor in the US Department of Defense, on leave from Stanford. I was mainly involved in matters related to the 2022 National Defense Strategy, a principal theme of which is deterrence. I frequently found myself thinking about Jervis's contributions and sometimes attempting to convey them in one way or another in a meeting or memo.[5]

This is not so surprising, given that the US foreign policy machine is making a hard turn back to the problem of deterrence between nuclear-armed, major power competitors. Jervis's *Perception and Misperception in International Politics* and "Cooperation Under the Security Dilemma" theorized about major powers unsure of each other's preferences over expansion, making decisions about how much to arm and whether to attack or expand into buffer territory. Although he drew on all manner of examples, his central motivation and application, particularly in chapter 3 of *Perception and Misperception*, was the US-Soviet competition. Should the United States arm up and posture forces to deter a Soviet Union bent on expansion and looking for any opportunity? Or would arming up coupled with an aggressive forward posture (and nuclear warfighting doctrines) make things worse by convincing Soviet leaders that the United States was itself an aggressive, expansionist type that was out to get them? In the latter case, a "spiral" of hostile beliefs might be especially dangerous between nuclear-armed adversaries worried about the other side's hair trigger and tragically unnecessary.

Although he did not commit to one or the other position for the US-Soviet case in *Perception and Misperception*, Jervis suggested that in general a common psychological bias favors spirals to unnecessary conflict. To use a topical example, the argument would be that US foreign policy makers could not imagine that Russian leaders would actually feel threatened by NATO expansion and alliance-friendly talks with Ukraine. Surely Russian president Vladimir Putin must realize that NATO would never attack Russia. His concerns regarding Ukraine must therefore be expansionist, or "greedy" in Charles Glaser's terminology, rather than defensive and motivated by security concerns. In this kind of account, then, costly conflict is purely a mistake on the supposition that Russian motives *are* purely defensive, as are US and NATO motives.[6]

Of course, I don't know exactly how Jervis would have applied a security dilemma analysis to this case. I doubt that he would go all the way to a "pure security seekers in conflict due to a psychological bias" interpretation. One of the great features of his scholarship was his deep appreciation for the complexity of reasons for state leaders' choices in foreign policy: not either-or but "well, could be some of this, and some of that, or one or the other. And hard to be certain based on the evidence we have."[7]

In an alternative account, Putin *is* "greedy" with respect to Ukraine. And the United States is fundamentally revisionist with respect to both Ukraine and Putin's regime, in the sense that its leaders have preferences over Ukraine's and Russia's regime types that are at odds with Putin's preferences. Each one knows this about the other. Given his own nationalist views and their domestic political utility, Putin would prefer Ukraine under Moscow's thumb and even as part of a greater Russia, wholly independent of external security concerns. Ukrainian leaders knew this full well. Subscribing to a different nationalist vision, they wanted, and want now, arms and alliance support to resist Russian coercion. Simply on grounds of preferences over types of regimes—and independent of national security concerns in a strict sense—the US and NATO powers would prefer to see a solidly democratic Ukraine that is aligned politically and economically with the West.

In turn, a more solidly democratic and Western-leaning Ukraine is intrinsically threatening to Putin's dictatorship, independent of military concerns about invasion. US, Ukrainian, and at least some other NATO state leaderships are clearly revisionists from Putin's perspective. They would ideally like to see Putin's authoritarian regime gone. They cannot commit themselves not to support, at the very least verbally, Russian opposition to Putin in the event of a mass uprising. Mass uprisings are a mortal fear of all modern dictatorships, even those that are relatively secure for the moment. For Putin, a democratic Ukraine is a bad example, even without a formal alliance.

In this account, costly conflict is not driven by misapprehension of essentially defensive intentions. Instead, it is driven by commonly known conflicting preferences that are difficult to accommodate because of commitment problems that are tricky to resolve in an anarchical environment. Maybe there was a hypothetical deal in which the United States would have agreed to try to limit Ukraine's military capability and, in one way or another, reassure Moscow on the alliance question. But Putin expressed justified skepticism about the credibility and feasibility of such deals to deliver, alliance or not. Crushing Ukraine's military before its missile capabilities improved and/or replacing the regime with one more under his control, with a new constitution more to his liking, may have looked to Putin like a surer guarantee, despite the costs and risks (which he clearly underestimated).[8]

I think that this type of account works better than a psychological-bias spiral model interpretation not only in regard to Russia's war against Ukraine but also for dangerous contemporary conflicts between the United States and other authoritarian regimes with whom it has major policy disagreements—China (especially in regard to Taiwan), North Korea, and Iran, in particular.[9]

To degrees that surely differ across cases, a lack of understanding the other side's perspective might exacerbate the (correct) perception of conflicting interests and adversary malevolence, making deals involving commitments harder to reach. It is probably both-and rather than either-or.

Jervis's original treatment in chapter 3 of *Perception and Misperception* suggests this. He notes that there is an underlying structural problem that is made worse by the dynamic implications of a psychological bias that is layered on top of it. I am arguing that the underlying structural problem typically depends on conflicting preferences that are not derivative of security concerns or anarchy.[10] But this does not mean that costly conflict between "greedy" states is not tragic or something that needs no explanation. States have disagreements all the time, with sources that are not fundamentally derivative of security concerns. And most of the time, they implicitly abide by or explicitly cut deals.

Jervis was fond of using Akira Kurosawa's film *Rashomon* as an analogy: different leaders see and interpret the same events in radically different ways, which can make interstate communication prone to error and basic misunderstandings. My impression is that one can go further. Even inside a government, it is all *Rashomon* all the way down. This is not primarily because of psychological biases but rather because different offices are necessarily and appropriately seeing and attending to different streams of information. By efficient organizational design, they have different responsibilities and thus incentives, which can in turn affect (and impair) communication. Both between states and within them, organizing collective action is incredibly difficult.

Jervis made foundational contributions by developing one important class of reasons for why this is so—reasons related to leader psychology. A promising agenda for future inquiry might involve a closer look at how organizational structures and career incentives affect what leaders can and cannot say about the relationship between their own actions and those of other states, as well as the inferences each one draws about the other.

NOTES

1. Robert Jervis, *The Logic of Images in International Relations* (Princeton University Press, 1970).

2. Robert Jervis, *Perception and Misperception in International Politics* (Princeton University Press, 1976); Jervis, "Cooperation Under the Security Dilemma," *World Politics* 30, no. 2 (1978), 167–214.

3. Robert Jervis, *The Illogic of American Nuclear Strategy* (Cornell University Press, 1984); Jervis, *The Meaning of the Nuclear Revolution* (Cornell University Press, 1989).

4. Jervis, *The Logic of Images in International Relations.*

5. An anecdote: As I used the term "security dilemma" in one conversation, my interlocutor (a highly capable and impressive officer) nodded vigorously in recognition and said, "Yes! We need to create security dilemmas for the adversary!" This, to be clear, is not at all what Jervis had in mind by the term. In my limited experience, receptivity to Jervis's concept was patchy, although I think much less for reasons of psychological bias than because of organizational incentives.

6. Charles L. Glaser, *Rational Theory of International Politics* (Princeton University Press, 2010). In Robert Jervis, "Was the Cold War a Security Dilemma?," *Journal of Cold War Studies* 3, no. 1 (2001), 36–60, Jervis ultimately argued that the answer is "no." He says that the Soviets fundamentally wanted to revise the international system. They were "greedy" rather than status quo types, which drove the United States to undertake costly policies of deterrence and also to aim to undermine the Soviet Union to gain peace and breathing room. I see this as consistent with the alternative model sketched next, and I would add that one needs to go further to explain the costly conflict. The existence of conflicting interests is not enough by itself.

7. In a March 2014 comment during Putin's intervention in eastern Ukraine, Jervis recommended negotiating a deal that would attempt to commit the United States and European Union to a "form of flexible neutrality" for Ukraine, "something akin to Austria during the Cold War," so as to take account of Russian interests and greater military power in the locale. He did not specifically mention the psychological bias argument and treated the problem mainly as a matter of negotiating a compromise between parties with conflicting interests. The term "sleepwalkers" may suggest, however, that he at least thought that Western diplomats were being unrealistic. Robert Jervis, "The New Sleepwalkers," *The European: Das Debatten-Magazin*, May 9, 2014. Jervis and Mira Rapp-Hooper, "Perception and Misperception on the Korean Peninsula: How Unwanted Wars Begin," *Foreign Affairs*, May/June 2018; this article puts more stress on the psychological bias that he linked to the security dilemma. See also Kathy Gilsinan, "North Korean Nukes and the Grand International-Relations Experiment in Asia: The Scholar Robert Jervis Discusses His Theory of the Security Dilemma, and How Trump Is Testing It," *The Atlantic*, March 18, 2017, https://www.theatlantic.com/international/archive/2017/03/security -dilemma-north-korea/520023/.

8. With adjustments for tense, this paragraph and the two before it come from the version written in December 2021 for the online ISSF Tribute to Jervis. I would add that the commitment problem in this case was and remains two-sided. How could Ukraine or its supporters trust that Putin would not take advantage of any arms deal ("demilitarization") for political or military coercion and interference?

9. For some elaboration, see James D. Fearon, "Two States, Two Types, Two Actions," *Security Studies* 20, no. 3 (2011): 431–40; Fearon, "The Big Problem with the North Koreans Isn't That We Can't Trust Them. It's That They Can't Trust Us," [not my title] *Washington Post*, August 16, 2017, https://www.washingtonpost.com/news/monkey-cage/wp /2017/08/16/the-big-problem-with-north-korea-isnt-that-we-cant-trust-them-its-that- they-cant-trust-us/; and Fearon, "Cooperation, Conflict, and the Costs of Anarchy," *International Organization* 72, no. 3 (2018): 524–60. For related analyses, see Lindsay Hundley, "Ideology and International Conflict," unpublished manuscript, https://www .lindsayhundley.com/research; Gideon Rachman, "Russia and China's Plans for a New World Order," *Financial Times*, January 23, 2022; Elsa B, Kania, "The Regime Security Dilemma in US-China Relations," *The Strategist*, Australian Strategic Policy Institute, March 21, 2019. For developed versions of this kind of account of war to prevent nuclear acquisition, see Alexandre Debs and Nuno Monteiro, "Known Unknowns: Power Shifts,

Uncertainty, and War," *International Organization* 68, no. 1 (2014): 1–31; Muhammet A. Bas and Andrew J. Coe, "A Dynamic Theory of Nuclear Proliferation and Preventive War," *International Organization* 70, no. 4 (2016): 655–85; and Andrew J. Coe, "Containing Rogues," *Journal of Politics* 80, no. 4 (2018): 1197–210.

10.   Randall L. Schweller, "Neorealism's Status Quo Bias: What Security Dilemma?," *Security Studies* 5, no. 3 (1996): 90–121; Andrew H. Kydd, "Sheep in Sheep's Clothing: Why Security Seekers Do Not Fight Each Other," *Security Studies* 7, no. 1 (1997): 114–54; and Kydd, *Trust and Mistrust in International Relations* (Princeton University Press, 2005) argue similarly.

13

SCHOLARLY SILVERBACK AND FOUNDER OF THE FIELD OF POLITICAL PSYCHOLOGY

ROSE McDERMOTT

This is a tribute that I desperately hoped I would never have to write. I am heartbroken over the loss of my mentor, Robert Jervis. In a world driven by social media, public expressions of grief too often feel performative, displaying a theatricality that is so at odds with the empty feeling of authentic loss. By contrast, the experience of real grief, however painful, constitutes a kind of sacred honor, proof of a relationship of real depth, value, and meaning in a world captivated by trivial shiny things. Robert Jervis forged me; he so deeply formed my intellect, and in many ways my character, that I would have to forget my very self in order to overlook his formative impact on me.

Robert Jervis was the first one to bring me to H-Diplo, as he invited me to so many other things, offering articles in journals that came with stipends when he knew I needed "real money," as well as introductions to other communities such as the STTL list administered by his friend Robert Art. As a published but admittedly armchair anthropologist (albeit of the biological persuasion), I often noticed the interactions on that list to follow a certain pattern: more often than not, Robert Jervis would start a thread, throwing a shot across the bow to see what others thought or how they might react. Frequently, it seemed like the responses were designed as much to get his attention and validation, and thus achieve status within the community, as to actually discuss the substance of the issue.

Among those who study primates, an individual like this in the gorilla community is called a "silverback." This is usually an older gorilla who manages to keep everyone else in line. The silverback organizes a given group; he is the one who protects the group, even if he is killed in the process. The silverback naturally captures everyone's attention, but his role is much larger and wider than being the organizing force of a group. He helps resolve conflicts among members of the troop, directs movement and provides guidance to feeding sites, and is the one designated to ensure the welfare of every member of the group. In the area of international relations and particularly in the subfield of security studies, Jervis was a silverback in all the ways that count: he forged new paths; he directed the field; he protected the vulnerable; and importantly, he swatted back the flies and locusts.

Jervis functioned as a silverback for the wider international relations community in myriad ways. He created community by bringing together people who might not otherwise have found each other or spent time together. In this way, he provided the cement by which everyone remained connected to others through their mutual attachment to him. Over the course of the last fourteen months of his life, he organized weekly Zoom lunches that brought together a disparate group of individuals from different backgrounds to talk about current events. In this, as in so many other ways, he was the glue that held the group together.

Jervis's reach was much broader than his immediate students and colleagues, however; he had widespread connections in the intelligence, government, and military communities. Jervis did not just create community. He established an entire field of study, and the depth and quality of his work in the area of political psychology gave it legitimacy.[1] Before Jervis, there were scholars, most notably V. O. Key[2] (1966) and Campbell et al. (1960), who applied psychology to politics.[3] However, this work focused almost exclusively on the arena of American politics, concentrating on mass political behavior in general and voting behavior in particular. Other influential scholars, such as Harold Lasswell, did examine the role of individuals, exploring the nature of leadership, but their work similarly focused on domestic leaders and less on international relations. Moreover, Lasswell and others, such as Alexander George, concentrated on how dysfunctional aspects of personality might influence outcomes.[4]

Jervis's perspective was quite unique because he leveraged studies in social psychology that examined how most people behave, without pathologizing the various processes under examination. Jervis was, however, cleverly able to trace how particular thought patterns and strategies could nonetheless lead to not only suboptimal but also, importantly, predictable outcomes. Such specificity was not possible using the more idiosyncratic psychoanalytic models favored by Lasswell, George, and others of the previous generation most heavily influenced by Freudian thought. Without question, he shaped the direction of the field in powerful ways, most significantly by giving credibility to the study of the role individuals play in directing large-scale outcomes. He taught and offered advice and guidance, both intellectual and professional, to generations of students, who themselves have gone on to pass his lessons on to their students. In addition, he protected junior scholars, helping them with their work, passing along opportunities for jobs and fellowships, offering advice and guidance, and providing reassurance and encouragement. I admit I feel very sad for the students to come who will only know of Jervis through his written work and videos of his presentations on YouTube. Yet his incredible support was not restricted only to junior scholars.

Rather, his advice and support came with a lifetime guarantee. Long after I finished my degree and even after I got tenure, I relied on Jervis for help and advice. Indeed, although I originally felt a bit embarrassed at doing so, every time I had a problem I couldn't figure out or solve, particularly hard ethical quandaries (and this would happen at least two or three times a year over the past twenty-five years), I would call him and ask for his help. Without fail, Jervis would provide unique insight as well as comfort and help me figure out what to do to or how to begin to address the concern. Inevitably, he never once led me astray. This is not to say that I never disagreed with him; I continue to think there was more motivated bias in the George W. Bush administration's assessment of weapons of mass destruction going into the war in Iraq than Jervis believed.[5] But it is to say that his professional advice never steered me wrong. The one time I went against his advice (and he understood why and accepted it without question or argument) was a disaster, and I never did it again. I admit I now feel like a bit of an orphan, having nowhere to turn when presented with challenges I am not able to resolve on my own.

Above and beyond the call of any reasonable expectation, Jervis remained my dependable lender of last resort until the day he died. I remain bereft.

In all these kinds of ways, Robert Jervis was a true silverback: strong, protective, loyal, dependable, and possessing flawless instincts. In nature, once a silverback dies, the group tends to break up, with individuals going their own way, dissipating into smaller collectives. In some groups, a new silverback may arise, but many perish as the troop dissolves. Significantly, the death of a silverback raises the rate of infanticide as in-group members kill their young. In this way, it is incumbent on all of us, as a community, to make sure that Jervis's legacy includes the kind of decency and kindness to each other and our students that he embodied throughout his long and influential career so that we do not lose more young scholars than we should to discouragement and lack of direction.

One of the first posts to STTL after Jervis died was appropriately titled "WWJD: What Would Jervis Do?" And, indeed, now without him, each of us has to make our own decisions about what to think and how to manage our careers without his sage advice and encouragement, although luckily we can still be inspired by his writings and talks on YouTube. But the question remains and can help guide the ways we seek answers.

Jervis was not one given to sentiment, but my primary, and often overwhelming, feeling since Jervis died is one of profound, even breathtaking, gratitude. There really are no words adequate to describe the depth of my gratitude to him and for him. I am so grateful I knew him, so grateful I was able to study with him and benefit from his wisdom and generosity for so many years. I feel so privileged and so fortunate to have crossed his orbit; the trajectory of my own career in political psychology would simply not have been possible without his pathbreaking work and endless and enduring support.

In short, there is absolutely no way I would be the person I am now without his work, influence, and mentorship. It is not an overstatement to say that he not only pioneered but also legitimated the use of psychology in the study of politics. Although others before him used psychology to understand mass political behavior, Jervis was really the first one to systematically extract theories and ideas from psychology to help illuminate leader behavior, judgment, and decision making in an integrated deductive fashion.[6] Earlier work that relied on psychology to help explain political outcomes tended either to rely on case studies from a psychoanalytic perspective, such as Alexander and Juliette George's magisterial *Woodrow Wilson and Colonel House*,[7] or focus primarily on the study of mass political behavior, such as the work of Paul Lazarsfeld.[8] Jervis was among the first to provide a more systematic deductive application of models of social and cognitive psychology to international politics.

When I started graduate school, every single person I spoke to in the field told me I would be "crazy" to do political psychology; I was repeatedly told that there was absolutely no future in the field. As an aside, those same people would point to Jervis as the exception that proved the rule, but each one made clear that the field only had room for one person doing psychology. Anyone else would be superfluous. What these same individuals failed to realize is that Jervis himself would manage to legitimize the field, paving the road so that others could follow. This was possible for several different reasons, among many other possibilities. One of the most important factors in my mind is that Jervis established and maintained credibility in standard international relations theory in work that had little to do with psychology. Specifically, his early work on the security dilemma (1978)[9] remains a classic in the field but also forced the hardcore security crowd to recognize and take him seriously as a traditional international relations theorist. Importantly, he kept contributing to standard security studies, especially in his pathbreaking work on nuclear weapons, including the book *The Meaning of the Nuclear Revolution*, which won the prestigious Grawemeyer Award in 1990.[10] His contributions to other areas of international relations were so significant that they demanded attention to the novel ways he applied psychology to the study of politics.

Second, Jervis's approach to the integration of psychology into political science in general and international relations in particular did differ in meaningful ways from past explorations. It is not just that he studied individuals rather than mass behavior, such as voting. It was not just that he applied his work in the new domain of international relations and not American politics. It was also that he relied on the kind of systematic studies that had been and were being generated during the heyday of social psychology. Rather than focus on older psychoanalytic models that required deep knowledge of an individual, often focused on motivated biases, Jervis brought to bear the work on unmotivated biases that appeared more universal in their manifestation. This is the work that permeates *Perception and Misperception in International Relations*. Notably, in his revised version many years later, which he undertook after I invited him to give a lecture at Brown, he recognized the fact that the moment in time during which the original work was written privileged these cognitive biases to the neglect of emotional factors. Work on emotion in decision making that came to light after *Perception* was published showed a new way to examine the role of emotion that did not depend on the earlier psychoanalytic theories.[11] In his new preface, Jervis wrestled with whether or not such work might have fundamentally changed his conclusions and decided that, as interesting as it was, it did not undermine his earlier work.

Third, and perhaps most meaningful, Jervis himself was not a restrictive gatekeeper. Rather, he was more inclusive, welcoming, and hopeful about the future of political psychology than many of the detractors, believing that political science in general and political psychology in particular could become a bigger tent, encompassing work on individuals and elites as readily as research on mass public opinion and examining judgment and decision making as well as regime type or other structural factors.

When my other dissertation adviser, Amos Tversky, died in 1996, a number of us asked him before he died, "What will we do without you?" His answer was as simple as it was eloquent and instructive: "Trust your memory of me." And so it is with Robert Jervis; we will have to trust our memory of him, which is decidedly poorer than his actual presence. One of the things that I noticed about this tendency with Amos is how tricky memory can be. It elides and transforms over time, shifting shape as the edges meld with the thoughts and experiences that occur afterward until it is not entirely clear what we actually remember and what thoughts we have infused with the power of reflection and the weight of emotion. But this is also the beauty and genius of Amos's instruction: he knew that. He knew that part of what memory is and part of what it does is to integrate what we know with what we learn and what we want. It is not, indeed, that time heals all wounds, for it most definitely does not always do that. Rather, time softens memory so that the associations between thoughts and feelings and experiences broaden and deepen, and it becomes more difficult to know where the memory ends and where it simply becomes inextricably interwoven into the fabric of our consciousness. The memory of the other becomes less distinct as it becomes incorporated into how we think about and approach the world. In this way, the other simply becomes part of who we are over time.

I am not sure I was ever able to trust my memory of Amos, but what I have been able to do and still often do is ask myself how Amos would have approached a particular question or problem. Just shifting that perspective often opens new ideas and avenues of inquiry for me. Similarly, I am sure I will not be able to trust my memory of Jervis because he was so much more than my experience of him. I always felt like I was trying to understand the next version of the software but I hadn't quite gotten the necessary upgrade yet. So at Windows X, I was not fully capable of understanding Windows X + 1. Indeed, part of what is so ineffably sad about Jervis's loss is how much knowledge went with him.

Ironically, what I do feel I can trust is not so much the thoughts and ideas that Jervis so continually and seemingly effortlessly generated but the feeling his work has always given me. For someone whose early work almost completely eschewed emotion, I nonetheless always found his work exciting, inspiring, and motivating. Jervis always provided a unique and interesting take on whatever he was working on, even if it appeared to be well-trodden ground. Without ego, he remained well aware of his status and the power and influence that granted him, and he never took that strength for granted or abused or took advantage of it. In addition, he also recognized the importance his work might have in the wider world, whether though policy circles directly, through his students, or as a result of his critical work with the Historical Review Committee for the CIA.[12] The sense of passion, devotion, and commitment to issues that matter and the work itself remain central to my sense of Jervis's character.

Robert Jervis is the last person who would have wanted a hagiographic remembrance. Like any other human, he was not perfect. He could be socially awkward, and he did not suffer fools lightly, if at all. He applied his high standards to others as well as himself, and it remains an impossible task to strive to achieve such heights of productivity, much less quality. But he provided an exemplary model of how to live a life of authenticity, serving others while following his own interests. At the end of his life, he also provided stunning lessons in how to die with open-eyed dignity, generosity, and grace, continuing to engage regularly and substantively, without any evident self-pity, with his community, and offering help and support to those he cared about. He taught me a great deal about how to think, how to work, and how to treat others. One of the things he modeled most eloquently was the importance of honesty, even when the information may not be positive or pleasant. In that regard, I feel very fortunate that I was not left with important things unsaid; he knew how grateful I was to him for all he did for me. What I did not tell him but what I suspect he knew is how much I will miss him for the rest of my life.

NOTES

1. There are many examples of this, but perhaps the most influential was Robert Jervis, *Perception and Misperception in International Politics* (Princeton University Press, 2017).

2. V. O. Key, *The Responsible Electorate: Rationality in Presidential Voting 1936–1960.* (Harvard University Press, 1966).

3. Harold Lasswell, *Power and Personality* (Transaction, originally 1948); Angus Campbell et al., *The American Voter* (University of Chicago Press, 1960).

4. Harold Lasswell, "Psychopathology and Politics," *Journal of Nervous and Mental Disease* 74, no. 5 (1931): 676; Alexander L. George and Juliette L. George, *Woodrow Wilson and Colonel House: A Personality Study* (Plunkett Lake, 2019).

5. Robert Jervis, *Why Intelligence Fails: Lessons from the Iranian Revolution and the Iraq War* (Cornell University Press, 2019).

6. Robert Jervis, "Hypotheses on Misperception," *World Politics* 20, no. 3 (1968): 454–79.

7. George and George, *Woodrow Wilson and Colonel House.*

8. Paul F. Lazarsfeld and Robert King Merton, *Mass Communication, Popular Taste and Organized Social Action* (Bobbs-Merrill, College Division, 1948).

9. Robert Jervis, "Cooperation Under the Security Dilemma," *World Politics* 30, no. 2 (1978): 167–214.

10. Robert Jervis, *The Illogic of American Nuclear Strategy* (Cornell University Press, 1984); Jervis, *The Meaning of the Nuclear Revolution: Statecraft and the Prospect of Armageddon* (Cornell University Press, 1989).

11. Jennifer Lerner et al., "Emotion and Decision Making," *Annual Review of Psychology* 66 (2015): 799–823; Elizabeth A. Phelps, Karolina M. Lempert, and Peter Sokol-Hessner, "Emotion and Decision Making: Multiple Modulatory Neural Circuits," *Annual Review of Neuroscience* 37 (2014): 263–87.

12. See the essays in this volume by Richard H. Immerman, Melvyn P. Leffler, and Janice Gross Stein.

14

A PSYCHOLOGY OF RATIONAL SIGNALING

JONATHAN MERCER

Robert Jervis's approach to international relations was social, psychological, and rational.[1] Not rational the way economists usually think about it or rational the way psychologists used to think about it. For Jervis, as for Daniel Kahneman, proving that policymakers were not rational (as commonly defined) was somewhat akin to proving that people did not have fur.[2] The challenge was to understand how people think and behave and then to use that understanding to provide insight into how people should think and behave, especially in strategic settings. In a passage that Jervis highlighted, Thomas Schelling wrote that "the principles relevant to *successful* play, the *strategic* principles, the propositions of a *normative* theory, cannot be derived by purely analytical means from a priori considerations."[3] Any theory that is useful in strategic settings must be based on how people reason.

Much of Jervis's research stems from this simple and radical insight, which he first developed in *The Logic of Images in International Relations*: because effective signaling depends on beliefs and theories, a rational approach to signaling cannot exclude beliefs and theories. Jervis identified two principles. First, analysts must distinguish between behavior that is known to be an attempt at persuasion (that is, a signal) and behavior that is telling because it is not an attempt at persuasion (that is, an index). Second, a rational approach to signaling depends on understanding the logic of inference.[4]

SIGNALS AND INDICES

The Nobel laureate Michael Spence hailed Jervis's introduction of the distinction between "indices" and "signals."[5] My first meeting with Jervis demonstrated the utility of this distinction beyond economics and international politics. Hoping for a letter of recommendation, I expressed how pleased I was that I received an A– in his course. Jervis responded that it was indeed an A– but barely. That was a signal: an intersubjectively understood shot across the bow. It was also textbook: clear, unambiguous, and credible. Several years later, Elizabeth Kier and I were writing an article on precedents and Jervis FedExed a large package stuffed with xeroxed newspaper articles that were in some way connected to precedents. I was not surprised that he had a file of newspaper clippings on precedents, but his generosity in sending them was revealing. That was an index.

SIGNALS DEPEND ON INTERSUBJECTIVE BELIEFS

A signal is a known attempt at persuasion. Diplomats agree that certain words or actions carry certain meanings, as Jervis argues: "Signals are not natural; they are conventional. That is, they consist of statements and actions that the sender and receiver have endowed with meaning in order to accomplish certain goals." When confronting the prospect of a nuclear war, the dispersal of one's long-range bombers has no military significance; that is why the United States has intercontinental ballistic missiles and submarines. Yet the dispersal of aircraft is accepted as a signal that the United States is preparing for nuclear war. Jervis suggested that in principle one could simply raise a flag with an image of a mushroom cloud on it to convey the same meaning.[6] But conventions change slowly. One could announce that raising a flag carries the meaning of a dispersal of bombers, but the success of the signal depends on others accepting that meaning.

Signals that depend on common historical interpretations—no matter how obvious they seem to the sender—provide more room for error than diplomatic code. What is obvious to the sender of a signal may not be obvious to its recipient, "especially when he does not share your history, values, norms, and theories."[7] The belief that obviousness is natural and that one's signal must be clear to the other can be attributed, in part, to our difficulty in not seeing something we have already seen. The more time one devotes to one's own plans or the more one has thought about how to signal a message, the more likely one will think the pattern is obvious to others.[8] People overestimate the ease with which a tune they tap with their fingers will be understood by others; once the song is in your head, it's hard to imagine not hearing it.[9] The clues predicting a crime become obvious once one knows who committed it.[10] Diplomats employ archaic, formal expressions because they are archaic, formal, and therefore come with precise meanings.

INDICES DEPEND ON SUBJECTIVE BELIEFS

An index is behavior that one believes either cannot be manipulated to project an image or is not being manipulated. As Jervis writes, "Indices are statements or actions that carry some inherent evidence that the image projected is correct because they are believed to be inextricably linked to the actor's capabilities or intentions."[11] Spence captures Jervis's distinction between signals and indices as having two parts: "The primary distinction is between manipulable and nonmanipulable characteristics or attributes or activities. A second is between activities of which the sender is aware and those of which he is not."[12] One can be aware of an activity that others recognize as an index but be unable to influence it. Spence notes that "unalterable attributes are called indices. The perspiration on the forehead of the nervous job applicant is an index."[13] The distinction is not rooted in "words" versus "deeds," and it stands independent of cost. Instead, indices capture a type of behavior that observers believe reliably distinguishes the characteristics of actors.

Whereas signals depend on intersubjective beliefs, indices depend on subjective beliefs. One might use domestic political systems as indices. If one believes that dictatorships link to peace or that democracies link to war, then these political systems provide an index of one's likely foreign policy. If one believes that an actor's past behavior reveals its future behavior, so that past retreats anticipate future retreats or conversely, and that past retreats anticipate future resolution, then past behavior is an index. In each case, an observer's beliefs and theories mediate between behavior and interpretation. Observers might also use a diplomat's alcohol-induced behavior as an index.[14] Statements that one assumes are not calculated to influence or are intended to influence one audience but not another might be seen as especially revealing. Eavesdropping on private communications or secretly watching another's behavior might be interpreted as revealing the true beliefs, preferences, or characteristics of that actor.

Actors know that they can probably project the image they desire by becoming that image. A state wishing to project an image of a peaceful state can abolish its military, or a state wishing to project an image of resolve can start a major war. Behavior that is too costly or too important to be a signal is an index. Jervis assumed that rational actors attend to the costs and benefits of projecting images: "To engage in a major war merely to show that one has a great deal of resolve is unusual because the costs are apt to outweigh the gains." If one begins a major war to project the false image of resolution, then the image is no longer false. Jervis captured this idea when he notes that cost does not merely reflect characteristics of an actor; it can change that actor. The growth of neo-isolationism in response to the Vietnam War suggested to Jervis that even victory there would be Pyrrhic if other states concluded that the US public would not again accept fighting such a war.[15]

Indices are influential because they are thought to be beyond manipulation, not because they are beyond manipulation. If an actor knows what the other side is using or is likely to use as an index—and this might be the uncontrollable temper of a decision maker, information based on secret wiretaps, or information obtained by torturing prisoners—then one can deceive an enemy. Tempers can be faked, wiretaps can be discovered, and operatives who will be captured and tortured can be given false information.[16] Rational actors fool other rational actors by knowing what they believe, not by knowing what they ought to believe. Indices depend on subjective understanding of how behavior and beliefs link to policies.

Cost does not distinguish an index from a signal. Indices can be costly (starting a war reveals one's resolve) or cheap (personality or regime type reveals preferences). What is intended as a signal may be read as an index. The late 2008 public absence of North Korean dictator Kim Jong Il prompted speculation that he was dead or sick, which led the North Koreans to release several photographs of the leader that were meant to show that he was still in control. It was a signal, but analysts also used the information to draw conclusions at odds with what the North Koreans intended. One analyst remarked, "The fact that the North is going to such lengths to demonstrate that Kim Jong-il is O.K. is, ironically, a sign that his health is not normal."[17] Other analysts interpreted the photographs to suggest that Kim had suffered a stroke: his left hand appeared immobile, and he was not wearing his shoes that made him taller.[18] Jervis's distinction depends on the intentions of the sender as well as the beliefs and theories of the audience. The sender and the receiver are two sides of the same coin, and a rational approach to signaling must address both the logic of signaling and the logic of inference.

LOGIC OF INFERENCE

Assuming that another person thinks what you think or shares the same theories is not sensible. According to Jervis, "Perception is laden with interpretation and theory. Almost no inferences—perhaps none at all—are self-evident in the sense that all people under all circumstances looking at the information would draw the same conclusion. Thus, knowing how theorists read a signal does not tell us how the perceiver does."[19] Naïve actors assume that everyone thinks the same way and holds the same beliefs; rational actors know that beliefs and theories necessarily influence interpretations of evidence. Because my best move depends on your move and your move depends on your beliefs about me, a rational approach to signaling must address how actors make inferences.

BELIEFS AND INTERPRETATIONS

People necessarily use beliefs, theories, and expectations to determine what counts as evidence and how to interpret that evidence. For example, Jervis's assessment of the CIA's failure to predict the 1979 Iranian Revolution focused on the US view that a fundamentalist religion could not be a serious political force. CIA analysts and academics understood opposition to the Shah "in terms of a liberal, modernizing, middle class" that was consistent with "prevailing social science theories."[20] The influence that beliefs and theories have on the interpretation of evidence is also evident in the CIA's failure to recognize that in 2003 Iraq had no weapons of mass destruction.[21] These were failures, but one can pick any success and show how beliefs and theories made possible the correct interpretations.

BELIEFS CAN CREATE REALITY

Schelling's discussion of coordination games and various bargaining strategies captures the central role beliefs and manipulation of beliefs play in signaling.[22] Schelling imagined the brink of war as a curved slope, where the further down the slope one goes, the steeper it becomes and the greater the risk of a mutually undesirable outcome so that diplomacy becomes a competition in risk taking. Whereas Schelling implied that the environment is natural and thus actors are able to manipulate the level of acceptable risk, Jervis emphasized that actors' beliefs construct their environment. Beliefs matter not simply in the sense that actors must know that they are bargaining over a specific issue or that they risk a mutually undesirable outcome. Beliefs determine the slope of the curve. Do they think it is relatively flat or very steep? Do they think conditions are stable or do they expect an ice storm? And what do they think the other thinks? Jervis observes, "If each stares at the slope for a long time, and knows that others are also staring at it, its shape will change."[23] Beliefs can create reality.

The influence of beliefs on reality varies. If two states believe that a limited nuclear war is impossible, then it probably is.[24] A belief that nuclear war can be kept limited is a necessary (though not sufficient) condition for doing so. Because beliefs can shape reality, actors have incentives to influence the beliefs of others. If I have premised my force posture on the ability to fight (and win) a limited nuclear war, then I need to persuade you that such a war is possible. If I believe that you believe that nuclear war cannot be limited, then your belief governs.

Disbelieving another's belief is always possible but not always practical. Jervis found the arguments for nuclear superiority to be illogical: what matters is the number of cities one can annihilate, not the number of times the same city can be struck. Because nuclear weapons are absolute, it makes no difference whether one has one thousand or ten thousand. The difficulty with this argument, as Jervis acknowledged, is that if people believe that nuclear weapons give one a bargaining advantage, then they do. Conversely, if I believe that nuclear weapons convey no bargaining leverage, and you believe that I believe this, then you gain no advantage from having more weapons. Just as one can change the slope of a curve by staring at it, Jervis noted that one's beliefs change the value of nuclear weapons: "By changing actors' beliefs about the utility of 'superiority,' strategic analysis can actually change this utility."[25] Utility is not deduced from objective properties. A rational approach to signaling depends on calculations about costs and benefits, but one cannot assess the benefits of nuclear superiority, the value of a reputation, the importance of a precedent, or the cost of violating international law without considering actors' beliefs. Beliefs create utility.

RETURNING TO COST

Since cost is one way that actors assess a signal's credibility, the emphasis that rationalists place on cost is appropriate. But assessments of cost are not objective; they typically depend on beliefs. What one analyst views as a cost, another analyst might view as a benefit. If an actor believes, as did Soviet leader Joseph Stalin, that spending vast amounts on defense is good for business, then massive defense spending is an index of capitalist greed and not of resolve.[26] During the Vietnam War, Assistant Secretary of Defense John McNaughton advanced the "good doctor" theory: as long as US leaders made a good faith effort to defend South Vietnam and accepted many casualties, then defeat would not harm the reputation of the United States.[27] Although the Soviets were impressed that Americans would sacrifice so much for something the Soviets viewed as tangential to US interests, Iraq's president Saddam Hussein apparently drew the opposite conclusion.[28]

Accurately assessing cost independent of beliefs is impossible. Different assessments of cost mean different assessments of credibility. If I think that dictatorships can bluff without suffering any domestic political consequences and you think that they risk political consequences if they bluff, then our assessments of cost and of credibility will differ.

Even when observers agree that a signal is costly, they can still disagree over the signal's meaning. Roberta Wohlstetter noted that even the clearest signal, such as the attack on Pearl Harbor, led to different interpretations among General Douglas MacArthur's officers over what it meant for the US position in the Philippines: they all read the Pearl Harbor signal, they debated with each other, they had time to prepare, and yet the Japanese attack on MacArthur's forces still surprised them.[29] Costly behavior might reveal *something* about an actor, but Jervis notes that "often it is not clear exactly what is being revealed, what is intended to be revealed, and what others will think is being revealed."[30] And of course, the possibility of deception is ever present. Actors know that cost can impart credibility, which is why one actor will attempt to persuade others that it views its behavior as costly.[31]

RATIONALITY AND SIGNALING

Jervis understood that one cannot develop a theory of rational signaling— if by rational signaling one means a way in which one should always send or read a signal—for the same reason that one cannot develop a rational theory of chess. Unless one assumes the conditions that allow that theory to work, i.e., that I know what my chess opponent thinks and I know what inference they will draw from my moves, the best one can do is to understand the game's principles. This insight seems so obvious now that many of us take it for granted. Although it represents only part of Jervis's scholarship, it also captures part of his brilliance.

NOTES

1. I thank Elizabeth Kier for her comments and James Davis for organizing a Festschrift for Jervis, from which this essay is based. See James W. Davis, ed., *Psychology, Strategy and Conflict: Perceptions of Insecurity in International Relations* (Routledge, 2012).

2. Michael Lewis, *The Undoing Project* (Norton, 2017), 286.

3. Thomas C. Schelling, *The Strategy of Conflict* (Harvard University Press, 1960), 162–63. Also see Robert Jervis, "Signaling and Perception," in *Political Psychology*, ed. K. R. Monroe (Lawrence Erlbaum, 2002), 293–314, quote on 293.

4. Robert Jervis, *The Logic of Images in International Relations* (Princeton University Press, 1970). Reprinted with a new preface, Columbia University Press, 1989.

5. A. Michael Spence, "Signaling in Retrospect and the Informational Structure of Markets," *American Economic Review* 92, no. 3 (2002): 434–59, see 434.

6. Jervis, *The Logic of Images*, 139, 229.
7. Jervis, *The Logic of Images*, 141.
8. Robert Jervis, "Hypotheses on Misperception," *World Politics* 20, no. 3 (1968): 454–79.
9. Elizabeth Newton, "Overconfidence in the Communication of Intent: Heard and Unheard Melodies" (PhD diss., Stanford University, 1990).
10. Robert Jervis, "Reports, Politics, and Intelligence Failures: The Case of Iraq," *Journal of Strategic Studies* 29, no. 1 (2006): 3–52.
11. Jervis, *The Logic of Images*, 18.
12. A. Michael Spence, *Market Signaling: Informational Transfer in Hiring and Related Screening Processes* (Harvard University Press, 1974), 10.
13. Spence, *Market Signaling*, 11.
14. Jervis, *The Logic of Images*, 32–36.
15. Jervis, *The Logic of Images*, 28–29, 271.
16. Jervis, *The Logic of Images*, 43–49.
17. Ryoo Kihl-jae quoted in Choe Sang-Hun, "North Korea Tries to Show Its Leader Is Healthy and in Control," *New York Times*, November 7, 2008, A6.
18. Choe, "North Korea Tries to Show Its Leader Is Healthy and in Control."
19. Jervis, "Signaling and Perception," 297–98.
20. Robert Jervis, *Why Intelligence Fails: Lessons from the Iranian Revolution and the Iraq War* (Cornell University Press, 2010), 23.
21. See the essays by Richard H. Immerman, Michael Warner, Melvyn P. Leffler, and Dipali Mukhopadhyay in the section "Robert Jervis as Public Intellectual," as well as that of Janice Gross Stein, in this volume.
22. Schelling, *Strategy of Conflict*.
23. Jervis, *The Logic of Images*, 242.
24. Robert Jervis, *The Illogic of American Nuclear Strategy* (Cornell University Press, 1984).
25. Jervis, *Illogic of American Nuclear Strategy*, 231–32.
26. Jervis, "Signaling and Perception," 301.
27. Quoted in Benjamin T. Harrison and Christopher L. Mosher, "John T. McNaughton and Vietnam: The Early Years as Assistant Secretary of Defense, 1964–1965," *History* 92, no. 38 (2007): 496–514, 503.
28. Ted Hopf, *Peripheral Visions: Deterrence Theory and American Foreign Policy in the Third World, 1965–1990* (University of Michigan Press, 1994); Kevin M. Woods, *Iraqi Perspectives Project: A View of Operation Iraqi Freedom from Saddam's Senior Leadership* (US Joint Forces Command, Joint Center for Operational Analysis, 2006), viii.
29. Roberta Wohlstetter, *Pearl Harbor: Warning and Decision* (Stanford University Press, 1962).
30. Jervis, "Signaling and Perception," 298.
31. Jervis, *The Logic of Images*, 47.

15

THE CONSUMMATE FOX

PHILIP E. TETLOCK

I first met Robert Jervis in 1984.[1] It was a formal setting. Jervis introduced himself as a scholar who had emerged from the neorealist theoretical tradition of Kenneth Waltz but who was also curious about how foibles of human psychology could exacerbate security dilemmas. Our relationship was initially asymmetric. I knew who Jervis was, having eagerly devoured his already-classic 1976 book, *Perception and Misperception in International Politics*, in graduate school.[2] But Jervis had no idea who I was. Nor should he have. I was twelve years younger, just getting tenure in a different field, and Jervis was moving into the midcareer phase of his rapidly rising academic trajectory.

The occasion was the first meeting of a pretentiously named committee, the Committee for the Prevention of Nuclear War, sponsored by the National Academy of Sciences and generously funded by two large foundations. The committee had been formed because of widespread worry among many in academia and the policy world that the first-term Reagan administration was recklessly raising the risks of nuclear war through its policy mix of massive defense buildup and moralistic rhetoric.

Jervis was no defender of the Reagan administration (indeed, I recall that there were no defenders on the committee—a point that Jervis pointedly made to zero effect). He thought the hard-line deterrence and even compellence theorists were wrong and that the risks of a misperception-driven, conflict-spiral escalation into war were greater than the risks of

Soviet leaders detecting US weakness and pushing too far. But he was skeptical of confident claims about what the future holds. And so was I. Indeed, I was already in the early stages of launching the first of a series of forecasting tournaments that elicited 20,000-plus expert judgments on a wide array of political, military, and economic trends and would be summarized in a book published in 2005.[3] Of course, I also tried to get numbers out of Jervis, but he balked at the questions in the first-round tournament—questions about the ideological leanings of the general party secretary who was likely to succeed Konstantin Chernenko's successor (perhaps Mikhail Gorbachev) or on the consequences of that leadership transition for US-Soviet relations.

I suspect Jervis initially found me annoying: a pushy young research psychologist from Berkeley who was trying to reduce the complexities of his assessment of a rapidly evolving situation to betting odds. But Jervis was a forgiving and generous soul—and he tolerated many annoying intrusions over the next thirty-five years.

I relied on the second chapter of *Perception and Misperception* as a framework for my first crude pilot tournament, which asked mostly Sovietologists about likely policy directions of the post-Chernenko politburo.[4] The conflict-spiral theorists among them expected an exacerbation of tit-for-tat hostilities. Reagan was making things worse. By contrast, the deterrence theorists expected continued deadlock. Neither side expected the scope of Gorbachev's glasnost and perestroika initiatives: dramatic domestic liberalization accompanied by an end to the Cold War. Curiously though, neither side saw much reason to change their minds after the fact. Spiral theorists pointed to the crumbling Soviet economy as the driver of Gorbachev's moves. If anything, the Reagan administration was either irrelevant or an impediment to better relations. And deterrence theorists suspected that the Soviet leaders had blinked: they saw that they could not match the Reagan defense buildup. In short, no one got it right, but everyone in retrospect claimed vindication. Here was a pattern of data that was strikingly consistent with the psychological arguments that Jervis developed in *Perception and Misperception*: biased assimilation of evidence in the service of one's pet theory of politics.

There was nothing dissonant, in Jervis's capacious mind, about admiring the elegance of both Waltzian system-level arguments and the research of Daniel Kahneman and Amos Tversky. In multiple publications, these researchers were busily demonstrating an array of systematic deviations from rationality that were rooted in the workings of the human mind and that Jervis used to help make sense of world politics.[5] Policymakers were often too quick to make up their minds and too slow to change them. Jervis was an epistemic pragmatist whose worldview had room for both Waltz and Kahneman. Jervis felt that if the goal is to understand messy real-world phenomena—like major intelligence successes and failures—one cannot afford to be picky about the provenance of good ideas.

This is another way of saying that Robert Jervis was more fox than hedgehog—to invoke Isaiah Berlin's stylized classification of intellectuals: "the fox knows many things but the hedgehog knows one big thing."[6] Even so, Jervis was always alert to false dichotomies. He saw the distinction more as a matter of degree, not of kind. And he was right. Twenty-one years later, in 2005, when I published the first-generation, geopolitical forecasting tournaments in *Expert Political Judgment: How Good Is It? How Can We Know?*, I found that the best indicator of accuracy among experts was their location along a hedgehog-fox gauge of thinking style.[7]

Jervis's foxiness manifested itself in many ways but nowhere more clearly than in his work on system effects[8] and intelligence failures.[9] Well-intentioned policies often have perverse consequences because policymakers default into simplistic linear modes of thinking; they fail to think about interaction effects in which the effects of A on B depend on a host of moderator variables. Even the interaction effects are unstable because parties adapt to each other, creating positive or negative feedback loop forms of causation.

Jervis had a remarkable capacity for what Albert Hirschman once called self-subversive thinking.[10] And this all too rare trait was operating at full throttle in one of his final essays, published in the *Proceedings of the National Academy of Science* in 2022.[11] Jervis devoted decades of labor to helping the US intelligence community conduct postmortems of intelligence failures. But he was deeply skeptical of how much was being learned—or even of how much could be learned—from these efforts.[12] And here his thinking was deeply psychological. People judge analysis and decisions by the outcomes that follow in their wake, not by the appropriateness of the cognitive processes behind them. If everything works out well, we applaud the analysts and decision makers and see no need for a postmortem; if not, there will be a strong presumption that faulty thinking lay behind the mess and that it had better be ferreted out and corrected. All of this makes sense until one stops and wonders how likely is it that the correlation between process and outcome is a perfect one.

It is extremely unlikely. And the implication is that postmortem analysts should expect to find many cases in which decision makers were doing a fine job—processing the available data in normatively defensible ways—but picking options that in retrospect look bad, even disastrous. Sometimes the best that the best forecasters can achieve is to be only slightly less wrong than consensus opinion. Let's call this Jervis's First Postmortem Principle: the world that analysts are struggling to make sense of is simply not very predictable. Hindsight bias makes it hard to appreciate how clueless even the smartest observers appear to be before we all know the outcomes that follow from pursuing the chosen policy option. This principle implies that we will often judge intelligence failures too harshly, working from the tacit, usually false, premise that we somehow would have seen the future much more clearly.

To this we should add Jervis's Second Postmortem Principle: policymakers are wary of analysts (or anyone else) trying to usurp their policy prerogatives. With notable exceptions, policymakers behave exactly as cognitive dissonance theory predicts. Jervis saw that theory as a good first-order approximation of how people wrestle with conflicting evidence and discordant values. Like their fellow human beings, policymakers do not like to make trade-offs and prefer intelligence analysts who provide convenient justifications for current policies—or at least do not undermine those policies. The stage has now been set for a kabuki dance. On one side, analysts pretend to forecast by offering statements that sound as though they shed light on the consequences of pursuing various policy options but that are too vague ever to be falsified by hindsight-tainted postmortem committees. On the other side, policymakers pretend to listen, which is a necessary part of their due-diligence ritual that often helps to persuade postmortem committees to judge their mistakes less harshly.

Because Jervis was a more nuanced and less cynical soul than I, I am 85 percent sure that he would cringe at certain phrases in the previous paragraph. So I hasten to add that there are, of course, many courageous, insightful intelligence analysts and thoughtful policymakers. But an interlocking system of political-psychological forces makes it hard for virtue to prevail. Hindsight and confirmation biases are both psychologically pervasive and potent, which means they will pop up at each point in the process: analyst, policymaker, and postmortem panel. And politically, even in less bitterly partisan times, all the players can anticipate the blame-game dynamics before they arise, and they position themselves accordingly in either a defensive or offensive crouch.

It is testimony to Jervis's tenacity that he devoted so much professional effort to clearing out these Augean stables, knowing full well that the likelihood of lasting implementation of his demanding intellectual prescriptions was close to zero. Implementation would require depoliticizing an inherently political process. And that is a task that feels almost as quixotic as the forecasting tournaments that I launched to pin down pundits' predictions.[13] Jervis would have appreciated the irony. In our very different ways, we were both rubbing against the grain of human nature.

NOTES

1.   I appreciate the helpful comments of Richard Immerman on an earlier draft of this essay.

2.   Robert Jervis, *Perception and Misperception in International Politics* (Princeton University Press, 1976).

3.   Philip E. Tetlock, *Expert Political Judgment: How Good Is It? How Can We Know?* (Princeton University Press, 2005).

4.   Jervis, *Perception and Misperception in International Politics.*

5.   Daniel Kahneman, *Thinking Fast and Slow* (MacMillan, 2011); Amos Tversky and Derek J. Koehler, "Support Theory: A Nonextensional Representation of Subjective Probability," *Psychological Review* 101, no. 4 (1994): 547–67.

6.   Isaiah Berlin, *The Hedgehog and the Fox: An Essay on Tolstoy's View of History* (Princeton University Press, 1950).

7.   Tetlock, *Expert Political Judgment.*

8.   Robert Jervis, *System Effects: Complexity in Political and Social Life* (Princeton University Press, 1998).

9.   Robert Jervis, *Why Intelligence Fails: Lessons from the Iranian Revolution and the Iraq War* (Cornell University Press, 2010).

10.   Albert O. Hirschman, *A Propensity to Self-Subversion* (Harvard University Press, 1995).

11.   Robert Jervis, "Why Postmortems Fail," *Proceedings of the National Academy of Sciences* 119, no. 3 (2022): e2116638118.

12.   See the chapter on Jervis's postmortems by Richard H. Immerman in this volume.

13.   Philip E. Tetlock, *Superforecasting: The Art and Science of Prediction* (Crown, 2015).

16

JACK OF ALL TRADES, MASTER OF ALL

JAMES GOLDGEIER AND ELIZABETH N. SAUNDERS

We're from different generations, and we were never formally his students, but we both found ourselves drawn to Robert Jervis and his work. Other colleagues and students have written eloquently about his wide-ranging intellectual curiosity, his mentorship, and his many, many contributions to our field. But perhaps one more tribute can help tally the debt we owe Jervis in international relations because our work would not have been the same without his pathbreaking efforts. Jervis not only shaped us as individual scholars but also had profound effects on our work together. When writing jointly, we have often had conversations with each other that begin with some version of "What would Jervis say about this?"

Jim's dissertation work and first book focused on Soviet leaders; Elizabeth's dissertation and first book addressed US presidents and the use of force. Each project was heavily dependent on Jervis's classic *Perception and Misperception in International Politics*.[1]

In the late 1980s, Jim was trying to assess the approach Soviet leaders took to international bargaining. The literature at the time was oriented toward understanding Soviet foreign policy largely as a constant, informed by history, culture, and ideology. Jim was trying to come up with an explanation for why, in his view, Soviet leaders differed in important ways in their foreign policy behavior, so naturally, he turned to Jervis. Reading back through *Perception and Misperception*, he became completely absorbed in the short five-page appendix to chapter 6. "Especially for a statesman who rises to power through the political processes (as opposed to a career diplomat)," wrote Jervis, "domestic politics has supplied both his basic political concepts and the more detailed lessons about what strategies and tactics are appropriate to reach desired goals."[2] There it was. At that moment, Jim knew exactly how to make sense of what he was finding in studying Soviet leaders from Stalin to Gorbachev.

Elizabeth still returns regularly to her well-loved, dog-eared copy of that book, particularly chapter 4, which outlines what makes foreign policy decision makers different. It helps put in perspective charges that decision makers are "biased" or "out of touch." Jervis argued that consistency "can largely be understood in terms of the strong tendency for people to see what they expect to see and to assimilate incoming information to pre-existing images." But this was not an automatic strike against the quality of their decision making, any more than it was a guarantee of success. Jervis warned that "scholars too often apply the labels of close-mindedness and cognitive distortion without understanding the necessary role of pre-existing beliefs in the perception and interpretation of new information."[3]

Jervis argued that biases are what make decision makers who they are—as citizens, we want them to have shortcuts and prior experience they can draw on in crises, lenses through which to quickly sort the vast incoming array of information so they can make decisions under pressure. These biases can be pernicious and do not necessarily lead to good decisions, and indeed, they can lead to pathologies in decision making.[4] But they also play a vital role in efficient decision making. The recent revival of interest in elite decision making confirms and extends Jervis's influence in this area of research.[5]

Jervis also showed how the study of individuals can be systematic. His discussion of the deterrence and spiral models in chapter 3 of *Perception and Misperception in International Politics* is influential for more reasons than there are words in the English language. One reason is that we can explain how mental models affect decision making with a parsimonious theory of two such models. One can argue about the details, but it is hard not to admire the theoretical simplicity of his argument about how different leaders think in crises.

Jervis did not shy away from questioning his own biases or asking hard questions about what might blind him to evidence that did not support his line of thinking. He was relentless in asking questions like "How would we know?" In fact, he wrote an article about whether leaders matter with that very question in its title.[6] All educators try to teach students to address the issue of how they would know if they were wrong, but Jervis practiced what he preached, even in the (many, many) areas in which he had well-known arguments. He thought hard about how to think about historical evidence and what it could and could not tell us about different models of the world.

Jervis's influential work on so many major areas of international relations—the nuclear revolution, deterrence theory, the role of individuals and political psychology—is an enormous contribution to the field.[7] But Jervis also played many other roles—editor of the Cornell Studies in Security Affairs series, founder of H-Diplo/ISSF, chair of the CIA's Historical Review Panel—that influenced, directly or indirectly, so many scholars, including a huge number of PhD students and junior faculty who were not officially under his tutelage at Columbia. He was generous with his encyclopedic knowledge of multiple disciplines, dropping highly specific references or pointers to historical evidence into reviews. An irony is that his work on individuals stressed the role of specific knowledge, but he had so much of it that he qualified as a jack of all trades, master of all.

Echoing so many other tributes, we also fell under the spell of Jervis's intellectual energy and curiosity. It was, of course, impossible to say no to Jervis. When he reached out to us to write for an H-Diplo roundtable on presidential tapes, we immediately (well almost immediately) said yes.[8] What's fascinating about the tapes is the fact that although they seem straightforward—the scholar as fly on the wall listening in to government conversations—what makes them most interesting is what is not straightforward at all about them. Which conversations were taped, and which were not? Perhaps most importantly, what did participants take away from the conversations that we as scholars are listening to?

One of our favorite articles is Fred I. Greenstein and Richard H. Immerman's article on the meeting to discuss Laos between President Dwight Eisenhower and President-Elect John F. Kennedy the day before the latter was inaugurated.[9] Four individuals wrote up their notes from the meeting, and each of them came away from the conversation with different beliefs about what was said. A tape of that meeting would tell us what we think was said, but that is not as relevant as what the participants thought was said—their perceptions and misperceptions. The disparate notes from that meeting offer a cautionary tale for scholars and one that we understand better thanks to the insights of Robert Jervis.

To say that Robert Jervis will be missed in the field of international relations is to say the sky is blue. But there can be no doubt that when confronting new research questions, evaluating historical evidence, or watching international events, we and so many others will continue to ask ourselves, "What would Jervis say?"

NOTES

1. James M. Goldgeier, *Leadership Style and Soviet Foreign Policy: Stalin, Khrushchev, Brezhnev, Gorbachev* (Johns Hopkins University Press, 1994); Elizabeth N. Saunders, *Leaders at War: How Presidents Shape Military Interventions* (Cornell University Press, 2011); Robert Jervis, *Perception and Misperception in International Politics* (Princeton University Press, 1976).

2. Jervis, *Perception and Misperception*, 283.

3. Jervis, *Perception and Misperception*, 117.

4. Cautionary tales include Philip E. Tetlock, *Expert Political Judgment: How Good Is It? How Can We Know?* (Princeton University Press, 2017, rev. ed.); Dominic D. P. Johnson, *Overconfidence and War: The Havoc and Glory of Positive Illusions* (Harvard University Press, 2004).

5. Among others, see Emilie M. Hafner-Burton, D. Alex Hughes, and David G. Victor, "The Cognitive Revolution and the Political Psychology of Elite Decision Making," *Perspectives on Politics* 11, no. 2 (2013): 368–86; Hafner-Burton et al., "The Behavioral Revolution and International Relations," *International Organization* 71, no. S1 (2017): S1–31; Keren Yarhi-Milo, *Knowing the Adversary: Leaders, Intelligence, and Assessment of Intentions in International Relations* (Princeton University Press, 2014); Joshua D. Kertzer, "Re-Assessing Elite-Public Gaps in Political Behavior," *American Journal of Political Science* 66, no. 3 (2020): 539–53. For reviews, see Daniel Krcmaric, Stephen C. Nelson, and Andrew Roberts, "Studying Leaders and Elites: The Personal Biography Approach," *Annual Review of Political Science* 23, no. 1 (2020): 133–51; Saunders, "Elites in the Making and Breaking of Foreign Policy," *Annual Review of Political Science* 25 (2022): 219–40.

6. Robert Jervis, "Do Leaders Matter and How Would We Know?" *Security Studies* 22, no. 2 (2013): 153–79.

7. In addition to *Perception and Misperception in International Politics*, other major works by Jervis that have had tremendous influence across time include *The Logic of Images in International Relations* (Princeton University Press, 1970); "Cooperation Under the

Security Dilemma," *World Politics* 30, no. 2 (1978): 167–214; *The Illogic of American Nuclear Strategy* (Cornell University Press, 1984); *The Meaning of the Nuclear Revolution: Statecraft and the Prospect of Armageddon* (Cornell University Press, 1989); and *System Effects: Complexity in Political and Social Life* (Princeton University Press, 1997). Even his lesser known works are gems; see for example his article, "The Impact of the Korean War on the Cold War," *Journal of Conflict Resolution* 24, no. 4 (1980): 563–92.

8.   Matthew Evangelista et al., *Forum 25 on the Importance of White House Presidential Tapes in Scholarship*, ed. Robert Jervis and Diane Labrosse, H-Diplo/ISSF, November 2, 2020, https://issforum.org/forums/25-tapes.

9.   Fred I. Greenstein and Richard H. Immerman, "What Did Eisenhower Tell Kennedy About Indochina? The Politics of Misperception," *Journal of American History* 79, no. 2 (1992): 568–87.

III

ROBERT JERVIS AND THE PRACTICE OF STATECRAFT

Nuclear Weapons, Intelligence, and Beyond

❖

17

POLITICAL PSYCHOLOGY AND
THE ANALYSIS OF INTELLIGENCE FAILURES

JANICE GROSS STEIN

obert Jervis was the rarest of academics, a field maker. With the
publication of *Perception and Misperception in International Politics* in 1976, he brought the cognitive revolution in psychology
into the analysis of decision making and strategy in international politics.[1] Political psychology had a long-standing and rich tradition in international politics, but Jervis's disciplined empirical study of how decision
makers think about the world, frame problems, and process information
began a fertile program of research that continues to produce new and
important results. Like so many others, I have often been influenced
by Jervis's work and by his unfailingly generous commentary on mine.
Many colleagues who are remembering his work will write about Jervis's
extraordinary contribution to the analysis of how foreign policy decision
makers think.[2]

Jervis made a more specialized but equally important scholarly contribution to the analysis of intelligence. This was a field of inquiry where he
not only analyzed but also actively engaged for decades. He contributed
not only as a scholar but also as an expert who worked to improve the performance and accountability of the intelligence community. Jervis chaired
the CIA's Historical Review Panel and wrote postmortems for the agency.
His report on why the intelligence community was slow to see that the
Shah of Iran might fall identified a number of important errors. Jervis
also led a small team that analyzed the overestimation of Iraq's weapons

of mass destruction in 2002–2003 and found that many of the errors he had identified earlier recurred.[3] He pushed hard to improve processes of declassification and for higher standards of transparency. Much of the improvement over the past two decades in the declassification of documents is the result of Jervis's persistent efforts.

Intelligence was an obvious area of study for Jervis given his deep interest in processes of perception and inference, the impact of beliefs on the interpretation of signals in a context of uncertainty and ambiguity, and the high costs of error.[4] Intelligence services, he argued, "are unusual in that their major errors are believed to be so consequential."[5] Jervis published seminal studies of the intelligence estimates from 2002–2003 regarding whether or not Iraq's president Saddam Hussein had weapons of mass destruction and of the National Intelligence Estimate of Iran's nuclear program in 2007.[6]

One of the core controversies that erupted almost immediately after the 2003 outbreak of the Iraq War was whether US intelligence had been politicized by the Bush administration in the run-up to the invasion and whether that was the central cause of the failure. The allegation was fueled not only by the failure after the fighting had stopped to find any unconventional weapons but also by the processes used by the administration in the period before the war. The governments of the United Kingdom and the United States established commissions of inquiry, but these inquiries only fueled the controversy.[7]

In his review of all these postmortems, Jervis made the important theoretical and methodological point that intelligence failures are ordinary. They are ordinary, he said, because intelligence is "a game between hiders and finders, and the former usually have the easier job." Failures are as old, he noted, as the reports by the spies that Moses sent to the land of Israel that overestimated the strengths of their adversaries. The ordinariness of intelligence failures, an artifact of cognitive and institutional processes, should sound a cautionary note. Decision makers, he concluded, should make their strategies less sensitive to accurate intelligence.[8]

How routine are intelligence failures? For scholars or anyone else to answer this question, we would need a careful coding of all intelligence investigations as either successes or failures before we could make that inference.[9] The obstacles to doing that kind of analysis are quickly obvious. Intelligence agencies rarely release any information about their successes, often because they do not wish to inadvertently expose either their sources or their methods of operation. Review panels and scholars alike consequently draw heavily on a set of cases that is biased toward failure. As a result, they cannot systematically discriminate whether the patterns they find in intelligence failure are also present when intelligence analysis succeeds and whether or not intelligence analysts engaged in what Jervis called "blameworthy errors."[10]

Jervis made a second counterintuitive argument that made political scientists instinctively uncomfortable. Inaccurate conclusions are not necessarily the result of flawed process. Reasoning backward from an incorrect analysis to a flawed process is a pervasive challenge not only in scholarly research but also in the findings of review panels. As Jervis noted with some acerbity, "Oxygen is not a cause of intelligence failure despite its being present in all such cases."[11] Throughout all the streams of his work, Jervis would point again and again to the strong bias that relying only on cases of failure and reasoning back from outcome to process introduces into the scholarly assessment of intelligence.

Nevertheless, Jervis identified important flaws in the processes of intelligence in 2002–2003. He found that many of the judgments of the intelligence community were stated with excessive certainty and that they failed to consider alternative explanations.[12] He remained unpersuaded, however, that better processes would have produced such a significant difference in the estimates that the policy outcome would have changed, and he traced the failure to deeply embedded cognitive beliefs grounded in the past experience of intelligence analysts.

All the major review panels rejected the proposition that intelligence failed because the analysts were subject to political pressure by leaders who had already made up their minds to go to war. Some scholars disagreed strongly. The most compelling challenge came from Joshua Rovner who systematically reviewed alternative explanations, looked carefully at the evidence, and rejected the alternatives to polarization as unconvincing.[13]

In *Fixing the Facts*, Rovner argued that none of the explanations that has been provided—changes in the evidence, time pressures, the limits of collection, routine bureaucratic politics, or psychological biases—is a sufficient explanation of the failure to assess Saddam's unconventional weapons more accurately. He traced the increasing alarm in the intelligence estimates in the summer of 2002 to the politicization of the relationship with the intelligence community by the White House. The most senior administration officials—Vice President Dick Cheney, Secretary of Defense Donald Rumsfeld, and National Security Adviser Condoleezza Rice—all spoke with increasing frequency about Saddam as a threat and warned that he was pursuing unconventional capabilities.[14] Behind closed doors, policymakers repeatedly questioned analysts, subtly signaling their displeasure at what they were hearing and hinting that they wanted different answers.

In London as well as in Washington, already committed political leaders and their advisers used intelligence information to persuade skeptical political opponents and doubting publics. By bringing intelligence evidence into the public debate, Rovner concluded, both governments were able to forge a policy consensus and overcome domestic opposition. The two governments politicized intelligence by downplaying dissent within their agencies, exaggerating the certainty of their threat assessments, and claiming that intelligence overwhelming supported their preferred policy options.[15]

Jervis disagreed but only to a degree. In the arguments that he developed, he paid scrupulous attention to alternative explanations and disconfirming evidence. Rereading his analysis, it is impossible not to be struck by how carefully he qualified his conclusions and how actively he searched for evidence that would challenge his own interpretation. He ultimately concluded that politicization was not the primary driver of failure, "although definitive judgments are impossible because of the multiple and subtle effects that can be at work."[16]

Jervis began his analysis with a detailed summary of the arguments *in favor* of the politicization of intelligence. He disentangled the different forms that politicization could take and agreed that leaders in London and Washington distorted intelligence estimates to garner public support. Senior intelligence officials, he acknowledged, also engaged in questionable behavior: "officials in the US and the UK engaged in 'cherry picking' and 'stove piping,'" highlighting supportive evidence and the delivery of selected raw intelligence directly to policymakers and bypassing analysts who could evaluate the information. This was politicization, Jervis affirmed, although not the more "insidious" kind of pressure from political leaders on intelligence officials to provide analyses that support their decisions.[17]

Jervis then provided additional evidence that the review panels missed, evidence that challenged his disagreement with the argument of politicization. He noted, for example, that the failure of US forces to search for weapons of mass destruction (WMD) as they moved through Iraq during the attack was troubling. Had these weapons been stockpiled, they could have fallen into the hands of adversaries. He concludes, "I cannot explain this failure, but the rest of the US occupation points to incompetence."[18] The evidence he cited is clearly inconsistent with his preferred interpretation, and he was candid in acknowledging that he could not explain the anomaly. It is rare that even the most careful scholars draw on evidence and make arguments that their critics have overlooked.

In support of his preferred interpretation, Jervis then cited confidential interviews that he had done with analysts who did not blame the errors they made on political pressure.[19] He also observed that agencies in all the major countries, even those that actively opposed the war, concluded that Iraq had active WMD programs, yet there was no evidence of political pressure in several of the countries that reached the same conclusion.[20] Moreover, the CIA was able to resist political pressure throughout 2002 and into 2003 right up to the attack when it consistently denied that there was significant evidence that Saddam might turn over WMD to al-Qaeda or other terrorists groups. There was consistent pressure, Jervis argued, but it was not the principal factor that drove intelligence estimates of Iraq's WMD.

Jervis then went on to qualify his own conclusion. That he rejected a general explanation of the politicization of intelligence did not mean, he concluded, that political pressure played no role. At the very least, "it created . . . an atmosphere that was not conducive to critical analysis and that encouraged judgments of excessive certainty." Using counterfactual reasoning as a key methodological tool, he then concluded that "the best evidence of politicization has not been noted by the reports . . . probably because it was something that did not happen: it appears that the ICs [intelligence communities] did not make any [re]assessments once UN Monitoring and Verification Commission (UNMOVIC) inspections resumed and found no traces of WMD."[21] They failed to do so, Jervis reasoned, because it was then obvious that both governments were bent on war and would dismiss any revisions to the estimates.

In November of 2020, my colleague Jon Lindsay and I were teaching an undergraduate course on intelligence, and we invited Rovner and Jervis to join the virtual class to reconsider their debate on the politicization of intelligence. Both graciously accepted, and what followed was remarkable modeling by both scholars of what they had each urged the intelligence community to do. They both asked themselves what kind of evidence would convince them that their original analyses needed to be revised. When it was his turn, Jervis carefully reviewed evidence that had come out in the ensuing decade and concluded that, yes, "late in the fall of 2002, when it became clear that the White House was going to war, the intelligence community felt that the ship had sailed, that they could have no influence, and they gave up. In the last period, intelligence was politicized."[22]

Politicization, Jervis still maintained, was not the basic cause of the flawed estimates. The fundamental drivers of error were the fear of repeating the mistake they had made in the past when intelligence analysts had missed Saddam's programs—"overlearning" from their earlier error—and the strength of the belief that Saddam "was consistent, coherent and unchanging" in his determination to acquire WMD. That belief was so strong and so embedded that it led to confirmation bias.[23] Both of these errors led to the minimizing of the uncertainty that characterized the estimates.[24] These were classic errors that Jervis had identified in his earlier postmortems and scholarship and that all the principal review panels found as well.[25] And, as he had noted as long as three decades ago and yet again in reviewing these estimates, there is no easy fix for this problem: "There is no such thing as 'letting the facts speak for themselves' or drawing inferences without using beliefs about the world; it is inevitable that the perception and interpretation of new information will be influenced by established ideas."[26]

The controversy continued when the National Intelligence Estimate (NIE) on Iran's nuclear program was released in November 2007. This NIE was seen by its critics as a mirror image of the NIE on Iraq that was released in October 2002. As Jervis observed, critics argued that the key judgments were both incompetent and politicized—incompetent because they implied that that the Iran nuclear program had halted, even though a footnote made clear that the halt only applied to warhead design and manufacture,[27] and politicized because the intelligence community was trying to thwart a misguided policy that might lead to war.

Again, Jervis rejected the argument that the estimate was politicized and drew on his "personal experiences and discussions," evidence that he acknowledges was far from fully acceptable but necessary because he worried that it would be years before the relevant documents were released. He carefully walked through the anomalies and alternative arguments that challenged his own and marshalled the strongest possible case against his own interpretation. Then he drew on the evidence that he did have. The people who wrote the estimate were sufficiently "low down the food chain," he claimed, "that they would not push the evidence around." Nor was the estimate altered by people "high enough up to take a broad political view." The estimate was changed when startling evidence came in that Iran had halted part of its program.[28]

The intelligence community, Jervis concluded, "had written an estimate in secret, taking great care to vet the sources, and to 'red team' the conclusions and to see that nothing leaked only to have the White House break [Senator Mitch] McConnell's promise and leave them defenseless against attacks to which they could not publicly respond."[29] Charges of politicization apparently flew both ways as analysts complained to Jervis that the White House had deliberately laid a trap, while policymakers complained to him that they had been set up. Both groups told Jervis how naïve he was when he defended one to the other. He acknowledged that the relationship between the two was "poisonous," a sequela of the original allegation that the White House had politicized the relationship five years earlier.[30]

Jervis drew two general conclusions from these interlinked episodes that speak more generally to some of the most important themes in his scholarship that will stand the test of time. Both relate to psychology and politics in the policy world. The first is how challenging it is to draw inferences about an adversary's intentions when the evidence is incomplete. "Intentions . . . often exist only in a few heads and are subject to rapid change," Jervis wrote. "The meticulous focus [on cause and effect] misses the larger truth. One might think that the IC might point this out, but to do so would be to imply that its contribution to policy must remain limited because of the high probability of error." Here Jervis points to a larger problem. Overconfidence is built into the intelligence community's dialogue with the policy community. That challenge can be managed but never solved.

The second conclusion is even more challenging—and sobering—for those who propose simple solutions to complex policy and institutional problems. "The fundamental reason for the intelligence failures in Iraq," Jervis argued, "was that the assumptions [about Saddam's intentions] and inferences were reasonable, much more so than the alternatives."[31] They were reasonable because Saddam had vigorously pursued WMD in the past, had significant incentives to build the programs, and had skilled technicians and a good procurement network. Saddam's goals were contradictory, his beliefs were difficult for US analysts to imagine, and his need to achieve relief from sanctions was not consistent with his need to maintain a strategic deterrent against Iran.[32] Jervis reasoned that "Saddam's policy was foolish and self-defeating and this goes a long way to explaining the intelligence failure. When the situation is this bizarre, it is not likely to be understood. . . . No conceivable fix would have led to the correct judgment."[33] More than a decade later and with access to the full Saddam archive, Jervis concluded that Saddam remained an enigma that we understand even less well now than we did then.[34]

Jervis spent decades thinking hard about how people responsible for national security thought, how they processed information, how they dealt with evidence, and how they made inferences. Steeped in history and worried about the serious consequences of error, he tested his ideas again and again against historical evidence and, in many ways, was his own fiercest critic. In the field of intelligence, he could test what he knew in something approaching real time and try to improve both process and outcome. And so when the opportunity came along, he took it. His writing about intelligence is granular, detailed, at times uncharacteristically personal, sophisticated, deep, and some of his finest scholarship in what was an extraordinary scholarly career. What shines through his scholarship is the recognition that almost every solution to a problem creates another, often unforeseen problem. I carefully qualified that last sentence because that is exactly what Jervis would have done.

NOTES

1.   Robert Jervis, *Perception and Misperception in International Politics* (Princeton University Press, 1976).

2.   Appropriately, this is the title of one of his recent books. Robert Jervis, *How Statesmen Think: The Psychology of International Politics* (Princeton University Press, 2017).

3. Jervis summarized these activities in his "Reports, Politics, and Intelligence Failures: the Case of Iraq," *Journal of Strategic Studies* 29, no. 1 (2006): 3–52, n. 1. His report on the failure to anticipate the Shah of Iran was declassified as CIA-RDP86B00269R00110011003-4.

4. Robert Jervis, "Understanding Beliefs," *Political Psychology* 27, no. 5 (2006): 641–63.

5. Jervis, "Reports, Politics, and Intelligence Failures," 6.

6. Robert Jervis, *Why Intelligence Fails: Lessons from the Iranian Revolution and the Iraq War* (Cornell University Press, 2010); Jervis, "Reports, Politics, and Intelligence Failures"; Jervis, "The November 2007 Iran Nuclear NIE: Immediate Aftermath, Intelligence and National Security," *Intelligence and National Security* 36, no. 2 (2021): 222–25.

7. For official reviews, see Department of Defence Inspector-General, "Review of the Pre-Iraqi War Activities of the Under Secretary of Defense for Policy," February 9, 2007, http://www.dodig.mil/fo/Foia/pre-iraqi.htm; Report of a Committee of Privy Counselors, *Review of Intelligence on Weapons of Mass Destruction* (Stationary Office, 2004, hereafter the Butler Report); Commission on the Intelligence Capabilities of the United States Regarding Weapons of Mass Destruction, "Report to the President of the United States," March 31, 2005, http://www.gpoaccess.gov/wmd/ (hereafter the WMD Report); "Report of the Select Committee on Intelligence on the U.S. Intelligence Community's Prewar Intelligence Assessments on Iraq," July 9, 2004, http://www.gpoaccess.gov /serialsecretreports/ira.html (hereafter the SSCI Report). See also David Kay, "Iraq's Weapons of Mass Destruction," Miller Center Report 20 (Spring/Summer 2004); and "Comprehensive Report of the Special Advisor to the DCI on Iraq's WMD, with Addendums (Duelfer Report)," April 25, 2005, https://www.govinfo.gov/app/details /GPO-DUELFERREPORT.

8. Jervis, *Reports, Politics, and Intelligence Failures*, 10–12.

9. There are a few exceptions when intelligence successes are celebrated. David Robarge, "Getting It Right: CIA Analysis of the 1967 Arab-Israeli War," *Studies in Intelligence* 49, no. 1 (2005): 1–8.

10. Jervis, *Reports, Politics, and Intelligence Failures*, 14.

11. Jervis, *Reports, Politics, and Intelligence Failures*, 19.

12. Jervis, *Reports, Politics, and Intelligence Failures*, 14–15.

13. Joshua Rovner, *Fixing the Facts: National Security and the Politics of Intelligence* (Cornell University Press, 2011): 156–62.

14. Secretary of State Colin Powell became more important in early 2003 when he testified at the United Nations.

15. Rovner, *Fixing the Facts*, 160–61, 94.

16. Jervis, *Reports, Politics, and Intelligence Failures*, 33

17. Jervis, *Reports, Politics, and Intelligence Failures*, 33, n. 7; 34.

18. Jervis, *Reports, Politics, and Intelligence Failures*, 33, n. 57.

19. Jervis, *Reports, Politics, and Intelligence Failures*, 35.

20. There were some discrepancies among allied services. See Alan Barnes, "Getting It Right: Canadian Intelligence Assessments on Iraq, 2002–2003," *Intelligence and National Security* 35, no. 7 (2020): 925–53. Canadian intelligence did not get it quite as "right" as Barnes suggests. I think Jervis got this more right than wrong.

21. Jervis, *Reports, Politics, and Intelligence Failures*, 36, 37.

22. Virtual discussion with Joshua Rovner, Jon Lindsay, and Janice Gross Stein, November 9, 2020.

23. Jervis, *Perception and Misperception in International Politics*, chap. 6.

24. Jervis, *Reports, Politics, and Intelligence Failures*, 22, 23. The Butler Report in particular concluded that analysts leaned toward worst-case analysis because they feared underestimating the threat more than they feared overestimating it. Butler Report, 139.

25. Jervis, *Perception and Misperception in International Politics*, chap. 4. With varying degrees of emphasis, the SSCI, the WMD, and the Butler reports agree. They all cite systematic bias against underestimation of the threat, the expression of judgments with excessive certainty, a failure to report continuing dissent and disagreement as spring turned to summer and fall in 2002, and lack of care in reporting levels of certainty to policymakers. The Butler Report, 13, makes an especially strong argument about the sloppy language of likelihood. The SSCI found that the NIE "layered" assessments on top of earlier judgments without bringing forward the uncertainties, a basic violation of the calculation of cumulative probabilities. SSCI Report, 22.

26. Jervis, *Reports, Politics, and Intelligence Failures*, 23–24.

27. Jervis, "The November 2007 Iran Nuclear NIE," 222.

28. Jervis, "The November 2007 Iran Nuclear NIE," 222.

29. Jervis, "The November 2007 Iran Nuclear NIE," 224. For a superb analysis of the drafting of the NIE, see Vann H. Van Diepen, "Reevaluating the 'Externals' and 'Internals' of the 2007 Iran Nuclear NIE," *Intelligence and National Security* 36, no. 2 (2021): 176–207.

30. Virtual discussion with Joshua Rovner, Jon Lindsay, and Janice Gross Stein, November 9, 2020.

31. Jervis, *Reports, Politics, and Intelligence Failures*, 11, 42.

32. Duelfer Report, 34.

33. Jervis, *Reports, Politics, and Intelligence Failures*, 44, 46.

34. Virtual discussion with Joshua Rovner, Jon Lindsay, and Janice Gross Stein, November 9, 2020.

18

THE SOCIAL DILEMMAS OF
TECHNOLOGICAL INNOVATION

ROBERT F. TRAGER

Researchers at a small drug company, Collaborations Pharmaceuticals in Raleigh, North Carolina, recently stumbled upon something that surprised them. The company searches for new medicines using artificial intelligence techniques designed to avoid potentially toxic molecules. What if, the researchers asked, they instead searched *for* toxic molecules? Six hours from the time they started the search, they had generated a list of forty thousand potential toxins. Some of these were known toxins, like the odorless, tasteless nerve agent VX—a large enough amount to be visible can be lethal when it touches the skin. But the researchers also uncovered many other agents that were predicted to be orders of magnitude *more toxic* than VX. They did not publish the list.[1]

This case highlights the fact that although technological progress is opening new possibilities for human flourishing, a growing list of technologies is challenging global security. DNA printing allows pathogens to be produced and modified. Lethal autonomous weapons facilitate the deployment of large-scale, targeted violence, potentially with diminished attribution of perpetrators. Both of these technologies are diffusing to ever-widening circles of actors. The misalignment of artificial intelligence systems with human values is difficult to detect and poses a variety of risks; such misalignments may already have caused political polarization within countries and between them. Advanced forms of artificial intelligence are supercharging other domains of science and may well produce new destruction-dominant technologies.

Robert Jervis took up the challenge of theorizing the impacts of technology throughout his career. The relationship between changing material possibilities and the social world fascinated him. He seemed to take as given that social worlds are objects of enormous complexity, and yet one could look for relatively simple, decisive influences of technology. Thus, one wonders how he would understand the social impacts of technological change today. Would he see fundamental shifts requiring new theory? Or do the theories that helped to make sense of earlier eras apply just as well today?

This is not a question Jervis would have taken lightly; he believed in the possibility of fundamental change. In the nuclear age, he inveighed against "conventionalization,"[2] treating a world with nuclear weapons like one without them. But what would he make of a world in which the binary distinction between conventional and unconventional breaks down? As lethal autonomous weapons become much more sophisticated than they are now, perhaps the same sorts of weapons that are regularly used on the battlefield could be scaled up to cause mass casualty attacks. It is unclear how norms governing use would function in such an environment.[3]

Indeed, Jervis criticized analysts of world affairs on many occasions for not appreciating the various social implications of differing technologies. In the case of biological weapons, for instance, he believed that "one reason why American preparations for defense against biological weapons has been misguided is that even experts have seen biological agents within the frame established by earlier attempts to deal with chemical weapons, despite the two differing in crucial ways."[4] He also thought that technology influenced the security dilemma, which would be heightened when offensive technologies are advantaged over defensive ones or the two cannot be distinguished.[5] Mobilization races, he thought, could create strong incentives to strike first and thus heighten the probability of war.[6] He thought modern technology made wars last longer.[7]

In the case of nuclear weapons, Jervis thought that they had caused a "revolution" in international affairs for two essential reasons: the mutual vulnerability of rivals and the continuing permeability of levels of violence. Unlike conventional conflicts, in a potentially nuclear conflict, one side does not become less vulnerable if it is winning the war. Both sides maintain the ability to harm the other until both are destroyed. But this does not mean that when both sides possess a reliable second strike, the sides can assume that nuclear weapons would never be used in an ongoing conventional conflict. The possibility of escalation, he thought, was due to the fog of war, human conflict psychology, and the dynamics of crises. The implication was that the nuclear balance could never be so stable that countries would freely engage in conventional conflict. Jervis thought that countries would generally be much more reticent to engage in conflict of any sort as a result of the danger of escalation to nuclear destruction. And he thought that this situation was reasonably satisfactory. He recognized the benefit of some risk that crises would get out of control: it meant crises would be avoided. In effect, he accepted some risk of nuclear catastrophe.[8]

Cyber capabilities, meanwhile, pose "special problems in the uncertainties and ambiguities involved in, and related to the lack of shared understandings about what would constitute escalation." Cyber and, perhaps, other new technologies heighten the tension between secrecy and deterrence. Adversaries have an incentive to announce their capabilities in order to extract concessions, but doing so makes the capabilities much less effective. Cyber vulnerabilities, once discovered, can usually be patched. Yet Jervis thought that the prospects for cyber arms control agreements were "dim." States would be restrained by deterrence in initiating attacks but not in developing the capability to attack.[9]

Although he recognized the great influence of technology on the character of international order, Jervis was not a technological determinist. "The future," he argued, "is probably unknowable because it will depend in part on how important actors think and behave."[10] He argued that "at least as important as technology are decision-makers' choices of strategy and beliefs about the offense-defense balance."[11] This followed because he believed that there would often be many social responses to a given material situation.

As a social theorist, Jervis tried to make room for agency, writing, "it would make no sense to criticize decisions if one believed that technology in fact *had* to determine events and the political leaders could not control their country's arms posture."[12] Yet, he was not convinced that there was a better social equilibrium than the variety of mutually assured destruction (MAD) that he defined. He spent a great deal of time looking for something better. Unfortunately, he concluded: "Human thought cannot change physical realities, but can it extricate us from the predicament we have created? My conclusion is that it cannot. MAD is here to stay, no matter how much we dislike or fear it. We live in the 'best of all possible worlds.' Furthermore, even if this is not all for the best, it is not as bad as we often believe."[13]

He thought it was right that we continue to search for better equilibria. He just did not believe that the search would bear fruit. Finally, he recognized that even a world without nuclear weapons would still be a world in which they could be rebuilt. In that case, their very absence might tempt some actor to try to build them in secret, and thus even if they were eliminated, the threat of nuclear devastation would remain.

Thus, nuclear capabilities were a revolution, one that led to living in the "awful situation" of being under the threat of destruction, but it was a state of affairs from which he did not think we could escape. "As long as we live," he wrote, "we will live under the threat of nuclear destruction."[14] Was Jervis right to be sanguine about the predicament of MAD? For his time, he seemed to be. But the history of MAD does not give us high statistical confidence that such a situation is stable over the long run.

Jervis did not, however, believe that other recent technologies had fundamentally changed international politics. For instance, he did not consider cyber capabilities to be a revolution. So where would the emerging capabilities of today fit on this continuum? Should we expect the near future to represent another break from the past or a smooth evolution? Would Jervis predict a revolution in international affairs resulting from developments in bioengineering, nanotechnologies, autonomous weapons, or another form of advanced artificial intelligence? Of course, it is impossible to answer these questions with a high degree of confidence.

Following the logic of the nuclear revolution, one could contend that the very dangers and vulnerabilities that these technologies imply will make the world safer—or at least not less safe because mutual vulnerability is already the state of affairs. Yet, much of Jervis's thinking was preoccupied with the two superpowers of the Cold War. Would his view change if the proliferation of certain technologies could not be controlled? Software, for instance, is usually easy to copy and thus easy to spread. Will new technologies advantage the offense or the defense? On the one hand, artificial intelligence may make the oceans "transparent," undermining defense by undermining the credibility of second strikes. On the other hand, autonomous technologies may enable second strikes that would not otherwise have been credible.

Although he was open to the possibility that new technologies could change fundamental strategic variables, Jervis did not think it likely that they would do so. The two fundamental forces that he viewed as shaping the international order of his time—mutual vulnerability and the slippery slope from one level of violence to another in wartime—seem likely to be with us for some time. This seems to argue for continuity. Yet there are factors that might lead to a different judgment. These include the seemingly increasing numbers of actors in the circle of mutual vulnerability, the potential challenges to attribution of attacks or even knowledge that an attack has occurred, the potential for large changes in the offense-defense balance, and other factors.

In some sense, perhaps the Cold War era was the easy task for social theorists. In contrast to today, technological developments were relatively stable. The theorists of that time could consider known technologies. Now, social theorists must consider technologies that may be around the corner because the potential of these technologies motivates the political actors of today. Potentially heightening security dilemma dynamics, the technology races of today will arguably have more impact on national capabilities. During the Cold War, much technological competition involved competition over appearances for the sake of status rather than fundamental changes in the balance of power. This led to feats that were impressive but had little direct material benefit. The clearest example is the period from 1957 to 1962 when, at the program's height, the United States spent over 4 percent of the federal budget on space flight—sending people to the moon.[15] Today, the United States, China, and other actors are openly competing in the field of artificial intelligence, an area of technology that is likely to have farther-reaching impacts.

We cannot know what Jervis would have written about the technological developments of today. We know that he would not have been dogmatic. Certainly, we can wish that he were here to help us think through the social responses. We know he would have done so with analysis from all angles, lively wit, unending historical comparisons, and a cataloguer's knowledge of follies, both human and social scientific.

NOTES

1. Fabio Urbina et al., "Dual Use of Artificial-Intelligence-Powered Drug Discovery," *Nature Machine Intelligence* 4, no. 3 (2022): 189–91.

2. Hans Morgenthau, "The Fallacy of Thinking Conventionally About Nuclear Weapons," in *Arms Control and Technological Innovation*, ed. David Carlton and Carlo Schaerf (Wiley, 1976): 256–64.

3. Robert F. Trager and Laura M. Luca, "Killer Robots Are Here—and We Need to Regulate Them," *Foreign Policy*, May 11, 2022, https://foreignpolicy.com/2022/05/11/killer-robots-lethal-autonomous-weapons-systems-ukraine-libya-regulation/.

4. Robert Jervis, *Perception and Misperception in International Politics* (Princeton University Press, 2017), 53.

5. Robert Jervis, "Security Regimes," *International Organization* 36, no. 2 (1982): 357–74; Jervis, "Cooperation Under the Security Dilemma," *World Politics* 30, no. 2 (1978): 167–214.

6. Jervis, "Cooperation Under the Security Dilemma," 212; see also Dan Reiter, "Exploding the Powder Keg Myth: Preemptive Wars Almost Never Happen," *International Security* 20, no. 2 (1995): 5–34.

7. Robert Jervis, "The Political Effects of Nuclear Weapons: A Comment," *International Security* 13, no. 2 (1988): 80–90, 86.

8. Robert Jervis, *The Meaning of the Nuclear Revolution: Statecraft and the Prospect of Armageddon* (Cornell University Press, 1989).

9. Robert Jervis, "Some Thoughts on Deterrence in the Cyber Era," *Journal of Information Warfare* 15, no. 2 (2016): 66, 72.

10. Jervis, "Some Thoughts on Deterrence in the Cyber Era," 73.

11. Robert Jervis, "Strategic Theory: What's New and What's True," *Journal of Strategic Studies* 9, no. 44 (1986): 153.

12. Robert Jervis, "Technology, Politics, and Choice," *Journal of International Affairs* 39, no. 1 (1985): 192.

13. Robert Jervis, "MAD Is the Best Possible Deterrence," *Bulletin of the Atomic Scientists* 41, no. 3 (1985): 43–45.

14. Jervis, "MAD Is the Best Possible Deterrence."

15. Joslyn Barnhart, "Emerging Technologies, Prestige Motivations and the Dynamics of International Competition," Centre for the Governance of AI, Working Paper, January 12, 2012, 2, https://www.governance.ai/research-paper/emerging-technologies-prestige-motivations-and-the-dynamics-of-international-competition.

19

COMPLEXITY, NONLINEARITY, AND OTHER ESSENTIAL JERVISIAN INSIGHTS ON INTERNATIONAL SECURITY PROBLEMS

CYNTHIA ROBERTS

In his thinking about causation and concern about effects, Robert Jervis is to international relations what Charles Darwin is to evolutionary biology and Richard Feynman is to theoretical physics—a pioneer whose original and unique contributions to the discipline and the subfields that he championed made a lasting mark. Like Darwin,[1] who showed how the natural selection of small, inherited variations increase the ability to compete, adapt, and survive, Jervis revealed that the international objectives of actors, such as deterrence and coercion, depend not only on credibility and material incentives to make threats potent but also fundamentally on how the actors see the world and how they employ strategic signaling to influence others' perceptions of them.

Jervis's work progressed further to show that a full understanding of international politics requires identifying not only actors' beliefs about the world and how behavior is perceived but also recognizing that international relations is a complex system that generates both direct and nonlinear second- and third-order effects that may not be immediately obvious.[2] Jervis invoked Darwin to emphasize the "need to take more seriously the notion that we are in a system and to look for the dynamics that are at work." "Nothing in biology makes sense," he quoted the distinguished geneticist Theodosius Dobzhansky as writing, "except in the light of evolution." Likewise, Jervis argued, "very little in social and political life makes sense except in the light of systemic processes. Exploring them gives us new possibilities for understanding and effective action; in their absence we are likely to flounder."[3] Best known is Jervis's explanation of the security dilemma as the means by which a state tries to increase its security decrease the security of others. This dynamic provides the rational foundation for the spiral model in which interactions among security seekers can paradoxically fuel dangerous international competition.[4] Jervis appreciated the continuing importance of deterrence and threats of punishment against aggression but sought to underscore how mistaking a security seeker for an aggressor leads to the wrong remedy when reassurance would be preferable. Relevant for contemporary great-power challenges, Jervis's historical analysis showed that the (first) Cold War was not the product of a security dilemma, although some elements of security dilemmas were present and intensified the conflict.[5]

Like Feynman,[6] Bob Jervis was a theoretical genius whose insights were enriched by and ranged across multiple disciplines and domains. Both scholars deeply appreciated the importance of empirical tests and devoted considerable intellectual energy to significant policy challenges. For Feynman, it was the Manhattan Project, Los Alamos, and the *Challenger* space shuttle disaster commission. Jervis wrote intelligence reviews and postmortems of key intelligence failures, including the unanticipated fall of the Shah of Iran in 1979 and the claim that Iraq had active weapons of mass destruction programs in 2002. He chaired the CIA's Historical Review Panel and was at the center of the most important debate about the nuclear age (which I discuss in more detail later).[7]

Feynman observed that "the first principle is that you must not fool yourself, and you are the easiest person to fool."[8] Jervis agreed, and his insights about misperceptions and beliefs help uncover why leaders fool themselves into taking avoidable costly actions. "It is all well and good to talk about credibility, punishment, and reward in the abstract," he noted, "but as they work out in the real world, they depend on what the targets value, believe, and think about the state's behavior."[9] One area, explored in the ensuing pages, is whether it is possible to make chance generate coercive leverage by encouraging others to believe that your disposition, emotions (e.g., being aggrieved, suffering from frustrated ambition and insecurity[10]), and particular situation predispose you to adopt postures and manipulate risks in ways that include crossing the threshold into limited nuclear strikes.[11]

As others have observed, some of Jervis's most interesting and important theoretical insights emerge from arguments he had with himself.[12] Scientific theory such as evolution is foundational, but Jervis also pointedly drew on Stephen Jay Gould (another scholar lost too early to cancer) to debate whether the future is driven by cycles or arrows, by patterns or contingency.[13] Like Gould, Jervis found that each perspective has an element of truth: "The operation of natural selection does not preclude a large role for chance and accidents. Had certain life forms been destroyed or others survived eons ago—and there are no general principles or scientific laws that precluded this—life would have evolved very differently." Jervis contended that international politics also "fit this pattern," although he acknowledges that this observation is impossible to prove.[14] Moreover, Jervis maintains, "if our laws are not timeless—if history resembles an arrow—some of what we have learned will not help us understand the future." As an example, Jervis cited alliance theory that predicted NATO's dissolution after the end of the Cold War against the notion that the roles and motivations for alliances can change and, one might add, continue to evolve.[15]

The parallels with Gould are further evident in the development of Jervis's thinking about international relations as a complex adaptive system, which also draws on insights from Charles Perrow and Garrett Hardin, reflecting Jervis's inimitable rich interdisciplinary research and analysis.[16] Seeking to explain how systems work and why they so often produce unintended consequences, Jervis underscored the tendency of interconnections influenced by previous interactions and positive and negative feedback loops to produce unexpected second- and third-order effects. A crucial advance beyond Perrow, closer to Werner Heisenberg,[17] is recognizing that system effects are strongly influenced by how actors perceive the system and strategize as well as how interactions add complexity and change the environment so that subsequent actions take place in different conditions.[18]

POLICY IMPLICATIONS OF
COPING WITH SYSTEM EFFECTS

Disturbing a complex system will produce several changes that require coping with unpredictability. Jervis illuminates this common problem in political life by drawing on Hardin's insight about the impossibility of locating a specific agent that will do only one thing because of the unintended consequences. "*We can never do merely one thing*," Hardin admonished. "Wishing to kill insects, we may put an end to the singing of birds. Wishing to 'get there' faster we insult our lungs with smog."[19] Jervis could not resist underscoring the effect by providing a long list of additional wide-ranging examples, including how

> redundant safety equipment makes some accidents less likely but increases the chances of others due to the operators' greater confidence and the interaction effects among the devices; placing a spy in the adversary's camp not only gains valuable information but also leaves the actor vulnerable to deception if the spy is discovered; . . . allowing the sale of an antibaldness medicine without a prescription may be dangerous because people no longer have to see a doctor, who in some cases would have determined that the loss of hair was a symptom of a more serious problem; flying small formations of planes over Hiroshima to practice dropping the atomic bomb accustomed the population to air raid warnings that turned out to be false alarms, thereby reducing the number of people who took cover on August 6.[20]

Jervis's point that "most actions, no matter how well targeted, will have multiple effects" bears repeating.[21] Sometimes the effects are readily evident, as when cuts to oil imports to punish Russia for its aggression against Ukraine initially led to significantly higher prices and greater gains to Moscow's coffers until alternative sources of supply could stabilize the market. However, not all side effects are negative, as witnessed by the historic turning point [*Zeitenwende*] in German security policy starting in 2022 that includes plans to spend €649 billion on German defense over five years, send heavy weapons to Ukraine, and end Germany's dependence on Russian energy.

Like Jervis, the Prussian general and military theorist Carl von Clausewitz also focused on the interactive nature of war and nonlinearity, "the interplay of possibilities, probabilities, good luck and bad" that contribute to uncertainty in war. He famously insisted that "no other activity is so continuously or universally bound up with chance" as war, where "the facts are seldom fully known" and where "everything is uncertain . . .

all military action is entwined with psychological forces and effects" and "war consists of a continuous interaction of opposites."[22] Security specialists are most familiar with Clausewitz's linear insights, such as concentrating one's forces on the "center of gravity [*Schwerpunkt*]." However, writing almost two centuries before Jervis, Clausewitz argued that it was a mistake to focus explanations solely on immediate aims and effects because "in war, as in life generally, all parts of the whole are interconnected and thus the effects produced, however small their cause, must influence all subsequent military operations and modify their final outcome to some degree, however slight."[23] Such feedback effects even led Clausewitz to limit his important claim that war is the instrument of policy to the extent that the "original political objects can greatly alter during the course of the war and may finally change entirely since they are influenced by events and their probable consequences."[24]

Of course, as Richard Betts observed, "Clausewitz recognized nonlinearity, but he still believed in strategy."[25] So, too, did Jervis. Typically arguing with himself, he acknowledged that "it is hard to measure [the] . . . frequency" of complex interactions and their unintended consequences. In his landmark study of system effects and complexity, Jervis pointedly cited Albert Hirschman's insight that "straightforward effects are common and often dominate perverse ones" noting that otherwise "it would be hard to see how society, progress, or any stable human interaction could develop."[26]

The necessary conclusion is that even if complexity and nonlinearity are neither absolute nor all-encompassing, policymakers must develop purposeful policy that accounts for their effects. Recognizing that international politics operates in complex adaptive systems, Jervis suggested that effective action is often possible by employing multiple policies that constrain and work with the dynamics of the system. To produce a desired change, the actor must appreciate the need to do several things, whether "Doing Things in 'Twos'"[27] or other combinations, and sometimes take indirect actions to moderate the effects of direct means.

Evidently in recognition of the system effects reverberating from Russia's war in Ukraine, the Biden administration and some NATO allies were arming Ukraine while simultaneously deterring Moscow from escalating to nuclear use and reassuring the Kremlin that Washington and NATO did not seek to become direct combatants or promote regime change in

Russia. The administration even publicly reinforced its private messaging to the Kremlin that the United States played no role in the June 2023 armed mutiny led by the Wagner Group's Yevgeny Prigozhin and that it viewed it as an internal Russian matter. Yet in another twist, the CIA director could not resist announcing that the agency hoped to exploit "disaffection" with Russian president Putin's war and used this rare opportunity to post on a popular Russian messaging platform that the CIA was open to recruit Russian intelligence sources.[28] The administration also was careful to avoid the bias of ignoring negative evidence,[29] tracking not only what Russia was doing with its forces but also what it was not doing—such as not taking pre-combat dispersal steps to operationalize nuclear warheads by transporting them from storage to the front for mating with tactical nuclear delivery systems.

The split in the Biden administration between the risk tolerant "push harder" and risk averse "tread cautiously" camps initially favored the latter leading the administration to cancel a scheduled routine nuclear test at the start of the war, slow-walk the supply of some advanced weapons (e.g., long-range Army Tactical Missile Systems) and judge some tactical support measures (e.g., a no-fly zone) as falling too close to a red line that could trigger significant Russian escalation. The objective was to increase assistance incrementally so as to slowly "boil the frog," a metaphor to avoid a significant single move that could provoke the frog to jump out of the pot or provoke Moscow into the type of major escalation that would propel Putin to employ nuclear weapons or deliberately strike NATO member states.[30]

Nonetheless, despite some realists' view that the United States had low stakes in Ukraine and should avoid paying high costs, many American policymakers seem convinced that failure to support a partner like Ukraine, struggling to defend itself from Russian aggression, would undermine US credibility to defend other allies. This follows Jervis's contention that "beliefs about resolve, credibility, and controllability were central to the Cold War," and such beliefs recur because empirical evidence is lacking to rule them out. Jervis reminds us that one of the reasons that Presidents John F. Kennedy and Lyndon Johnson decided to fight in Vietnam was to convince others that the United States would not abandon Berlin and that the United States needed to stay in Berlin "to deter larger attacks on West Germany."[31]

The significant incremental increases in the level of assistance to Ukraine do not just show the benefits of a defense pact, even one short of NATO membership. Europe's support for Ukraine (especially by states like Germany, France, and Italy that have had strong domestic ties to Moscow) and Finland's and Sweden's rapid NATO accession also reflect strong systemic effects. These outcomes parallel China's and Iran's deepening relationship with Russia and Teheran's entry in July 2023 as a full member to the Shanghai Cooperation Organization (SCO). As Jervis argued, "the international system can polarize as alliances spread consistency throughout it."[32]

That Ukraine failed to gain bargaining leverage to force an early wartime admission into NATO, despite significant assistance from many members of the Alliance, is not surprising. Following Jervis's logic, as the supplicant [*demandeur*], Ukraine needs the support of NATO more than the reverse, and it has no outside options that would give credibility to threats to defect from the partnership if the Alliance's backing is not forthcoming. The hard truth for Kyiv is that "vulnerability . . . can be a bargaining asset, but only if the other [side] needs the state."[33] Arguments to fast-track Ukraine into NATO vary in form, some through dispensations forswearing the use of force to recover Crimea and other regions analogous to the Federal Republic of Germany (FRG) in 1955, which deferred reunification to gain security guarantees and NATO membership.[34] However, their common foundation—as evident in the problematic comparison to the NATO accession of the FRG—is rooted more in moral than strategic logic. Ukraine's security position will not be resolved quickly or by Israeli-style security guarantees offered in lieu of rapid NATO accession,[35] at least not without the equivalent nuclear backstop.

JERVIS AND THE BOMB

The current attempt to both engage in and simultaneously contain a full-blown "competition in risk-taking" over Ukraine leads us to a third area in which Jervis made a foundational contribution: the meaning and effects of the atomic bomb. Jervis's *The Meaning of the Nuclear Revolution* is a pathbreaking study of the implications of nuclear weapon states in the condition of mutual assured destruction (MAD) and a focal point for continuing debate over strategy and the nuclear age. Jervis's core claim was one he defended to the end of his life, that "MAD is a fact, not a policy."[36] Mutual vulnerability meant the risk of mutual suicide because there was no meaningful defense; MAD theorists contend that these facts decrease the chance of a nuclear war. Even the "shadow of mutual vulnerability" (what Jervis calls MAD 4) strongly influenced the beliefs of political leaders who "never had any faith that all-out war would lead to anything other than utter devastation."[37]

Jervis, like other scholars (notably Kenneth Waltz[38] and Charles Glaser[39]), openly recognized that the theory of the nuclear revolution is normative and prescriptive and contended that states would be better off if they followed it. Nonetheless, he acknowledged that in practice actors have struggled to escape MAD more than he initially expected.[40] To his credit, Jervis encouraged and engaged serious challenges to the theory.[41] In developing this work, he acknowledged not only the important influence of prior contributions by Bernard Brodie and Thomas Schelling[42] but also that the theory needs refinement in view of new empirical evidence. In particular, the nuclear revolution theory overoptimistically predicted not only "peace between the superpowers, [but also that] crises will be rare, neither side will be eager to press bargaining advantages to the limit, the status quo will be relatively easy to maintain, and political outcomes will not be closely related to either the nuclear or the conventional balance."[43]

Jervis underestimated the efforts by states and policymakers to gain strategic advantages while arms racing as well as the extent to which new technologies and other advances could assist such efforts, particularly by the United States, which is presently the only major power with the resources and capabilities to pursue the objective of damage limitation. Nevertheless, even the United States has struggled with strategic defense and has to face Russia's (and potentially China's) determined efforts to deny the United States significant possibilities for damage limitation while preserving the condition of mutual vulnerability. An example is Moscow's development of the Poseidon intercontinental, nuclear-powered, nuclear-armed autonomous torpedo that is designed for massive destruction of coastal cities. China also is moving away from its minimal deterrent posture and more determined to preserve an assured retaliation capability despite the US pursuit of technological advances and other means to erode it.

Finally, Jervis recognized that although mutual second-strike capabilities decreased the chance of nuclear war, they "also made it safer for either side to engage in provocations at lower levels of violence."[44] The latest and most dangerous manifestation of this stability-instability paradox is evident in Russia's prosecution of war against Ukraine and hybrid warfare (e.g., sabotage operations) against Europe while making persistent nuclear threats to deter the United States and NATO from joining as full combatants. As mentioned, for their part, the United States and several NATO allies are significantly aiding Ukraine while warning (and reassuring) Russia that the United States does not seek a Russia-NATO war which would likely lead to nuclear escalation. Washington has publicly signaled that "any use of nuclear weapons in this conflict on any scale would be completely unacceptable to us as well as the rest of the world and would entail severe consequences."[45] It is also likely that some U.S. policymakers fear that a defeat in Ukraine will weaken deterrence for the Baltic states and Taiwan.

Jervis did not live to give us his interpretation of the latest US/NATO-Russian crisis over the war in Ukraine, with its frequent Russian nuclear saber-rattling. One of his last publications was titled "The Nuclear Age: During and After the Cold War," when it was already evident that force could again "be used to change borders in Eastern Europe."[46] Like Schelling, Jervis appreciated that the "threat that leaves something to chance" and "the danger that things will get out of control" are "ways of bringing pressure to bear in a crisis."[47]

Jervis continued to insist, however, that leaders' awareness of the possibility that they could stumble into war played a large role in keeping them further from the brink. He observed a tendency for cautious behavior when the danger of nuclear war arose in contrast to "standard theories of bargaining [that] would lead us to expect states to have been bolder and more assertive than they were, and partly because of their caution they never saw situations as hopeless."[48]

Is that prevailing sense of caution still true today as regional flashpoints erupt and will it hold into the future? Jervis laid important foundations for future research on deterrence and wars in the shadow and under repeated threats to employ nuclear weapons. This is fortunate given that the era of multipolar nuclear rivalry has already arrived and spans multiple regions. If Jervis is right, nuclear deterrence or a nuclear taboo will continue to hold, despite crises involving nuclear-armed states and security competition aiming to break the stalemate. He laid down the marker that this fortuitous outcome will occur because the drivers of significant continuity—whether common beliefs about the basic facts created by nuclear weapons, path dependence, or self-fulfilling prophecies—prove stronger than the countervailing impulses.[49]

To be sure, Jervis's work also indicates some important causes of deterrence failure,[50] and it has to be expected that any nuclear use would have second- and third-order system effects, in line with Jervis's theory about international politics. One set of problems underpinning nonlinear drivers of nuclear escalation involves the nexus of misperceptions, biases, and emotions that could motivate leaders to take higher risks under the pressures of stress or to avert perceived hopeless losses. Jervis held that "fear is usually a more potent motivator [for risk taking] than the desire for expansion."[51] Fearing defeat, especially if facing rapid collapse, leaders may feel compelled to gamble for survival or resurrection.[52]

Another area of concern involves what could happen if the caution that Jervis attributed to nuclear powers to resist the temptation to push bargaining advantages does not hold and starts to erode either gradually or in a rush. An impulse for this could be a weakening position and concomitant slippage in leverage during an ongoing conflict beneath the nuclear threshold or an incentive to preempt a perceived imminent large-scale conventional attack. For instance, frustrated by Russian combat ineptness and the susceptibility of the Kremlin to the proverbial boiled-frog tactic, some Russian civilian experts and military analysts from the General Staff are urging the government to ratchet up the level of risk, lower the nuclear threshold, and possibly even employ limited nuclear strikes—though it is unclear whether these would be demonstration strikes for coercive purposes, limited to discrete tactical objectives, or done to achieve strategic effects.[53]

It is important to note that even the limited use of nuclear weapons can vary from a defensive combat action on one battlefield to a more substantial regional strike to gain operational or strategic advantage in an ongoing conventional fight and that the ultimate result could still lead to uncontrollable escalation. Moreover, constraints resulting from prior decisions about the size of the nuclear force, design of the force posture, and effectiveness of nuclear command, control, and communications

(NC3) structures affect available capabilities for warfighting and the range or lack of options for bargaining and intentional escalation in wartime. States with ample limited nuclear options should be more likely to press their bargaining advantages or cross the nuclear threshold when they have high stakes.

Strap in. We are in a new run of the experiment on whether nuclear weapons make the world safer because they increase the costs of war and reduce the probability of major-power war or make the world more dangerous because erroneous beliefs and miscalculations in a fragile balance of terror in nuclear multipolarity could lead actors to stumble over the brink. In his many writings, Robert Jervis asked the right questions, challenged much conventional wisdom, and expertly guided us toward compelling new explanations. Yet Jervis understood that the future will not necessarily resemble the past and that there is always more work to be done.

NOTES

1. Charles Darwin, *The Origin of Species by Means of Natural Selection; or the Preservation of Favoured Races in the Struggle for Life*, 6th ed. (J. Murray, 1872).

2. System effects, second-order effects, and third-order effects reflect direct, indirect, and unintended consequences of changes in a system. Nonlinearity (such as the exponential spread of an infectious disease) is often prevalent in complex adaptive systems, allowing small changes to lead to large effects. Moreover, given feedback effects, actors may change their behavior in response to changes in the adaptive system, adding complexity and uncertainty.

3. Robert Jervis, *System Effects: Complexity in Social and Political Life* (Princeton University Press, 1997), 295.

4. Robert Jervis, "Cooperation Under the Security Dilemma," *World Politics* 30, no. 2 (1978): 167–214.

5. Robert Jervis, "Was the Cold War a Security Dilemma?," *Journal of Cold War Studies* 3, no. 1 (2001): 36–60.

6. Those who are disinclined to study Feynman's papers on quantum mechanics or his lectures on physics or computation can still enjoy reading Richard P. Feynman, *The Pleasure of Finding Things Out: The Best Short Works of Richard P. Feynman* (Basic, 2005); and James Gleick, *Genius: The Life and Science of Richard Feynman* (Vintage, 1993).

7. See also the essays by Richard H. Immerman, Melvyn P. Leffler, Dipali Mukhopadhyay, and Janice Gross Stein in this volume.

8. Richard P. Feynman, "'Cargo Cult Science' Caltech 1974 Commencement Address," *Engineering and Science* 37, no. 7 (1974): 12

9. Robert Jervis, *How Statesmen Think: The Psychology of International Politics* (Princeton University Press, 2017), 10. On a personal note, I still recall meeting Jervis for the first time as an early lesson in how inferences can succumb to the representativeness fallacy. Jervis rushed in late to a Columbia experts' seminar on arms control dressed in his trademark khakis and Izod T-shirt, looking more like a goateed hippy just off the magic bus from Kathmandu than a distinguished professor. As the graduate student rapporteur of the seminar, I probably scowled disapprovingly, until he introduced himself. Could this person really be the author of one of the most compelling books I had read in the field—*Perception and Misperception in International Politics*? I struggled with my own attribution bias! One of my mentors at Columbia, Warner Schilling, gruffly complained that after Jervis arrived, the students were all seeing biases everywhere. "Whatever happened to normal error?" he demanded to know. In fact, it is well known that in *Perception and Misperception*, Jervis had set a high bar for determining the existence of bias in decision making. Bob and Warner were actually alike in their meticulous attention to historical detail, appreciation of pluralism in methods, and generous encouragement of young scholars.

10. These are emotional characteristics that CIA director (and former Russia hand) William Burns has frequently attributed to Vladimir Putin. See, for example, William J. Burns, "A World Transformed and the Role of Intelligence," 59th Ditchley Annual Lecture, July 1, 2023, https://www.russiamatters.org/analysis/world-transformed-and -role-intelligence-cia-director-william-j-burns-delivers-59th.

11. For a useful recent discussion, see Reid B. C. Pauly and Rose McDermott, "The Psychology of Nuclear Brinkmanship," *International Security* 47, no. 3 (2023): 9–51; and the H-Diplo|RJISSF roundtable review of the article with contributions by Jacques E. Hymans, Marika Landau-Wells, Joshua Rovner, and Janice Gross Stein, H-Diplo | Robert Jervis International Security Studies Forum Policy Roundtable II-5 on "The Psychology of Nuclear Brinkmanship," August 4, 2023, https://issforum.org/to/jprII-5.

12. For similar observations of this Jervis trait, see Jack Snyder, "Both Fox and Hedgehog: The Art of Nesting Structural and Perceptual Perspectives," in *Psychology, Strategy and Conflict*, ed. James W. Davis (Routledge, 2013), 13–24 at 14, and Marc Trachtenberg, "Robert Jervis and the Nuclear Question," in Davis, *Psychology, Strategy and Conflict*, 101–20 at 116.

13. Stephen Jay Gould, *Time's Arrow, Time's Cycle: Myth and Metaphor in the Discovery of Geological Time* (Harvard University Press, 1987).

14. Robert Jervis, "The Future of World Politics: Will It Resemble the Past?," *International Security* 16, no. 3 (1991): 39–73 at 43.

15. Jervis, "The Future of World Politics," 45.

16. Charles Perrow, *Normal Accidents: Living with High Risk Technologies* (Princeton University Press, 1984, rev. ed., 1999); and Garrett Hardin, "The Tragedy of the Commons," *Science* 162, no. 3859 (1968): 1243–48.

17. Werner Heisenberg, *Encounters with Einstein and Other Essays on People, Places and Particles* (Princeton University Press, 1989); and Aya Furuta, "One Thing Is Certain: Heisenberg's Uncertainty Principle Is Not Dead," *Scientific American*, March 8, 2012, https:// www.scientificamerican.com/article/heisenbergs-uncertainty-principle-is-not-dead/.

18. Jervis, *System Effects*. Jervis starts to develop the theoretical insights in *The Logic of Images in International Relations* (Princeton University Press, 1970) and in *Perception and Misperception in International Politics* (Princeton University Press, 1976).

19. Jervis added the emphasis, *System Effects*, 10.

20. Jervis, *System Effects*, 11.

21. Jervis, *System Effects*, 11.

22. Carl von Clausewitz, *On War*, ed. and trans. Michael Howard and Peter Paret (Princeton University Press, 1976), 85, 86, 156, 134, 136.

23. Clausewitz, *On War*, 158. For an insightful discussion, see Alan D. Beyerchen, "Clausewitz, Nonlinearity, and the Unpredictability of War," *International Security* 17, no. 3 (1992): 59–90.

24. Clausewitz, *On War*, 92.

25. Richard K. Betts, "Is Strategy an Illusion?," *International Security* 25, no. 2 (2000): 21.

26. Jervis, *System Effects*, 67–68; Albert O. Hirschman, *The Rhetoric of Reaction* (Harvard University Press, 1991).

27. Jervis, *System Effects*, 271–79.

28. Burns, "A World Transformed."

29. Jervis, *How Statesmen Think*, 223.

30. David E. Sanger et al., "Ukraine Wants the U.S. to Send More Powerful Weapons. Biden Is Not So Sure," *New York Times*, September 17, 2022; and Joshua Yaffa, "Inside the U.S. Effort to Arm Ukraine," *New Yorker*, October 17, 2022.

31. Robert Jervis, "The Nuclear Age: During and After the Cold War," in *Before and After the Fall: World Politics and the End of the Cold War*, ed. Nuno P. Monteiro and Fritz Bartel (Cambridge University Press, 2021), chap. 6 at 131; and Jervis, Keren Yarhi-Milo, and Don Casler, "Redefining the Debate Over Reputation and Credibility in International Security: Promises and Limits of New Scholarship," *World Politics* 73, no. 1 (2021): 167–203.

32. Jervis, *System Effects*, 213.

33. Jervis, *System Effects*, 195, 203.

34. François Heisbourg, "How to End a War: Some Historical Lessons for Ukraine," *Survival* 65, no. 4 (2023): 1–18. It is worth noting that German membership was considered vital to the Alliance and yet Germany still had to concede Königsberg while Estonia had no choice but to agree that Ivangorod would remain separated from Narva. Most recently, Finland surely abandoned hope of regaining Karelia and other territories seized by the USSR before joining NATO. (Only Porkkala was returned in 1956.)

35. "Biden Interview on Fareed Zakaria GPS," CNN, July 9, 2023, https://www.cnn.com/videos /tv/2023/07/09/exp-gps-0709-president-biden-on-nato-membership-and-ukraine.cnn.

36. Robert Jervis, *The Meaning of the Nuclear Revolution: Statecraft and the Prospect of Armageddon* (Cornell University Press, 1989), 74.

37. Jervis, "The Nuclear Age," 123.

38. Kenneth N. Waltz, "Nuclear Myths and Political Realities," *American Political Science Review* 84, no. 3 (1990): 730–45.

39. Charles L. Glaser, *Analyzing Strategic Nuclear Policy* (Princeton University Press, 1990); and Glaser and Steve Fetter, "Should the United States Reject MAD? Damage Limitation

and US Nuclear Strategy Toward China," *International Security* 41, no. 1 (2016): 49–98. See also Glaser, "Nuclear Revolution Theory Marches Forward," in *Book Review Roundtable: The Meaning of the Nuclear Revolution 30 Years Later* (Texas National Security Review, April 30, 2020), 20–30.

40. Robert Jervis, *The Illogic of American Nuclear Strategy* (Cornell University Press, 1984); and Jervis, *The Meaning of the Nuclear Revolution: Statecraft and the Prospect of Armageddon* (Cornell University Press, 1989). See also Robert Jervis, "Author Response: Reflection on *The Meaning of the Nuclear Revolution*, 30 Years Later," in *Book Review Roundtable: The Meaning of the Nuclear Revolution 30 Years Later* (Texas National Security Review, April 30, 2020). For critiques, see Scott D. Sagan, *Moving Targets: Nuclear Strategy and National Security* (Princeton University Press, 1989); Brendan Rittenhouse Green, *The Revolution That Failed: Nuclear Competition, Arms Control, and the Cold War* (Cambridge University Press, 2020); Green and Austin Long, "The MAD Who Wasn't There: Soviet Reactions to the Late Cold War Nuclear Balance," *Security Studies* 26, no. 4 (2017): 606–41; Long and Green, "Stalking the Secure Second Strike: Intelligence, Counterforce, and Nuclear Strategy," *Journal of Strategic Studies* 38, no. 1–2 (2014): 38–73; Keir A. Lieber and Daryl G. Press, "The New Era of Counterforce: Technological Change and the Future of Nuclear Deterrence," *International Security* 41, no. 4 (2017): 9–49; and Lieber and Press, *The Myth of the Nuclear Revolution: Power Politics in the Atomic Age* (Cornell University Press, 2020).

41. Jervis, "Author Response." See also the citations in note 40.

42. Bernard Brodie, ed., *The Absolute Weapon* (Harcourt, Brace, 1946); and Thomas C. Schelling, *The Strategy of Conflict* (Harvard University Press, 1960).

43. Jervis, *The Meaning of the Nuclear Revolution*, 45.

44. Jervis, *System Effects*, 12, citing Glenn H. Snyder, "The Balance of Power and the Balance of Terror," in *The Balance of Power*, ed. Paul Seabury (Chandler, 1965), 184–201.

45. Joseph R. Biden, "What America Will and Will Not Do in Ukraine," *New York Times*, May 31, 2022. See also Robert Jervis, *The Logic of Images in International Relations* (Princeton University Press, 1970); Jervis, "Signaling and Perception: Projecting Images and Drawing Inferences," in *How Statesmen Think*, chap. 5, 107–24.

46. Jervis, "The Nuclear Age," 118.

47. Thomas C. Schelling, *The Strategy of Conflict* (Harvard University Press, 1960), chap. 8; and Jervis, *System Effects*, 279. See also Alexander L. George and Richard Smoke, *Deterrence in American Foreign Policy: Theory and Practice* (Columbia University Press, 1974).

48. Jervis, *How Statesmen Think*, 232.

49. Jervis, "The Nuclear Age," 117.

50. For example, Jervis, *How Statesmen Think*, chap. 9, 191–215.

51. Robert Jervis, "Political Implications of Loss Aversion," *Political Psychology* 13, no. 2 (1992): 187–204 at 194.

52. George W. Downs and David M. Rocke, "Conflict, Agency, and Gambling for Resurrection: The Principal-Agent Problem Goes to War," *American Journal of Political Science* 38, no. 2 (1994): 362–80; and Hein Goemans, *War and Punishment: The Causes of War Termination and the First World War* (Princeton University Press, 2000).

53.   See especially Sergei Karaganov, "Primenenie yadernogo oruzhiia mozhet uberech' chelovechestvo ot global'noi katastrofy [The Use of Nuclear Weapons Can Save Humanity from a Global Catastrophe]," *Profil*, June 13, 2023. Karaganov is the honorary chairman of the Russian Council on Foreign and Defense Policy (SVOP) and chairman of the editorial board of *Russia in Global Affairs*, which reprinted this provocative article on its website in Russian and English under the title, "A Difficult but Necessary Decision." The journal's well-known editor-in-chief, Feodor Lukyanov, subsequently published a range of responses from other experts. Strikingly, on July 13, twenty prominent members of SVOP then published a statement that denounced nuclear blackmail and any use of nuclear weapons in combat. "O prizyvakh k razviazyvaniiu yadernoi voiny [On Calls to Unleash Nuclear War]," July 13, 2023, https://svop.ru/main/48156/. See also critical views in "Yadernaia voina—plokhoe sredstvo resheniia problem," *Kommersant*, June 21, 2023. Among the notable articles on this topic recently published in the Russian General Staff journal, *Military Thought*, is one coauthored by the deputy commander of the Russian Strategic Missile Forces (RVSN): Lieutenant-General I. R. Fazletdinov and Colonel (ret) V. I. Lumpov, "Rol' Raketnykh Voisk Strategicheskogo Naznacheniia v Protivodeistvii Strategicheskoi Mnogosfernoi Operatsii NATO [The Role of the Strategic Missile Forces in Countering NATO's Strategic Multi-Domain Operation]," *Voennaia mysl'*, no. 3 (March 2023): 53–63.

20

BRIDGING THE GAP BETWEEN PUBLIC
DISCOURSE AND SECRET INTELLIGENCE

RICHARD K. BETTS

My first encounter with Robert Jervis was half a century ago, as a first-year graduate student in his Government 230 seminar on theories of international politics. The syllabus was an ideal voluminous survey of the literature, and I cribbed from it six years later when, as a lecturer, I taught the course after Jervis's departure for UCLA. I recall Jervis's class in particular because Peter Katzenstein was in it (auditing?) and he regularly dominated the class discussion, but I remember it most clearly because of my pride in getting an A from Jervis—before the prevalence of grade inflation! I was a late bloomer academically and didn't take such a grade for granted. Many years later, at Jervis's sixtieth birthday party, I was gratified to see that he was a bit of a late bloomer too. At the party, he displayed copies of his old report cards from the Fieldston School, and I was pleasantly surprised to see a lot of B grades. Maybe for selfish reasons, I liked to think that he affirmed the notion that creativity and great intellectual achievements do not depend on early performance according to standard metrics.

I had only infrequent contact with Jervis for the next twenty years, but we shared an interest in developing the academic study of intelligence. He was arguably the dean of this field, which only emerged in a serious way at the end of the 1970s when waves of declassification began to provide reliable empirical material for study. He came to the subject through his work in political psychology, whereas I came to it via work on the staff of the original Senate investigation of US intelligence agencies (the Church Committee). This combination fueled some cross-fertilization, and we crossed paths occasionally in purveying our academic insights as consultants in the intelligence community. Although I've been primarily a policy analyst, Jervis was the consummate theorist, but unlike some eminent theorists, he was eager to apply his ideas to policy when opportunities arose and without the naiveté often found among cloistered academics about what constitutes real policy relevance.

Two examples illustrate how Jervis was one of the rare professors who succeeded in applying academic research and expertise to the policy process, a mission that is widely honored in principle but much less in practice. Most significant was his role in doing a large postmortem study on the causes of the American intelligence failure before the Iranian Revolution and hostage crisis of the late 1970s.[1] With the support of the intelligence agencies, he investigated how the analysts had operated, interpreted evidence, and made judgments and the ways in which cognitive and methodological limitations affected their products and the influence of those products. This was a lengthy and detailed exercise that attracted significant attention within the intelligence community. Its value was reflected in the frequency with which Jervis was called on in subsequent years to consult on other matters at high levels in the CIA and the intelligence community. Many years later, much of the study was declassified and Jervis plugged it into his book *Why Intelligence Fails: Lessons from the Iranian Revolution and the Iraq War*,[2] thus reversing the direction in which knowledge and insight flow between academia and the secret world.

A related example a quarter century after the original Iran study was a postmortem on the National Intelligence Estimate before the second war against Iraq, in which the estimate concluding that Iraq's president Saddam Hussein had biological and chemical weapons of mass destruction and an ongoing nuclear weapon development program proved wrong. This was a team exercise, with Jervis leading three other outside scholars (myself included) to assess how and why the analytical process broke down. Our work received enough attention at high levels that former Director of Central Intelligence George Tenet included some of its language (without attribution) in his memoirs. Jervis was also able to use enough of the conclusions from the exercise without violating classification that he could produce an article about it in *The Journal of Strategic Studies* soon afterward, in addition to the book mentioned earlier.[3]

Both examples showed Jervis's mastery of merging two normally quite separate worlds: academic expertise and public service involving secret information. This is, to say the least, a delicate and rare combination of activity, one that in principle should be honored by the two communities, which are both supposedly dedicated to discovering truth but which seldom interact enough to profit materially from each other's advantages in knowledge. As a practical matter, many academics are reluctant to become involved with secret intelligence agencies either out of ignorance of what they really do or fear that association might damage their reputations with colleagues for ideological reasons. Jervis did not worry about that, and his professional stature did not suffer. He succeeded in significant ways in bringing his expertise on psychology and international politics—the main basis of his academic status—into the awareness of government professionals. In recent decades, the surprising extent to which the CIA's and other agencies' training programs for analysts have placed serious emphasis on methodological issues involving cognitive processes and biases was probably driven to some degree by Bob's influence.

Perhaps because of the productive linkage among his academic expertise on psychology, his deep grounding in diplomatic history, and his access to professional insiders in the intelligence community who were engaged in analysis, Jervis was one of the leaders, arguably *the* leader, of the growing group of scholars who began to study and publish in a knowledgeable way about intelligence. Before the late 1970s, literature on the subject was mostly limited to work by journalists who were only lightly informed by reliable data or reliant on the assertions of insiders willing to ignore secrecy agreements or muckraking memoirs by dissident intelligence officers. The loosening of classification restraints in the last quarter of the twentieth century enabled study with greater depth and confidence of accuracy. Bob served on the editorial boards of both of the principal journals in the developing field: *Intelligence and National Security* and *Journal of Intelligence and Counterintelligence*. Within his discipline of political science, he was the most prestigious figure to work on the subject.

As influential as he was in policy circles compared to most academics, there were limits to how Jervis navigated the Washington world. Probably because of his work with the CIA, Jervis was apparently on a list of potential appointees in the incoming Clinton administration at the end of 1992 when I got a call from someone on the transition staff who was compiling information and opinions about candidates. I assume that I was contacted because I had previously spent fourteen years in the

Washington policy milieu, including several months on leave from the Brookings Institution as a foreign policy advisor in Walter Mondale's presidential campaign, and had some connections among insiders. I gave Jervis a strong recommendation, but then the caller asked, "Is he quirky?" I responded, "What do you mean?" He answered that he'd heard that Jervis dressed "unconventionally." What could I say, other than that unconventional was conventional in the academic world, and I knew Jervis was happy to dress appropriately when circumstances required because I had heard that he dressed up for the opera. I mention this only because in the various reminiscences about Jervis that I've heard in the days after his death, fondly humorous remarks about his clothing choices seem to pop up.

Another aspect of Jervis's personality that I kidded him about whenever possible was his Manhattanite provincialism—that is, his view, which is typical of many raised in the city, that it is the only place to be and, indeed, that there is scant reason ever to go anywhere else. This was a trait Jervis flaunted, albeit with an eye twinkle. An international affairs expert who had to be dragged into foreign travel—indeed, I don't believe he ever went to Asia—is unusual. When Harvard tried to recruit Jervis in the late 1980s, Samuel Huntington, originally a New Yorker himself, lamented to me that conversation had revealed they couldn't entice him because of his attachment to "the high life in Manhattan."

One of our colleagues once characterized Jervis as a "conflict avoider." At the time, this sounded like criticism for unwillingness to embrace contention forthrightly. Like our colleague, I too tend to prefer frank confrontation in most cases, but I wouldn't criticize the difference in Jervis's inclination if such it was. He did not avoid polite debate and was quite adept at making critical points indirectly or stepping up to aggressive argumentation on the rare occasions when importance and effectiveness demanded it. The milder diplomatic style may well have underwritten his success in leading the profession, and in any case, it had a strongly admirable side. As Ken Prewitt said in a Zoom meeting soon after Jervis's death, Jervis was a man who had no enemies. That was something unusual and laudable.

I owe many sorts of thanks to Jervis. He was a personal friend for the past thirty-plus years since I came to Columbia despite the many demands on his time not just as a professor called on by administrators more than most but as a leader of the profession outside. I had to love him because he appreciated my work more than many others. We often (definitely not always) shared a similar tilt in attitudes toward contending arguments, and when Jervis agreed with me in a debate with others, I took special comfort and confidence in my position. He is one of two especially eminent political scientists (Huntington the other) who supported my career progress and had faith in my work despite its not being in step with the main methodological trends of recent times. He was instrumental in getting me to Columbia at a time when I was, in a sense, damaged goods, the president of another great university having just vetoed my appointment after it had been voted by its government department. He supported me beyond the call of duty several times along the way in my career—something doubtless legions of his friends, colleagues, and disciples would also say.

These recollections dwell on Bob Jervis's personal relationship more than his intellectual influence on me. The latter was not so much in specific matters of research as in simply being a model of theoretical innovation, intellectual breadth, and erudition. If any critic ever mounted a major attack on any of Jervis's ideas or writings, let alone a telling one, I missed it. Jervis and I shared the devotion to accumulating, annotating, and relying heavily on books, which used to be typical of academics but has become less so in the computer age. His appreciation of the empirical discipline that psychology and history should impose on political science rang ever truer in the heyday of rational choice theory and emulation of economics. That Jervis was chosen as president of the American Political Science Association at the same time that the latter trends were ascendant (and that he supported as a fellow traveler and intellectual pluralist) is especially powerful testimony to his stature. Indeed, he had no enemies—personally, intellectually, or professionally.

NOTES

1. See Richard H. Immerman's chapter in this volume.
2. Robert Jervis, *Why Intelligence Fails: Lessons from the Iranian Revolution and the Iraq War* (Cornell University Press, 2010).
3. Robert Jervis, "Reports, Politics, and Intelligence Failures," *Journal of Strategic Studies* 29 (2006): 3–52.

IV

ROBERT JERVIS, HISTORY, AND HISTORIANS

21

THEORIST AND METHODOLOGIST

JACK S. LEVY

The passing of Robert Jervis is a devastating loss for the profession and a personal loss for so many. Jervis touched everyone he met with his kindness, generosity, integrity, and humor, as well as the power of his intellect. I was never Bob's student or close colleague at Columbia. Yet his work on misperception, learning, signaling, deterrence, conflict spirals, and offense-defense theory, among other topics, had a greater impact on my intellectual development than that of any other scholar. Bob influenced my career in other ways as well. He welcomed me to his Columbia faculty seminars in international relations and political psychology when I first arrived at Rutgers in 1989, which helped integrate me into the terrific international relations community at Columbia. Later, Bob arranged for me to teach PhD seminars in the department. These opportunities made my intellectual life much more interesting and rewarding.

For the last half century, Jervis was one of the most influential scholars in the international relations field—and for many of us, he was *the* most influential. The breadth of Jervis's contributions to the study of international relations and foreign policy is stunning, ranging across all levels of analysis from individual psychology to organizational politics and processes to the dynamics of international systems and the nuclear revolution.[1] With other contributors to this volume covering many of these topics, I focus here on the often neglected importance of social science methodology in much of Jervis's research. First, however, I want to make some brief comments highlighting the interdisciplinary nature of Jervis's scholarly orientation and influence and his role in the development of the subfield of the political psychology of international relations.

The scope of Jervis's scholarly contributions extends beyond international relations to other fields of political science and to other disciplines as well. In fact, it is hard to think of many political scientists with a stronger interdisciplinary orientation. This is evident in Jervis's first book, *The Logic of Images in International Relations*, where he wrote in the acknowledgments that the two greatest influences on that study were the economist Thomas Schelling and the sociologist Erving Goffman.[2] In *Perception and Misperception in International Politics*, Jervis built both on a wide range of theoretical and experimental research in social psychology to formulate his theoretical arguments and on an unparalleled familiarity with secondary (and often primary) sources in diplomatic history to illustrate those patterns. This interdisciplinary breadth is also clear to readers of *System Effects*, which draws on extensive readings in evolutionary biology, ecology, ethology, sociology, organization theory, and other fields.

Jervis's scholarly work both influenced other disciplines and was informed by them. As one example, the important conceptual distinction in *The Logic of Images* between signals (which can easily be manipulated by the sender) and indices (which are not manipulable) was not only central to later work on costly signaling in international relations but also incorporated by the economist Michael Spence into his formal theory of economic signaling, which led to Spence's 2001 Nobel Memorial Prize in Economic Sciences.[3]

The core of *The Logic of Images* involves deductive theorizing about strategic interaction between states in the context of uncertainty and incentives for strategic deceit. A central theme in the book is that all signals, costly and otherwise, are infused with meaning and interpreted through different analytic lenses by different receivers with different worldviews and different formative experiences.[4] Jervis develops this line of argument more fully in his subsequent research on the psychology of perception, beginning with his 1976 book *Perception and Misperception in International Politics*.

Perception and Misperception is one of the most influential publications in the international relations field of the last half century. Before the 1960s, the study of psychology and foreign policy was mainly the province of social psychologists and personality theorists.[5] Jervis's 1976 book synthesizes many disparate propositions and findings in social psychology into a more integrated theoretical framework. The book marks the birth of the systematic study of the psychology of foreign policy and international relations. *Perception and Misperception* also marks an important advance in the relatively new field of foreign policy analysis, where early efforts to develop theoretical frameworks gave relatively little role to psychological factors.[6] The study of the psychology of foreign policy and international interactions has subsequently occupied an increasingly important place in international relations, accelerating significantly in the past decade. Although research has shifted in a more experimental direction, Jervis's theoretical insights continue to guide the subfield. Jervis contributed further to the broader study of political psychology in both political science and social psychology through his role as coeditor of the first edition of the *Handbook of Political Psychology*.[7]

Jervis also interacted on a regular basis with diplomatic historians.[8] He published his work in history journals. These publications generally involve the application of core international relations concepts to consequential historical episodes. Jervis's numerous writings on the Cold War are a good example. He asked, for example, whether the Cold War was a security dilemma.[9] In this and other studies, Jervis used theory to help better understand history while using history to refine our theoretical concepts. The same is true of Jervis's writings on the Concert of Europe, where he engaged the question of the extent to which the Concert constituted traditional balance of power politics or a new kind of security regime.[10]

This ongoing interaction with diplomatic historians helped shape Jervis's views of the differences (and similarities) between diplomatic historians and international relations scholars who were trained in political science in their respective studies of essentially the same subject matter. Particularly notable is an exchange on this topic with the historian Paul Schroeder (and others), where Jervis articulated many of his views on the philosophy of science and on how one goes about what he regarded as the primary task of establishing causation in historical research.[11] I return to those ideas later. Jervis also served as a coeditor of a volume of some of Schroeder's most important articles.[12] After Schroeder's death in 2020,

Jervis (along with Diane Labrosse) organized a forum on the importance of Schroeder's scholarship both for diplomatic history and for international relations.[13]

In the process of engaging with scholarly work in multiple disciplines, Jervis was exposed to a variety of methodologies and theoretical orientations. Although Jervis is widely and correctly regarded as one of the leading theoreticians of international relations, the methodological sophistication of much of his work and some important lessons we can draw from it are often overlooked. The term "methodology" has acquired multiple meanings, but if we define the concept broadly to include issues of philosophy of science and research design, Jervis was a social science methodologist as well as a theoretician.

One theme running through many of Jervis's theoretical analyses is the importance of constructing and testing alternative explanations for observed behavior and of specifying in advance what kinds of evidence would be most useful in validating one causal explanation over another. This idea runs throughout *Perception and Misperception*, beginning with the statement in the introduction that the neglect of structural explanations leads to "over-psychologizing" behavior that can be better explained by political variables.[14] Jervis was well aware of the difficulties associated with constructing research designs that effectively distinguish among different alternative explanations. A good example comes from chapter 6 on "How Decision-Makers Learn from History." Jervis hypothesized that decision makers sometimes use historical analogies to guide their policy preferences, attributing a causal role to those analogies. But Jervis highlighted two leading threats to valid causal inference. In one, the causal arrow is reversed, with leaders strategically selecting a historical analogy that bolsters their preexisting policy preferences. In the second, a third variable shapes both historical lessons and current preferences, so that the inference of a causal relationship between historical analogies and policy preferences is spurious. Jervis then outlined a series of comparisons that can help distinguish among these competing explanations.

Jervis subsequently reflected on his analysis of learning from history in his study of differences between diplomatic historians and international relations scholars. He contrasted his approach in *Perception and Misperception* with historian Ernest May's analysis in *Lessons of the Past*.[15] After noting the greater value political scientists place on theoretical generalization, Jervis again emphasized the importance of ruling out alternative explanations for validating causal claims. Referring to the different methodological approaches of the two disciplines, Jervis argued that his "excursions" (into comparisons to eliminate alternative explanations) are "irrelevant if not confusing" for historians but critical in establishing causation for political scientists.[16]

This line of argument reflects another underlying difference between the two disciplines: political scientists treat a historical case not as an end in itself, as historians generally do, but as an instance of a broader class of phenomena. The political scientist always asks, "What is this a case of?" This led Jervis to note another fundamental difference in the nature of explanation in the two disciplines. For historians, "explanation is more deeply embedded in the description" and in fact inseparable from that description, whereas political scientists insist on a much sharper separation between explanation and description. When political scientists read history, Jervis argued, they are "annoyed that the discussion of what happened is entangled with an analysis of why it happened." This annoyance reflects the social science principle that a theoretical explanation must be constructed independently of the data on which it is to be tested.[17]

Another good example of the priority Jervis placed on the kinds of research designs most useful in empirically discriminating among alternative explanations for observed phenomena is his study of the causal impact of individual leaders, which is a natural follow-up to his earlier study of the sources of individual perception and misperception. In fact, the importance of research design is reflected in the second half of the title of his article, "Do Leaders Matter and How Would We Know?"[18] Jervis identified several possible reasons why individuals might not matter: they might come to power with the same values and beliefs; they might be socialized once they take office; or they might be constrained (or enabled) by international or domestic pressures (or opportunities). He suggested the kinds of comparisons that might empirically differentiate among these rival explanations. But he also noted the limits of comparison as a methodology for determining whether and how much leaders matter. Jervis noted, among other things, the difficulty of assessing the various ways in which the situations faced by different leaders are different, complicating efforts to rule out the alternative explanation that situational differences explain variations in behavior.[19]

Jervis then briefly considered the possible utility of counterfactual analysis to analyze whether a different leader, if they had been in power, would have acted in the same way. Jervis suggested that counterfactuals might be useful if the imagined leader in the counterfactual world was a plausible one given the politics of the country and if the hypothetical change in leaders was the only thing that changed.[20] In an earlier commentary on counterfactuals, however, after writing that counterfactuals are both "useful and tricky," Jervis expressed skepticism. He emphasized the interconnectedness of the world and the impossibility of changing just one thing and argued that counterfactuals "cannot be employed to help us imagine a world that is like our own in all ways except for one."[21]

This emphasis on the interconnectedness of the world and the resulting causal complexity,[22] along with the argument that political scientists place greater value than do historians on "explicit, parsimonious theorizing," generated another interesting line of argument. Jervis argued that because historians explore historical cases in much more detail than do international relations scholars with political science training, historians are generally more willing to embrace causal complexity. As such, Jervis argued that "historians are less troubled than political scientists by multiple sufficient causation—i.e., the possibility that the same outcome or behavior can be produced by different causes and through quite different pathways." Jervis went on to say that the possibility of multiple causal pathways is a "real problem" for political science because it is a "menace to one of its prime methodologies."[23]

This is an extremely important point, although Jervis did not elaborate. What I think he was getting at is that multiple sufficient causation is not easily analyzed through multiple regression analysis or related statistical techniques, which are the bedrock of quantitative statistical studies in social science.[24] The importance of causal factors that rarely have an impact but are overwhelmingly important when they arise is difficult to capture through methods that measure average causal effects. These kinds of concerns about the limitations of standard regression models for dealing with causal complexity led some social scientists to adopt Boolean and related fuzzy-set methods.[25]

Although Jervis embraced many aspects of qualitative methodology in the study of international relations, he also recognized some of its limitations and noted particular aspects of historical methodology that international relations scholars would do well to emulate. He emphasized the advantages of parsimonious explanation but conceded that it limits our ability to explain individual cases.[26] He embraced the importance of the comparative method and noted the costs to historiography in failing to make more use of it (comparative history being an exception), but he acknowledged the importance of temporal sequence. Jervis criticized the common practice among international relations scholars of conducting comparative cases studies based on the assumption that sequential cases are independent. He argued that international relations scholars would benefit from paying more attention to chronology and to the interdependence of sequential historical episodes, and from exploring the extent to which one set of events influences subsequent perceptions and behavior and through what mechanisms.

Another example of Jervis's concern with issues of research design involves his emphasis on the importance of case selection. He argued that "dogs that do not bark"—events that do not occur despite theoretical predictions that they should occur—can be quite revealing, as Sherlock Holmes famously recognized in "The Hound of the Baskervilles."[27] Given the potential importance of such nonevents or "negative cases," Jervis emphasized the standard injunction to avoid selecting on the dependent variable.[28] In his extensive work on intelligence failure, in academic writings and for the policy community, Jervis criticized the common tendency of students of intelligence failure to focus exclusively on cases of intelligence failure and to neglect cases of intelligence success. He repeatedly pleaded for more attention to the latter as a means of better understanding the former through theoretically guided comparisons.[29]

One can find other examples of Jervis's emphasis on the importance of case selection in his book *System Effects*. Jervis addressed the key balance of power proposition that states balance against concentrations of power or threat. If this is correct, he argued, strong powers increasing in strength should anticipate that their growing power or threatening behavior might induce other states to balance against them. Consequently, potentially dominant states might avoid aggressive actions and behave more moderately. However, there are other potential sources of moderation. How much causal weight do we attribute to the anticipation of balancing? We might look at a larger number of cases, but because moderation induced by the anticipation of balancing leaves few traces in the historical record (though primary sources might be revealing), we cannot count all of the cases in which it plays an important role.[30]

This argument has important implications for a standard research practice for testing the hypothesis that great powers tend to balance against stronger powers or the greatest threat. In this design, the researcher examines a number of wars and assesses the extent to which great powers engage in balancing against the hegemonic threat. But this neglects the many but uncertain number of cases in which the strongest power refrains from aggressive behavior to avoid the anticipated balancing by others. Balancing plays a central causal role in the outcome, but the practice of selecting on wars and not including nonwars underestimates the causal impact of balancing.

Jervis's commitment to social science methodology is also evident in his policy-relevant writings and consulting. He worked with the Central Intelligence Agency on the question of the sources of intelligence failure. He was tasked with conducting detailed studies of US intelligence failures associated with the 1979 Iranian Revolution and the 2003 Iraq War.[31] One of his central conclusions was that a major cause of intelligence failure is that intelligence analysts do not think like social scientists—and that they should be trained to do so. Jervis wrote the following:

> Intelligence and postmortems on failures can benefit from using standard social science methods. . . . In many cases both intelligence and criticisms of it have only a weak understanding of the links between evidence and inferences. . . . They do not formulate testable hypotheses and so often rely on beliefs that cannot be falsified, leave crucial assumptions unexplicated and unexamined, fail to ask what evidence should be present if their arguments are correct, ignore the diagnostic value of absent evidence, and fail to employ the comparative method and so assert causation without looking at instances in which the supposed causal factor was absent as well as at cases in which it is present.[32]

One should not infer from Jervis's commitment to social science methodology that he was excessively optimistic that following proper methods would always lead to accurate conclusions about the nature of cause and effect in international politics. The theoretical insights developed in *System Effects*, which Jervis regarded as his most important book,[33] have enormously important methodological implications. Building on theories of complexity, Jervis emphasized that everything is connected to everything else; "we can never do merely one thing"; causal relationships are often interactive; nonlinear relationships, third-party behavior, and negative and positive feedback generate unintended consequences; and actors coevolve with their environments. All of this can make it difficult to trace causation, especially when actors are guided in part by their own theories of how the world works. These considerations led Jervis to recognize the limitations of knowledge, to be cautious in his own claims, and to always be alert to evidence that would require a modification of his views.[34] This epistemological stance, along with his personal attributes, help to explain the quality of humility in Jervis that many have noted in their remembrances.[35]

In conclusion, it is fair to say that Jervis was first and foremost a theoretician but one who loved history and who was committed to "bridging the gap" and using theory to inform policy. He recognized, however, that good policy requires good theory, that good theory requires empirical validation, and that this process must be guided by appropriate research designs. In this critical sense, Robert Jervis was a social science methodologist as well as a theoretician.[36]

NOTES

1. Robert Jervis, *Perception and Misperception in International Politics* (Princeton University Press, 1976; 2nd ed., 2017); Jervis, *Why Intelligence Fails: Lessons from the Iranian Revolution and the Iraq War* (Cornell University Press, 2010); Jervis, *System Effects: Complexity in Political and Social Life* (Princeton University Press, 1997); Jervis, *The Meaning of the Nuclear Revolution* (Cornell University Press, 1989).

2. Robert Jervis, *The Logic of Images in International Relations* (Princeton University Press, 1970).

3. Michael Spence, *Market Signaling: Informational Transfer in Hiring and Related Screening Processes* (Harvard University Press, 1974).

4. This has important methodological implications for the study of the sending and receiving of signals and suggests some limitations of rational choice models.

5. A useful review that influenced Jervis is Joseph de Rivera, *The Psychological Dimension of Foreign Policy* (Charles E. Merrill, 1968).

6. Influential early work in the theory of foreign policy includes Richard C. Snyder, H. W. Bruck, and Burton Sapin, *Foreign Policy Decision-Making* (Palgrave, 1962); Graham T. Allison, *Essence of Decision: Explaining the Cuban Missile Crisis* (Little Brown, 1971).

7. David O. Sears, Leonie Huddy, and Robert Jervis, eds., *The Oxford Handbook of Political Psychology* (Oxford University Press, 2003). The *Handbook* is now in its third edition.

8. Jervis was the founding editor of the International Security Studies Forum (ISSF) in 2009, linking up with H-Diplo. H-Diplo/ISSF has provided the central platform for interactions between diplomatic/international historians and international relations scholars trained in political science. In honor of Jervis's founding role and tireless work, in January 2023, ISSF was renamed the Robert Jervis International Security Studies Forum (RJISSF; https://issforum.org/). See Diane Labrosse's chapter in this volume. In the 1990s, Jervis worked with Paul Kennedy at Yale to bring together diplomatic historians at Yale and political scientists at Columbia (and some affiliates) for discussions of World War I. See the chapter in this volume by Volker Berghahn and Paul Kennedy's online essay, "Robert Jervis: My Diplomatic History Buddy," in "Tribute to the Life, Scholarship, and Legacy of Robert Jervis, Part I," ed. Richard H. Immerman, Diane Labrosse, and Marc Trachtenberg, *H-Diplo/ISSF*, February 4, 2022, https://issforum.org/ISSF/PDF/ISSF -Jervis-Tribute-1.pdf. Few if any political scientists can match Jervis's familiarity with historical details associated with the outbreak and diplomacy of World War I.

9. Robert Jervis, "Was the Cold War a Security Dilemma?," *Journal of Cold War Studies*, 3, no. 1 (2001): 36–60.

10. Robert Jervis, "A Political Science Perspective on the Balance of Power and the Concert," *American Historical Review* 97, no. 3 (1992): 716–24.

11. Robert Jervis, "International History and International Politics: Why Are They Studied Differently?," and Paul W. Schroeder, "International History: Why Historians Do It Differently Than Political Scientists," in *Bridges and Boundaries: Historians, Political Scientists, and the Study of International Relations*, ed. Colin Elman and Miriam Fendius Elman (MIT Press, 2001).

12. Paul W. Schroeder, *Systems, Stability, and Statecraft: Essays on the International History of Modern Europe*, ed. David Wetzel, Robert Jervis, and Jack S. Levy (Palgrave Macmillan, 2004).

13. Robert Jervis et al., "Forum 28 on The Importance of Paul Schroeder's Scholarship to the Fields of International Relations and Diplomatic History," ed. Jervis and Diane N. Labrosse, *H-Diplo/RJISSF*, September 10, 2021, https://issforum.org/forums/28#PDF.

14. Jervis, *Perception and Misperception*, 4.

15. Ernest R. May, *"Lessons" of the Past: The Use and Abuse of History in American Foreign Policy* (Oxford University Press, 1973).

16. Jervis, "International History and International Politics," 394–95.

17. Jervis, "International History and International Politics," 394–96.

18. Robert Jervis, "Do Leaders Matter and How Would We Know?," *Security Studies* 22, no. 2 (2013): 153–79.

19. In this context, Jervis notes in "Do Leaders Matter?," 158, that "methodologically, the deaths of leaders (especially from natural causes) are a godsend because they usually eliminate this possibility of endogeneity" (different situations enabling or constraining the rise of particular kinds of leaders). He notes, however, that even this natural experiment (not his term) is not perfect. New leaders may want to continue the policies of a

popular president or to differentiate themselves from unpopular presidents even if they agree with some of their policies.

20. Jervis, "Do Leaders Matter?," 160.

21. Robert Jervis, "Counterfactuals, Causation, and Complexity," in *Counterfactual Thought Experiments in World Politics: Logical, Methodological, and Psychological Perspectives*, ed. Philip E. Tetlock and Aaron Belkin (Princeton University Press, 1996), 316.

22. These were central themes in Jervis, *System Effects*.

23. Jervis, "International History and International Politics," 392. Note that this statement goes beyond the common argument that events have multiple causes. The concept of "sufficient causation" suggests that there are two or more sets of causes, and that the presence of any one of these combinations of causes guarantees the outcome.

24. The same is true for hypotheses involving necessary conditions. True, one can add interaction terms to capture causal complexity, but such models would face problems of statistical separation.

25. Charles C. Ragin, *The Comparative Method: Moving Beyond Qualitative and Quantitative Strategies* (University of California Press, 1987); Ragin, *Fuzzy-Set Social Science* (University of Chicago Press, 2000).

26. Despite Jervis's interest in history, interactions with historians, and publications in history journals, his preference for reasonably parsimonious explanations (but certainly not monocausal ones) is clear from his earliest scholarly days. As he wrote in the first chapter of his first book, "one of the best routes to international relations theory does not lie in an attempt to deal with all the significant variables operating in any case, but rather in the attempt to see what the world would look like if only a few dominant influences were at work." Jervis, *Logic of Images*, 15–16.

27. Jervis, "International History and International Politics," 390–402.

28. The warning against selecting on the dependent variable is drilled into all graduate students in political science but often without an important qualification. If a hypothesis posits a necessary condition for an outcome, the only observations that can falsify the hypothesis are those where a particular outcome of the dependent variable occurs despite the absence of its hypothesized necessary condition. This means that an optimal research design for testing necessary condition hypotheses involves selecting on positive instances of the dependent variable.

29. Jervis, *Why Intelligence Fails*.

30. Jervis, *System Effects*, 139.

31. See the essays by Richard H. Immerman, Michael Warner, Melvyn P. Leffler, and Dipali Mukhopadhyay in the section "Robert Jervis as Public Intellectual: Post Mortems and the CIA's Historical Review Panel," as well as that of Janice Gross Stein in this volume.

32. Jervis, *Why Intelligence Fails*, 3.

33. Robert Jervis, "How I Got Here," H-Diplo Essay 198 on Learning the Scholar's Craft: Reflections of Historians and International Relations, March 4, 2020, 7, https://hdiplo .org/to/E198.

34. This latter point informs Jervis's explanation for the US intelligence community's erroneous conclusions, prior to the 2003 Iraq War, regarding Iraq's possible development of

weapons of mass destruction (WMD). Jervis argued that the problem was not so much intelligence analysts' initial estimate that Iraq had an ongoing WMD program but their failure to ask the question "How would we know if we were wrong?" and to actively search for information that might contradict their initial estimate. Jervis, *Why Intelligence Fails*.

35. I am struck by Jervis's description of the evolution of his thinking about the deterrence model and the spiral model, in "How I Got Here," 4. Jervis wrote that he began his analysis of the two models as alternative descriptions of and prescriptions for the Cold War "with a strong bias toward deterrence." But after further theoretical refection, writing *Perception and Misperception*, and immersion in many historical cases, he gained "more sympathy for the spiral model." He concluded, "In the end, while I continue to study and teach about the Cold War, my conclusions remain fluid." Jervis was always eager to push his arguments as far as theory, logic, and evidence would allow but not beyond.

36. I made this argument a few years ago at a conference honoring Jervis's scholarly contributions. Jervis was amused and responded that "most people do not think of me as a methodologist."

22

READING ROBERT JERVIS

VLADISLAV ZUBOK

At one point in 1983, I discovered the work of Robert Jervis by rummaging through American political science journals in a special secret section of the Library of the Institute for US and Canadian Studies (ISKAN). I became involved in research on nuclear strategy and arms control, eminently topical subjects during the time of the "second Cold War" and the heightened tensions between NATO and the Warsaw Pact. It was a year of great anxiety. At one meeting of the institute's senior scholars, I was stunned to learn that they were earnestly discussing the possibility of a first nuclear strike by the Reagan administration. It is hard for me now to remember the date, but it was probably after the Soviets accidentally shot down the KAL-008 passenger plane near Sakhalin on September 1, 1983, which triggered outrage in the United States—from President Ronald Reagan and Secretary of State George Schultz to the general public. At some point, one ISKAN expert said something along the lines of: "Anyone who at least once visited New York City should understand that Americans would never start a nuclear war." This essentially ended the debate.

Jervis's writings on perception and misperception hit the nail on the head for me.[1] They resonated with the discussions we had at ISKAN about American intentions. I also liked the clarity of his language: he reasoned together with the reader, not condescendingly; did not abuse political science lingo; and unlike some other scholars, showed empathy with those on the other side of the conflict.

The next stage of my familiarization with Jervis's works occurred during much brighter times. Soviet leader Mikhail Gorbachev was trying to lead the Soviet Union out of the Cold War. In the winter of 1988–1989, the ISKAN sent me on a "scholarly leave" to Washington for six months. The atmosphere inside the Soviet Embassy compound, where I resided, was still one of a besieged fortress, and perestroika had yet to penetrate its gates. My supervisor, Andrei Kokoshin, called his US colleagues at the Brookings Institution, and they offered me, a young scholar, a nice arrangement: I could sit in a reading room on 1775 Massachusetts Avenue and read historical and political science journals in a cozy library.

Notwithstanding my love for numbers during my school years, many of the articles were full of jargon and math that I struggled to understand. Jervis's publications impressed me again: they were lucid in logic and accessible in expression.[2] I was a trained historian, not a political scientist. Yet much to my surprise, I learned more from Jervis about how to interpret international history than from the work of many of historians, Russian and Western. For me, Jervis was a historian's political scientist. Reading his secondary sources made me wonder how he found time to read so much in so many subsections of international political history. He dipped into primary sources to prove that the Korean War, not preexisting causes, had created the phenomenon of the high-pitched Cold War on American soil and in the minds of US policymakers.

Jervis went against the "revisionist" New Left in doing this but also against the deterministic current that continues to dominate political science today. How many contemporary international relations scholars dip into a fresh volume in the *Foreign Relations of the United States* series in order to corroborate or falsify their conclusions? And how many send their manuscripts to a group of leading historians in order to consult with them on those conclusions? In *The Meaning of the Nuclear Revolution*, Jervis wrote that the analysis should take into account what statesmen and military do not do as well as what they do: "As we know . . . dogs that do not bark can provide crucial evidence. But as we also know . . . most people are slow to realize this. Things that have not happened do not call attention to themselves and are easy to overlook."[3] How many scholars today dare to add to their arguments "evidence" from the Sherlock Holmes mysteries? Jervis also used the Bible and Mark Twain's witticisms to clarify his theoretical points on contingency and human agency.

Above all, Jervis was keen on the peculiarities of human cognition and the roots of misperceptions and errors. For a young scholar from the Soviet Union, where a supposedly omniscient and infallible politburo ruled, the latter aspect was particularly fascinating and revealing. Even at that time, I suspected that a "rational actor" in politics existed only in the imagination of theorists, just like "classes" existed in Marxist schemes. Inside the Soviet compound, I could see a model of different behavior: everyone from the KGB officers to the wives of diplomats acted like perfect Soviet conformists in public, yet their material interests were far from the "socialist" ideals. They behaved rather like frugal and pragmatic shoppers, and their main material idol was the US dollar, a key to the treasure trove of American consumer goods. This rational consumption model, however, did not prevent them from entertaining the most hilarious anti-American stereotypes, as if they lived not in the US capital but in an isolated ideological cul-de-sac. Life inside the compound made me think about the rationality and logic of all this, and Jervis came to my assistance.

Sometime in the spring of 1989, I had a chance to meet Bob Jervis for the first time. It was at one of the conferences I was invited to, probably at Columbia University. With his special sensitivity for history and his personal experience (he traveled to the Soviet Union for the first time in 1961), Jervis realized early on that Gorbachev's "new thinking" pointed to a fundamental change. He argued that Gorbachev's support for abolishing the danger of nuclear war, and his pronouncement that the principles of nonuse of force in international affairs, "may be the most important development in word politics since 1945." He did not analyze the objectives at that point because of their novelty. Nevertheless, he prudently expressed doubt that they would lead to the abolition of nuclear weapons.[4]

A quarter of a century later, when I focused my research on the Soviet collapse, my approach was again influenced by Jervis, perhaps even more than I realized. Just like him, I was fascinated by the role of contingency and human agency, rapid change, and misperception in history. Like him, I read Nassim Nicholas Taleb's popular work and remained skeptical regarding the conceptual vagueness of "black swans."[5] All his life, Jervis studied the impact of ideas, observations, and intelligence on political decisions, and I did the same when sorting through mammoth amounts of evidence from 1989 to 1991 on the behavior of Gorbachev and his successor, Boris Yeltsin. In 2006, Jervis wrote, "Gorbachev followed his reforms only because he expected them to revitalize rather than destroy the Soviet Union. If he had known what he was actually accomplishing, he would not have done it."[6]

In my investigation, I could recognize that both Gorbachev and Yeltsin consistently asserted that their policies remained the only available alternatives that could preserve the Soviet Union—and yet those policies were aimed in two completely incompatible directions. It was only when I finished my book on the Soviet collapse that I discovered the quotation that Bob had used from Charles Kurzman about the Iranian Revolution of 1979: "the revolution suddenly went from being unthinkable to being inevitable."[7] This was exactly what happened in Moscow in 1989–1990. In any case, I used a similar phrase in describing the shift of perceptions on the Soviet collapse in the West and in Russia.

My book came out only one month before Jervis passed away, so he did not read it.[8] For me, this compounded the sadness about his death because he would have been a fantastic reader and critic. No doubt, he would have found all kinds of shortcomings in my arguments: confirmation bias, excessive hindsight, insufficient testing of alternative hypotheses, and more. Still, he would have been intensely interested in the subject, as he had always been with regard to monumental historical events that had occurred in opposition to all of the predictions of social and political scientists.

Most political scientists do not prioritize this unpredictability and contingency as much as Jervis did. The mainstream of political science today is not prepared to interpret rapid, not to mention calamitous, changes. As I am writing this essay, I am thinking about a recent article by my friend, the Italian political scientist Giovanni Orsina. He points to the three fallacies in Western political science literature today: using history for illustrative purposes; ignoring anthropology and psychology in favor of rational agency; and equating modernization, as well as democracy, with a "natural law."[9] Bob was a lifelong liberal democrat, yet his writings reveal a scholar who was deeply sensitized to historic experience, curious about the illogical nature of human thinking, especially decision making, and never triumphalist about "Western values" or the collective wisdom of the "international community." His critical and realistic voice is badly missed.

One of the lessons that Jervis drew from his studies of international history is the danger of "overlearning" from the past. "A recent and important event is likely to leave a deep imprint on people," wrote Jervis in 2006, "especially if they were in error."[10] Not only individuals but also bureaucracies, organizations, and network institutions like the Western commentariat find this lesson extremely hard to follow. The "overlearning" effect shaped multiple developments in contemporary international politics. US officials during the presidency of George H. W. Bush "overlearned" from the failure of détente, and the reductionist lessons that they drew made them remain skeptical of Soviet reforms even when they saw revolutionary changes, such as the 1989 Round Table Talks in Poland and economic reforms and announcement of competitive elections in the Soviet Union during the first months of 1989. The administration of Bush's son, George W. Bush, "overlearned" from the catastrophe of 9/11 and allowed themselves to be guided not by rational calculus but by a toxic brew of fear, arrogance of American power, and a hubris that was rooted in a belief in exceptional American greatness. This led the United States into another quagmire of "democracy building" in Iraq and Afghanistan.[11]

And in Russia, the same "overlearning" effect, tinged by the sense of a colossal failure of the 1990s, made the Russian president Vladimir Putin come to the conclusion that the invasion of Ukraine was the only option to preempt NATO expansion into Ukraine and the Western challenge to the legitimacy of his regime. This invasion, in turn, brought forward everything that the Western commentariat had "overlearned" from the Munich appeasement of German dictator Adolf Hitler in 1938, peppered with quotations of the military theorist Carl von Clausewitz.

Failure of reason is human, common, and unexceptional. As long as humans make estimates and decisions, they will repeat the same mistakes again and again. Jervis knew this very well, but the realization did not diminish his respect for social science, expertise, and its predictive power. Nor did it diminish his determination to bring to the attention of policymakers, scholars, and the public the ubiquitous errors to which we are all vulnerable in an effort to at least mitigate the consequences of them. In this, Robert Jervis offered yet another good lesson for all of us who continue to observe and study human history.

NOTES

1. Most notably, Robert Jervis, *Perception and Misperception in International Politics* (Princeton University Press, 1976). This book appeared in new editions in 2015 and 2017.

2. See, for instance, Robert Jervis, *The Meaning of the Nuclear Revolution: Statecraft and the Prospect of Armageddon* (Cornell University Press, 1989), and Jervis, "The Political Influence of Nuclear Weapons," *International Security* 13 (1988): 80–90.

3. Jervis, *The Meaning of the Nuclear Revolution*, 154.

4. Jervis, *The Meaning of the Nuclear Revolution*, ix.

5. Nassim Taleb, *The Black Swan: The Impact of the Highly Improbable* (Penguin, 2010).

6. Robert Jervis, "Black Swans in Politics," *Critical Review* 21, no. 4 (2009): 485.

7. Charles Kurzman, *The Unthinkable Revolution in Iran* (Harvard University Press, 2004). Quoted in Jervis, "Black Swans," 486.

8. Vladislav Zubok, *Collapse: The Fall of the Soviet Union* (Yale University Press, 2021).

9. Giovanni Orsina, "Political Science as a Modernist Project," unpublished manuscript, courtesy of the author, 2022.

10. Robert Jervis, "Reports, Politics, and Intelligence Failures: The Case of Iraq," *Journal of Strategic Studies* 29, no. 1 (2006): 3–52, 28–29.

11. Melvyn P. Leffler, *Confronting Saddam Hussein: George W. Bush and the Invasion of Iraq* (Oxford University Press, 2023).

23

REMEMBERING ROBERT JERVIS

MARC TRACHTENBERG

R obert Jervis's death still does not seem real to me. He certainly remains very much alive in my mind. His impact on the way I have come to understand international politics was enormous, but that was not the only way he made a difference in my life.

I got to know Jervis more or less by accident. In 1982, when I was teaching history at the University of Pennsylvania, I was asked to organize a conference on military history. The department wanted to curry favor with a wealthy potential donor who happened to be interested in that field. I could scarcely refuse to take on that job, but I had no idea who to invite. As it turned out, at about that time, an archivist at the National Archives in Washington put me in touch with David Rosenberg, whom I asked for advice. David suggested that I arrange to meet Steve Van Evera, then at Princeton, and it was Steve who told me about Robert Jervis.

So I got in touch with Jervis, and he invited me to attend a workshop he was running at Columbia. It was there that I learned the little I know about cognitive psychology and especially about how the ideas developed by Amos Tversky and Daniel Kahneman could throw light on how international politics works. I eventually got to know Jervis quite well. He and I taught a couple of graduate classes together at Columbia around 1989. In those classes, we tried to bring the historical and political science perspectives together—to try to understand the differences between the two fields, the limitations of each approach, and what each could learn from the other. Those classes—"King Kong meets Godzilla" classes, I used to call them—were among the best and most interesting classes I ever got to teach.[1]

What struck me the most as I came to know Jervis better was the way he approached history. My personal experience with political scientists over the years had not been very positive. As a general rule, I did not like the way they used history. They did not seem to have much feel for history as a field with an intellectual personality of its own. Their assumption seemed to be that history might have a certain importance as a source of information about the past, but digging up the facts was not to their mind an intellectually challenging process. When it came to doing the real thinking—to getting at the deeper questions about why things worked the way they did—the historians, it was tacitly assumed, did not have a major role to play. And of course we historians reacted more or less as you would expect and did not have a particularly high regard for the political scientists. In the eight years I spent as a graduate student in history at Berkeley, I had had practically nothing to do with them.

But Jervis followed his own drummer, in this regard as in so many other ways, and his approach to history was very different. He actually understood that historians were concerned, in their own way, with basic "theoretical" issues, although few historians would actually use that word. That is, Jervis understood that historical analysis was concerned not just with the facts but with larger questions—in the case of our own field, with the fundamental question of what makes for war or for a stable international system but also, albeit in an even more indirect way, with the great question of how in general policy should be formulated and conducted.

That respect for history as a discipline, it seems to me today, might have had something to do with Jervis's basic view that our understanding of reality is very much a product of the way evidence about the world is processed in our minds, so that in interpreting historical reality, the *thinking* the historian does is of fundamental importance. Or as Jervis himself put it in a really wonderful sentence, "there is no reality to be described that is independent of people's beliefs about it."[2] That approach, of course, is very much at odds with the positivist view that dominates so much of what passes for "social science"—at odds, that is, with the generally unexamined but intellectually untenable assumption that "the facts" have a kind of elemental quality and can be made to "speak for themselves."[3]

You can hardly imagine how gratifying it was for me to deal with some-one from another field who seemed to understand and appreciate what people like me were doing—especially someone who, I soon learned, was a giant in his own field. In fact, when I began to get some sense of Jervis's standing in political science, I was kind of amazed. It was quite extraor-dinary that someone of his stature could be so unassuming and so easy to relate to. Top people in any field tend to be corrupted by their own success; they tend to be a little too full of themselves, a little too convinced that they already have all the answers. But Jervis was not cut from that cloth at all—quite the opposite in fact.

It is hard to separate Jervis's intellectual persona from what he was like as a human being. The two blend together in my mind. His scholarly style—open-ended, not just undogmatic but antidogmatic, developing ideas that he well knew could at best capture only part of the truth—was of a piece with his personal modesty and approachability. The ideas he came up with had little to do with any strongly held set of beliefs about how international politics worked. Instead, he read widely—amazingly widely in fact (and to this day I don't know where he found the time to do everything he did)—and what he read would often spark certain thoughts. He would then create file folders for particular ideas, and when he came across some new piece of evidence that related to that particular idea, he would put it in the corresponding folder. (He once showed me those fold-ers in a filing cabinet in his office.) When dealing with a particular issue when writing a book or article, he would pull the corresponding folder and was ready to go.[4] The stimulus came not just from works of history, which he read avidly, but also from works in many other fields (psychol-ogy, economics, even evolutionary biology). You can probably see that method in action most clearly in his book *System Effects*.[5]

For Jervis, the ideas came so easily that he would often just stick them into something he was writing, without making a big deal over them. The most striking example is a point he made in a footnote in his first book, *The Logic of Images in International Politics*: "As will be discussed later, high costs are often involved if it is later discovered that the actor's sig-nals were designed to be misleading. *Indeed, if there were no such costs associated with issuing misleading signals, there would be no reason for receivers to place any faith in them*."[6] The point he made in that italicized sentence was quite extraordinary. This was the first time, I believe, that any international relations scholar had made this point—and I spent some time looking into this issue. Even Thomas Schelling had not gone quite that far. And that argument about what we would now call "costly signaling" would go on to play a fundamental role in contemporary international relations theory. But my point here is not just that this was an important idea. My more basic point has to do with the very casual way in which Jervis introduced it —that it was presented in a *footnote*. Ideas came so easily to him that he could scarcely bring himself to trumpet their importance.[7]

One of Jervis's key ideas was that it is much harder to interpret reality than people think—that the process of understanding the world is anything but straightforward. For him that point applied not just to political actors but also to scholars. And it carried over into a certain skepticism about theorizing. Jervis's view, of course, was not that theoretical work was worthless but that, in doing that kind of work, scholars were on much thinner ice than they realized. And that helps explain why he thought historical work was so important. There are some political scientists who think that getting the history right does not matter all that much. I remember Alexander George once telling me, "I know this will shock you, Marc, but for me as a theorist what's important is that an interpretation of the past be plausible. It's less important that it be accurate." I am not sure whether that was his real view or if he was just trying to be provocative. But a number of theorists, even the most famous ones (like Schelling), did seem to take the view that historical accuracy did not matter all that much.[8]

Jervis, however, was different. For him, it *was* very important to understand what had actually happened. And it was for that reason that he went into the historical sources so deeply—not just the accounts written by professional historians but even the documents like those published in the *Foreign Relations of the United States* series. The historical sources provided a kind of intellectual ballast; they helped keep the theorizing down to earth and in touch with political reality.

All this carried over to the way Jervis related to students, especially graduate students. For me, it was always a pleasure to meet with his group at Columbia, which was intellectually serious but more relaxed and friendlier than similar groups elsewhere, and I think that had a lot to do with what Bob Jervis was like as a person. Although he is gone now, you can still get a sense for what he was like—and for why so many of us feel about him the way we do—by watching videos of him in action. A number of them have been posted on YouTube.[9] If you watch him give a talk or have a conversation with someone, you'll understand why so many of us feel that our intellectual world seems so much colder and emptier now that he's gone.

NOTES

1. See the essay by James McAllister in this volume.

2. Robert Jervis, *The Illogic of American Nuclear Strategy* (Cornell University Press, 1984), 38.

3. For Jervis's own take on this issue, see his essay "International Politics and Diplomatic History: Fruitful Differences," H-Diplo/International Security Studies Forum (ISSF), March 12, 2010, https://issforum.org/ISSF/PDF/ISSF-Jervis-InaguralAddress.pdf. This was based on a talk he gave at Williams College in 2009 and was the very first essay published in the ISSF.

4. He describes this method in Robert Jervis, "Change, Surprise, and the Hiding Hand," in *Journeys Through World Politics: Autobiographical Reflections of Thirty-Four Academic Travelers*, ed. Joseph Kruzel and James N. Rosenau (Lexington, 1989), 394.

5. Robert Jervis, *System Effects: Complexity in Political and Social Life* (Princeton University Press, 1997).

6. Robert Jervis, *The Logic of Images in International Relations* (Princeton University Press, 1970), 18, n. 2; emphasis added. He went on to develop that point in the text. See especially 19–20.

7. Compare, for example, what Schelling wrote about the originality of Bob's first book with what Jervis said about the same subject. "I tend to think," Schelling wrote, "that *The Logic of Images in International Relations* has had more influence on me than anything else Bob has written. That's partly because the ideas were absolutely new to me. The analysis focused on something I hadn't thought about." Thomas C. Schelling, "Foreword," in *Psychology, Strategy and Conflict: Perceptions of Insecurity in International Relations*, ed. James W. Davis (Routledge, 2013), xi. But Jervis's view was very different. The *Logic of Images* book, he said, had simply "combined Tom's ideas with those of Erving Goffman's *Presentation of Self in Everyday Life*." It was true, he noted, that Schelling "later said that he thought my book was entirely original and could not see where the thoughts came from, but the answer was largely in his own work." Robert Jervis, "Thomas C. Schelling: A Reminiscence," War on the Rocks, December 28, 2016, https://warontherocks .com/2016/12/thomas-c-schelling-a-reminiscence/. He made the same point in his ISSF essay in the "Learning the Scholar's Craft" series. Robert Jervis, "How I Got Here," H-Diplo/ISSF, March 4, 2020, 4, https://hdiplo.org/to/E198. I personally agree with Schelling about the extraordinary originality of that book, but this was not a case of false

modesty on Jervis's part. Given the almost effortless way in which ideas took shape in his mind, my guess is that it was hard for him to see them as particularly impressive or original.

8. See Marc Trachtenberg, "The Accidental War Question" (unpublished), 17–20, https://www.sscnet.ucla.edu/polisci/faculty/trachtenberg/cv/inadvertent.pdf. Note also Thomas Schelling, *Arms and Influence* (Yale University Press, 1966), xxiii.

9. See, for example, three of his lectures: "How Statesmen Think: The Psychology of International Politics," Woodrow Wilson Center, April 2019, https://www.youtube.com/watch?v =XLLcoTe5Olc; "Why Intelligence Fails: Lessons from the Iranian Revolution and the Iraq War," Duke University Law School, September 2010, https://www.youtube.com /watch?v=QmPy91_AkEc; and "Why We Get Things Wrong" (with Paul Pillar), Georgetown University Center for Security Studies, April 2015, https://www.youtube.com /watch?v=W1zow5yFS7w. Note also his conversations with Harry Kreisler (University of California Berkeley, November 2005), https://www.youtube.com/watch?v=tmmXaSDFcSI, and Gideon Rose (*Foreign Affairs*, March 2014), https://www.youtube.com/watch?v =g5oOL_a3ZfA.

24

LEARNING FROM HISTORY

DEBORAH WELCH LARSON

On July 8, 2021, during the US withdrawal from Afghanistan, in a testy response to a journalist's question about parallels with the aftermath of the US withdrawal from South Vietnam, President Joe Biden asserted that "there's going to be no circumstance where you see people being lifted off the roof of an embassy," as had happened in 1975 after the North Vietnamese completed their conquest of South Vietnam. Although Biden was determined to withdraw US forces from Afghanistan, he surely did not want the chaos and loss of life that occurred when desperate Afghanis clung to the wheels of US military aircraft to escape.[1] Though much remains to be learned about this US intelligence failure, the American withdrawal from Afghanistan illustrates the inability of policymakers to learn from history, an inadequacy pointed out by Robert Jervis in his famous 1976 book, *Perception and Misperception in International Politics*.[2]

I had the pleasure and privilege of being Jervis's colleague at Columbia from 1984 to 1988. He had many amazing ideas, but I would like to focus here on the contribution of *Perception and Misperception in International Politics*. Indeed, the book changed the international relations field. Amazingly, *Perception and Misperception* comprised only half of his 1968 PhD dissertation at University of California, Berkeley. The other half was published in 1970 as the *Logic of Images in International Relations*—another pathbreaking work but in a different field of signaling and deception.[3]

As the title suggests, the focus of *Perception and Misperception* is on perception rather than beliefs. Previous work applying social psychology to international relations had focused on belief systems, such as the operational code.[4] The work on belief systems tried to explain foreign policy in terms of beliefs—the need to maintain consistency among beliefs and the role of beliefs as a prism in interpreting experience. Scholars looked for correlation between elite beliefs and state behavior.

Perception used vision as a metaphor for policymakers' interpretation of information. This metaphor was extremely useful because it focused analysis squarely on *accuracy*. Just as there can be optical illusions, so too can there be inaccurate estimates of other states' intentions and behavior—misperception.[5] The classic work on international relations by Hans J. Morgenthau, Arnold Wolfers, and Henry Kissinger had highlighted irrational or misguided state foreign policies, but these were usually the result of domestic politics or political culture rather than to policymakers' biases and omissions.[6]

Comparing interpretations of information about the international system to visual perception opened up many new ways of understanding foreign-policy decision making. For example, it became more important to divide policymaking into stages—the reception, interpretation, and implementation of information. Errors and biases could occur at any of those stages of information processing. On a wider scale, Jervis viewed foreign-policy decision making as embedded in levels of analysis, including the international environment, domestic politics, and the bureaucracy, as well as the individual. It was important to disaggregate causality, to avoid blaming individual policymakers when the problem was poor implementation by bureaucratic actors, for example.[7]

Misperception could account for otherwise puzzling occurrences in international relations and foreign policy, such as the collapse of US-Soviet détente in the 1970s or the Vietnam War. Moreover, Jervis argued that misperceptions were predictable. They could account for patterns in international relations across time periods and situations. Misperception was not just a matter of individual pathology. With knowledge of types of errors, policymakers could learn to make better decisions.

Jervis's book made it possible to connect the psychological study of international relations with the "cognitive revolution" in social psychology that took root in the 1950s and 1960s. In the book, Jervis expresses frustration that existing work applying social psychology to international relations emphasized emotional causes such as wishful thinking and defense mechanisms over cognitive factors, overlooking uncertainty, complexity, and confusion.[8]

The cognitive revolution applied concepts and research methods of cognitive psychology to social interactions.[9] What made the cognitive revolution possible was the comparison of the human mind to a computer in processing information. The new cognitive social psychology looked at sequential stages of information processing—reception, interpretation, inference, storage in memory, and retrieval.

So did *Perception and Misperception*. Jervis argued that people tend to see what they expect to see and to assimilate new information to preexisting beliefs. One of the examples in the book involves an anthropologist taking a forest dweller to a park where there are grasslands. He discovers that the man perceives the buffalo in the distance as insects because, in the forest, he never had to make allowances for distance.[10]

Jervis highlighted the importance of memory. Policymakers store information in memory under the categories and ideas they had at the time. When they try to develop innovative policies, they can't easily recall relevant information because it is stored in memory in a different place.[11] Jervis gives the example of the British Navy's difficulty during World War I in comparing the effectiveness of convoying and patrolling as defense against German submarine attacks on British merchant ships. The British Navy had stored information on the destruction of submarines by the types of vessels involved rather than the activities in which they were engaged.[12]

As part of the cognitive revolution, psychologists stressed that errors and biases could result from normal cognitive processes that were accurate and useful most of the time but that, in a different context, resulted in error.[13] In his discussion of cognitive consistency theory, Jervis stresses that it is normal and appropriate for foreign-policy decision makers to make inferences and judgments based on their preexisting beliefs. Information is usually ambiguous and susceptible to multiple interpretations. Beliefs that are grounded in experience are useful in understanding new cases.[14]

This explains why the release of new evidence after the Cold War has not eliminated debates among historians or political scientists about

Soviet motives. The same documents may be interpreted in different ways depending on one's beliefs about the determinants of Soviet foreign policy.[15]

Jervis relates consistency-seeking by policymakers to scientific epistemology. Scientists are also prone to interpret the evidence in light of their theories. There are no "facts" independent of preexisting theories. Because evidence is susceptible to differing interpretations, scientists would be unable to carry out their inquiry without having theories. It would be irrational and bad science for scientists to discard well-grounded theories quickly, on the basis of a few pieces of discrepant evidence.[16]

We could not function in everyday life if we were constantly testing and reevaluating our beliefs. Consequently, we should not be too quick to condemn past leaders for being too close-minded. In the British debate over appeasement of Adolf Hitler, the British prime minister, Neville Chamberlain, and the British permanent undersecretary, Robert Vansittart, were both dogmatic but reached opposite conclusions about Germany's intentions. Those who were right often reasoned no more logically than those who were wrong. That Japan would attack a much more powerful United States at Pearl Harbor or that Hitler would declare war on the United States was highly improbable and is puzzling in hindsight.[17]

But Jervis also provides several tests as to when consistency-seeking is excessive and violates reality testing. This would include instances when decision makers fail to look for relevant evidence that is readily available or when a leader refuses to read or discuss some information that casts a preferred policy into question.[18]

Conversely, people's belief systems are sometimes more consistent than is warranted, leading to belief-system overkill. People believe that all good things go together, and they avoid recognizing that even a favored policy may have some bad side effects. There may be no good option. As Jervis wrote of the test-ban debate in the 1950s: "People who favored a nuclear test-ban believed that testing created a serious medical danger, would not lead to major weapons improvements, and was a source of international tension. Those who opposed the treaty usually took the opposite position on all three issues. Yet neither logic nor experience indicates that there should be any such relationship. The health risks of testing are in no way connected with the military advantages, and a priori we should not expect any correlation between people's views on these questions."[19]

In short, policymakers avoid recognizing the need to make value trade-offs.[20] In the Obama administration, those policymakers who favored aiding the moderate opposition in the Syrian civil war were confident that the United States could distinguish the moderates from the extremists and that weapons would not fall into the hands of the enemy. Those who opposed US involvement contended that failure to provide aid to the opposition to the Syrian president Bashar al-Assad would not escalate the situation or result in strengthening terrorist groups.[21]

If policymakers recognize that their preferred policy will have costs or side effects, they might be able to make adjustments in advance to compensate. At least they would not be surprised by unintended consequences, which could exceed the benefits.

One of Jervis's original ideas was the idea of the evoked set—that foreign policymakers' interpretation of information can be colored by their current preoccupations and that this could lead to misunderstanding and misperception. For example, before the Japanese attack on Pearl Harbor on December 7, 1941, Washington officials warned Lieutenant General Walter Short to expect "hostile action," meaning "attack on American possessions from without." But General Short, who was concerned about the risk of sabotage, did not interpret the warning as referring to an attack on Pearl Harbor.[22]

In chapter 6 of *Perception and Misperception*, "How Decision-Makers Learn from History," Jervis anticipated many of the insights of schema theory. Schema theory is about how people use stored knowledge to make sense out of new information.[23] Jervis argued that learning from experience creates perceptual predispositions—tendencies to see the world in certain ways. Decision makers view current events as analogous to past cases with which they are familiar. Policymakers draw oversimplified lessons from the past—they tend to believe that the most salient aspects of the situation led to the outcome, failing to search more deeply for the causes. Accordingly, decision makers are drawn to repeat policies that succeeded while avoiding those that failed. Although seemingly rational, merely copying what worked does not take into consideration contingent conditions that affect outcomes. The past case can be fundamentally different from the present situation. In any case, a successful policy may have turned out well due to chance factors. A failed policy may have achieved the best that could have been expected.[24]

Not all experience is useful or informative. Leaders are unduly influenced by their firsthand experience. This includes their encounters with foreign leaders after brief summit meetings. On the one hand, as a result of misplaced confidence that they have understood their foreign counterpart, leaders' future judgments may be less accurate. On the other hand, policymakers rarely believe that the similar experiences of other states can offer any useful lessons for their state, even though careful study could help them prevent fiascoes and costly failures.[25]

One insight from *Perception and Misperception* that I often use in my lectures is that foreign policymakers fail to understand how others could perceive them as a threat. Leaders know that they mean other states no harm—and they assume that their intentions are obvious to others.[26] A recent example is the failure of US and NATO leaders to understand how President Vladimir Putin might have felt threatened by increased US military assistance to Ukraine, which fought a Russian-supported insurgency by separatists in southeastern Ukraine before Russia's invasion in 2022..

Another widely applicable insight that *Perception and Misperception* provides is that we tend to overestimate how centralized and coordinated the other's behavior is—failing to take into consideration the role of internal bureaucratic conflicts, foul-ups, accidents, and so on. Often when analysts worry about the significance of an apparent sudden shift in a state's policy, the cause is a military commander acting independently or competition between bureaucratic agencies rather than attempts to send a signal.[27] This can apply to states like China, where the foreign policymaking process is a "black box."

Just about every psychological theory relevant to decision making can be found in *Perception and Misperception*, including cognitive dissonance theory, attribution theory, cognitive consistency theory, and schema theory. By using an eclectic set of social psychological theories, Jervis is able to show broad convergence of findings upon the determinants of perceptions.

One of the reasons that the book had such an impact were the many colorful and vivid examples taken from a variety of disciplines, such as diplomatic history, but also espionage, the philosophy of science, and literature. Without historical and other examples, it is difficult to determine whether laboratory findings have any validity in the real world. In the laboratory, the subjects are usually students dealing with simple topics that they care little about. It is another matter to find out that experienced, highly competent foreign policy leaders who are dealing with consequential issues make systematic errors.[28]

As I have learned from experience, it is difficult to come up with examples of psychological processes. Jervis made it seem effortless, largely because he was a voracious reader with remarkable powers of retention. Every time that I would mention to him a book that I had read, he had already read it and a few more. His widespread reading and knowledge of history gave Jervis an intuitive sense for what theories are likely to be correct and a commonsense view of what leaders do.

If policymakers tend to be closed to new information and to see what they expect to see, Jervis demonstrated the opposite. He was remarkably open to new information, theories, and approaches. Jervis was an intellectual magpie. He generated ideas from many diverse sources—current events, diplomatic history, newspapers, magazines—as well as political science.

Jervis often weighed the opposite point of view to determine when it might be valid. He believed in the hypothetico-deductive method, whereby the researcher should consider what would happen if a hypothesis were correct as well as what might falsify the hypothesis. Perhaps because of his pathbreaking work on how policymakers assimilate information to their preexisting beliefs, Jervis was concerned with avoiding confirmation bias. Reality is often contradictory, as he argued in his later book on systems theory.[29] Different paths can lead to the same result.

My last meeting with Jervis was at an April 27, 2021, Zoom meeting sponsored by *Political Science Quarterly* where I summarized an article that I had written on President Donald J. Trump's foreign policy. As a discussant, Jervis characteristically had many insightful, well-informed comments on Trump's policy toward Russia and China and on Biden's reaction to this legacy. I was struck by his comment that Biden was a gambler and that he was taking big risks in withdrawing from Afghanistan. Little had been written in the mainstream press about the potential risk that a US withdrawal would lead to the swift collapse of the Islamic Republic of Afghanistan. But Robert Jervis, as a student of the history of US withdrawal from Vietnam, correctly predicted the outcome.

NOTES

1. "Racing to Get Out as Fear and Desperation Set In," *New York Times*, August 17, 2021; Michael D. Shear et al., "Miscue After Miscue, Exit Plan Unravels," *New York Times*, August 22, 2021, 1.

2. Robert Jervis, *Perception and Misperception in International Politics* (Princeton University Press, 1976).

3. Robert Jervis, *The Logic of Images in International Relations* (Princeton University Press, 1970).

4. Ole R. Holstl, "The Belief System and National Images: A Case Study," *Journal of Conflict Resolution* 6, no. 3 (1962): 244–52, https://doi.org/10.1177%2F002200276200600306; Holsti, "Cognitive Dynamics and Images of the Enemy: Dulles and Russia," in *Enemies in Politics*, ed. David J. Finlay, Ole R. Holsti, and Richard Fagen (Rand McNally, 1967); Alexander L. George, "The 'Operational Code': A Neglected Approach to the Study of Political Leaders and Decision-Making," *International Studies Quarterly* 13, no. 2 (1969): 190–222. https://doi.org/10.2307/3013944. See Deborah Welch Larson, "The Role of Belief Systems and Schemas in Foreign Policy Decision-Making," *Political Psychology* 15, no. 1 (1994): 17–33, https://doi.org/10.2307/3791437.

5. Jervis, *Perception and Misperception*, 7.

6. Arnold Wolfers, *Britain and France Between Two Wars* (Norton, 1966); Hans J. Morgenthau, *Politics Among Nations: The Struggle for Power and Peace*, 7th ed., rev. Kenneth W. Thompson and W. David Clinton (McGraw-Hill, 2006).

7. Jervis, *Perception and Misperception*, 15–19.

8. Jervis, *Perception and Misperception*, 3.

9. George A. Miller, "The Magical Number Seven, Plus or Minus Two: Some Limits on Our Capacity for Processing Information," *Psychological Review* 63, no. 2 (1956): 81–97, https://psycnet.apa.org/doi/10.1037/h0043158; Ulric Neisser, *Cognitive Psychology* (Appleton-Century Crofts, 1967); Jerome S. Bruner, Jacqueline J. Goodnow, and George A. Austin, *A Study of Thinking* (Wiley, 1956); Marvin Minsky, "Steps Toward Artificial Intelligence," *Proceedings of the IRE* 49, no. 1 (1969): 8–29, https://doi.org/10.1109/JRPROC.1961.287775.

10. Jervis, *Perception and Misperception*, 148–49; Colin Turnbull, *The Forest People* (Simon and Schuster, 1961), 252–53.

11. Jervis, *Perception and Misperception*, 162–63.

12. Arthur J. Marder, *From the Dreadnought to Scapa Flow*, vol. 5, *Victory and Aftermath (January 1918–June 1919)* (Oxford University Press, 1970), 99–100.

13. Daniel Kahneman, Paul Slovic, and Amos Tversky, eds., *Judgment Under Uncertainty: Heuristics and Biases* (Cambridge University Press, 1982).

14. Jervis, *Perception and Misperception*, 161–62.

15. William C. Wohlforth, "New Evidence on Moscow's Cold War: Ambiguity in Search of Theory," *Diplomatic History* 21, no. 2 (1997): 229–42, https://doi.org/10.1111/0145-2096.00066.

16. Jervis, *Perception and Misperception*, 156–62.

17. Jervis, *Perception and Misperception*, 175–76, 178–81.

18. Jervis, *Perception and Misperception*, 172–73.

19. Jervis, *Perception and Misperception*, 129.

20. Jervis, *Perception and Misperception*, 128–42.

21. Robert M. Gates, *Exercise of Power: American Failures, Successes, and a New path Forward in the Post-Cold War World* (Alfred A. Knopf, 2020), 305–13.

22. Robert Wohlstetter, *Pearl Harbor: Warning and Decision* (Stanford University Press, 1962), 74, cited in Jervis, *Perception and Misperception*, 206–7.

23. Susan T. Fiske and Patricia W. Linville, "What Does the Schema Concept Buy Us," *Personality and Social Psychology Bulletin* 6, no. 4 (1980): 543–47; Shelley E. Taylor and Jennifer Crocker, "Schematic Bases of Social Information Processing," in *Social Cognition: The Ontario Symposium*, ed. E. Tory Higgins, C. Peter Herman, and Mark P. Zanna (Lawrence Erlbaum, 1981); David E. Rumelhart and Andrew Ortony, "The Representation of Knowledge in Memory," in *Schooling and the Acquisition of Knowledge*, ed. Richard C. Anders, Rand J. Spiro, and William Montague (Lawrence Erlbaum Associates, 1977). For application to international relations, see Deborah Welch Larson, *Origins of Containment: A Psychological Explanation* (Princeton University Press, 1985), 50–57; Yuen Foong Khong, *Analogies at War* (Princeton University Press, 1992).

24. Jervis, *Perception and Misperception*, 228–32.

25. Jervis, *Perception and Misperception*, 243–46.

26. Jervis, *Perception and Misperception*, 354–55.

27. Jervis, *Perception and Misperception*, 319–21.

28. Jervis, *Perception and Misperception*, 4–5.

29. Robert Jervis, *System Effects: Complexity in Political and Social Life* (Princeton University Press, 1997).

25

AN APPRECIATION

JAMES McALLISTER

U ndoubtedly like many others in the community of political scientists and international historians, after the passing of Robert Jervis I spent much time revisiting his scholarship. Even for those who have long known that he was one of the true intellectual giants of political science and international relations, it is simply awe inspiring to systematically go through his curriculum vitae and appreciate how much scholarship he produced on so many different topics for over five decades. Future intellectual historians trying to understand the disciplines of political science and international relations in the post–Vietnam War era will spend much of their time grappling with Jervis's contributions and all of the related research projects he inspired others to pursue. Of course, the wide range of Jervis's scholarship will present a difficult challenge to anyone who takes on the project because of the sheer number of the areas of inquiry they will have to master in order to fully appreciate his seminal contributions to everything from political psychology to the nuclear revolution to systems theory.[1]

Without the abundant evidence of his generosity and kindness that will be presented in volumes such as this one and the many others that will appear in the years to come, a future historian would surely be forgiven for assuming that Jervis must have been singularly focused on his own individual scholarship, indifferent to the teaching and mentoring of graduate students and unconcerned with providing collective goods to wider academic communities. If Jervis had displayed any of those qualities, it would have been completely understandable and would not have diminished the greatness of his scholarship at all. But what is truly remarkable when considering Jervis's life and legacy is how much time and energy he devoted to his students and colleagues, the strong intellectual communities he fostered and created, and how he used his influence to build essential connections between international relations theorists and historians of American foreign policy and world politics. It is not at all an accident that the online tributes to Jervis were organized by two historians and were published on H-Diplo/International Security Studies Forum (ISSF), a venue that he founded in partnership with H-Diplo and one that would not have existed or flourished without his leadership.[2]

I first met Jervis in the fall of 1988 when I enrolled as a graduate student in the Columbia Department of Political Science. The department, then as now, was one of the very best in the world, and it admitted many highly intelligent, intellectually combative, and remarkably confident graduate students. Of course, it also admitted a few students like myself who lacked all of these qualities and had no business being in a graduate program that contained brilliant students like Randy Schweller, Tom Christensen, Victor Cha, Jon Mercer, and far too many others to mention. I took two lecture courses with Jervis that semester, his introduction to international relations theory course and his course on nuclear strategy. What I remember most about both courses, in addition to the extensive and often quirky reading lists, is Jervis's unique teaching style. Lectures never proceeded in a chronological or formulaic manner, and many of his most insightful remarks flowed from complex questions posed to him by students. Although only a small portion of the fairly large class could actively participate, Jervis always held the entire audience in a state of rapt attention that made the classes feel like intimate seminars. Needless to say, it was also impossible for anyone in those classes not to appreciate how privileged they were to have the opportunity to study these topics with Robert Jervis himself.

Despite my appreciation for the great courses I took with Jervis and the other superb members of Columbia's political science faculty, at the end of my first year, I was highly doubtful that I would continue in the program. I did not even enroll for the fall semester. Leaving aside purely personal factors, it increasingly dawned on me that my passion for studying the history of American foreign policy and the Cold War was far more intense than my interest in the theoretical concerns of political science at this time. Although I recognized their importance, discussions of methodology and research design always left me uninterested. Indeed, I would not have argued with anyone who told me that I had no business at all being in a political science department; in fact, I had already privately come to that conclusion myself. It was at that moment of complete resignation that I signed up for a seminar course in the spring of 1990 that Jervis was coteaching with Marc Trachtenberg, who at the time was in the history department at the University of Pennsylvania.

It is impossible to overestimate the impact that seminar had on my life. Being in a classroom with two tremendous scholars from different disciplines examining the fundamental issues of war and peace in the twentieth century was a transformative experience. In a course filled almost entirely with aspiring political scientists, we had insightful and passionate debates over the origins of the First World War, the strengths and weaknesses of A. J. Taylor's *The Origins of the Second World War*, and several key moments and crises of the Cold War.[3] The point of the course was not to learn the historiography of crucial events but to understand how much historical arguments like Taylor's were rooted in implicit theories of world politics and to demonstrate how theoretical debates in international relations often turned on historical interpretations that were false, misleading, or incomplete. Perhaps most importantly, working with primary documents made it clear that there was absolutely no reason why students of international relations in political science departments should be content with being passive consumers of secondary historical accounts. International relations theorists could approach history with their own disciplinary concerns and also immerse themselves in the same documentary sources and archives used by historians. Although Trachtenberg's influential book *History and Strategy* was not be published until the following year, the concluding sentences of that book captured exactly the atmosphere that was present throughout the semester: "A process of cross-fertilization and intellectual interaction is just beginning to get off the ground, but already the people involved have the sense that this sort of thing is tremendously valuable. It may be odd for a historian to predict the future, but even now you can feel a certain momentum: clearly something important is taking shape on that border area where history and political science meet."[4]

Jervis obviously thought as insightfully as anyone about the nature of the "border area" where the fields of history and political science meet. In a lecture he delivered at Williams College in 2009 to a distinguished group of scholars, one almost equally composed of historians and political scientists, Jervis began by noting what brought everyone together: "For all of our differences, we share a fascination with the patterns, idiosyncrasies, and changes in cross-border relations." The body of the lecture then proceeded to expertly lay out in an informal manner all of the deep philosophical differences that constituted the border area that separated the two disciplines. It would have been easy for Jervis to minimize or obscure how fundamental those differences were, but his concluding message was that the border between the two disciplines could not and should not be expected to dissolve: "These differences produce tensions between political scientists and international historians that we should not expect to be resolved. Indeed, they should not be because the diversity of perspectives benefits us all. The point is not to convert others to our viewpoint, but to understand theirs."[5]

If borders between intellectual disciplines were in some sense inevitable and even desirable, what exactly could be done to increase the frequency and fruitfulness of encounters between historians and political scientists? Always a pluralist who valued innovative scholarship from all theoretical and historical perspectives, Jervis characteristically did not offer a simple answer to a complex issue. Although the philosophical divide between the two disciplines could not be resolved or wished away, Jervis did many significant and practical things to make those borders more porous throughout his career. For example, along with Robert Art (and later joined by Stephen Walt), Jervis founded the Cornell Studies in Security Affairs imprint with Cornell University Press in the early 1980s. It is hard to exaggerate the role that the prestigious series has played and continues to play in fostering the careers of political scientists, including my own, whose research is more historical and less quantitative than has long been the norm in political science departments.

Of course, one of Jervis's enduring legacies will surely be H-Diplo/ISSF, which he founded and guided from 2009 to his passing.[6] The creation of a community for international relations scholars that would be comparable to the role that H-Diplo had long played for historians was and is a remarkable achievement. Bob often illustrated debates between structural and contingent explanations of events by citing McGeorge Bundy's famous Vietnam-era line that "Pleikus are like streetcars," which suggested that the bombing of an American military installation by Vietcong forces in February 1965 was merely a rationale rather than a cause of the subsequent military escalation by the Johnson administration.[7] However, in the case of ISSF, it is very hard to construct a plausible counterfactual that the forum would have either come into being or flourished in the way it has without Bob's vision and leadership. I had the great privilege of working with him in the early years of ISSF as a managing editor and can attest to the active role he played in guiding all of its activities. It also did not take me long to discover that the most effective way to garner participation from very busy scholars was to start every invitation with some form of the sentence, "I am working with Bob Jervis on. . . ." Over the past decade, and particularly after the election of Donald Trump, ISSF has developed into the most vital online scholarly community for informed theoretical, historical, and policy-relevant discussions of America's role in the world. The border between international relations scholars and historians is still there, but Bob's vision of ISSF has made it much easier for everyone to cross over and familiarize themselves with the latest research and disciplinary debates on both sides.

Political scientists and international historians have suffered a great loss with the passing of Bob Jervis, but his pathbreaking scholarship, his intellectual values and integrity, and the kindness and generosity he displayed to so many will never be forgotten.

NOTES

1. Simply compiling a short list of Jervis's most influential works raises agonizing dilemmas of inclusion and exclusion. Beyond the obvious books and articles that have appeared on everyone's syllabi for decades, like *Perception and Misperception* or "Cooperation Under the Security Dilemma," it is important to emphasize the importance of his articles that brilliantly combined his intellectual interests in international relations theory, diplomatic history, and American foreign policy. An early and generally underappreciated example of this combination is Robert Jervis, "The Impact of the Korean War on the Cold War," *Journal of Conflict Resolution* 34 (1980): 563–92. Other important examples of this approach include "From Balance to Concert: A Study in International Security Cooperation," *World Politics* 38 (1985): 58–79; "Realism, Game Theory, and Cooperation," *World*

Politics 40 (1988): 317–49; and "Was the Cold War a Security Dilemma?" *Journal of Cold War Studies* 3 (2001): 36–60.

2. *H-Diplo|ISSF Tribute to the Life, Scholarship, and Legacy of Robert Jervis*, organized by Richard H. Immerman, Marc Trachtenberg, and Diane N. Labrosse, Part I, February 4, 2022, https://issforum.org/ISSF/PDF/ISSF-Jervis-Tribute-1.pdf; Part 2, August 25, 2022, https://issforum.org/ISSF/PDF/ISSF-Jervis-Tribute-2.pdf. On Jervis's influence on the origin and evolution of H-Diplo/ISSF, see the essay by Labrosse in this volume.

3. A. J. P. Taylor, *The Origins of the Second World War* (Atheneum, 1962).

4. Marc Trachtenberg, *History and Strategy* (Princeton University Press, 1991), 286.

5. Robert Jervis, "International Politics and Diplomatic History: Fruitful Differences," H-Diplo/ISSF Essays, no. 1, March 12, 2010, https://issforum.org/essays/essay-1-jervis-inagural.

6. In honor of Jervis's founding role and vision, H-Diplo/ISSF has been renamed H-Diplo/RJISSF (the Robert Jervis International Security Studies Forum).

7. McGeorge Bundy cited in David Halberstam, *The Best and the Brightest* (Random House, 1969), 533.

26

PERCEPTIONS AND MISPERCEPTIONS AND THE OUTBREAK OF WORLD WAR I

Memories of an Interdisciplinary Scholarly Relationship

VOLKER R. BERGHAHN

A s the recent Columbia University conference in his memory in March 2023 and the many other tributes to his life and work in the press and online have demonstrated, Robert Jervis's influence on the fields of international relations, political science, and political psychology was enormous. However, as I argue in this chapter, he also had a keen interest in historical scholarship and in debates on history. I benefited from Jervis's openness to historical studies when I arrived at Columbia from Brown University in 1998. Jervis was one of the first colleagues to reach out to me and help me integrate myself into a large and very complex institution in New York City. This integration was facilitated from my end by the fact that I had not been trained in the Rankean tradition of political and diplomatic history that claimed to describe past events and processes "how they had in fact happened." Instead, I had been part of a generational shift that occurred in the 1960s and 1970s toward the social sciences. The quest was no longer merely to be a historian who told empathetic stories but to be one who rigorously conceptualized one's research and who had read both Karl Marx and Max Weber as well as other major social scientists.

The other person with whom I was in close contact after my arrival at Columbia was Paul Kennedy at Yale, who approached history from the perspective of grand strategy and the policies and attitudes of military and political elites. When this trio began to exchange ideas about cooperation, funding for workshops was more easily available than it is today, and so Jervis, Kennedy, and I organized day-long seminars that brought our Columbia doctoral students together with Kennedy's for invariably lively and fruitful exchanges on research projects and methodological debates. When these funds dried up around the time of the Great Recession of 2007–2008, Bob and I continued our conversations, and I attended his workshops at Columbia's Saltzman Institute of War and Peace Studies.

With the approach of the hundredth anniversary of the outbreak of World War I, dozens of historical books and articles began to appear, with Christopher Clark's 2013 *The Sleepwalkers*[1] becoming a bestseller whose title gave his interpretation of the Crisis of July 1914 away and immediately unleashed sharp disagreement.[2] Harking back to the events of the Fritz Fischer Debate of the 1960s and 1970s,[3] Clark was challenged by historians in Europe and the United States who questioned his argument that all European powers had sleepwalked into the abyss of World War I and that hence all participant powers and their leaders were responsible for the unfolding catastrophe.

Because this chapter is not merely a personal memoir of my academic interactions with Jervis but also an attempt to integrate them with more recent work on the July Crisis of 1914, I shall come back to the latest findings in this field later in the chapter. There is also the earlier research on this crisis to be remembered that goes back to the 1920s, when there was a sharp split between, on the one hand, apologetic and defensive German scholarship as far as Germany's responsibility was concerned and, on the other hand, Western European and American analyses that tended to make Germany and Austria-Hungary directly responsible for pushing the world over the brink.[4] These differences of opinion continued after 1945, when West German historians returned to the positions of the interwar years and also played down continuities with the Hitler dictatorship that many West German historians viewed as an "accident in the works." Western scholarship, by contrast, resumed its earlier positions that focused on the responsibility of the Central Powers and the argument that Germany had taken a special path, *Sonderweg*, into the twentieth century that culminated in the Nazi dictatorship and its launching of World War II.[5]

These exchanges of the 1950s were greatly enlivened when the Hamburg University historian Fritz Fischer for the first time gained access to the files of the Imperial government, now kept in the East German archives. He examined the expansionist war aims that were being discussed in

Berlin during World War I.[6] Although primarily dealing with those war aims, Fischer argued in his first chapter that they had been formulated before 1914 and that the war was unleashed by Berlin in July 1914 in order to implement them. Fischer's argument of a continuity between Imperial foreign policy led to an enormous uproar among West German historians. The vigorous public debate that followed was quickly also taken up outside West Germany. This development not only led to the unearthing of more new documents on the July Crisis but it also put Fischer under pressure to elaborate on the first chapter of his study of German war aims and his view of German responsibility for the war. This complementary book appeared in German in 1969 and in an English translation in 1975 under the title *War of Illusions*.[7]

I am quite certain that Jervis not only followed this particular international debate but also—and his papers may contain some evidence of this—was intrigued by the title of Fischer's voluminous study. After all, the Hamburg historian and his protagonists (being sharply criticized by their disbelieving colleagues at the University of Hamburg and elsewhere) asserted that in order to explain the attitudes and decisions of the German (and Austro-Hungarian) policymakers, one had to grapple with their perceptions and misperceptions as well as their miscalculations before and after the outbreak of war in July 1914.

Jervis was bound to have been intrigued by the new evidence that Fischer and his supporters had found in the archives. After all, he had been working at this time on his own major study titled *Perception and Misperception in International Politics* in which, deriving from his interest in security dilemmas, he inserted political psychology into the study of international relations and was interested in the role of individual decision makers in international politics and their socialization and formative experiences.[8] Jervis wanted to capture the complexities of international relations and the decisions that were being made by real people with their quirks and flaws. Moreover, there were also the often unintended consequences of their labors. Finally, with his judgment that policymakers were often being driven by fear as well as by opportunities to be exploited, Jervis was also preoccupied with wars that were preventive or preemptive. Because these were all issues that could be found in Fischer's *War of Illusions*, Bob's book, the first edition of which appeared in 1976, contains many references to historical studies of the pre-1914 period.

A close look at *Perception and Misperception,* however, will show that Bob's understanding of the field and its political-psychological aspects was not narrowly focused on Europe but comprehensive and global. It is not easy to keep up with him in his book, as he moves from case studies on the dynamics of the Cold War to conflicts on the periphery of great-power politics and back to Europe in the early modern period and nineteenth century. Yet if one adds it all up, his references to World War I and its origins are strikingly frequent. Thus, he starts on page 15 with a quote by Reich Chancellor Theobald von Bethmann Hollweg on the general disposition toward a major war. He adds that even Chancellor Otto von Bismarck's diplomacy of "glittering skill" could not alter the forces that were more powerful than the founder of the German empire of 1871.[9] Jervis was certainly interested in tsarist Russia and the role it played in escalating the crisis after the assassinations of Archduke Ferdinand and his wife in Sarajevo on June 28, 1914, by Serb nationalists by siding with Serbia in its defensive war against Austria-Hungary.[10] Nevertheless, on balance, his analysis of the summer of 1914 was clearly tilted toward Berlin and London.

In both cases, Jervis looked not only at the foreign policies of Germany and Great Britain but also at the domestic pressures on each of the governments. Above all, he examined how suspicions between the two countries intensified and how the rapid expansion of the German navy after 1898 led key experts in the British Foreign Office to suspect that the Germans were aiming to replace Britain in its preeminent position. At the same time, Germany's leaders failed to appreciate Germany's strength, which caused much fear among its neighbors.[11] Hence Berlin's strategic location on Britain's doorstep in the North Sea meant that even minor territorial ambitions had a major impact on how other powers, Britain in particular, perceived (and perhaps also misperceived) the Hohenzollern monarchy.

Still, as Jervis continued to stress, London's fears did not result in efforts to negotiate a formal military alliance with France, Germany's archenemy. Instead, British leaders merely sought cooperation in an effort to contain Kaiser Wilhelm II and his entourage of military officers and ministers. Overall, Jervis opted for a spiral theory that began with a naval arms race in 1898 that Admiral Alfred von Tirpitz had started and then lost by 1912 and that thereafter was replaced by an arms race on land with Germany and Austria-Hungary as land powers facing republican France and tsarist Russia.

During the debate on the war's origins, when St. Petersburg's policies temporarily became a focus of his research, Jervis invited the historian Marc Trachtenberg to a seminar discussion at the Saltzman Institute. The latter had written on the "inadvertent war" of 1914, arguing that the Russian decision to mobilize at the end of July was tantamount to a declaration of war and that the tsarist leadership understood the implications of this at the time.[12] Trachtenberg's analysis also included Bethmann Hollweg's maneuvers during the last days of peace, but he then kept his eyes on St. Petersburg's supposedly preemptive strategy. He concluded that there was little evidence to support the argument that things had just run out of control. To be sure, there were misperceptions and also miscalculations, but Russia's decision to go to war was not an irrational one.

Bob's main interest continued to be in Germany and Britain. As to the gradual escalation of the July Crisis, he clearly perceived the spiral dynamics of the Anglo-German arms race since the late 1890s. Since many relevant sources on those early years were available in translations of relevant German research, Jervis was spared having to wrestle with the original German academic prose, with its tapeworm sentences and convoluted participle constructions. In this respect, English-language studies were more accessible to him because their authors took pride in writing short, "crisp" sentences. If there is a thread running through Jervis's analysis, it is London's reluctance to make firm promises of support to France. If isolationism and explicit abstention from alliance commitments ended in the very early years of the twentieth century, all that was on offer from London by 1904 was an Entente Cordiale with France, which was expanded in 1907 to the Triple Entente with Russia.

Always interested in the psychological effects of policy decisions, Jervis quoted from the memoirs of the British foreign secretary Sir Edward Grey that "the increase in armaments that is intended in each nation to produce consciousness of strength, and a sense of security, does not produce these effects. On the contrary, it produces a consciousness of the strength of other nations and a sense of fear. Fear begets suspicion and distrust and evil imaginings of all sort, till each Government feels it would be criminal and a betrayal of its own country not to take every precaution, while every Government regards every precaution of every other Government as evidence of hostile intent."[13]

It seems that this observation by a historical key figure such as Grey reinforced Jervis's belief that it is worthwhile to discuss the impact of perceptions and misperceptions of security concerns and the existence of fear also in regard to other cases and the East-West Conflict after 1945 in particular.

When it came to the final weeks of peace in July 1914, Jervis continued his interest in the attempts by the British leadership to prevent a great-power conflict that, in turn, was misperceived by Wilhelm II and his advisors. They assumed that Britain would keep out of a war on the European continent, whereas others badly underestimated Britain as a major military opponent of Germany. This miscalculation explains the surprise and dismay in Berlin when Britain abandoned its years of continental non-commitment and not only entered the war on the side of the French, Belgians, and Russians and began to dispatch the British Expeditionary Force to the Western Front but also, on September 6, 1914, signed and published the Treaty of London, the firm alliance agreement that bound each of its members not to sign a separate peace agreement (NSPA) with the enemy and therefore to fight until all signatories agreed to conclude a peace treaty.

Mira Rapp-Hooper, one of Jervis's doctoral students, had studied history as an undergraduate and, having noticed the significance of NSPA in the seminars and being intrigued by the formulation of British and German policy during the July Crisis, decided to sign up for an independent study with me with the aim of scouring the relevant documents and secondary literature on the outbreak of World War I and the early months of the conflict.[14] By the end of the semester, she had submitted several excellent papers and a concluding comprehensive one on those dramatic weeks of decision making in Berlin and London with special attention to perceptions, misperceptions, and miscalculations. Working further in the Foreign Office archives in London and finding lower-level papers and correspondence, she decided to weave her material into a larger scholarly article on NSPAs, published in December 2014 in *Security Studies* under the title "Ambivalent Albion, Ambitious Ally: Britain's Decision for No Separate Peace in 1914."[15]

A brief summary of the latest historical research on the decisions of the German government in 1914 provides the foundations for Rapp-Hooper's analysis of British policymaking in August and September of 1914. The background to the July Crisis is provided by the fallout from the infamous War Council of December 8, 1912, that both Fischer and John Roehl examined and how the kaiser cancelled the plan to unleash a war against Serbia for fear that this would escalate into a world war that would also draw in Britain.[16] When the assassination crisis of June 28, 1914, began to escalate into a major confrontation, however, Wilhelm II did not want to pull in his horns again (*umfallen*), as he had done in 1912. Then, on July 28, the German ambassador in London cabled that Grey was willing to launch a last-minute mediation effort, whereupon Wilhelm ordered a halt to the planned German invasion of Belgium to which Helmuth von Moltke, his chief of the general staff, reacted with something like a nervous breakdown. When the news from London was corrected a few hours later and his generals were ready to invade Belgium, Wilhelm II, now in a great panic, received yet another telegram on July 30 that the British king, George V, had sent to Prince Heinrich, the Kaiser's brother. In it, George suggested that the Austro-Hungarian advance into Serbia be stopped. When this telegram was hand-delivered to Bethmann Hollweg in the middle of the night, with the request to transmit it to Vienna, the Reich chancellor ignored it and the attack on Belgrade continued.

No less important, Wilhelm II now signed the mobilization order and the German invasion of Belgium began. In light of his experiences during the Franco-Prussian War of 1870–1871, the elder Helmuth von Moltke had warned against a "people's war" among the great powers that no one would win.[17] In 1914, encouraged by the Schlieffen Plan, his nephew with the same name deemed a lightning war against France, followed by a subsequent swift movement of Germany's armies to the east and another lightning war against Russia, still winnable.[18] The trouble was that this German strategy foundered by mid-September in Belgium and northern France during the Battle of the Marne.

There is now further evidence that, unlike his comrades who did not understand the full implications of this momentous military setback, General Erich von Falkenhayn actually concluded that the war had been lost at this early point.[19] It seems that this in turn caused Bethmann Hollweg to put out secret diplomatic feelers to London in the hope that an armistice could be concluded. Although these peace feelers were likely to be genuine, London not only thought them untrustworthy but also was now bound by the London NSPA, with France and Belgium resisting all negotiations.[20] And so the war continued until November 1918 after a number of other attempts at mediation had also failed.

Jervis encouraged Rapp-Hooper to publish her findings. Yet his own attitude toward the July Crisis was in line with the caution that marked his work more generally. Although many of his colleagues came up with firm conclusions on a particular international crisis, Jervis remained more skeptical. To be sure, he was interested in the building of models, such as the spiral and deterrence ones with regard to the origins of major wars, but when asked about the one or the other, he tended to prevaricate and continued to wrestle with the problems that in his mind did not provide clear-cut answers.

If this was Jervis's more hesitant approach to international relations, I would like to conclude with a story that historians love to tell (don't they?). It indicates that however close Jervis's cooperation with historians and with me, in particular, was and despite the fact that both his work and that of his students relied on historical sources, those studies were written within a distinctly international relations framework. It also underscores the point made earlier about Rapp-Hooper's long and illuminating article in *Security Studies*, which is clearly conceptualized as an international relations piece of research. It is not an essay using the methods of history but devotes most of its effort to conceptualizing and hypothesizing about the uses and traps of NSPAs.

The story involves an experience I had when Jervis invited me to be a member of a doctoral examination committee of one of his students. When we met for those two, often tense hours, my international relations colleagues had an extensive discussion of the theories and methods that the candidate had applied. When it was my turn, I asked her about the historical parts of the dissertation and about the empirical evidence that she had been bringing to bear. After we had recommended the award of the degree, I received an email a few weeks later from the newly minted PhD. She wrote that she had been so glad to have had an opportunity to discuss the historical parts of her dissertation because the archival sources that she had found were just as important to her as the theories that she had examined. I am sure Bob would have agreed that however interdisciplinary we try to be, there are always limits to our quest, of which he was nevertheless a persistent practitioner. His *Perception and Misperception* will continue to have a lasting impact on international relations and other social science disciplines, including history.

NOTES

1. Christopher Clark, *The Sleepwalkers: How Europe Went to War in 1914* (Harper, 2014).

2. See, for example, Gerd Krumeich, *Juli 1914. Eine Bilanz* (Schoeningh, 2013).

3. Fritz Fischer, *Germany's Aims in the First World War* (Norton, 1967). I outline the debate below.

4. See, for example, Georg G. Iggers, *The German Conception of History* (Wesleyan University Press, 1983).

5. See, for example, Helmut Walser Smith, "When the Sonderweg Debate Left Us," *German Studies Review* 31, no. 2 (2008): 225–40; Jürgen Kocka, "Looking Back on the Sonderweg," *Central European History* 31 (2018): 137–42.

6. Fischer, *Germany's Aims in the First World War*.

7. Fritz Fischer, *War of Illusions: German Policies from 1911 to 1914* (Norton, 1975).

8. Robert Jervis, *Perception and Misperception in International Politics* (Princeton University Press, 1976). The text of the second edition, which was published in 2017, remained unchanged, but it contains a ninety-page preface in which he looks back on the reception of his book during some forty years of debate and also provides further information on the conception and aims of his work. Because my essay is concerned with Bob's interactions with historical research of the 1970s, his new preface is indirectly relevant here and is therefore not part of this analysis.

9. Jervis, *Perception and Misperception*, 23.

10. For the most detailed recent account of this event and its fallout, see Gerhard Hirschfeld, *Sarajewo. 28. Juni 1914* (Landeszentrale fuer politische Bildung Thuringia, 2020).

11. See, for example, Volker R. Berghahn, *Germany and the Approach of War in 1914* (Macmillan, 1973).

12. Marc Trachtenberg, "The Meaning of Mobilization in 1914," *International Security* 15 (1990/1991): 120–50. Trachtenberg later joined the UCLA Political Science Department.

13. Jervis, *Perception and Misperception*, 65.

14. See Mira Rapp-Hooper's touching essay on Jervis in Richard H. Immerman, Marc Trachtenberg, and Diane N. Labrosse, eds., *H-Diplo|ISSF Tribute to the Life, Scholarship, and Legacy of Robert Jervis: Part I*, February 4, 2022, https://issforum.org/to/JervisTribute-1.

15. Mira Rapp-Hooper, "Ambivalent Albion, Ambitious Ally: Britain's Decision for No Separate Peace in 1914," *Security Studies* 23, no. 4 (2014): 814–44. I would like to thank Dr. Rapp-Hooper for making this article available for me and also for her most helpful comments on this essay and on my efforts to understand Robert Jervis's work.

16. John C. G. Roehl, "1914: Wilhelm II," in *Deutschland. Globalgesellschaft einer Nation*, ed. Andreas Fahrmeier (Beck, 2020).

17. On the elder Moltke's warnings against a major war, see Stig Foerster, ed., *Vor dem Sprung ins Dunkle* (Schoeningh, 2016).

18. See Gerhard Ritter, *The Schlieffen Plan: Critique of a Myth* (Praeger, 1958).

19. See, for example, Holger Herwig, *The Marne 1914: The Opening of World War I and the Battle That Changed the World* (Random House, 2009); Holger Afflerbach, *Auf des Messers Schneide: Wie das Deutsche Reich den Ersten Weltkrieg verlor* (Beck, 2018).

20. Rapp-Hooper, "Ambivalent Albion," 831.

V

ROBERT JERVIS AS PUBLIC INTELLECTUAL

❖

Bob Jervis in classic form giving an animated talk at the National Defense University, Washington, DC, in 2019.

27

THE ART AND SCIENCE
OF THE POSTMORTEM

RICHARD H. IMMERMAN

Although I cannot claim to have been a student of Robert Jervis, I came close. I initially met him sometime in 1987—it must have been late summer or fall. By that time, although a tenured professor in history, my attraction to political science and international relations had become hard to miss. (Jervis probably more than anyone else in either discipline persuaded even the most skeptical historian that although history and international relations represented two "sides," each illuminated and profited from the other). I had majored in government as an undergraduate, and my first job after receiving my PhD was in the politics department at Princeton. There I worked with Fred Greenstein, who introduced me to political psychology. Greenstein, however, concentrated on personality and politics. He recognized that for the kind of projects I wanted to pursue, I should learn about the cognitive dimension as well.

So at Greenstein's suggestion, when I applied for a fellowship that funded training in a different discipline, I recruited Jervis to be my mentor. I knew of him only because I had read his already-iconic *Perception and Misperception in International Politics*.[1] He didn't know me from a hole in the ground. (Or so I thought. As I would rapidly learn, Jervis read anything and everything; he even had a book of mine in his indescribably cluttered office. When undergoing treatment for his cancer, he rejected my advice that he go for walks in Central Park because, exhausted from the treatments he was receiving, his priority was conserving his energy for reading.) Jervis characteristically agreed to help me out, I received the fellowship, and virtually overnight he became integral to my life.

Jervis made it easy for me to become not only his mentee but also his friend and colleague. We all know how difficult academics can be, especially those who have reached the exalted heights that Jervis already had and who keep the impossibly hectic schedule that he did. Nevertheless, he was warm, welcoming, compassionate, and patient almost to a fault. He never seemed to be in a rush, even when I was. His inquisitiveness was boundless, and he always had one more question to ask. Often it was about a book in my field that he had read and I sheepishly had to admit I had not. Although a private person, he would also ask about my family or some other personal matter. Later he would ask about my father, who, as fate would have it, ended up sharing a law office suite with Bob's father. Over the following years, he would go out of his way to compliment me for something I'd written or buck me up if I received a less-than-sterling review, always in a peer-to-peer manner. I appreciated Jervis's use of the adjective "marvelous" so much that I resented Billy Crystal's mocking it. For the record, I thought Jervis funnier than Crystal. Warm, welcoming, compassionate, and patient—that was Bob Jervis.

And oh so smart. Yet like everything else about Jervis, he "carried" his intelligence with ease. Over the course of the two-year fellowship, I spent countless hours with Jervis at Columbia. Among the first substantive conversations we had was about his classic article, "Cooperation Under the Security Dilemma," which to my embarrassment I had not yet read.[2] It is brilliant and, as is the case with so much of Jervis's writing, remarkably accessible. Often after reading something he wrote, I thought to myself, why had I not thought of that? Why hadn't anyone? Of course I knew the answer.

That conversation, during which Jervis ping-ponged back and forth between "Cooperation Under the Security Dilemma" and *Perception and Misperception*, dramatically revised my conception of Cold War history (which I revised again a decade later after reading his article "Was the Cold War a Security Dilemma?"[3]). We followed up that conversation with one about *The Logic of Images*.[4] He asked me how much I knew about signaling. Only a little, I answered. Within an hour's time, I knew a great deal more. I cannot even begin to capture our conversations about *The Meaning of the Nuclear Revolution*, which he was wrapping up at the time and for which he would win the Grawemeyer Award.[5] Jervis's explanation of the questions that drove him to write *The Meaning of the Nuclear Revolution* prompted me to reread Bernard Brodie's *The Absolute Weapon*, which it turned out Dwight D. Eisenhower had read in draft when, serendipitously for this book, he was president of Columbia University, and thus became vital for my work on Eisenhower's strategy once he reached the White House.[6] Jervis consistently identified questions that in retrospect were commonsensical yet that only he thought to ask and answer.

Jervis graciously introduced me to his colleagues at Columbia. He was confident that I could learn from them and, perhaps, because I was a historian, that they could learn a little from me. He also invited me (Bob never insisted) to attend several of his graduate seminars. I rarely said anything. I listened and consumed—as would any historian of US foreign relations after his initial introduction to unfamiliar theories. Jervis's classes weren't electric; that was not his style. I nonetheless hung on every word he said, which were uniformly intelligible even to an international relations neophyte like me. Jervis's seminars resembled an extended, informal conversation that because of his knowledge, skill, and preparation covered the spectrum of core issues. Several years later, he invited me, along with Marc Trachtenberg and several other historians, to attend James McAllister's dissertation defense. What a fabulous experience that was, for James above all but only slightly less so for the rest of us.[7] And what better evidence could there be of the generosity and thoughtfulness that Jervis rained on his students—on top of his wisdom, stimulation, and inspiration.

Yet the highlights of my visits to Columbia were the late-afternoon seminars that he hosted. These were distinct from the lunches and brown bags, ultimately dubbed "Jervis lunches," that his Columbia colleagues and graduate students write about effusively in this volume and that were continuations of what he began at UCLA.[8] Jervis's ability to lead a discussion without dominating it was uncanny. If there was no reading that he thought appropriate for his selected subject, he wrote a paper on it. I'm sure he was among the first to apply prospect theory to the Vietnam War, and I do not believe that he ever published that paper, which was substantial. He conceived of it solely as a vehicle to collect his thoughts and provoke our thinking. I never again read a document the same way that I had before attending these seminars.

I must interject, and this is not simply a sidebar, that Jervis taught me about the necessity of serving cookies at what one might call extracurricular meetings. I almost ran afoul of the federal government's ethics rules when, later, as an assistant deputy director of national intelligence (ADDNI), I insisted on applying the lesson that I learned from Jervis. The Office of the Director of National Intelligence's (ODNI) Office of Legal Counsel warned me that, should I request reimbursement for refreshments for a workshop I convened with former presidential briefers, I risked violating legislation enacted in the wake of Vice President Dick Cheney's January 2001 meeting with his energy task force. To me, Bob's rule was sacrosanct; I paid for the cookies out of my personal research funds.

This anecdote is more than a sidebar because it links my relationship to Jervis with my appointment as an ADDNI. And that appointment deepened both our relationship and my perspective on Jervis's insights about the US intelligence enterprise and the postmortems for which he was so renowned. I had examined a CIA covert action prior to my having had any direct contact with Jervis, but my focus was on the agency as an implementer of policy. That was par for a historian's course. I attribute the evolution of my concern with the dynamics of intelligence analysis and with intelligence reports and estimates as inputs into the formulation of policy largely to my reading and discussions of Jervis's work. Surprisingly in retrospect, his stint as a CIA consultant during the Jimmy Carter years never came up during our early conversations. That may have been because he rigorously adhered to the strictures of his security clearances. His postmortem on the fall of the Shah had not yet been declassified. Further, he was just beginning to publish on intelligence when I came to know him, a subject that was still peripheral to me. I was writing a book with Robert Bowie, however, and we became very close. Bowie, as Carter's director of the National Foreign Assessment Center (the short-lived product of the merger of the CIA's Directorate of Intelligence and the National Intelligence Officers), had hired Jervis to write the postmortem on the CIA's estimates about Iran and the Shah. After one of Jervis's afternoon seminars that Bowie attended, he told me about it and the reason for his selection of Jervis. We discussed it on multiple subsequent occasions in the context of our writing about decision-making processes. I don't recall when I first discussed it with Jervis.

During those years, Jervis increasingly turned his attention to the study of US intelligence.[9] I read everything he wrote, drawn to his arguments about how hard it is for intelligence analysts to reach accurate judgments in light of the universe of uncertainty in which they operate and the ambiguity of their sources, the gaps in their sources, and often the unreliability of their sources. Then there are their beliefs and preconceptions. Inspired by his logic, evidence, and theoretical insights, I all but adopted Jervis's interests and concerns. More by circumstance than by design, he reprised his role as my mentor.

Accordingly, Jervis's scholarship on intelligence was in large part responsible for my grasping the opportunity to serve as the assistant deputy director of national intelligence for analytic integrity and standards when offered the position in 2007. The authors of the 2004 Intelligence Reform and Terrorism Prevention Act (IRTPA) that created my office designed it to address precisely the shortcomings in the analytic process that Jervis had identified in his writings.[10] He had begun to argue that these shortcomings could be mitigated albeit not resolved through more effective exploitation of historical and social science methods. (*Why Intelligence Fails* did not come out until 2010, but he foreshadowed his arguments in earlier articles and papers, and we had discussed them extensively.[11]) Not many of those outside the intelligence community (IC) and too few inside it were as interested as Bob was in what my staff and I were doing. Repeatedly he would take the train down to Langley, Virginia, to talk, after which we would go to dinner to talk some more. Often he would use these "sessions" to pull out a copy of a document that he wanted to show—and give—to me. He never lost sight of my scholarly agenda.

Of course, he never lost sight of his own scholarly agenda. When at Langley, Jervis would meet with his friends in both the CIA and ODNI's National Intelligence Council. They were his friends, but they were also primary sources. He was like a kid in a candy store, but what a kid and what a store. No scholar had the sources within the IC that Jervis did because those sources within the IC trusted him like no other scholar. An exemplar is the special issue of the journal *Intelligence and National Security*, which Jervis helped to organize and to which he contributed an essay. More than a half-dozen essays by commentators on and participants in the production of the 2007 National Intelligence Estimate (NIE) on Iran's nuclear program composed the symposium. They included myself, my boss Thomas Fingar, at the time the deputy director of national intelligence for analysis, and Vann Van Diepen, the national intelligence officer whom Jervis held in particularly high regard and who served as the NIE's chief drafter. Jervis conceived of the project as an instrument to educate scholars, policymakers, and the public.[12]

Indeed, the nexus that Jervis established with the IC was anything but a one-way street. He was passionate about encouraging intelligence officials to draw on scholars both for their subject-matter and methodological expertise, and he used his personal relationships to promote such outreach at every opportunity. Further, for decades, he chaired the CIA's Historical Review Panel (which was renamed the Historical Advisory Panel after his tenure ended when the Donald Trump administration sought to disband the committee). For over half of that time, I chaired the State Department's Historical Advisory Committee and hence had a birds-eye view of Jervis's heroic efforts to enhance the transparency of the CIA by making public, through special projects as well as through the *Foreign Relations of the United States* (FRUS) series, documents that had previously been classified, most notably those that acknowledged a covert action. Jervis fully appreciated that the release of these documents would better inform American citizens even as they became grist for scholarship that would better inform government officials.[13]

As Bowie explained after that seminar in the 1980s, it was because of Jervis's scholarly expertise, his sensitivity to the challenges that intelligence analysts confront in pursuit of "getting it right," and, simply put, his patriotism that he invited Jervis to prepare the now legendary postmortem on the 1979 fall of the Shah of Iran. Jervis's scholarship was so eclectic as to defy explanation beyond his astoundingly inquisitive and fertile mind.[14] I am nevertheless confident that the research and writing that he did for the postmortem on the fall of the Shah served as a catalyst for the greater attention that Jervis paid to intelligence from the 1980s up to the tragic day that he passed away. That postmortem, combined with the equally important and influential one he wrote on the IC's flawed 2002 NIE and related assessments of Iraq's weapons of mass destruction (WMD) program, served as the foundation for his capstone book, *Why Intelligence Fails*. Initially published in 2010, it became an instant classic.[15]

It also cemented Jervis's reputation, to quote Richard Betts in this volume, as the "dean" of intelligence studies in the United States.[16]

——— ✺ ———

Many of the contributors to this volume predictably and appropriately highlight and comment on both of these postmortems and *Why Intelligence Fails* as integral to Jervis's legacy and illustrative of "the Jervis effect." In the paragraphs and outline that follow, I contextualize these postmortems by providing what in my judgment is a revealing supplement to them that is far less known. I stumbled upon this document while reviewing my email correspondence with Jervis (I very much regret that I did not archive this correspondence more systematically) after his passing. Writing to me on an unrelated personal matter in February 2011, he attached what he titled "Post-mortem Plan and Questions." He explained, "I'm helping the IC with the Egypt postmortem," adding that "I'm not sure what that will entail." He planned to travel down to the CIA's campus in Langley later that week to discuss the project. "I am not at all sure they will do it right," he concluded.[17]

That concluding sentence signals Jervis's approach to the assignment, his priorities, and his expertise. By 2011, his experience with postmortems was extensive. I lack sources and evidence to compare his experience with that of others, but especially in terms of the time and effort he put into them and their rigor, he almost certainly was in a league of his own. Hence when he worried about whether "they will do it right," he had a reliable baseline from which to judge. What is more, without minimizing the intellectual satisfaction that Jervis received from these projects and the extent to which they influenced his own scholarship, his goal from the outset, as is evident from his work plan (see the plan at the end of this chapter), was for these postmortems to serve the interests of the IC by provoking introspection and providing lessons learned. (Jervis appreciated the distinction between the dedicated postmortems to which he contributed and the case studies produced by the CIA's lessons-learned program, which, with rare exceptions, collected dust on the CIA library's shelves.) The first bullet point of his outline described the production of a postmortem as "a way of increasing IC capacity."[18]

As he made explicit in "Why Postmortems Fail," however, Jervis was under no illusion that his postmortems were likely to alter dramatically how the CIA went about doing its business. He never wavered from this goal of increasing IC capacity.[19]

Jervis did not subsequently write anything about this postmortem, nor did he speak about it, at least not to me. It may never have been completed. If it was, the political environment, then and now, bodes ill for its declassification. Because we were communicating over email, Jervis identified the subject only as "Egypt." Yet it's easy to infer the specifics. Encouraged by the overthrow of Tunisia's president Zine El Abidine Ben Ali on January 14, 2011, antigovernment protests erupted on Egypt's National Police Day two weeks later. Tens of thousands of protestors gathered in Cairo and other cities, and their numbers and reach grew over the following days. The long-time Egyptian president, Hosni Mubarak, responded with curfews, violent repression, and even a few concessions. The protests only intensified. On February 11, Mubarak resigned, and on February 13, Egypt's Supreme Council of the Armed Forces dissolved parliament, suspended the constitution, and declared that it would exercise governing power for six months or until a new election and a referendum on the constitution could be held.[20] I received Jervis's email with the attached work plan for the Egyptian postmortem the following day, precisely a month after the anti-Mubarak protests first broke out.

The logic of examining the reporting and analyses of the Egyptian Revolution from start to finish and the weeks if not months leading up to it is compelling. Still, I have no way of knowing when the IC decided to prepare a postmortem on it or who in the IC solicited Jervis's assistance. What is certain is that he had little advance notice prior to putting together his recommendations about how to proceed and what questions to address. Further, he makes explicit in the document that he sent to me, which he labeled "revised," that he had not received a briefing on either the intended scope of the project or the time and resources that the IC budgeted for it. Was it to be completed "quick and dirty or slower," and how far back in time should it begin?[21] Most fundamentally, who was the intended audience, and what did the IC expect the project to yield? Would the CIA's Product Evaluation Staff or the ODNI's Office of Analytic Integrity and Standards contribute? Perhaps the CIA's Center for the Study of Intelligence might also?

Notwithstanding the imprecision of the charge, the work plan shows that Jervis was able in probably less than a week to take with him to Langley an extraordinarily constructive document because it reflected his prior experience, his extraordinary scholarship, and his profound understanding of the IC's organization and mission. The plan is insightful and sophisticated. It also anticipates areas in which the IC's work and its work product regarding Egypt likely came up short and, therefore, the IC should seek to improve in the future.

Jervis's destination that Thursday must have been the Langley campus. The CIA's Original Headquarters Building (OHB) continues to house the National Intelligence Council (NIC) even though NIEs are products of the ODNI, and the CIA remains responsible for most of the all-source intelligence products that a postmortem on the Egyptian Revolution would doubtless feature. Undeterred by the all-but-certain traffic, Jervis probably at a minimum planned to visit the headquarters of the ODNI at Liberty Crossing II near Virginia's Tyson's Corner, the Defense Intelligence Agency at Joint Base Anacostia–Bolling in Washington, and the National Security Agency in Fort Meade, Maryland.

The reason for these visits goes beyond their reporting on Egypt. As his work plan makes clear, Jervis understood the need to assess the extent to which different IC elements and offices collaborated with one another and shared information; whether these different elements and offices and, for that matter, individual analysts differed in their judgments; and what, if any, peer-review process was conducted of any of the products, internally within the elements and offices or jointly. Jervis would have wanted to ensure that the postmortem team had license to interview analysts and office managers as well as access to a comprehensive set of products.

Some of Jervis's most salient questions related to concerns that he had long held and expressed. When assessing the CIA's estimates of the stability of and threats to the Shah's regime in Iran, he had been struck by the paucity of resources and expertise that the agency had devoted to the issue and the compartmentalization of those analysts who "worked" it.[22] Only someone who remained as engaged with the IC as Jervis was over the subsequent three decades would sufficiently have appreciated the extent to which that challenge remained. He advised that the postmortem investigate whether the resources—based on both analytic and collection requirements—were adequate and, even if they were, whether the same could be said about the level of expertise and language capabilities. Did the IC's emphasis on counterterrorism come at the expense of its attention to more traditional threats, and compared to regional targets such as Iran and Iraq, had the community relegated relatively stable Egypt to something of a "backwater" status? In this regard, Jervis wrote that the postmortem must evaluate the pre-crisis reporting as much as, if not more than, that beginning on January 14 and keep a careful lookout for antecedents that analysts had identified, mistaken as precedents, or ignored.

Further, that reporting had to drill down below the level of Mubarak, his regime, and his supporters. Because "our policy was to encourage democracy, but of a top-down, elite driven type [underscoring in the original]," he asked, did that lead the IC "to an underestimate of the possibilities of unrest from the bottom?" Even if they did not underestimate these possibilities, did they communicate the prospect of a revolution with the language required to get the attention of policymakers? Had analysts become so risk averse since Iraq that they omitted from their estimates scenarios that they judged unlikely or, because of gaps in their intelligence, in which they had low confidence? Perhaps even more importantly, were they derelict in their duty by shielding policymakers from discomforting "news"? Did they speak truth to power?

To the murky issue of politicization, Jervis directly linked the questions that he formulated regarding the prospect that the IC had assessed a revolution from below as unlikely because it followed the lead of policymakers. Although disputes about whether intelligence is politicized have raged since the Vietnam War, they became central to the historiography of President George W. Bush's decision to take the United States into a "war of choice" in Iraq, most notably in terms of the production and consequence of the 2003 NIE on Iraq's WMD program. Jervis was among those scholars who argued that although the NIE and attendant products were seriously flawed and riddled with misjudgments, the intelligence on the Iraqi president Saddam Hussein and WMD had not been seriously politicized, despite the efforts by Bush administration officials to do so. It did not need to be, he explained, because the IC (the NIC was no exception) suffered from the same preconceptions that pervaded the administration and, what is more, its judgments were reasonable given the deficient quality of the intelligence reporting.[23]

This postmortem that was "assigned" to Jervis in February 2011, he consequently recognized, could not avoid considering that the intelligence on Egypt had been politicized. He had not revised his judgment that, as professionals, analysts were far less vulnerable to skewing their conclusions so that they conformed to policymakers' preferences than many observers, including scholars, contended. As he wrote in his work plan, his concern was "not politicization in the normal sense, but [the] impact of policy on what intelligence was thinking about (& what it was ignoring)." Put another way, Jervis understood that too often poor tradecraft was mistaken for politicization. By searching for signs of the latter, the postmortem could expose the former, which he deemed far more pervasive and fundamental. The postmortem that Jervis hoped the IC would produce would hold the IC's reporting on Egypt to the analytic tradecraft standards (surfacing underlying assumptions, identifying alternate scenarios, and more) that had been established and institutionalized after the NIE on Iraq's WMD debacle.[24]

<hr />

Topping the list of these standards was the quality, reliability, and scope of the intelligence itself—the evidence. More than he had at the time of the Iranian Revolution, Jervis had come to appreciate that the IC's employment of the term "all-source" intelligence did not necessarily mean that judgments emerged from intelligence from all sources. It too rarely did. Collaboration among agencies and the integration of their respective "silos" remained aspirational, and information sharing was a work in progress. The postmortem thus had to evaluate whether policymakers were receiving the right intelligence in the right form and at the right time. That included open-source intelligence. There would be much value added to a postmortem, Jervis's work plan underscored, if it addressed analysts' long-standing fetishization of "secret intelligence." The postmortem should not only assess how and how much analysts drew on open sources but also compare this intelligence to that collected by covert means. To Jervis, conducting a content analysis of the press coverage could prove very illuminating, and he even provided examples of columns.

The emphasis that Jervis placed on exploring how much analysts had drawn on open sources was inseparable from what became something of a pet peeve of his—analytic outreach.[25] Owing largely to his countless interactions and friendships with IC, particularly CIA, analysts, Jervis was acutely aware of their discomfort with and even aversion to sounding out scholars and others from the unclassified universe for their knowledge. He theorized that although they recognized the benefits of learning from academics, journalists, businesspeople, and parallel experts from the private sector without security clearances, they feared that the more intimate their conversations became, the greater the opportunities for classified information to slip out. As a result of these cost-benefit calculations, they avoided reaching beyond the IC for expertise, or if they did find themselves at a gathering of outside experts, they did not ask questions or say a word. Jervis had been present at such gatherings and observed this dynamic. He repeatedly commented to me on his frustration. Therefore, it came as no surprise to me that he wanted the postmortem to address among its first questions whether "outside experts [were] called? Who? When?" Pushing further, he deemed it important to learn whether the analysts had a Rolodex of experts, and he specified who should be in it. To Jervis, analytic outreach was integral to all-source intelligence.

I encourage readers to review Jervis's plan and his questions for themselves. The document, which follows in toto, offers something of the negative of the postmortems that he published and with which most of us are familiar. Some day we may learn that this postmortem was written, and if so and if it is declassified, it would be highly instructive to juxtapose it with the ones on the fall of the Shah and Iraq's WMD program. We could therefore judge for ourselves, to return to the question that Bob posed in his email to me, whether "they" got it "right." But even if his work plan came to naught, it provides a unique window into Bob Jervis's remarkable mind, his unsurpassed understanding of the world of intelligence, and his often overlooked effort to serve America's national interests.

POST-MORTEM PLAN AND QUESTIONS

Robert Jervis revised (2/14/11)

I. Objectives, Methods, and Questions

1) Both a post-mortem & a way of increasing IC capacity. Working with evaluation staffs and possibly CIA's CSI.

2) Need to look at past false alarms, and, perhaps more importantly, search for cases where alarm wasn't sounded but in retrospect they look like Tunisia or Egypt at some stage. Minor—past immolations & incidents. What was the analysis following June death & protest?

3) Scope—partly a matter of resources, but also of how much time. Quick & dirty or slower? How much description and "plot summary" to establish the record is desired? How wide and far back in time should one look?

4) How to avoid distracting those on front lines?

5) Performance during crisis included?

6) What can reasonably be expected—e.g., can the IC be expected to say more than this could be trouble? Obvious problems in knowing more than foreign leaders (or potential revolutionaries).

7) Is the team—& am I—expected to make recommendations?

8) Who is the audience? IC leadership; rank-and-file; Congress?

II. What to look for

1) Level of effort (both collection & analysis)—numbers at home & in the field (& how many spoke/read Arabic?). But would more resources have been likely to have made a difference?

2) North Africa and even Egypt seen as backwater? Did they have interested customers?

3) Were "good" reports held at low or medium levels?

4) Was there peer review?

5) Any outside experts called? Who? When?

5a) Did analysts have a Rolodex of people like Robert Springborg (at Naval Postgraduate School, no less) or Ragui Assaad (Minnesota—NYTimes of 2/6/11)?

6) Compare intelligence to what open sources were saying.

6a) Track number of column-inches of coverage in NYT and a few other outlets, starting with June death & protests.

7) How and how much were open sources used?

7a) Do we really do all-source intelligence?

8) Reports from the military (US or T/E)?

9) Were we too focused on counter-terrorism?

10) Underlying assumptions about stability & role of security forces? We hadn't seen major revolutions recently (the "color revolutions" are a partial exception)—had we come to see revolutions as unlikely?

11) Ways to track feedback & expectations among protesters.

12) Did we share assessments with allies—and they with us?

13) Did analysis become more cautious after Iraq? Did analysts feel that anything they said had to be even more grounded in reports from the field?

14) Differences within IC?

15) Differences between offices or individual analysts?

16) Role of review process—did anyone raise basic questions?

17) Inhibitions against intelligence on friends?

18) Inhibitions against bringing bad news, especially when top officials have enough problems?

19) Any insights from failed states project?

20) Were assumptions made explicit—e.g., on role of security services? Need to "show work".

21) Perhaps most important—what was the quality of the pre-crisis reporting? How much did it go deeper & beyond the field reporting? How much did it take account of the work and views of scholars, journalists, and business people? Analysis of military? Any research papers?

22) Related—was our analysis skewed by the fact that our policy was to encourage democracy, but of a top-down, elite driven type, which could have led to a lack of attention to & an underestimate of the possibilities of unrest from the bottom? Not politicization in the normal sense, but impact of policy on what intelligence was thinking about (& what it was ignoring).

23) Did we track impact of rising food prices? Any other indicators of a) discontent (i.e., poll data as in Slackman NYTimes article) or b) things we thought would generate discontent & unrest?

24) Any routine internal evaluations?

25) Did we track Mubarak's health and how it—and his perceptions of it—might influence his behavior (and how other's perceptions of it might affect theirs)?

26) Did we have research reports on security forces, Brotherhood, etc.
27) Did we track the protests in the spring & how they may have increased the protesters' capacity? See, e.g., the <u>NYT</u> article of 2/14.

III. How to do it?

1) Level of effort internally.
2) Extent and nature of my involvement.
3) Possible use of an external team to review draft reports—both fully cleared & 1-day secret.

NOTES

1. Robert Jervis, *Perception and Misperception in International Politics* (Princeton University Press, 1976).
2. Robert Jervis, "Cooperation Under the Security Dilemma," *World Politics* 30 (1978): 167–214.
3. Robert Jervis, "Was the Cold War a Security Dilemma?" *Journal of Cold War Studies* 3 (2001): 36–60.
4. Robert Jervis, *The Logic of Images in International Relations* (Princeton University Press, 1970).
5. Robert Jervis, *The Meaning of the Nuclear Revolution* (Cornell University Press, 1989).
6. Frederick Dunn et al., The Absolute Weapon: Atomic Power and World Order (Harcourt Brace, 1946).
7. See James McAllister, "An Appreciation," in this volume.
8. See Tanya Putnam, "The Jervis Lunches," and Arthur A. Stein, "Bob Jervis at UCLA," in this in Richard H. Immerman, Diane Labrosse, and Marc Trachtenberg, eds., "Tribute to the Life, Scholarship, and Legacy of Robert Jervis, Part I," *H-Diplo/ISSF*, February 4, 2022, https://issforum.org/ISSF/PDF/ISSF-Jervis-Tribute-1.pdf.
9. See Robert Jervis, "What's Wrong with the Intelligence Process?," *International Journal of Intelligence and Counterintelligence* 1 (1986): 28–41; Jervis, "Intelligence and Foreign Policy: A Review Essay," *Intelligence Security* 11 (1986–1987): 141–61; and Jervis, "Strategic Intelligence and Effective Policy," in *Security and Intelligence: New Perspectives for the 1990s*, ed. Stuart Farson, David Stafford, and Wesley Wark (Frank Cass, 1991).
10. Public Law 108–458, Intelligence Reform and Terrorism Prevention Act, December 17, 2004, https://www.archives.gov/files/declassification/pidb/legislation/pdfs/public-law-108-458.pdf. See section 1020 in particular.
11. Robert Jervis, *Why Intelligence Fails: Lessons from the Iranian Revolution and the Iraq War* (Cornell University Press, 2010). See also Jervis, "Reports, Politics, and Intelligence Failures," *Journal of Strategic Studies* 29 (2006): 3–52; and Jervis, "The Politics and Psychology of Intelligence Reform," *The Forum* 4 (2006): DOI:10.2202/1540-8884.1108.

12. "Anatomy of a Controversy: The 2007 Iran Nuclear NIE," special issue of *Intelligence and National Security* 36 (2021), https://www.tandfonline.com/toc/fint20/36/2?nav=tocList. Robert Jervis and James Wirtz later coedited this symposium for a volume published by Routledge with a revised title. Robert Jervis and James Wirtz, eds., *The 2007 Iran Nuclear Estimate Revisited: Anatomy of a Controversy* (Routledge, 2002).

13. See Melvyn P. Leffler, "The CIA's Historical Review Panel," and Michael Warner, "Robert Jervis and Official History," in this volume.

14. See Paul K. MacDonald's introductory essay to this volume.

15. Robert Jervis, *Why Intelligence Fails: Lessons from the Iranian Revolution and the Iraq War* (Cornell University Press, 2010). See also Jervis, "Reports, Politics, and Intelligence Failures," *Journal of Strategic Studies* 29 (2006): 3–52.

16. See Richard K. Betts, "Bridging the Gap Between Public Discourse and Secret Intelligence," in this volume.

17. Jervis email to Immerman with attachment, February 14, 2011 (author's possession).

18. Jervis email to Immerman, February 14, 2011.

19. Robert Jervis, "Why Postmortems Fail," *PNAS* 119 (January 13, 2022), https://www.pnas.org/doi/full/10.1073/pnas.2116638118.

20. Project on Middle East Political Science (POMEPS), "Arab Uprising: The State of the Egyptian Uprising," *POMEPS Briefings* 6 (September 7, 2011), https://www.pomeps.org/wp-content/uploads/2011/09/POMEPS_BriefBooklet6_Egypt_web.pdf/.

21. Unless otherwise noted, quotes are from the draft work plan appended below.

22. Jervis, *Why Intelligence Fails*, 52–54.

23. In addition to *Why Intelligence Fails*, 131–36; 171–74, see Robert Jervis "Reports, Politics, and Intelligence Failures: The Case of Iraq," *Journal of Strategic Studies* 29 (2006): 3–52. For an opposing argument, see Joshua Rovner, *Fixing the Facts: National Security and the Politics of Intelligence* (Cornell University Press, 2011), 139–84. Illustrative of his attitude toward scholarship and support of that of others, *Fixing the Facts* was a volume in the Cornell Studies in Security Affairs series that Jervis cofounded and coedited. See Roger Haydon, "Robert Jervis: Colleague and Friend," in Immerman, et.al., in Richard H. Immerman, Diane Labrosse, and Marc Trachtenberg, eds., "Tribute to the Life, Scholarship, and Legacy of Robert Jervis," Part I. See also in this volume Janice Gross Stein, "Political Psychology and the Analysis of Intelligence Failures."

24. In part because of our conversations, but only in part, Jervis, probably more than most scholars of intelligence, appreciated the importance of the analytic standards that the director of national intelligence approved in 2007. Intelligence Community Directive (ICD) 203, "Analytic Standards," June 21, 2007, https://www.dni.gov/files/documents/ICD/ICD%20203%20Analytic%20Standards%20pdf-unclassified.pdf; the standards were revised and expanded in 2015, ICD 203, "Analytic Standards," January 2, 2015, https://www.dni.gov/files/documents/ICD/ICD%20203%20Analytic%20Standards.pdf.

25. As one of the contributors to the drafting of the intelligence community's initial directive on analytic outreach, I discussed it with Jervis on multiple occasions. ICD 205, "Analytic Outreach," effective July 16, 2008, https://www.dni.gov/files/documents/ICD/ICD_205.pdf.

28

ROBERT JERVIS AND OFFICIAL HISTORY

MICHAEL WARNER

Men and nations do behave wisely
once they have exhausted all other alternatives.

—ABBA EBAN (UNITED NATIONS ADDRESS BY ABBA EBAN, JUNE 6, 1967)

I met Robert Jervis a quarter century ago in an unlikely setting: the headquarters of the Central Intelligence Agency (CIA).[1] He had consented to join the Agency's Historical Review Panel (HRP); I served as acting chief of the CIA History Staff. I liked him right away and would learn a lot from his acumen and his example. I believe he learned a few things from me; at least he was always gracious and appreciative. Herein hangs a tale, as the storytellers say, though it requires a fair-sized preface.

The records classification system that Jervis saw firsthand on the HRP derived from the American experiences in two world wars. The US military did not formally classify documents in World War I, and when normalcy returned in the 1920s, nearly everything in the files just sat there until it was gradually culled or shipped to the National Archives. World War II fell out differently. America's British allies taught US officials modern methods of signals intelligence, and with that came ways to sorting and restricting documents according to the sensitivity of the sources and methods involved in their production or use.

After World War II, such sensitive documents could not be left to the normal ravages of bureaucracy; i.e., the transience of officeholders and the need to free up file drawers by disposing of the obsolescent and embarrassing, combined with the haphazard preservation of the curious or seemingly significant. Many classified files sat for decades, while the exigencies of the Cold War doubled, trebled, and quadrupled the volume of records and the need for file space. By the 1970s, the employees who had produced the earlier strata of records had retired, and the departments and agencies that owned the records had scant interest or means to hire the expertise required to sort through decades-old documents in a systematic fashion.

Legislative remedies to this dilemma proved unavailing. The Freedom of Information Act (FOIA; 1966) provided a mechanism to declassify important records in relatively small volumes—if and when requestors asked for them. Soon after, however, the Privacy Act (1974) restricted the government's ability to release records naming average American citizens and even most federal employees. What legislation giveth, legislation taketh away. Not for the first time had good intentions gone awry in the world of historical review and declassification.

Director of Central Intelligence (DCI) William Casey found a partial solution, at least for his agency. He convinced Congress that many CIA files should be exempt from FOIA because they were so sensitive that reviewing them for declassification was futile. In return, he offered up most of the records from his former agency, the wartime Office of Strategic Services (OSS). Congress kept its end of the bargain, granting an "operational files exemption" for some CIA records and for 1984.[2] And Casey did his part, shipping thousands of linear feet of OSS recrds to the National Archives. This looked like a win for the taxpayers (allowing the agency to employ its declassification resources more efficiently) and for the historians (who could study an intelligence service from its birth in 1941 to its demise and disposition after 1945).

The end of the Cold War caused some rethinking in the intelligence community, particularly at the CIA. Just before the formal end of the Soviet Union in late 1991, DCI Robert Gates publicly pledged to declassify agency records on several well-known operations, such as the Bay of Pigs invasion and the coups in Iran and Guatemala in the 1950s. He backed up his promise with resources as well, rejuvenating a small office called the Center for the Study of Intelligence (CSI), augmenting it with a modest history staff that was soon doubled in size (which is how I was hired) and also adding to it a new Historical Review Group (HRG) that was dedicated to releasing the covert action files flagged by those new agency historians.[3]

But no good deed goes unpunished. Just as the HRG set to work, a tendentious film depiction of the Kennedy assassination revived old conspiracy theories and caused a controversy that media outlets amplified to the point where several members of Congress demanded that the CIA release records related to the Warren Commission's investigation of the president's murder. Agency personnel who had been detailed to reviewing files on Cold War records suddenly found themselves hunting through anything and everything possibly related to the plotline of an axe-grinding B movie. The CIA had no one else to dedicate to this task because experts in decades-old records and declassification policies are by definition rare. Thus, the US government set aside an effort to reveal the details of real conspiracies (which is what most covert actions truly are) to spend taxpayer money documenting a fictional conspiracy.

The CIA tried again in the mid-1990s, after the Kennedy assassination rumors went dormant for lack of evidence. By now, the CSI with its historians and reviewers had gained some runtime, learning how to find old files and how to review them safely and efficiently. A new head of CSI, Brian Latell, wisely decided that the agency's historical review effort needed some scholarly counsel (and legitimacy), and thus he devised the idea of recruiting academic historians for a Historical Review Panel (HRP). The CSI modeled this committee on the State Department's Historical Advisory Committee, an activist body of diplomatic historians who consulted with the Office of the Historian in its compilation of State Department's estimable *Foreign Relations of the United States* series. Unfortunately, the maiden voyage of the HRP ended poorly. Ushered in to meet with the DCI, one of the scholars took the opportunity to complain about the CIA's lack of declassification. That particular DCI had scant patience for aggravations of any kind, and he nearly threw the eminent historian (and with him the director of CSI) headlong from his office.

Enter Robert Jervis, who soon after this accepted our invitation to chair a revamped HRP. He brought a different approach. He looked grandfatherly and acted that way as well: patient, kind, and logical. But he shared a guiding vision informed by his study of international relations and state behavior. He knew that scholars in his field (and others as well) depended on good source material, which is to say on good history, which in turn relied on access to documents. In short, if scholars collectively were to make sense of the Cold War—especially its nuclear dynamic—they needed to understand the intelligence that informed leaders' decisions and then implemented their orders.

Here I must confess I had hitherto paid little attention to international relations as a field. Historians, we learned in our training, were to stick to the documents and timelines, eschewing "generalization" as hasty and even biased.

Jervis and I intersected at just this point. I had heard of him, of course, but had not appreciated his significance. We quickly found that we shared a desire for the agency to raise the productivity (and the stature) of its declassification effort. I wanted more historians in that great beyond that we called "academia" to understand what had happened in the Cold War. Jervis wanted international relations to mature its theories and approaches by considering some of the most momentous events in living memory.

The rest of the agency took time to grasp our view that it shared a corporate interest in openness. I did my best to keep the CSI and the agency's leadership interested in the HRP and, for a time, scheduled and hosted its meetings. Jervis appreciated the opportunity and played along despite my junior status and anonymity in academic circles. He asked good questions of briefers. He persisted in explaining what should be done.[4] But once again, an outside event managed to complicate tailored declassification of important records.

This time the intention was laudable, if flawed in its execution. In 1995, President Bill Clinton issued Executive Order 12958, mandating sweeping, automatic declassification of older federal records. Naturally the military and intelligence departments and agencies held certain exemptions, but even they had to release (by their standards) prodigious numbers of documents. Though Clinton's order would result in many millions of pages going to the National Archives, the archivists there were not resourced or trained to process them for public viewing. And so they sat among hundreds of millions of pages of backlogged records for years, "declassified" but unavailable.[5] But that is another story.

The agency geared up to comply with this new mandate in the late 1990s. Years of flat budgets and increasing requirements, however, had squeezed agency resources. The inevitable consolidation of records management and review functions that followed meant that the mandatory declassification managers cast envious eyes on the CIA's Historical Review Group, with its cadre of trained declassifiers. Who better to staff the mandatory review effort, which after all complied with an Executive Order, instead of merely satisfying Professor Jervis and his colleagues on the HRP? Any bureaucracy will choose the mandatory over the optional.

Even then, Jervis did not give up. Voluntary, tailored declassification survived, and progress, though halting, was made.[6] By September 11, 2001, the HRP and voluntary declassification had enough momentum to survive the inevitable surge to even higher priorities.[7] Jervis had kept on going, and by the early 2000s, I could boast to public audiences that the CIA was the most open major intelligence service in the world and could rattle off declassified histories, files, and collections to make my case.

I took a rotation to the new Office of the Director of National Intelligence (ODNI) in the mid-2000s, which meant that I formally parted ways with the HRP. From my post at ODNI, however, I did help Jervis to land some extra work. By 2007, I was teaching intelligence to graduate students as an adjunct professor and found his writing on the blown Iraq weapons of mass destruction (WMD) analysis to be useful in the classroom.[8] This was right when ODNI was completing a new WMD estimate (on Iran), and I suggested that Jervis and his Columbia colleague Richard Betts be asked to comment on the draft. The subsequent National Intelligence Estimate has been defended and critiqued by many observers (including former president George W. Bush in his memoirs), so I'll leave them the chore of saying how much credit Jervis earned for his role.[9]

Teaching gave me another appreciation for Jervis's contributions. As an intelligence historian, it struck me that certain "patterns" recurred over and over in the employment of intelligence. I began to hypothesize about how states predictably built and used their spies and agencies in similar ways. In short, I found myself "generalizing"; learning from the rigor of Jervis's work in the field while teaching at Columbia for a semester, I was able to compare notes with him for once on his home turf, typically in his remarkable office in the gloriously shabby suite of the School of International and Public Affairs (SIPA).

The issues and problems of official declassification had not changed, but by now, a lot of records had been released through mandatory programs, FOIA requests, and yes, voluntary releases. By the 2010s, the agency was opening up its records on its own momentum and perhaps no longer needed Jervis to shepherd the HRP.[10] This was exactly the point. That is what was supposed to happen—the agency had institutionalized openness. Today it is still arguably the most open intelligence service anywhere. Ironically, its good example inspired a competitor for that title at the National Security Agency (NSA), of all places, which now rivals the CIA in the volume of its releases.

⁂

Robert Jervis had a small but direct role in opening the NSA as well. In the middle of the last decade, his interests widened to include cyber strategy and policy. This was when those matters had come under high-level scrutiny in the executive and legislative branches. Leaders in both arenas wondered how the United States could deter the growing scope and severity of state-sponsored, malicious cyber behavior that ranged from attacks on private corporations to an online campaign by the Islamic State to fears that peer competitors would hold the critical infrastructure of the United States at risk.

With Jervis's expertise in international perception and deterrence issues, not to mention his security clearances, he was naturally invited down to Washington to participate in workshops on cyber deterrence. One such workshop was held at my new institutional home, the US Cyber Command (USCYBERCOM), in 2015.

The actual event made no breakthrough on the cyber deterrence front (that would await a clearer differentiation of the strategic "environments"—nuclear, conventional, and cyber—and the strategies aligned to each). Nonetheless, two events around it held a certain importance because they occurred where USCYBERCOM lived, which is to say on the main campus of the NSA.

First, the NSA's records review and declassification effort at that time was run by an enlightened senior executive, David Sherman. He jumped at the chance to meet Jervis when I suggested it, and the two had an engaging conversation about what more the NSA could be doing to add clarity to the documents being released by the CIA and ODNI (especially the Presidential Daily Briefs from the 1960s that would soon be released).

The second event that day held more symbolic value. As we strolled the labyrinthine corridors between one meeting and the next, someone at the NSA pulled the fire alarm. We found the nearest exit, of course, which meant I still carried some classified notes I had just taken.

I had no choice but to approach the guard at the building entrance and ask him to hold my notes while we waited in the parking lot for the all clear. While the fire alarm shrieked at us, Jervis enjoyed the ensuing dialogue:

"I can't hold your notes, sir," the guard politely replied.

"Okay. Then can I carry the notes outside?" I asked in return.

"No, sir. You cannot carry classified material out of the building."

"Then can I take the notes back to my office for safekeeping?"

"No, sir. Not during a fire alarm."

"Well, then," I offered, "either you hold my notes until the alarm stops or let me carry them outside, or you let me take them to my office. You pick one of those options."

At this point, the poor guard relented and grudgingly held my notebook for the next twenty minutes, letting a bemused Jervis and me wait with the NSA and USCYBERCOM workforces in the parking lot.

Stripped of its modest comedic merit, our encounter neatly encapsulated Jervis's approach to declassification. He and I shared Abba Eban's (paraphrased) impression that the federal government, like that harried entrance guard, generally desires to do the right thing. It just needs some gentle persuasion—backed up by airtight logic—to realize that it has exhausted its alternatives and that openness, though uncomfortable, is not only possible but wise in the end.

NOTES

1. The opinions expressed above are those of the author alone and do not reflect official positions of any US government entity.
2. See 50 US Code § 3141.
3. J. Kenneth McDonald, foreword to Mary S. McAuliffe, ed., *CIA Documents on the Cuban Missile Crisis, 1962* (Central Intelligence Agency, 1992).
4. Jervis talked about his time with the HRP in a 2019 podcast; see Robert Jervis and Francis J. Gavin, "An Interview with Robert Jervis—Reflections on Political Science, Politics,

and Policy," *War on the Rocks*, August 12, 2019, https://warontherocks.com/2019/08
/an-interview-with-robert-jervis-reflections-on-political-science-politics-and-policy/.

5. "The December 29, 2009 Presidential Memorandum accompanying EO 13526 specified
a December 31, 2013 deadline for making available to the public the declassified records
within the approximately 400 [million] pages currently backlogged (that is, currently
accessioned but not yet fully processed for release) at the National Archives and Records
Administration (NARA) and under the [National Declassification Center]"; National
Archives and Records Administration, "Bi-annual Report on Operations of the National
Declassification Center Reporting Period: January 1, 2010–December 31, 2010," https://
www.archives.gov/declassification/ndc/reports/2010-biannual-january1-december31
.pdf.

6. Publicly released minutes of HRP meetings, which were never classified, can be found at
various sites on the internet.

7. Richard H. Immerman has reflected on this phase of the HRP's life in "The Incomparable Robert Jervis," in *ISSF Tribute to the Life, Scholarship, and Legacy of Robert Jervis:
Part I*, ed. Immerman, Diane N. Labrosse, and Marc Trachtenberg, February 4, 2022, 9,
https://issforum.org/to/JervisTribute-1.

8. Robert Jervis, "Reports, Politics, and Intelligence Failures: The Case of Iraq," *Journal of
Strategic Studies* 29, no. 1 (2006): 3–52.

9. For his own account, see Robert Jervis, "The November 2007 Iran nuclear NIE: Immediate Aftermath," *Intelligence and National Security* 36, no. 2 (2021): 222–25.

10. "A spokesman for the C.I.A [in 2006] said that the agency had released 26 million pages
of documents to the National Archives since 1998 and that it was 'committed to the highest quality process' for deciding what should be secret." Scott Shane, "US Reclassifies
Many Documents in Secret Review," *New York Times*, February 21, 2006.

29

THE CIA's HISTORICAL REVIEW PANEL

MELVYN P. LEFFLER

I will let other colleagues and friends comment on the significance of Robert Jervis's scholarly contributions. I want to write a few words about Bob, the man I got to know when we served together for more than fifteen years on the Historical Review Panel for the director of the CIA. Jervis chaired the committee when I joined it around the year 2000. It had been through a stormy history, and he was seeking to resurrect its legitimacy and demonstrate its efficacy. We met twice a year, usually for two days. Prior to that time, I had been acquainted with Jervis's scholarly contributions, especially his book on perception and misperception in international politics and his writings on nuclear strategy, deterrence, and the security dilemma.[1] But I don't think I had ever met Bob prior to our work on the advisory committee.

For fifteen years or more, we labored with other committee members to do a little good to promote declassification and transparency, and I will talk about that shortly. But for me, the highlight of these duties was getting to know Robert Jervis, corresponding with him about books and articles, and garnering his comments and insights on my own writings. What I so admired about Jervis was his thoughtfulness, judicious disposition, modesty, and honesty. What I so admired about Jervis was his open-mindedness, his ability to change his mind, his readiness to acknowledge that he was wrong on a particular matter, and his determination to insist that he was right when the majority thought otherwise.

What I so admired about Jervis was that he was an international relations specialist who truly had a voracious interest in and insatiable appetite for history, who kept abreast of the most recent literature on a myriad of topics, and who was insistent on using historical scholarship carefully and imaginatively to question theoretical generalizations and to extrapolate lessons that might help policymakers. But Jervis always recognized that those exercises were fraught with challenges and imponderables.

What attracted Jervis to me was his humility in the face of complexity. What he told me privately was what he said publicly: the most important book he ever wrote was *System Effects*.[2] Significantly, the subtitle of this book is "Complexity in Political and Social Life." "Very little in social and political life," he concluded, "makes sense except in the light of systemic processes" (295). But the processes themselves, he explained, were inordinately complex: interactions cannot be understood "by explaining each alone; the fate of an actor's policy or strategy depends on those that are adopted by others; behavior alters the environment in ways that affect the trajectory of actors, outcomes, and environments" (60). These types of interactions, he argued, explain much of the puzzling behavior in international politics that captures the attention of scholars: "Intentions and outcomes often are very different, regulation is prone to misfire, and our standard methodologies are not likely to capture the dynamics at work" (60).

Simply stated, Jervis articulated and illustrated for me what a lifetime of scholarship also had taught me, and perhaps that is why I felt so attracted to him. Time and again, he reminded me that evidence is provocatively ambiguous, and the trade-offs that policymakers face are always agonizing. In his last essay, "Why Postmortems Fail," he stressed: do not start by blaming policymakers; remember that it is very hard to get inside their heads. Recognize, he emphasized, that hindsight privileges what we think should have been obvious and that, therefore, "confirmation bias" must be held in check. And keep in mind, he admonished, that people can be right for the wrong reasons and that people can be wrong for the right reasons.[3]

Jervis developed these thoughts as he grappled time and again with the failure of intelligence analysts to get things right. Why had they failed to foresee the fall of the Shah of Iran? Why had they failed to grasp that the Iraqi president Saddam Hussein had no weapons of mass destruction? Why had they failed to prepare for the assault on the US Capitol on January 6? I admired Jervis because he did not think that analysts and officials were stupid or foolish or cowardly; he knew many of them personally, and by the end of his life, he had trained some of them. Faced with the challenge of examining why things went wrong, Jervis advised "humility." Not only is it likely, he wrote, "that the case under consideration will be a difficult one, which means that correct judgments were not likely to have been obvious at the time, but even later conclusions are likely to be disputable. A good post-mortem then recognizes the ambiguities of the case, many of which may remain even after the best retrospective analysis."

To get things right, Jervis believed you needed to adopt good social science methods and you needed to have reliable evidence. He really cared about evidence, about historical documentation, and about understanding the peculiarities of a particular case—yes, its complexities—even as one tried to formulate generalizations and theoretical propositions. Year after year, Jervis steadfastly struggled with CIA officials to accelerate the declassification of critical documents. Sometimes, we met on Sunday nights at an "undisclosed location" near Dulles airport where the CIA rented a building and where we were allowed to read some of the most fascinating and contentious documents that had the CIA (and other agencies) warring with the compilers of the *Foreign Relations of the United States* series. Jervis loved reading those documents, and so did I and the other committee members. Jervis grasped their importance—and sometimes their irrelevance—for the larger subject under discussion.

When we met on subsequent days to talk with intelligence analysts or covert officers and questioned their determination to keep a particular document classified, Jervis was uncannily shrewd in explaining why a particular piece of information would not jeopardize sources or methods, and, even more importantly, why it would actually serve the interests of the agency and the government to have the information disclosed. He could illuminate why a particular piece of information would help explain why a seemingly stupid decision actually was not so foolish, given the information that was available. He could explain that a budgetary number that the agency or the government swore could not be disclosed actually was so small that it did not matter and that readers, in fact, would be amazed at how little was spent on a particular piece of a covert operation. I watched Jervis tangle with our interlocutors, and along with other committee members, I often tried to assist him, but he had his own unique manner of engagement. In my opinion, he was never really eloquent and never really argumentative, but straightforward, honest, self-deprecatory, illuminating, and often persuasive. Most of all, Jervis would insist that the agency and the government had an obligation under an act of Congress to disclose all materials that bore on substantive policy decisions. He emphasized that making the information available would help all of us assess policy successes and failures and understand them in their full complexity so that simplistic and foolish allegations of blame or ineptness would be seen in a larger context.

What was rewarding was that Jervis sometimes was successful. He had stature within the CIA because of his previous consulting and because of his gigantic reputation as a scholar and teacher. He had credibility because he was transparently so honest, so unvindictive, and so desirous of helping the agency through transparency. Time and again, year after year, we would meet for lunch with one director of the agency after another, with George Tenet, with General David Petraeus, and with Leon Panetta, and Jervis would say to them: you know you really have the ability to enhance the agency's credibility by being more transparent; or alternatively, you know you may need to deal with critical legislators or media inquiries if you deny a document that on the face of it should be disclosed because, for example, it already had been published by a foreign government or in a personal memoir. Jervis loved making the case for transparency; he was always polite and deferential but never cowed by authority.

Jervis's approach was always nonpolemical, nonpolitical. He talked in commonsense terminology. Understanding how systems worked or did not work, he constantly prodded CIA officials to meet with and collaborate more with the State Department. Over time, he succeeded at getting key officials in some of the agencies and departments actually to talk directly to one another. He even got the CIA and the State Department Historical Office to appoint a joint historian to examine CIA documents. He also helped push through the declassification of key documents that had held up important volumes of the *Foreign Relations of the United States* (FRUS) series, convinced the CIA that declassifying some early Presidential Daily Briefs would not compromise the security of the US government, and helped persuade agency officials to make the CIA's online CREST system of documents more readily available, to improve the agency's search engine for researchers, and to assess and declassify the oldest and most important documents from the agency's history.

Jervis knew very well that the committee's successes were always marginal and incremental. But what amazed me was his commitment and tenacity. After I had served on the committee for five or eight years—I don't really recall—he said he thought it was now time to pass on the chairmanship and inquired if I might take over if others agreed. I explained why I could not, or would not, and Jervis just continued in place year after year, long after I departed. He never resigned. Although President Donald Trump and his acolytes temporarily dismantled the committee and then reconstituted it without Jervis, in one of the last messages he wrote to me, he said he was looking forward to seeing the new panel continuing its work and was writing some suggestions about what needed to be done.

Until the last months of his life, Jervis remained engaged and enmeshed in scholarly dialogue and debate. He relished his interactions with historians and liked talking about lessons learned. We participated with Chinese and American scholars last June in a forum related to the applicability of the Cold War analogy to contemporary US-Chinese relations. Elected to the National Academy of Sciences in the spring of 2021, Jervis produced an essay for the academy's journal that I alluded to earlier titled "Why Postmortems Fail."[4] To a large extent, the essay summed up conclusions from much of his life's work and conveyed the modesty we all need to feel when confronted with the ambiguities of human behavior and the messiness of national interactions in a complex international system.

Bob Jervis had a strong moral compass, deep convictions, and wonderful values coupled with an ability to discuss matters dispassionately and intelligibly. He saw both the flaws and attributes of people and policymakers and possessed an ability to hold them accountable without attacking them personally. He was a brilliant man who worked prodigiously hard and who contributed invaluable insights to the fields of international history and international relations. He was forever participating in debates and critiquing books and articles, yet he was always fair-minded and levelheaded. He was a scholar I deeply admired, and he became a friend whose personal qualities I found exemplary. I will miss him.

NOTES

1. Robert Jervis, *Perception and Misperception in International Politics* (Princeton University Press, 1976); Jervis, *The Illogic of American Nuclear Strategy* (Cornell University Press, 1984); Jervis, *The Meaning of the Nuclear Revolution* (Cornell University Press, 1989); Jervis, "Cooperation Under the Security Dilemma," *World Politics* 30 (January 1978): 167–215.

2. Robert Jervis, *Systems Effects: Complexity in Political and Social Life* (Princeton University Press, 1997).

3. Robert Jervis, "Why Postmortems Fail," *PNAS* 119 (January 13, 2022), https://www.pnas.org/doi/full/10.1073/pnas.2116638118. See also Richard H. Immerman's essay in his volume.

4. Jervis, "Why Postmortems Fail."

30

LOWERING BARRIERS AND CONNECTING SCHOLARS THROUGH INNOVATIVE ONLINE PUBLICATIONS

H-Diplo/ISSF

DIANE N. LABROSSE

I t is fitting that the online tributes to Robert Jervis that form the basis of this book were first published on H-Diplo/ISSF. Jervis was the founding editor of the International Security Studies Forum (ISSF) in 2009 and worked tirelessly on its behalf until a week before his untimely death.[1] ISSF represents his vision of the endless potential of drawing international relations (IR) scholars and diplomatic historians into dialogue and interaction with each other. His goal was to increase the velocity of transdisciplinary academic communications and to lower the barriers to entering those discussions. Even more, it speaks to Jervis's legendary generosity and kindness, his boundless curiosity about and knowledge of diplomatic history, and his desire to push the boundaries of digital publication and scholarly engagement. In 2023, ISSF was renamed the Robert Jervis International Security Studies Forum (RJISSF) in honor of Jervis's dedication to this online forum, to which he contributed throughout his illness and until the days before his passing.[2] As of mid-2025, it is simply The Jervis Forum.

As so many of the tributes in this volume attest, Jervis was a giant who never pulled rank or issued orders. He set the bar very high with his dedication to H-Diplo/ISSF and his grasp of the unlimited possibilities of online publication. All of us who were fortunate enough to have worked with Jervis on the ISSF project were beneficiaries of his immense wisdom, courtesy, deep sense of collegiality and fairness, and extraordinary work ethic and drive.

Working with Jervis over the past thirteen years was a gift. The amount of work he did for ISSF, which represents a mere drop in the bucket of his scholarly and professional concerns, was nothing short of amazing.

WHAT IS H-DIPLO?

H-Diplo, the open-access online publication site and listserv for thousands of scholars of diplomatic history and foreign policy, was founded in the early 1990s.[3] As its managing editor, I was aware that Robert Jervis not only subscribed to H-Diplo but also judged it to be worthwhile. I knew that because he took the time to comment when he thought that we had published something that was valuable. Until the end, he sent notes such as "This is important" or "This is excellent."

From its founding, H-Diplo had an impressive and large roster of distinguished scholar-subscribers who wrote for us when asked. Jervis was unique, however, because as a political scientist he also actively participated in the intense online discussions, most of which concerned historical interpretations of volatile subjects like the dropping of the atomic bombs, the US war in Vietnam, US policy during the Cold War, 9/11 and its aftermath, and the like.

Starting in the early 2000s, the H-Diplo editors transformed a simple listserv network into the flagship diplomatic history website. We did so by publishing reviews and roundtables on important new books and articles, state-of-the-field essays, and original-content essays. We also highlighted the work of junior scholars and reached out to those at smaller institutions and across the globe. We realized that we could marry the speed of online publishing with the depth of print publications to change the way that new scholarship emerged and was discussed. Our book reviews appeared shortly after the books were published, and article reviews were published simultaneously with the articles themselves. The change was in part a response to the many subscribers who told us that they wanted to find a way to write reviews without waiting for up to two years for them to appear in a print journal. At the same time, our style guidelines and strict editing standards ensured that our reviews would be fair and respectful. Even better, we were not constrained by word limits. There was no paywall or entry fee; anyone with an internet connection could and still can join in. Meanwhile, we established contacts with the leading journals in the field, starting with *Diplomatic History* and the *Journal of Cold War Studies*, as well as with the major university presses. We also realized the cross-disciplinary possibilities of online publication and organized reviews of selected relevant IR works.

That Jervis, a giant in the field of international relations, supported H-Diplo in this transformation added immensely to its appeal and its growing reputation. One of our inaugural roundtables featured Fredrik Logevall's 2001 *Choosing War*.[4] Having never assigned a roundtable at that point, I asked around for the names of a few scholars who might want to write for us. Jervis's name was at the top of every list. To my surprise, Jervis almost immediately answered my invitation and agreed to review what he called an important work. (So too did Lloyd Gardner, Jeffrey Kimball, and Marilyn Young.) By the mid-2000s, thanks to the generosity of scholars across the globe, we were publishing over three hundred roundtables and reviews per year. Emerging scholars began to inform us that having their first book featured in an H-Diplo roundtable was a mark of distinction and an important part of their tenure files.

THE ORIGINS OF H-DIPLO/ISSF

In March 2009, at the behest of Jervis and on the behalf of a small group of international relations scholars, T. V. Paul, the chair of the International Security Studies Section (ISSS) of the International Studies Association, proposed creating an ISSS list analogous to H-Diplo that would review IR books as well as the articles in journals such as *Security Studies* and *International Security*. The initial idea was to create a sister list for H-Diplo that would appeal to international relations scholars and offer a place where security studies and the policy issues that grow out of this scholarship could meet. The H-Diplo model of speed plus depth, it was felt, would suit the mission perfectly. The initiative had the support of Sean M. Lynn-Jones, William C. Wohlforth, and a host of other notable scholars, journal editors, and center directors who joined the editorial board. The project was named the International Security Studies Forum.[5]

After a few weeks of discussions, and a frank assessment of the work involved in crafting a new list and a review program from scratch, we decided to graft ISSF onto H-Diplo as a subsidiary sister list. H-Diplo's experienced team of review editors, the late Tom Maddux and Seth Offenbach, had already demonstrated what a dedicated editorial team could do. George Fujii, our skilled web and production editor, had pioneered the publication of H-Diplo's pdf-formatted reviews and oversaw our web design. ISSF publications would be edited, formatted, and published on the ISSF website as well as H-Diplo, reach its large subscriber base, and be grounded upon H-Diplo's existing in-house publication program. In short, we could easily meet Jervis's larger goal of creating a space where historians of diplomacy and international relations scholars would be able to read each other's work, participate in cross-disciplinary panels, and follow the latest developments in both field.

The final details were hammered out in April 2009 at a conference on New Scholarship in American Foreign Relations that was graciously hosted by James McAllister at Williams College. Jervis delivered the keynote address, "International Politics and Diplomatic History: Fruitful Differences," which decisively justified the need for the new H-Diplo/ISSF partnership and the future benefits of cross-disciplinary engagement.[6] To illustrate the point, the conference featured four foundational roundtables, two on new diplomatic history books and two on new IR books, and engaged historians and international relations scholars alike.[7] The four roundtables were eventually published on H-Diplo and ISSF.

Then we got to work.

Over the years Jervis recruited highly talented international relations and security studies specialists as managing editors for ISSF, including Chris Ball, James McAllister, Frank Gavin, Joshua Rovner, Jennifer L. Erickson, and, currently, Joe Parent. They assigned policy roundtables and reviews of the security studies literature, thereby tapping ISSF's full potential. The result is a vast archive of international relations-related reviews, roundtables, policy debates, and forums.

After the first few years, in part to boost the number of ISSF publications, the H-Diplo team assumed more work and ISSF was fully merged with H-Diplo. Tom Maddux officially came over as commissioning editor, as did Seth Offenbach, Andrew Szarejko and, most recently, Daniel Hart. In 2017, Jervis and Frank Gavin convened a conference on the future of

ISSF that was generously hosted by Michael Horowitz and the University of Pennsylvania's Brown Center and Perry World House. That resulted in the addition of a new layer of expertise to ISSF with the creation of a large board of associate editors (AEs) who represented the cream of the new generation of international relations scholars and were charged with organizing roundtables and policy forums for the list.[8] For many years, Joshua Rovner and Stacie Goddard chaired the AE team, which is now overseen by Erickson and Matthew Fuhrmann. Chris Ball is now our production editor.

Thanks to these dedicated teams of editors and Jervis's steady and innovative leadership, H-Diplo/ISSF has consistently produced illuminating and germane publications and policy roundtables. As McAllister writes in his chapter, invitations that contained the phrases "Robert Jervis wonders if . . ." or "Robert Jervis will be writing the introduction . . ." were impossible to decline. In the beginning, Jervis maintained mostly an advisory role, but as ISSF took shape and expanded, his involvement deepened and resulted in daily or weekly communications with me. He not only wrote more reviews and introductions but also supported new series and gathered top scholars to write for us on specific, critical, topics.

JERVIS'S ISSF WRITINGS

A hallmark feature of H-Diplo/ISSF is its essays and series. Many were either conceived by Jervis or included an essay or introduction by him. No matter the topic, he always wrote something that was interesting and learned, and suggested a dynamic roster of contributors. His ISSF writings offered master classes that not only summed up the state of the field on the topic at hand but suggested new avenues for fruitful research. The history/IR nexus was the focus of much of that work, and he wrote with both audiences in mind, as few others could have done. What follows is a random and necessarily short selection of Jervis's ISSF work, which is intended to showcase the breadth and depth of his ISSF contributions.[9]

In 2014, Marc Trachtenberg wrote the article "Audience Costs in 1954?," which was sparked by Fredrik Logevall's Pulitzer Prize–winning book, *Embers of War*.[10] Jervis wrote a substantive response, noting that the Trachtenberg essay "sits fruitfully at the intersection of history and political science, and has much to offer in terms of both substance and method," before taking up three important points that allowed him to draw on both international relations theory and the historiography on the subject. He concluded by drawing on his work on signaling:

> As a political scientist, I seek parsimonious explanations and think there are important generalizations to be had, but they may not be simple ones.
>
> In all of this, the signals that are perceived may differ from those that are intended to be sent. As I noted, Nixon's alert in October 1969 not only failed to impress Soviet leaders, it was barely noticed. Trachtenberg shows that in 1954, far from believing that the bellicose statements of the Eisenhower administration might trap them into using military force, Chinese leaders thought that public opinion was holding the adminis- tration back. There was no fear that Eisenhower would have to intervene lest he show domestic opinion that he was failing to live up to his word; rather the fear was that after the November elections the administration would be less bound by public opinion. To some extent the state can con- trol the signals it sends, but it has much less influence over how they are received and interpreted. Those of us who have written deductive argu- ments about signaling make strong arguments about how signals ought to be interpreted, but, unfortunate as this is for decision-makers and the- orists, the theories that matter are those held by the perceiving states, and these are often different from those of scholars and, more importantly for the conduct of foreign policy, different from those held by the state doing the signaling.[11]

This exchange sparked a follow-up forum in which Trachtenberg and Bronwyn Lewis wrote original essays on "Audience Costs and the Viet- nam War," to which Richard Betts, Jervis, Fredrik Logevall, and John Mearsheimer wrote responses.

In his introduction, Jervis opened with his usual nod to both disci- plines, writing, "Bad wars make challenging history, as is clear from the papers by Bronwyn Lewis and Marc Trachtenberg. Although their focus is on audience costs, both this question and the case of American deci- sion-making in Vietnam raise and shed light on multiple theoretical questions. These two essays move us a significant step forward on several fronts." He concluded:

> As Trachtenberg, Lewis, and others have noted, even if it is domestic rather than foreign audiences whose reactions most concern presidents, and they are likely to focus much more on the substance of what the president has done than on whether or not it is consistent with what he has said. So to argue against the centrality of audience costs in the technical sense of the president fearing that he will be punished for not living up to his pledges does not mean that the reaction of domestic opinion is unimportant. My guess is that Nixon felt that he could abandon South Vietnam if need be because domestic opinion had written off that country, or at least felt that the U.S. had more than lived up to its obligation to try to save it. To the extent that domestic opinion was important in Johnson's decision, I think it was not that he believed that people would compare his words to his deeds, but the fear that, irrespective of what he or Kennedy had said, he would be blamed for losing South Vietnam. What was salient in his mind was the price the Democrats had paid for "losing China," even though Truman had not pledged to save it. Similarly, to say that Nixon's policy was not shaped by the manipulation and fear of audience costs is not to claim that public opinion was unimportant. Far from it; after the failure of his original policy of prevailing in Vietnam by linkage and feigning madness, it was the unwillingness of the domestic public to continue the war that carried the day. Domestic opinion and domestic politics were primary; it was just that audience costs in the narrow sense were at most a small part of this.[12]

In 2016, Joshua Rovner commissioned and chaired a large number of policy roundtables that were designed to be fast, deep, and jargon-free. The inaugural roundtable focused on the Chilcot Report.[13] Jervis wrote an essay, as did John Bew, Seth Center, James Ellison, William Inboden, Louise Kettle, and Rovner himself.[14] Jervis opened his essay, "The Mother of All Post-Mortems," as follows:

> The main news about the Chilcot Report is that the picture it paints is a familiar one. It seems to me that at least in its coverage of the run-up to the war, it largely confirms what most scholars had come to believe.

But that should not be a cause for disappointment, because the point of inquiries like this is to lay out the historical record and reach sensible judgments, not to be original.

He ended as follows:

If the 9/11 attacks did not "change everything" in the UK as they did in the US, for the former as well as the latter it reduced the tolerance for risk and made more salient low-probability but high-impact events. Contrary to both the common generalization that heightened tensions lead people to focus on the immediate future, and the normative claim that we are better off looking to the future, leaders in both counties were moved by fears, not of what was likely to happen soon, but for the longer-run. Indeed, it was clear that invading Iraq would increase the immediate risks. They mislead the public not about the danger they saw, but when they believed it might eventuate. Presumably their underlying assumption is that while they, being stewards of their countries' fates, were mature enough to give proper weight to the future, their publics were not.

In a 2018 roundtable organized by Stacie Goddard on Ron Robin's *The Cold War They Made: The Strategic Legacy of Roberta and Albert Wohlstetter*, Jervis framed his introductory comments with a discussion of his relationships with the famous couple and also justified the need for the forum:

Those outside of the field of national security policy may be skeptical that there needs to be a book about the careers and legacies of Albert and Roberta Wohlstetter, names that are not only unfamiliar to the general public, but may not be known to most students of international politics. But they were indeed important. Albert's death was marked by a memorial ceremony at the U.S. Senate, attended by numerous dignitaries including President Bill Clinton (181). Ron Robin has written a fascinating if critical study of them, filled with insight and details that even people like myself who thought we knew the full story will find intriguing. At the start, I should note that I know almost all the characters Robin discusses: I audited a course with Albert (following Robin's practice, I will use the Wohlstetters's first names to differentiate them) at Berkeley in 1965 and interacted with him while I was at UCLA in the late 1970s; I met Roberta on several occasions (I also corresponded with her, something I had forgotten until Robin kindly sent me a letter he found in her archives); I was a colleague of Bernard Brodie, Albert's fierce rival; and I know Paul Wolfowitz a bit, and was a colleague and remain a friend of Zalmay Khalilzad, two of Albert's most important students, each of whom receive chapter-length treatment. Taking advantage of the fact that there are three other reviewers in this Roundtable, I will concentrate on the Wohlstetters's contributions to nuclear strategy, which is the area I know best.[15]

In the summer of 2020, Jervis mused about organizing a discussion about the White House presidential tapes and suggested the roster of writers. In response, a few months later, H-Diplo published "The Importance of the White House Presidential Tapes and in Scholarship," which featured essays by Matthew Evangelista, James Goldgeier and Elizabeth Saunders, Luke Nichter, and Marc Trachtenberg.[16] In 2021, Jervis's questions about the effects on historical scholarship of the digitalization of archives resulted in "Scholars and Digital Archives: Living the Dream?" At Jervis's suggestion, Richard H. Immerman chaired and introduced the forum, which included essays by Matthew Connelly, Kaeten Mistry, Christopher J. Prom, and Joseph C. Wicentowski.[17]

The most important and far-reaching ISSF/H-Diplo publications have been our two series of essays on Donald Trump's presidency; a third is in the works. The first series, "America and the World: 2017 and Beyond," asked a group of historians and IR experts to consider what diplomatic history and IR theory could tell us about the likely future of the United States in the world and what tools and insights the H-Diplo/ISSF community could provide to make sense of a fundamentally evolving situation.[18] Jervis wrote the inaugural essay, "President Trump and IR Theory." His opening was a classic: "I never thought that I would write the phrase 'President Trump,' let alone link it to IR theory. But the former is a great opportunity for the latter. Scholars of international politics bemoan the fact that our sub-field cannot draw on the experimental method. Well, now we can."[19] In 2019, Columbia University Press published a selection of these essays in *Chaos in the Liberal Order: The Trump Presidency and International Politics in the Twenty-First Century*, which was edited by Robert Jervis, Francis J. Gavin, Joshua Rovner, and Diane Labrosse.[20]

The second series, "America and the World—The Effects of the Trump Presidency," kicked off in January 2021. Again, Jervis composed our inaugural essay, "The Trump Experiment Revisited." He wrote,

Four years ago I wrote that the Trump presidency would provide a test for many IR theories. It was clear from Trump's campaign and his personal style that both his policy preferences and his methods of operation were outside of the political mainstream, and indeed this was a major part of his appeal to voters, even if they did not necessarily approve or even know of the specific policies he was advocating. What made his period in office so valuable to IR scholars, even if they disapproved of him and what he sought to do, is that it provided insight into the classic arguments about how much freedom of action an American president has and the level of constraint domestic interests and the international system will apply. On this topic I found Kenneth Waltz's well-known levels of analysis framework particularly useful.

Here I want to discuss the results of the experiment and then turn briefly to what this means for the Biden presidency. Even in science, where scientists can clean their test tubes, the results of experiments often are unclear and susceptible to multiple interpretations. So in this case we should not be surprised that we—or at least I—see a muddy picture. One complication is that the experiment was not run under ideal conditions. Trump not only had unusual views, but was inexperienced in running a large and complex organization and had a short attention span for most issues. Richard Neustadt famously reported that President Harry Truman thought that his successor would not be able to manage the executive branch: "He'll sit here, and he'll say, 'Do this! Do that!' *And nothing will happen.*" Truman underestimated Eisenhower, but his prediction applies years later to Trump, in part because many of the people he appointed to high positions did not share his views.[21]

His cautious conclusion warrants quoting in full:

What this means is that we cannot fully judge the Trump experiment at the end of his term. The impact of what he has said and done will last longer and, for better and for worse, will carry over into the Biden presidency and perhaps beyond. The difference that Trump's idiosyncrasies have made is, then, yet to be fully determined. Furthermore, we may be misled by the use of the standard comparative method to judge the question I originally posed about how constrained Trump would find himself when he took power. The instances of continuity between Trump and Biden at first glance suggest that the former was not as innovative as it might seem. He instead was responding to pressures from the domestic or international environment that would have yielded a similar response, regardless of who was president, since Biden behaved as he did. While this may be true, it is also possible that Biden was able (or compelled) to act in this way only because Trump had charted a new course. As in so many cases of history and international politics, it is not easy to choose between these alternative explanations, and at this point all I can do is to raise the question.

In July 2023, Columbia University Press published a selection of those essays in *Chaos Reconsidered: The Liberal Order and the Future of International Politics*, edited by Robert Jervis, Diane Labrosse, Stacie Goddard, and Joshua Rovner.[22] In one of his final communications with me, Jervis sent the revised draft of his essay for the book.

As noted, Jervis encouraged new projects. In late 2019, we discussed a new series of essays that I was designing for H-Diplo called "Learning the Historian's Craft." I asked him to write for us and to suggest the names of international relations scholars, which would allow us to rename the series "Learning the Scholar's Craft: Reflections of Historians and International Relations Scholars" and cross-post it on ISSF. Jervis agreed; his wonderful essay, "How I Got Here," offers an engaging discussion of his formative years. (The essay is included as the final selection in this volume.)[23] Jervis concluded his essay with a statement that also summarizes the purpose of ISSF: "This enjoyment and stimulation that we hope leads to a collective better understanding of the world is of course the point of our shared enterprise."[24]

For some time, I had tried to convince Paul Schroeder, who at the time was in his early nineties, to write for us, and he agreed when Jervis sent a letter (a constant theme throughout the chapters in this book is that Jervis always sent missives or picked up the telephone when needed). Unfortunately other matters intervened, and Schroeder had to withdraw. Shortly after that, in December 2020, he passed away. Schroeder's death and the sense of loss that it created led us to create a new H-Diplo/ISSF series of retrospective appreciations of the scholarship of those major figures who are no longer here to write for the "Scholar's Craft" series.

At Jervis's suggestion, we opened the series with a tribute to Schroeder. Jervis planned to write the introduction and suggested that we find two diplomatic historians and two international relations specialists to write for us in order to encompass the full range of Schroeder's work. By the time the essays by Beatrice de Graaf, Jack Levy, T. G. Otte, and John A. Vasquez were edited and finalized, Jervis was struggling with his treatment and exhaustion. To his very great regret, he felt that he could not go ahead with the introduction. Marc Trachtenberg kindly agreed to step in, but just before publication, Jervis told us that he wanted to write a personal note and would find a way to do so.

His tribute, "Paul Schroeder: Bringing Moderation, Morality, and Progress Back In," was heartfelt and lovely, detailing the intense intellectual engagement of two giants over many decades. It was also bittersweet given Jervis's own situation. He wrote the lines that so many of his colleagues would apply to him only a few months later:

> The symposium on Paul Schroeder's scholarship was worthy of its subject, who made so many contributions to our understanding of international history and international politics. . . . I trust that the scholarly community and perhaps the interested public will continue to grapple with the issues he raised. I know my own research and understanding of the world would have been much simpler and cruder without his scholarship and conversation. He was a treasure and will be sorely missed.[25]

CODA

Like so many of those who have also written tributes, I was privileged to be in communication with Jervis until the last days of November 2021. We continued to discuss promising new works and to assign reviews and plan new series, while Jervis sent updates on his condition and his own projected deadlines for ISSF writings ("the cancer has read its Darwin," he wryly reported after a promising treatment had lost its efficacy). The amount of work he did during this period was astonishing.

What is also astonishing, in retrospect, is the fact that despite Jervis's regular and frank reports on his condition, I had the sense that things would somehow carry on indefinitely. This false sense of optimism[26] (wishful thinking, really) remained, even after the arrival of what would be Jervis's last note, along with a copy of his revised essay for our second Trump volume. He wrote that his situation "isn't good" after the failure of a recent treatment and that the new one had "only a 20 percent chance of working." "But," he added, "at least [the chances are] not 0, and all the nasty effects of the disease and the treatment are controllable," with the exception of the deep exhaustion that had dogged him from before his diagnosis.

I expected to receive a follow-up note the next week, as had occurred so many times during the roller-coaster reports over the course of Jervis's illness and treatments. Sadly, that note never arrived.

Bob Jervis was a treasure and will be sorely missed.

NOTES

1. The terms H-Diplo/ISSF and ISSF are used interchangeably here: ISSF editors work for H-Diplo/ISSF but are otherwise not affiliated with H-Diplo in any way; H-Diplo editors work for both H-Diplo and ISSF.

2. The Jervis Forum RJISSF will continue its mission thanks to the invaluable support of Dr. Keren Yarhi-Milo, Arnold A. Saltzman Professor of War and Peace Studies and dean of the School of International and Public Affairs at Columbia University; Professor Jack Snyder, Robert and Renée Belfer Professor of International Relations in the Department of Political Science and 2025–2026 director of the Harriman Institute at Columbia University; and Elizabeth N. Saunders, professor of Political Science and director of the Saltzman Institute of War and Peace Studies at Columbia University

3. It is part of the Humanities and Social Sciences Online network (H-Net), which is an independent, nonprofit scholarly association that offers an open academic space for scholars, teachers, advanced students, and related professionals. It is built around an online system of networks moderated by certified editors. Its "vision is of the humanities and social sciences transformed by the immense potential of digital technologies and oriented around moderated intellectual exchange, collaborative production, and the open dissemination of knowledge." See https://www.h-net.org/.

4. Fredrik Logevall, *Choosing War: The Lost Chance for Peace and the Escalation of War in Vietnam* (University of California Press, 1999).

5. It also had institutional sponsors and was associated with the A. Saltzman Institute of War and Peace Studies at Columbia University. See https://issforum.org/about.

6. Robert Jervis, "International Politics and Diplomatic History: Fruitful Differences," H-Diplo/ISSF, March 12, 2010, https://issforum.org/ISSF/PDF/ISSF-Jervis-Inagural Address.pdf.

7. For the full roster of panels and panelists, see https://leadership-studies.williams.edu /about-2/archived-events/. The roundtables were published on H-Diplo and ISSF during the week of May 18, 2009.

8. "Meet the Team," H-Diplo/ISSF, https://issforum.org/team.

9. A selected list of Bob's H-Diplo and ISSF work is included in Appendix III of Part I of Richard H. Immerman, Diane Labrosse, and Marc Trachtenberg, H-Diplo|ISSF "Tribute to the Life, Scholarship, and Legacy of Robert Jervis," February 4, 2022, 158-161; https:// issforum.org/ISSF/PDF/ISSF-Jervis-Tribute-1.pdf

10. Fredrik Logevall, *Embers of War: The Fall of an Empire and the Making of America's Vietnam* (Random House, 2012).

11. Marc Trachtenberg, "Audience Costs in 1954?," ed. Diane Labrosse, H-Diplo/ISSF, September 6, 2014, https://issforum.org/ISSF/PDF/ISSF-Forum-1.pdf.

12. H-Diplo/ISSF Forum on "Audience Costs and the Vietnam War," November 7, 2014, https://issforum.org/ISSF/PDF/ISSF-Forum-3.pdf. Jervis included references in this paragraph to his chapter "Signaling and Perception," in *Political Psychology*, ed. Kristen Monroe (Erlbaum, 2002), and his book *The Logic of Images in International Relations* (Princeton University Press, 1970).

13. The Chilcot Report of July 6, 2016, detailed the findings of the Iraq Inquiry, chaired by Sir John Chilcot, into the British role in the 2003 Iraq War.

14. H-Diplo/ISSF Policy Roundtable on the Chilcot Inquiry, September 18, 2016, https:// issforum.org/roundtables/policy/1-1-chilcot. See Richard Immerman's essay on Jervis and post-mortems in this volume.

15. H-Diplo/ISSF Roundtable, Volume X, No. 17 (2018) on Ron Robin. *The Cold War They Made: The Strategic Legacy of Roberta and Albert Wohlstetter*. Cambridge: Harvard University Press, 2017, November 19, 2018, http://issforum.org/ISSF/PDF/ISSF-Roundtable -10-17.pdf.

16. H-Diplo/ISSF Forum 25 on the Importance of White House Presidential Tapes in Scholarship, published on November 2, 2020, https://issforum.org/forums/25-tapes.

17. H-Diplo Forum on Scholars and Digital Archives: Living the Dream?, ed. Diane Labrosse, October 6, 2021, https://issforum.org/forums/Forum-2021-2.pdf.

18. "Policy Series: America and the World – 2017 and Beyond (Introduction)," January 2, 2017, https://issforum.org/roundtables/policy/1-5a-policy-series-introduction.

19. H-Diplo/ISSF Policy Series, "America and the World - 2017 and Beyond, Introductory Essay by Robert Jervis, 'President Trump and IR Theory,' " January 2, 2017, https://issforum .org/ISSF/PDF/Policy-Roundtable-1-5B.pdf.

20. Robert Jervis et al., eds., *Chaos in the Liberal Order: The Trump Presidency and International Politics in the Twenty-First Century* (Columbia University Press, 2018).

21. Robert Jervis, "The Trump Experiment Revisited," ed. Diane Labrosse, H-Diplo/ISSF Policy Series: America and the World; the Effects of the Trump Presidency, February 1, 2021, https://issforum.org/to/ps2021-7; in Robert Jervis et al., eds., *Chaos Reconsidered:*

The Liberal Order and the Future of International Politics (Columbia University Press, 2023). The quotation is from Richard Neustadt, *Presidential Power: The Politics of Leadership* (Wiley, 1960), 9; emphasis in the original.

22. Robert Jervis, Diane N. Labrosse, Stacie E. Goddard, and Joshua Rovner, eds., *Chaos Reconsidered: The Liberal Order and the Future of International Politics* (Columbia University Press, 2023).

23. The "Scholar's Craft" series now includes essays by over sixty distinguished scholars in both fields. They begin with Andrew Bacevich's story, and are available at https://issforum.org/category/essays/formation-essay/page/10.

24. Robert Jervis, "How I Got Here," Learning the Scholar's Craft Series, March 4, 2020, https://hdiplo.org/to/E198 and https://issforum.org/essays/PDF/E198.pdf.

25. Robert Jervis, "Paul Schroeder: Bringing Moderation, Morality, and Progress Back In," H-Diplo/ISSF Forum 28 on the Importance of Paul Schroeder's Scholarship to the Fields of International Relations and Diplomatic History, https://issforum.org/forums/28.

26. Keren Yarhi-Milo talks about a similar false sense of optimism at the end of her poignant essay in the coda of this book; those by Bob's former students like Rose McDermott, Mira Rapp-Hopper, and James Wirtz, speak volumes about Bob's courage and grace during his illness. McDermott's essay is included here; the latter two appear in volume 1 of the H-Diplo|ISSF tribute, https://issforum.org/ISSF/PDF/ISSF-Jervis-Tribute-1.pdf. All of the essays testify to what a fundamentally fine and decent man Bob was.

31

THE PUBLIC INTELLECTUAL

DIPALI MUKHOPADHYAY

first encountered Robert Jervis's work as a freshman at Yale University in Bradford Westerfield's Introduction to International Relations lecture. I would soon understand him to be one of the great theorists of our discipline, a scholar who could deconstruct, demystify, and even predict the most terrifying of human creations: war. Most scholars only dream of achieving this in a career, but for Bob, it was just the beginning.

Because Jervis refused a parochial approach to conceptualizing world politics, he immersed himself in the experiences of waging war, deterring catastrophe, and suing for peace with the mind of a political scientist but also of a psychologist, a historian, a sociologist, and so on. This, too, was a radical and profoundly productive analytical move in our field.

But perhaps most exceptionally, Jervis recognized that war is not an elegant idea or a clever game. It is a mess—of politics and power, struggle and suffering, death and destruction. And it is marked by a constellation of decisions, big and small, that are made in the real world by real people every minute of every day. This recognition positioned him to attain the status of public intellectual in the fullest sense of the term.

Jervis told the story of being a young boy in New York City at the dawn of the Cold War, sitting at the family dining table one morning in 1947. As his parents consumed their two newspapers for the day, young Bob wondered aloud whether or not the United States would retaliate against the Soviet Union given reports that an American spy plane had been shot down. In a 2005 conversation with Harry Kreisler at his alma mater, the University of California at Berkeley, he described his childhood as indelibly marked by the politics of days like that one and, ultimately, the emergent fear of a global catastrophe that would be worse than any had ever before imagined: "You couldn't escape the world. . . . It was enveloping," he recalled.[1]

So many in the academy conceive of our work in lofty terms, constructed to be deliberately esoteric, to keep the real world out even as we claim to explain it. Not Bob Jervis. He insisted that the work of the mind speak to and be connected with the larger body (and spirit) politic. He elevated the efforts of those engaged in the public square routinely and in no uncertain terms. He taught them in his classroom, vetted their ideas through correspondence, made room for them at his lunch table, and created space for them at Columbia University to rest, reflect, and regroup.

In Washington, political scientists are not the most popular bunch. But Bob was beloved, not just for his brilliant books but also for his quiet contributions to the relentless and often thankless work of policymaking. For Jervis, fieldwork was time spent in the corridors of the Pentagon and the halls of Langley, where he could collect new data, help workshop a concept or program, and gather some good beltway gossip on the way home. In the real world, those analysts, officers, bureaucrats, and diplomats were his students, his teachers, and his friends. He took their ideas and their work seriously and helped both to be better in the process.

Jervis's ability to engage policymakers so fruitfully derived from a deeply held intellectual humility, a corresponding openness to competing points of view, and a seemingly unlimited capacity to engender trust. He avoided dogmatism at every turn and, instead, found his curiosity stirred by the ways in which otherwise smart and well-meaning people disagreed with one another. In a conversation with Francis Gavin in 2019, Bob spoke about the value of disagreement as an intellectual space from which to ask interesting questions. He went on to describe his own uncertainty about the "right" answer to the thorniest of dilemmas: "I'm often really ambivalent on some major policy issues," he explained. "But the ambivalence then makes it easier to say, wait a minute, wait a minute, look, we really should ask, do some, use some of our standard social science methods on this, to see how the argument stands up."[2]

Academics are, by some mix of nature and conditioning, reluctant to reveal what they do not know. Instead, they often insist upon asserting themselves from a place of clarity, even certitude. It is precisely that air of certitude that can deter those in politics and policymaking from engaging with us. As Jervis explained, "I think one reason why my scholarship has been useful, not to people at the highest level, but the working level, is that it does not try to make moral judgments on the people. And that it doesn't try to pretend that we're smart. [That] we, in the academics, are smarter than the policymakers . . . the feeling that I would have done it better than those people. And I think that's just a terrible attitude. I mean, usually the answer is, no, you wouldn't have. And why would you think that you would have?"[3]

It was that self-awareness and modesty—and the decidedly nonjudgmental tenor of his approach—that made Jervis an indispensable sage to those at the highest levels of government struggling to understand what went wrong in the spirit of attempting to do better next time. His postmortem review of the Iraq War was exemplary in this regard. In my first job out of college at the Carnegie Endowment for International Peace, I found myself tasked with collecting and analyzing open-source materials on Iraq's weapons of mass destruction capability in the fall of 2002. The Endowment distinguished itself as one of the few institutions in Washington that stood in the breach as the country marched toward war.

A decade later, I would join the Columbia junior faculty and meet my senior colleagues—Richard Betts, Jack Snyder, and Jervis—who, as scholars of international security, had taken a similar stand that fateful fall. Alongside a number of their distinguished peers, they bought an advertisement in The New York Times in September 2002, declaring that "military force should be used only when it advances U.S. national interests. War in Iraq does not meet this standard." They raised the risks of war for American forces and neighboring countries. And they cautioned that intervention without a clear exit strategy would mean "a divided society that the United States would have to occupy and policy for many years to create a viable state." Ultimately, they urged the US government to focus, instead, on a robust, multilateral containment strategy for Iraq and to expend its energies and attention on the al-Qaeda network in the meantime.[4]

Needless to say, their warning went unheeded. But Jervis was never one to rest on the laurels of having been right about that most disastrous of geopolitical errors. Instead, he offered up his services to the US govern-ment to help it—and his fellow countrymen—understand how the United States and its allies managed to get Saddam's capabilities so wrong. In a 2010 talk at Duke Law School about his book *Why Intelligence Fails: Lessons from the Iranian Revolution and the Iraq War*, Jervis described post-mortems as "hard to do" because of the acute risk of being "polluted by hindsight." In that remark, he was referencing the ubiquitous (and smug) belief of many observers, myself included, that this grievous intelligence error had certainly been caused either by epic incompetence or malevo-lent manipulation. Bob went on to unravel this common misperception, admitting that he went into the review with the same presupposition alongside a deep disdain for the war's key protagonists that only further deepened that bias.

It was, he explained, only when he drew on his social scientific training and leveraged some "good old comparative method" that it became clear to him that politicization was not, in fact, a major, let alone the primary, explanation for the intelligence failure that undergirded the war's justi-fication. His conclusions delivered none of the "gotchya!" comeuppance that so many of us craved. Instead, drawing on his expertise in politi-cal psychology, he pointed to a set of background beliefs through which analysts filtered the evidence before them, arriving at the very reasonable conclusion that the Iraqi regime was engaged in subterfuge. As he put it, what we now know to be true simply was not believable: "the truth was implausible," he said. He detailed the ways in which both analysts and decision makers might have moved beyond the most obvious conclusion to arrive at something closer to the truth. He underscored, in particular, the value of forcing oneself into the posture of seeing events from the other's point of view and of seeking out the "negative evidence" and con-tending with the alternatives, however implausible they may seem.[5]

But ultimately, Jervis expressed a profound empathy for those who are tasked with such difficult and high-stakes work and made clear that he might well have made the same mistakes had he been in their position. His trademark humility spoke to the grave challenges inherent in the work of assessment and decision making and underscored why error is so frus-tratingly common. It is no wonder that this scholar, who was always pre-pared to concede his own limitations, uncertainties, and mistakes, helped so many of us understand why states, militaries, and armed groups—all of which are populated by fallible human beings—behave, interact, and collide as tragically as they so often do.

The grinding work of attempting—and often failing—to avoid tragedy is the work of many policymakers. And as a preeminent scholar of tragedy, Jervis made every effort to support them as best he could. He reflected in 2019, "I've never served full-time. And in a way, I very much do regret that. I don't think I would have made anything better. I think I would have learned a tremendous amount, both about the process and about the substance."[6] Jervis's innate understanding of human fallibility informed a profoundly pragmatic view of the world—his expectations of states and the humans that populated them remained forever moored in a reasoned analysis of what was possible, not ideal. That pragmatism did not, however, drive him to despair about the world. Rather, it pushed him to keep learning more and to support the rest of us in our efforts to do the same.

Bob often teased me about my version of fieldwork. He thought me a bit mad—and told me so—when I would head off to Afghanistan or return home from a trip to the Turkey-Syria border. "Ah, Kabul in the summer—just the place for a vacation," he emailed me in June 2017 as I prepared for a research trip.[7] But he tracked my moves closely, asked me questions at every turn, and did not let up, even when he was dying. On August 15, 2021, the day Kabul fell to the Taliban, like clockwork, I got a note from his wife, Kathe—she and Bob wanted to take me to lunch to know how I was doing. A month later, I received an email from Bob, who had been newly inducted to the National Academy of Sciences—it was a note to the academy president asking her to work with me to support Afghan scholars at risk.

And then, on October 27, I had my final time with Bob—we spent two hours in his living room, eating too many of Kathe's candied pecans while running our own postmortem of the military withdrawal and gaming out different scenarios of Taliban rule. I owed him more reading material when I learned from Keren Yarhi-Milo that he had drifted into a deep sleep. As a longtime scholar of Afghanistan, the events of that fall will haunt me for the rest of my days. Bob knew that the best way to support me in that time was to help me begin the process of asking the questions that would need to be answered in order for all of us to better understand what went wrong and why. He made room for my rage, fear, and sadness, even as he urged me forward to consider the next good question.

People toss around the term "public intellectual" too casually for my taste. The work of public intellectualism is not about writing essays in fancy newspapers or joining blue ribbon commissions in the capital. It is about honoring the unglorified sacrifices of service and supporting the banal efforts of bureaucracy. It is about championing those who are engaged in this work, contributing to their conversations as best one can, and speaking truth to power when necessary. Soon after Bob passed away, the world descended into yet another terrifying episode of war, reminding us all that peril is never far. I couldn't help but imagine how different our world might be if more great thinkers did this noble thing, this thing of being a true public intellectual the way Bob Jervis did it. May we all strive to do it better in his memory, and may he forever rest in peace.

NOTES

1. Robert Jervis, "American Foreign Policy in a New Era," Conversations with History Interview Series at University of California Berkeley, November 16, 2005, https://conversations .berkeley.edu/jervis_2005.

2. Francis J, Gavin, "An Interview with Robert Jervis: Reflections on Political Science, Politics, and Policy," *Horns of a Dilemma* podcast reprinted in War on the Rocks, August 12, 2019, https://warontherocks.com/2019/08/an-interview-with-robert-jervis-reflections-on -political-science-politics-and-policy/.

3. Gavin, "An Interview with Robert Jervis."

4. Robert J. Art et al., "War with Iraq Is Not in America's National Interest," *New York Times*, September 26, 2002, https://sadat.umd.edu/sites/sadat.umd.edu/files/iraq_war _ad_2002_2.pdf.

5. Robert Jervis, "Why Intelligence Fails: Lessons from the Iranian Revolution and the Iraq War," talk delivered at Duke University Law School, September 23, 2010, https://law.duke .edu/video/robert-jervis-why-intelligence-fails-lessons-iranian-revolution-iraq-war.

6. Gavin, "An Interview with Robert Jervis."

7. Private email communication with Robert Jervis, June 2017.

VI

ROBERT JERVIS AS COLLEAGUE, MENTOR, AND FRIEND

❖

CODA

To My Fellow Perceiver

KEREN YARHI-MILO

I t goes without saying that Robert Jervis was a giant in the field. He was a one-of-a-kind scholar whose work will forever shape how we think about international politics. But for me, he was a rare gift of a person who changed my life profoundly over the past twenty years. As a freshman at Columbia, I took my very first class in international relations with Jervis as my professor. Later on, he became one of my dissertation advisors even though I completed my PhD at the University of Pennsylvania while he taught at Columbia. Since then, he has read at least one draft of every paper that I have ever published. I even had the rare honor of coauthoring a paper with him shortly before he was diagnosed with cancer. Most recently, he was my colleague at Columbia and a core member of the Saltzman Institute of War and Peace Studies, of which I became the director in 2020. More than these titles, however, Jervis was a mentor, advocate, and second father to me.

I could write a book-length manuscript just on how Jervis influenced the field of international relations and my own work in particular. Thomas Christensen and I tried to summarize some of his key contributions in a recent *Foreign Affairs* piece.[1] Instead, in this tribute, I would like to highlight the aspects of Jervis's unparalleled personality that I believe will resonate with everyone who was fortunate enough to know him, work with him, and be his student. For the readers who did not have the chance to get to know Bob Jervis, I have no doubt that learning about what made him so special as a person will shed light on what made him such a brilliant scholar.

I'll start at the beginning, which was my first semester as an undergraduate student at Columbia. As I sat in the International Affairs Building, eagerly anticipating the start of my first session of Introduction to International Politics, Jervis began the class by going through newspaper articles, one of which was about the Arab-Israeli conflict. Using the article as a launching point, he kicked off a discussion about whether or not the conflict was a security dilemma. Admittedly, at this point in time, I had no idea who Jervis was, but that he spoke about the topic with so much passion and sensitivity sparked something that made me want to approach him and discuss the subject further. So although I was only a freshman, I joined the line of students waiting for a chance to chat with him during office hours. When I made it into his office, he asked me about my background. When I told him that I had served in Israeli intelligence, his eyes lit up and he grinned. Intrigued by one another, we started talking about biases in intelligence analysis, the role of intelligence in the Arab-Israeli peace process, and international relations more broadly. I left his office over an hour later and the rest was history. In reflecting back on the treasure trove of conversations that I had with Jervis each week during his office hours, I am reminded why I always tell my students to make an effort to get to know their professors.

For the next twenty years, Jervis would follow up every conversation we had by sending me something he had found useful or interesting in his prolific reading. I was not the only beneficiary of his rare and immense thoughtfulness. In fact, Jervis was known for this: looking through his office, which was filled with piles of books and papers strewn about, and finding something relevant to the topic at hand. Despite the seeming disorganization, he always knew exactly what he was looking for and would scan the document right there and then, handing you a copy at the close of the conversation, or attach it in an email a few days later. Other times, he would send you thoughtful and brilliant emails out of the blue, recalling an old conversation or referencing your work. How remarkable that in all of his nonstop reading, Jervis would think not just about his own work but also about how what he was reading could help his students, colleagues, and research in general. To take one example, just a week before he passed, Jervis sent me an email with a piece about British cabinet deliberations in the interwar period, something that I wrote about extensively in my first book.[2]

Beyond his genuine interest in helping others do their research, Jervis's unfailing ability to find something relevant to every conversation was borne out of his voracious reading. Jervis was up to date with every journal and every book—I really do not know any other scholar who read as much as he did. He read anything and everything that he thought could potentially be interesting. He even read articles he suspected to be awful and browsed through journals he did not think very highly of. Jervis would carve out time every other day to sit with his legs up on the chair, like a schoolboy, and jot down notes in the margins of whatever book or journal he had set out to read. (His handwriting is nearly impossible to decipher, but having these journals in my office now, I continue trying to figure out what his notes mean, knowing that each annotated scribble is an invaluable gem.) Impressively, he would also remember what he read and was able to recall the exact article and the details of an author's argument up until his very last day.

Though his field was political science, Bob was passionate about diplomatic history as well as work in political science that seriously engaged with historical case studies. In fact, this is one of the interests that the two of us bonded over. In combination with his avid curiosity, it should be no surprise that he loved to talk about the archives. Bob's singular passion for historical documents (at least among political scientists) is also why he agreed to head the CIA declassification board (known at the time as the Historical Review Panel), knowing how important it was for scholars to access files that could enable the building and testing of new theories in international relations. He would spend hours listening to students share about the archival jewels they had found. Any time that a document was declassified, he immediately and eagerly wanted to know everything about it. I will never forget Jervis's reaction when I first showed him the documents I collected from Jimmy Carter's Presidential Library, where one can still see Carter's handwritten notes in the margins on the weekly reports he received from his national security advisor, Zbigniew Brzezinski. Upon seeing the documents, Jervis's face lit up like a kid in a candy store and with a huge grin on his face he exclaimed, "This is just marvelous!!!" I hold this memory of Jervis most dearly because it captures his fantastic inquisitiveness and unquenchable thirst for knowledge.

Put simply, Jervis was unmatched as a mentor. He was there for me during the ups and downs of my career (and there have been many). When I told him during graduate school that I did not think I was cut out for academia, he unflinchingly sympathized with me, telling me he did not blame me for feeling this way. When I told him that I might have to quit my tenure-track job at Princeton due to my son's developmental delays, he could not have been more compassionate, sensitive, and supportive. At that time, we spoke every week as he helped me navigate the situation. When I decided to return to my work, he threw himself into helping me get back on track professionally. In addition to being an unparalleled advisor, Jervis was my number one advocate—most senior people in the field probably first heard of me or my work thanks to him and his many shout-outs. There is no doubt in my mind that I would not be where I am today without him having been there every step of the way.

Just before he was diagnosed with cancer, I had the rare privilege of coauthoring a piece with him. I call this a rare privilege because you can count on one hand the number of coauthors he had during his illustrious career. I feel lucky to have written a review piece in *World Politics* with him and Don Casler[3] precisely because it gave us a glimpse into Jervis's unique writing process—the output of which discerning readers will recognize as the "Jervisian" style—that was not easily shared. Indeed, part of Bob's aversion to coauthoring stemmed from the difficulty of matching his idiosyncratic habits to others' styles. Thus, Don and I were elated to be invited behind the curtain, and we learned so much from the honor of observing the process up close.

Jervis began every piece by collecting newspaper clips on items with a common theme. When a file got thick or heavy enough, he would decide that it was time to write about that topic. For him, these clippings were more than anecdotes—they were pieces of evidence that together painted a picture and hinted at a larger theoretical or empirical story. After examining his clippings, he would dictate his thoughts, recording himself as he talked through his ideas. The resulting transcript would already contain incredibly rich examples (because he had already collected them and based his argument on them) and a clean, well-articulated argument. That initial draft would then go through a very long process of editing until it was refined into publishable work. It was not just the dictation (rare in and of itself) that made his style so interesting, but also the peculiar way in which his process of research and writing resembled piecing together a jigsaw puzzle.

Considering that his remarkable writing was based on his dictation, it should come as no surprise that Jervis was also an exceedingly skilled communicator. Moreover, given his scholarly focus, he was very sensitive to the dynamics of perception and misperception. The way that he carried himself and interacted with others in professional settings reflected this sensitivity. Jervis knew that it was not only what you argued for or against but also how your words or actions were perceived (or misperceived) by others that mattered. Whenever Jervis spoke, everyone understood exactly the message he intended to get across because he had already factored in the myriad ways in which others might misunderstand him. Among Jervis's superpowers was his uncanny ability and instinct to think critically about his audience (and many times, it was not just one audience but multiple audiences). I sat with him in countless meetings during which sensitive issues came up or the audience was especially divided. While always honest and sincere, he knew how to craft an argument diplomatically and sensibly so that no one could possibly take his idea the wrong way. Not too long ago, in a particularly tense Arts and Sciences meeting, Jervis raised his hand, and I thought to myself, "What is he doing?" In that environment, I anticipated that there would be a huge blowback to whatever he might say (and especially to the particular suggestion that I suspected he would offer). Advocating for this bold course of action, Bob spoke elegantly and empathically. Much to my surprise, when he finished speaking, every single person in the previously polarized environment was nodding in agreement. Dazzled, I thought to myself, "How brilliant. Watch and learn, Keren." If his scholarship talked the talk about signaling and perception, then in his interpersonal interactions and communications, Jervis walked the walk.

As talented a writer as he was a communicator, Bob was also a community builder and expert convener—he absolutely loved bringing people together in both the field and across the university. Bob did not care about what methodology or subject matter expertise one had—he was enthusiastic to learn from everybody and saw the value in every piece of good scholarship. It did not matter to him whether you were an international relations scholar, historian, or political theorist; everyone was welcome at the infamous brown bag lunches that he hosted as often as twice a week. For Jervis, it was not enough simply to email an invitation. He would go around collecting faculty members by knocking on their doors and asking them if they were coming to lunch—no one could or would say no to Jervis, and so everyone came. Before the pandemic, room 1302 in the International Affairs Building would be filled with people from all different backgrounds and subfields discussing current events. During the pandemic, this tradition continued on Zoom all the way up until his very last week.

Jervis cared profoundly about the community he helped build at Columbia—about the Political Science Department, the School of International and Public Affairs, the Saltzman Institute, the Graduate School of Arts and Sciences, and Columbia University at large. Even as he was undergoing chemotherapy treatments, he was still attending faculty meetings and job talks—a true testament for how important Columbia was to him. Just as he was an expert in international relations, he was also a connoisseur in everything to do with the university; Jervis knew everything one possibly could in terms of budgeting, strategic planning, and internal politics. He put great effort into protecting the faculty and the students by making sure that Columbia maintained a high quality of education. He and I spent hours during his last months talking over Zoom about the university's plans to expand and restructure the college, two issues about which Jervis cared deeply and wanted to make sure were done right.

Jervis poured similar energy into caregiving for the field of political science as a whole, serving as a leader not just through his writing but also as president of the American Political Science Association, a board member of many journals, founder of the H-Diplo/International Security Studies Section Forum, and editor of the Cornell Studies in Security Affairs at Cornell University Press for many years (to name but a few roles). Most of what he did was to pave the way for younger scholars and give them the opportunity to get their work reviewed. Remarkably, he did it all for free, out of pure passion and devotion. Just as he was always going out of his way to help scholars along with their research, he also expended immense effort into creating a structural environment that would allow them to thrive.

Jervis and I were attracted to the same puzzles and patterns in world politics. Perhaps this was because I was his student, or maybe this is what brought us together to begin with. I remember many instances of us sitting at conferences, talks, or faculty meetings when another participant said something that caused us to look at each other and smile, each knowing that the other was thinking the exact same thing in reaction. "To my fellow perceiver" is how he signed my copy of *Perception and Misperception*. In sum, Bob Jervis was my go-to person. He was the first one I called or emailed about everything from a question about research to advice about my career to help with deliberating about what opportunities to say yes to or no to. My biggest joy was coming full circle and joining him at Columbia as a colleague—if we were not close enough before, this made us closer than ever.

When Bob told me confidentially that he had been diagnosed with stage four cancer, it was a déjà-vu moment for me, as my father had been diagnosed with cancer eight years earlier. It was a truly devastating blow. Jervis was generally brutally honest about his prognosis, but despite our own expertise on biases, we were both a bit guilty of false optimism at times. Knowing I only had a limited time left to enjoy his brilliance, wisdom, humor, and advice, I cherished every Zoom call and email correspondence, and I was delighted to see him in person when it was safe. He celebrated what turned out to be his last birthday in Central Park during spring 2021, surrounded by colleagues who adored him. I looked at him and how happy he was. I then turned to look around at the many faces that surrounded him, all of them filled with immense admiration layered with tears of both joy and sadness.

On December 9, 2021, the world lost its biggest mensch and the most astute observer of world politics. I lost a rare mentor and a father figure who profoundly shaped, and will forever continue to influence, my life and career.

Now that I serve as dean of a school Bob believed in so deeply, I would be lying if I said that I don't picture him in the audience every time I open a major event or convene a roundtable. I so wish he were here—to help me navigate the hard moments, to challenge and guide me through uncertainty, and to witness the milestones we have achieved. His absence is deeply felt. And yet, in so many ways, he is still with us—in the questions we ask, in the values we uphold, and in the community he helped create and so fiercely nurtured.

NOTES

1. Thomas J. Christensen and Keren Yarhi-Milo, "The Human Factor: How Robert Jervis Reshaped Our Understanding of International Politics," *Foreign Affairs*, January 7, 2022, https://www.foreignaffairs.com/articles/world/2022-01-07/human-factor.

2. Yarhi-Milo, *Knowing the Adversary: Leaders, Intelligence, and Assessment of Intentions in International Relations* (Princeton University Press, 2014).

3. Robert Jervis, Yarhi-Milo, and Don Casler, "Redefining the Debate Over Reputation and Credibility in International Security: Promises and Limits of New Scholarship," *World Politics* 73, no. 1 (2021): 167–203, https://doi.org/10.1017/S0043887120000246.

A photo of Bob reading in his office, surrounded by piles of books, in the Arnold A. Saltzman Institute of War and Peace Studies at Columbia University on November 11, 2019. This was a familiar sight to all who passed by Jervis's office. He read voraciously and widely, across fields and disciplines, and even schools of thought with which he disagreed. He was the quintessential scholar.

Permission granted by JD Work.

EPILOGUE

The Jervis Effect: The Scholarship and Legacy of Robert Jervis

RICHARD H. IMMERMAN, STACIE E. GODDARD, AND DIANE N. LABROSSE

T*he Jervis Effect* brings together thirty-five authors to honor Robert (Bob) Jervis, who died on December 9, 2021. Although it is always right and good to honor intellectual greatness, it might seem that there is little need for this volume. Jervis's work, after all, is capable of speaking for itself. As Paul MacDonald writes in his introduction, Jervis left us with an astonishing amount of material on a wide range of topics. He relied on a vast array of theoretical approaches and empirical methods. He was part political scientist, part psychologist, part historian, and part policy analyst. There is very little of the academic field—or very little of the policy world—that Jervis's work did not touch. We have also included Jervis's essay, "How I Got Here," which details his formative years, as an appendix.

Our authors tell this story of Jervis's remarkable scholarship and influence, and it is likely a story that many political scientists, historians, and other academics already know quite well. But if we only tell stories about his research, we risk obscuring as much as we reveal about Jervis's career. As James McAllister observes, "a future historian would surely be forgiven for assuming that Jervis must have been singularly focused on his own individual scholarship, indifferent to the teaching and mentoring of graduate students and unconcerned with providing collective goods to wider academic communities."[1] While *The Jervis Effect* pays due recognition to his research, with these essays, we also intend to help set the future historical record straight about who Jervis was as a person, a colleague, and a friend and especially to remind readers how he worked tirelessly to sustain our intellectual community.

Jervis was no isolated mind or prestige-seeking ego. The "Jervis Effect" that our authors speak about in their essays worked through his devotion to his students and colleagues, his commitment to public service, and his tireless efforts to build robust intellectual communities. Were the editors to construct a word cloud from these contributions, we would see as much reference to "kindness," "humility," "mentorship," and "polo shirts" (an ode to his always casual attire) as we would to "intellectual giant" and "genius." It is that unrelenting humanity and decency that is the secret behind the "Jervis Effect."

This book appropriately focuses on Jervis's scholarship; his theoretical, methodological, and interdisciplinary contributions to our understanding of international relations; the singular role he play in the evolution of "intelligence studies"; and his citizenship and influence as a public intellectual. Yet there were additional dimensions of his behavior, personality, and career that are also integral to his legacy. Discussions and assessments of these dimensions appeared in fifty-eight essays that appeared in the original two H-Diplo/ISSF online forums that honored Jervis after his passing, the majority of which form the backbone of this volume.[2] Drawing on the forum again, we use this epilogue to provide a snapshot of Jervis's mentorship, his collegiality and commitment to community, and his professionalism, which are perhaps lesser known but nevertheless vital components of his legacy that continue to inspire those who knew him and can serve as enduring models even to those who did not.

TO BE A "JERVIS STUDENT"

Many of the contributors to this volume were Jervis's formal students, most of whom undertook their doctoral degrees in Columbia's Political Science Department, where Jervis was a member of the faculty from 1980 to 2021.[3] The stories they tell paint a picture of a dedicated advisor. Far from holing himself up in his office (small and messy, his students all agree), he saw his office as a space of engagement. A student's comment might lead him to climb onto his desk, searching for the book that would help push forward a dissertation chapter. As Sara Moller writes, "you never knew what book or torn out news clipping he would pull out from the towering stacks that surrounded him, but which somehow never came crashing down."[4] He encouraged his students to follow his lead in harvesting ideas from all sorts of sources "newspapers, student papers and dissertations, manuscripts under review, new journal issues, declassified documents, [an] endless stream of library books, and everything else that caught his eye."[5]

Although much of these efforts occurred at Columbia, being a "Bob Jervis student" was never about belonging to an exclusive club. Jervis, as many of the contributors report, was an intellectual pluralist, and his own ecumenical style extended to his students. Remarkably, no two Jervis students look alike. Academia is full of mentors that attempt to recreate their advisees in their own image. In contrast, Jervis reveled in difference and even promoted it. The first part of the volume is a testimony to his pluralism. Here we find among his students realists mixed with constructivists, psychologists with historians, and quantitative and qualitative scholars.

And as many of the contributors to this volume attest, Jervis seemed inclined to admit anyone to his club of students, provided they expressed an interest in joining. As Richard Immerman wrote in introducing Part I of the H-Diplo/ISSF tribute, he made it easy for all of us to become his mentees.[6] Austin Long explains how, as an MIT student, he sent a cold email to Jervis asking for a copy of his not-yet-published analysis of the intelligence leading up to the Iraq War.[7] Within a day, Jervis responded. In the coda to this book, Keren Yarhi-Milo tells us that she met Jervis as a first-year undergraduate at Columbia, braving a line of graduate students to attend his office hours. In a familiar pattern, that initial meeting sparked a long and deep personal, collegial, and intellectual friendship.[8]

Although happily accommodating a plurality of intellectual interests, Jervis did place demands on his students. Students understood that he expected insatiable intellectual curiosity and, despite the level of complexity of politics and history, a drive toward mastery, as Robert Art describes.[9] Jervis's own relentless curiosity made him master of all things—theoretical, historical, and current. Our essay writers report that Jervis read "key journals from cover to cover each time they appeared."[10] His infamous filing system paired topics of interests with photocopies of relevant examples from secondary histories and newspapers. When the file got large enough, that is when it was time to write the article (or book!). Those of us who worked closely with Jervis were often awed by his command of historical detail and a bit frightened when we came to realize that he would expect the same capacity of his students. At least one of the editors of this volume attempted to find topics to research that they hoped would be outside of Jervis's expertise—such as the Schleswig-Holstein crisis—so as to avoid precise questions about the case.[11]

Jervis also expected his students to accept their own intellectual limits, which is not always an easy thing to do. But if Robert Jervis was a humble intellectual, then certainly the rest of us, as mere mortals, could accept our own academic limitations. He was both kind to his students and constructively critical of their work. Jervis never hesitated to tell us when we needed to do more to push our projects forward. If an argument was not flying, he would let us know, while at the same time helping us to improve it. He would never attempt to impose his own vision on the work of another but instead helped to develop the other's ideas. As the editor Roger Haydon reports, Jervis "was a genius at improving books that advanced arguments he didn't wholly believe but was sure the scholarly community had to confront. No 'what *I* would have written' from him."[12]

And our contributors agree that one never aged out of being a Jervis student. Jervis was not only a professor of political science but also a professor of the profession, a colleague guiding us all through the politics of our careers. He provided advice on everything from article and book manuscripts to teaching to department and college politics. Helen Milner, Richard Betts, Yarhi-Milo, and Arthur Stein all recall how Jervis helped steer them through the Byzantine systems of academic politics, negotiating committee assignments, university budgets, and hiring squabbles.[13] Yet whatever battles he fought, Jervis remained, as Betts tells us, "a man who had no enemies. That was something unusual and laudable."[14]

TO BUILD COMMUNITY

Asking most faculty about university service evokes eye rolls and grumbles. Jervis saw service—to his institutions and to the profession—as an integral part of his professional life. But he never served in academic administration (although, as his daughter wrote in his informal obituary, he embraced his role as "an enthusiastic provider of feedback to university administrators").[15] He even managed to avoid the role of department chair.

The service that Jervis preferred revolved around efforts to build community. In Columbia's Political Science Department, those efforts were legendary. Jervis organized informal seminars for his colleagues. He would select recent journal articles or book chapters that were related in some way, and "everyone would arrive prepared to discuss them over sandwiches and cookies."[16] In 2021, Columbia University designated those meetings as university seminars, which bring together Columbia faculty as well as political scientists, historians, and practitioners from around the country.

And then there were the infamous Jervis lunches, which began shortly after Jervis joined the faculty. Jervis would walk the halls of the Saltzman Institute of War and Peace Studies and the Political Science Department, reminding faculty that they, in fact, were mortal and needed to eat. Sometimes meeting in a restaurant, sometimes in the faculty club, but more often than not in some room in the International Affairs Building, faculty would gather to talk international politics, American politics, sports, and occasionally gossip. The gatherings had no defined research interests or political science subfields. As Tonya Putnam reports, the only entry requirements were "'intellectual curiosity and epistemological modesty,' as well as a willingness to check any inflated sense of hierarchy at the door."[17] When the pandemic came, the lunches did not end but instead migrated to Zoom, where they welcomed an even more expansive group, hungry for conversation and connection. He was, as Rose McDermott tells us, the "glue" that held our group together during a particularly bleak moment.[18]

Jervis shepherded the discipline of international relations as well and was particularly dedicated to facilitating conversations between political scientists and diplomatic historians. Jervis never downplayed the differences between the disciplines of political science and history, but he believed good scholarship on international relations required finding connections between these fields. While at Columbia, he worked with historians like Paul Kennedy and John Gaddis at Yale to organize workshops designed to bring together historians and political scientists and also allow graduate students to engage with some of the most preeminent scholars in both disciplines. As James Davis writes, "Imagine the exhilaration and sense of inadequacy that comes with extended and intense discussions of work in progress with the likes of McGeorge Bundy, Paul Schroeder, and Marc Trachtenberg! Not only was there the challenge of absorbing the substance of their historical arguments, but also there was the need to come to terms with the historical method and what often was a not-so-subtle critique of the discipline to which many of us had just committed ourselves."[19]

His efforts to cultivate this interdisciplinary community live on in the existence of H-Diplo's International Security Studies Forum (ISSF). H-Diplo, the open-access online publication site and listserv for thousands of scholars of diplomatic history and foreign policy, was founded in the early 1990s. Jervis, as Diane Labrosse details, was committed to supporting H-Diplo's mission of reviewing emerging scholarship, even in its infancy as a humble listserv, and he "actively participated in the intense online discussions, most of which concerned historical interpretations of volatile subjects like the dropping of the atomic bombs, the US war in Vietnam, US policy during the Cold War, 9/11, and the like."[20] His efforts were essential to launching and maintaining H-Diplo's sibling site, H-Diplo/ISSF, which, like Jervis himself, was committed to reviewing books and articles that crossed the boundaries between diplomatic history and political science. It is fitting, Labrosse notes, that the essays in this book were first published as tributes to Jervis on H-Diplo/ISSF. It is also fitting that shortly after Jervis passed away, ISSF was renamed RJISSF, the Robert Jervis International Security Studies Forum. It is now known simply as The Jervis Forum.

SOMETHING BEYOND ONESELF

Jervis's commitment to mentorship and community building were no accident. They were rooted in who he was as a human being. The contributions in this volume are filled with personal stories of how Jervis's empathy shaped not only his efforts to support his students and colleagues but also how he approached his scholarship.

Jervis understood that his colleagues and students needed to live more than a life of the mind. Jervis himself embraced his life outside of academia, attending opera with friends, spending time with his daughters, and always working in partnership with his wife, Kathe. His perspective meant that we could turn to Jervis to understand how we could most effectively negotiate the balance between our work and our families. He often actively intervened when he felt that his colleagues needed more support in order to make that balance possible. In this book's chapters, there are stories of Jervis helping colleagues figure out how to do their scholarship while caring for an ill child or parent.

Jervis also understood that, for many of his colleagues, politics were interwoven with the personal. Dipali Mukhopadhyay tells how, in August of 2021, Jervis reached out as Kabul fell. She tells us that "Bob knew that the best way to support me in that time was to help me begin the process of asking the questions that would need to be answered in order for all of us to better understand what went wrong and why. He made room for my rage, fear, and sadness, even as he urged me forward to consider the next good question."[21]

Jervis extended his empathy not only to colleagues but also to the policymakers who he studied. Jervis understood that the world was a complicated place and that all human beings—no matter how smart—are fallible. He opposed the US war in Iraq, but when he wrote the postmortem on that conflict, he argued that the intelligence was not politicized.[22] Intelligence officers may have made errors, but they were within the realm of the rational and comprehensible. We will all make mistakes when trying to analyze complex systems. The academics who proclaim they would have been right in hindsight miss the point entirely.

And Jervis did not simply sit on the sidelines. He did the hard work to demonstrate this empathy for the policymakers he studied. In the 1990s, as the US intelligence community somewhat begrudgingly accepted demands for increased transparency and declassification, Jervis accepted an invitation to chair the CIA's Historical Review Panel. Jervis's success, as Michael Warner details, lay in his ability to explain to the intelligence community the urgent need for transparency, that if "scholars collectively were to make sense of the Cold War—especially its nuclear dynamic—they needed to understand the intelligence that informed leaders' decisions and then implemented their orders."[23] The aim of declassification was not to allow scholars to second-guess policymakers' decisions. It was to show how scholars and policymakers could work together to reflect on past decision-making processes in hopes of identifying and avoiding catastrophic errors that could make the difference between war and peace.

CONCLUSION

In this brief epilogue, we have commented more on Jervis as mentor, colleague, and friend than as Jervis as a researcher. Our point is not that these roles were more important than his research; it is that these roles are inseparable.

This volume is about the "Jervis Effect," the immense intellectual legacy that Bob Jervis left. We want to do more here than describe the effect. Jervis himself would demand that we explain it, that we carefully tease out the causal mechanisms that underpin his lasting influence (to be clear, he would also wave off our attempts to explain his "legacy" or "influence"). Those causal mechanisms are not only or even primarily found in his books and articles. They are embedded in the relationships he so carefully cultivated, using his humor, his generosity, and yes, his genius. We will miss our friend and colleague but have no doubt that much of what he inspired in his work will remain with us and future generations.

NOTES

1.   See the essay by James McAllister in this volume.
2.   Richard H. Immerman, Diane N. Labrosse, and Marc Trachtenberg, eds., *H-Diplo | ISSF Tribute to the Life, Scholarship, and Legacy of Robert Jervis*: Part I, February 4, 2004, https://issforum.org/ISSF/PDF/ISSF-Jervis-Tribute-1.pdf; and Part II, August 25, 2004, https://issforum.org/ISSF/PDF/ISSF-Jervis-Tribute-2.pdf. The second part includes Alexa Jervis's touching obituary for her father, along with a series of photographs from Bob's life. We thank Kathe Jervis for her generosity in allowing us to feature these photos. Page constraints and this volume's framework required the omission of a number of the essays published in the online forum. We want to acknowledge those authors, each of whom contributed valuably to honoring Bob and explaining his remarkable legacy. We thank Robert Art, Ken Booth and Nicholas J. Wheeler, Peter Clement, Michael Cox, Timothy W. Crawford, Robert Dallek, John Lewis Gaddis, Brendan Rittenhouse Green,

Lori Helene Gronich, Hope M. Harrison, Tsuyoshi Hasegawa, Jonathan Haslam, Roger Haydon, Paul Kennedy, Warren Kimball, Stephen Krasner, Austin Long, John Mearsheimer, Helen V. Milner, Sara Bjerg Moller, Dianne Pfundstein Chamberlain, Tonya Putnam, Mira Rapp-Hooper, Joshua Rovner, Scott D. Sagan, Mark S. Sheetz, Arthur Stein, and James J. Wirtz.

3.   Not all of his students were from Columbia. Richard Betts, for example, took his first class with Jervis in Harvard's Government Department.

4.   Sara Bjerg Moller, "Remembering Bob Jervis," *Tribute to Bob Jervis*, Part II.

5.   Timothy W. Crawford, "How Bob Helped Me: Direct and Indirect Effects," *Tribute to Bob Jervis*, Part I.

6.   Richard H. Immerman, "The Incomparable Robert Jervis," *Tribute to Bob Jervis*, Part I.

7.   Austin Long, "Bob Jervis: Never a War Lord, Always My Hero," *Tribute to Bob Jervis*, Part II.

8.   See the coda by Keren Yarhi-Milo in this volume.

9.   Robert J. Art, "Remembrances of the Bob Jervis I Knew," *Tribute to Bob Jervis*, Part I.

10.   Helen V. Milner, "Memorial to Bob Jervis," *Tribute to Bob Jervis*, Part I.

11.   This editor failed in her efforts. Jervis was an expert in that case as well.

12.   Roger Haydon, "Robert Jervis: Colleague and Friend," *Tribute to Bob Jervis*, Part I.

13.   See notes 10 and 8, Richard K. Betts's essay in this volume, and Arthur A, Stein, "Bob Jervis at UCLA: A Rembrance," *Tribute to Bob Jervis*, Part I.

14.   Betts in this volume.

15.   See "Obituary for Robert Jervis," https://networks.h-net.org/node/28443/discussions /9270091/obituary-robert-jervis.

16.   Tonya Putnam, "Remembrance of Bob Jervis, "*Tribute to Bob Jervis*, Part I.

17.   Putnam is quoting Nolan McCarty, December 10, 2021, https://twitter.com/Nolan_Mc /status/1469489384705642502?cxt=HHwWjMCyiemz1uQoAAAA.

18.   See the essay by Rose McDermott in this volume.

19.   See the essay by James W. Davis in this volume.

20.   See the essay by Diane N. Labrosse in this volume.

21.   See the essay by Dipali Mukhopadhyay in this volume.

22.   For an overview, see Robert Jervis, "Iraq WMD: What Everyone Knows Is Wrong," in *Why Intelligence Fails* (Cornell University Press, 2010). For a discussion, see Richard Immerman's essay in this volume.

23.   See the essays by Michael Warner and Melvyn P. Leffler in this volume.

ACKNOWLEDGMENTS

The editors offer their profound thanks to Kathe Jervis for generously sharing the photographs that appear on the book's cover (Bob Jervis at home, reading) and the inset (Jervis teaching at Columbia University). The third photograph captures Jervis giving a talk at the National Defense University, Washington, DC, USA, CC BY 2.0, via Wikimedia Commons. The fourth shot, of Jervis reading in his office at Columbia University, is reproduced with permission ©2019 JD Work, https://issforum.org/admin/jervis-tribute-part-1.

We also thank Jason Rudd and Christopher Ball for their excellent work in creating the high-resolution versions of the photographs that appear in this volume, Chris Ball for his production work for the online versions of these essays, and Mia Tellman, MIA student at SIPA, Class of 2026, for compiling the index.

APPENDIX

HOW I GOT HERE

ROBERT JERVIS

For as long as I can remember—and long before I knew there was a field called political science with a specialization in international politics—I was intrigued by politics. This was due to a combination of what must have been my inborn nature, the strongly political atmosphere of New York in the 1940s and 1950s, and, perhaps most of all, "events, dear boy, events," in the words that Prime Minister Harold Macmillan used to explain to an interviewer why his policies had changed.[1] Since I was born in 1940, my first memories were of World War II and then the Cold War. The early years of the latter led me to the question I would grapple with later in exploring deterrence and the spiral model as explanations of and prescriptions for conflict.[2] In fact, I remember pestering my parents about what they thought the US should do in response to the Soviet Union shooting down what I thought were innocent American airplanes in the late 1940s (I would have been shocked had I been told that the Soviets were correct to label these spy missions). Needless to say, this question recurs not only in my scholarship, but, more importantly, in world politics. When I started writing this essay in late January 2020, the newspapers carried a story about the American strikes against Iranian-backed militias in Syria and Iraq in retaliation for a rocket barrage that killed an American contractor. "The key question" according to the American reporter, "is whether the American counter attack can end the cycle of violence or escalate it."[3]

In fifth grade I organized a few classmates to produce a current-events newsletter. A strange hobby, perhaps, but it was not out of sync with the spirit of the times, at least not in New York liberal circles. McCarthyism and the Korean War heightened our worries, and because friends of my parents were called before various congressional committees, the issues were more than abstract.

Two other influences were important. My older brother, with whom I am now quite close, beat me up quite regularly, including once knocking out a (loose) tooth. From this I developed a healthy respect for the use of force, paired with an understanding that it made sense to avoid conflict if possible. The other influence was my fierce loyalty to the Brooklyn Dodgers, who in this period would often come close to the holy grail of the World Series, only to falter at the end. This torment was compounded by the fact that almost everyone else in my school rooted for the New York Yankees, and the result was a sympathy for the underdog. Perhaps the most crushing memory, and the last time I cried over anything other than a death, was Bobby Thompson's home run that defeated the Dodgers in the 1951 playoffs. Given my later interest in deception in international politics, I was glad when the story came out that he managed this not only because of the short left field fence in the Polo Grounds but because the Giants had stolen the sign and knew he was getting a fastball.

Being a good liberal, I did my bit by handing out leaflets for Adlai Stevenson in 1952 and 1956 (not that this mattered much in Manhattan). While I later learned from political scientist Fred Greenstein and many historians that Dwight D. Eisenhower was very skilled, and was perhaps was a better president than Stevenson would have been,[4] I still have great admiration for him and so was gratified many years later when I was given the Adlai Stevenson chair at my university. As documents from the Eisenhower administration became available and I was able to compare my contemporary views with a less biased and more accurate understanding, I learned (a bit of) humility and an appreciation of the importance of preserving and studying the historical record.

Until my junior year at Oberlin College, my interests were much more driven by current events than by scholarship. This is not to say that my high school and college courses in history and political science were bad—I had one marvelous course in early modern European history in high school and great courses in American politics and European history at Oberlin—but they did not give me powerful analytical tools for understanding what was happening. But the Oberlin library put new books on display, and in quick succession, I stumbled upon Thomas Schelling's *Strategy of Conflict* and Glenn Snyder's *Deterrence and Defense.*[5] I had already been deeply interested in nuclear strategy, or rather in the raging debates about the "missile gap," the commonly believed "fact" that the Soviets had a great advantage over the United States in this domain, and its consequences. Indeed, for my own benefit, I had written a paper on this subject in 1959. The theoretical structure it lacked was supplied by the Schelling and Snyder books, which are now recognized as classics. Among their foundational ideas is the importance of strategic interaction, i.e., that when rational states act, they do so anticipating how others will respond, knowing that the others are similarly anticipating what the actor will do. This and the other tools that were developed in these books led me to a much deeper understanding not only of nuclear strategy but also of a wide range of international politics, both current and past.

Schelling and Snyder became very important figures later in my life. Serendipitously, Berkeley had given Snyder a two-year visiting appointment, and so I enthusiastically took his field survey course in the fall of 1962. He was a very good instructor, but in the classroom as in his writings, he was not flashy or self-promoting. This low-key stance did not fit with the Berkeley department's drive to get to the top of the professional ladder, and so it foolishly let him go, thereby missing out on his two later milestone books, *Conflict Among Nations* (coauthored with Paul Diesing) and *Alliance Politics.*[6] Not only did I learn a great deal from Snyder's lectures, but his reading list included chapters from Arnold Wolfers's *Discord and Collaboration.*[7] Here I discovered the work of a founder of American realism (although of course he and the others were European émigrés) that made analytical sense to me. I had been assigned Hans Morgenthau's *Politics Among Nations,*[8] and at the time, I found it discursive and vague. I have revised my critical judgment of some of Morgenthau's other writings, but my evaluation of his textbook remains the same. Wolfers's essays, on the other hand, were clean, clear, and incisive. I think they can be read today to great advantage. I was also deeply impressed with Snyder as a person. Unassuming, he always listened carefully to students, many of whom did not deserve this attention, would spend time mulling over ideas, and greatly encouraged me to pursue my own. I was able to return the favor many years later when I urged my colleagues at the University of North Carolina to consider Glenn for their opening—he had been in for a talk but his low-key manner had not impressed.

I also audited a course by the great European diplomatic historian Raymond Sontag. His lectures were marvelous, and I still turn to his *European Diplomatic History, 1871–1932*,[9] but I looked in vain for the sort of probing for explanations and causes that I had grown accustomed to from Snyder and the readings he had assigned. I was fascinated by the events Sontag recounted and his ability to make sense of them but frustrated by the narrative's blurring of the line between description and explanation and the lack of focus on bringing evidence to bear on theoretical propositions. This was simply a different way of approaching the material.[10] He, like Snyder, cared deeply about his students, however, and when I went to visit him in his office hours, I was struck by the fact that he wrote my name and interests on a card that he placed in his massive file. But he also indicated that much as he appreciated the interests of political scientists like myself in European diplomatic history, he did not think that they could shed much light on the subject.

My view of the history discipline was very much as an outsider, and I missed most of the fascinating cross-currents that David Hollinger saw as a history graduate student.[11] As he notes, Sontag was of the older school, and the emerging trends in intellectual, social, and cultural history that caught the imagination of the younger faculty and students did not enter in.

Two episodes at Berkeley embodied the interaction of doing and studying politics. Given my commitment to civil liberties and civil rights, I was an active participant in the Free Speech Movement (FSM). The right to speak and organize that we were defending in the FSM was intended to combat racial discrimination in various commercial establishments in San Francisco. Although I had been active in student government in high school and college (and had chosen Berkeley partly because of its students' role in the protests against the House Un-American Activities Committee meeting in San Francisco), the FSM was on a larger stage and played for more serious stakes. While I can't say that I had much influence, I was struck by the importance of dedication and commitment, the large role for folly and error, the significance of accidents and luck, and the difficulty of any one actor of understanding the whole picture; as a prime example of this point, almost none of us understood the political pressures Clark Kerr, the reviled president of the university, was under. I also saw that my own political instincts and calculations often proved flawed if not entirely wrong, which offered a nice lesson in humility. Unlike many of my colleagues, neither the FSM experience nor my opposition to the Vietnam War (see below) moved my general political views. These were already deeply anchored. Those with much less political experience were more strongly buffeted by these winds.

The second instance involved the reverse flow from studying to changing a policy position. In the spring of 1963, I took a course on revolutions from Chalmers Johnson, the brilliant scholar of Japan, whose own political position moved from the right to the far left without pausing in between, and I wrote a paper on what was then called internal war and what we would now call insurgency and counterinsurgency. This study of past cases and relevant theories convinced me that the US could not win the war in South Vietnam, at least at a reasonable price, as long as the border with North Vietnam remained unsealed. Unlike many of my liberal colleagues, however, I did not think that the war was immoral, that the North Vietnamese regime was benign, or that the marvelous solution of neutralization was available. My later research was to study the propensity of people to avoid difficult value trade-offs and the prevalence of rationalizations to ease the burdens of choice, but even then I saw that a negotiated solution, nice as it would be, was simply beyond reach. Like many in my generation, however, I am drawn back to the Vietnam War, teach about it, and have written a bit on it.[12] Here too the documents, first in the *Pentagon Papers* and later in the *Foreign Relations of the United States* volumes, tell us how much of the story we could not see at the time.[13]

As an aside, I should mention that although the Vietnam War did not have much impact on the political science discipline, my sense is that it did strongly affect the field of diplomatic history. On the positive side, it induced a more critical perspective on American foreign policy and a refusal to take official justifications at face value. So far, so good, but in my view, much of the field went too far in seeing American blundering as either uniquely American or the product of capitalism (with the implication that other economic and social systems would behave differently) and, relatedly, by transmuting moral condemnation into cheap moralism, with the implication that we academics not only know more than the policymakers at the time but are morally superior to them. Vietnam also contributed to the flight of historians from international political history.

Academic study, perhaps also combined with Vietnam, also affected my political views on the question that had preoccupied me from the beginning: whether, when, and how conflicts are best dealt with by threats or by conciliation, or, of course, how these approaches can be sequenced and interwoven. I started working on deterrence and the spiral model as alternative descriptions of and prescriptions for the Cold War with a strong bias toward deterrence. But immersion in the relevant theories, the analysis of perception and misperception, and a wide range of historical cases led me to have more sympathy for the spiral model. In the end, while I continue to study and teach about the Cold War, my conclusions remain fluid.[14]

As I continued to read history, I became more convinced that not only was chess a wildly inaccurate model for international politics (the rules are established and all play is open), but even poker (with its role for deception) is inadequate. In fact, actors often live in very different worlds, fail to perceive each other accurately, and, even more, do not appreciate this. The best picture is then provided by the Japanese short story and movie *Rashomon*, which reveals that each actor sees the situation very differently and usually in a self-serving manner.

It was thanks to Schelling, to whom I had sent my early work on signaling, that I owe the two years of research at Harvard's Center for International Affairs (CFIA) that was so important for my later career. To digress, I want to note that without disclaiming the virtues of the papers I had sent Schelling, getting this position involved a good bit of luck. Without it, my research and career would not have been nearly as successful. In those two years, I was able to complete my first book on signaling and deception (in retrospect, this would have been a much better title than *The Logic of Images in International Relations*[15]), which was built on the scholarship of Schelling and the imaginative sociologist Erving Goffman[16] and was a combination of rational choice and constructivism, both *avant la lettre*. Not surprisingly, it did not fit any of the categories in the field but did spark the interest of a PhD student of Schelling's in economics, Michael Spence, who went on to win a Nobel Prize for his approach to signaling.

An additional benefit of these years was meeting lifelong friends of my generation in political science and coming into close contact with three others. Schelling had brought me to Harvard, his written work was and remains a lodestar for mine, and we established a friendship that ended only with his death. The second was Kenneth Waltz, who, on his sabbatical year, had the office next to me at the CFIA. We talked literally every day, often for several hours (it got to the point where when his wife wanted to reach him, she phoned my office first). Talking to Waltz allowed me to pick up where I had left off with Glenn Snyder (the two of them were also good friends), and I realized in a combination of delight and horror how little of the field I had learned at Berkeley. Guided by Ken, and having the gift of being free of teaching and administration, I read and thought much more than I had before. His approach to rigorous social science theorizing and to the analysis of systems served me well in the rest of my career. I was overjoyed when, after retiring from Berkeley, Ken and his wife moved back to New York and he became an affiliate of the institute that had been founded by his mentor, Bill Fox.

The third friendship was with Samuel Williamson, an assistant professor in the history department. He taught me a great deal about the origins of World War I, pointed me to other important books in his field, and helped start the dialogue with history and historians that I have sought to maintain ever since. Williamson himself sank to becoming a university president but fortunately did not abandon scholarship, and anyone in early twentieth-century international politics should read his books and articles.[17]

Much of the rest of my career can be read in my CV, so here I just want to pick up a couple of themes. First is the continuing involvement with the field of history. Although I have not plumbed cases and trends to the depth of some of my colleagues and students,[18] continuing conversations with historians, especially Robert Dallek, John Gaddis, Mel Leffler, Paul Kennedy, Paul Schroeder, and Marc Trachtenberg, have enriched my life, my teaching, and my own writings. Rather than trying to summarize what I have learned from each, I will be content to say that in addition to developing a deep appreciation for the historian's craft, I have thought more about the contrast between the typical political science method of comparing cases in order to try to establish the causal efficacy of various factors (an approach that usually assumes that cases are independent of each other) and the historian's sensibility that the backbone of understanding is chronology and that events, trends, and "cases" (a term that historians would not use) are not independent but rather are strongly influenced by what has preceded them.

Throughout the rest of my career, academic scholarship and current politics continued to intersect and enrich each other.[19] Three instances stand out. First, when I became a consultant to the CIA in the fall of 1978, I rekindled my interest in nuclear strategy, which was then a subject to raging debates centering on the state of the nuclear balance and whether the Soviet leaders believed, to take part of the title of one influential article that grew out of an official study, that they "Could Fight and Win a Nuclear War."[20] I not only closely followed the public debates (and listened to, without being persuaded by, the hawkish arguments of the famed nuclear strategist Albert Wohlstetter)[21] but was now able to read many of the classified studies. These convinced me that official thinking was superficial and failed to come to grips with the insights of theorists like my UCLA colleague Bernard Brodie and the clear thinking of Tom Schelling. Instead, they viewed nuclear weapons within the intellectual framework of earlier eras in which military victory was possible, an error that Hans Morgenthau labeled "conventionalization,"[22] rather than grasping the implications of what I and others called the nuclear revolution.[23]

This led me to think more deeply about the subject, culminating in two books in which I sought to both intervene in the policy debate and lay out fairly rigorous analytical arguments. Their validity is of course subject to debate, as is their relevance for contemporary politics.[24] I cannot do justice to the issues here but just want to note that I would not have gotten deeply into these questions were it not for having to confront how they were playing out within the government.[25] This involvement not only carries the obvious risk that policy preferences will drive analysis but also brings out the tensions between the descriptive and the normative aspects of many of our theories.[26] As I was working at the CIA, it became apparent that, contrary that what had been foreseen, Iran was entering the throes of a revolution. Because Deputy CIA Director Robert Bowie was a former colleague who knew of my work on misperception, I was asked to write a postmortem. This was a fascinating experience that taught me quite a bit about how the government worked and led me to propose a similar study of the Iraq intelligence failure a generation later. Although the former had only a slight impact on the way the US did its intelligence business, the latter, combined with internal studies, did I think make a positive contribution, and I was able to mine both cases for insights into how individuals and organizations processed information under difficult circumstances.[27]

This pattern continued even without exposure to inside information. The election of President Donald Trump was not only an unpleasant surprise but also led me to think about how his term in office would test various IR theories. A few weeks after Rex Tillerson was appointed secretary of state, lecturing to my introductory undergraduate course led me to think that the arguments of Richard Neustadt on presidential power pointed to the likelihood that Tillerson would be extraordinarily weak.[28]

In light of the discussion of the gap between IR social science and policy relevance,[29] it is worth noting that my slight entrée into the policy world and even slighter influence has come much less through my writings on policy than by the fact that a range of middle-level officials are familiar with my academic writings (and also that a number of my students have gone into the government either at the working levels or for short-term political assignments).

Not all my research was sparked by policy concerns, however. My work on the dynamics of systems was not. Initially spawned by an invitation to contribute to Tom Schelling's *Festschrift*, it built on ideas of strategic interaction and Schelling's collection of marvelous essays explicating how collective outcomes could diverge from individual desires and actions,[30] to discuss selection effects and other ways in which the anticipations of how others would respond were central to a wide range of political and social patterns.[31] I later expanded this into *System Effects*, which I think is my most important book because it applies to so much of human (and animal) life.[32] Drawing not only on Schelling but also on psychology and, especially, ecology and evolution, I tried to elucidate the mechanisms that arise when multiple actors and influences are interconnected, often in ways that make tracing causation impossible before the fact and difficult afterward, confounding many of our standard notions about causation that are derived from the belief that we can compare cases holding all but one variable constant.[33] We then often see unintended consequences, nonlinearities, various forms of feedbacks, and coevolution of actors and their environments (to the extent that these can be meaningfully distinguished).

All of this is further complicated when the actors have their own ideas about the workings of the system. This perspective has parallels to historians' sense of the ironies of history and to the view that John Gaddis developed in his *Landscape of History*.[34] Not being anchored in pressing political science debates, this book has received less attention in the discipline than others I have written, but it has gained readers in other fields and been assigned in at least one medical school class. Its contribution is to expand our ways of thinking to deal with complexity; those who are intrigued can read the quotation that begins the book and do not have to read further if they see the dangerous oversimplification that it embodies.

Reading in the diverse fields that constituted my research and writing the book were great fun and led me to see the world in a different way. This enjoyment and stimulation that we hope leads to a collective better understanding of the world is of course the point of our shared enterprise.

NOTES

1. In fact, although the saying is well known, it may be apocryphal: Robert Harris, "As Macmillan Never Said," *The Telegraph*, June 4, 2002, https://www.telegraph.co.uk/comment/personal-view/3577416/As-Macmillan-never-said-thats-enough-quotations.html.

2. Robert Jervis, *Perception and Misperception in International Politics* (Princeton University Press, 1976; 2nd ed., 2017), chap. 3.

3. Julian E. Barnes, "U.S. Attacks Iranian-Backed Forces in Iraq and Syria in Retaliatory Strikes," *New York Times*, December 30, 2019.

4. Fred I. Greenstein, *The Hidden-Hand Presidency: Eisenhower as Leader* (Basic, 1962).

5. Thomas C, Schelling, *The Strategy of Conflict* (Harvard University Press, 1960); Glenn Herakd Snyder, *Deterrence and Defense: Toward a Theory of National Security* (Princeton University Press, 1961).

6. Glenn Herald Snyder and Paul Diesing, *Conflict Among Nations: Bargaining, Decision Making, and System Structure in International Crises* (Princeton University Press, 1977); Glenn Herald Snyder, *Alliance Politics* (Cornell University Press, 1997).

7. Arnold Wolfers, *Discord and Collaboration: Essays on International Politics* (Johns Hopkins University Press, 1965).

8. Hans Morgenthau, *Politics Among Nations*, 2nd ed. (Knopf, 1959).

9. Raymond J. Sontag, *European Diplomatic History, 1871–1932* (Appleton-Century-Crofts, 1933).

10. For my own discussions of the difference between international relations scholars and international historians, see "Diplomatic History and International Relations: Why Are They Studied So Differently?" in Miriam Fendius Elman and Colin Elman, eds., *Bridges and Boundries: Historians, Political Scientists, and the Study of International Relations* (MIT Press, 2001); and "International Politics and Diplomatic History: Fruitful Differences," H-Diplo, June 2009, https://issforum.org/ISSF/PDF/ISSF-Jervis-InauguralAddress.pdf.

11. David A. Hollinger, "Between Samuel Flagg Bemis and Perry Miller," February 8, 2020, https://hdiplo.org/to/E189.

12. Robert Jervis, "The Politics of Troop Withdrawal," *Diplomatic History* 34, no. 3 (2010): 507–16; "Audience Costs and Vietnam: A Comment on Lewis and Trachtenberg," H-Diplo/ISSF Forum, no. 3, November 2014, http://issforum.org/ISSF/PDF/ISSF-Forum-3.pdf.

13. Just to mention one fascinating study I draw on for my thinking and teaching about on diplomacy, see James G. Hershberg, *Marigold: The Lost Chance for Peace in Vietnam* (Stanford University Press, 2012).

14. Robert Jervis, "The Impact off the Korean War on the Cold War," *Journal of Conflict Resolution* 24 (1980): 563–92; Jervis, "Was the Cold War a Security Dilemma?," *Journal of Cold War Studies* 3 (2001): 36–60; Jervis, "Identity and the Cold War," in *The Cambridge History of the Cold War*, vol. 2, ed. Melvyn P. Leffler and Odd Arne Westad (Cambridge University Press, 2010).

15. Robert Jervis, *The Logic of Images in International Relations* (Princeton University Press, 1970; 2nd ed., Columbia University Press, 1989).

16. Erving Goffman, *The Presentation of Self in Everyday Life* (Doubleday, 1959).

17. See, for example, Samuel Williamson *The Politics of Grand Strategy: Britain and France Prepare for War, 1904–1914* (Ashfield, 1990); Williamson, *Austria-Hungary and the Origins of the First World War* (Macmillan, 1991); Williamson and Ernest May, "An Identity of Opinion: Historians and July 1914," *Journal of Modern History* 79 (2007): 335–87.

18. See, for example, Jack Snyder, *The Ideology of the Offensive* (Cornell University Press, 1984); Snyder, *Myths of Empire: Domestic Politics and International Affairs* (Cornell University Press, 1991); Jack S. Levy, *War in the Modern Great Power System, 1495–1975* (University Press of Kentucky, 1983) and articles too numerous to cite; James McAllister, *No Exit: America and the German Problem, 1943–1954* (Cornell University Press, 2001).

19. For more on this, see my "Politics and Political Science," *Annual Review of Political Science* 21 (2018): 1–19.

20. Richard Pipes, "Why the Soviet Union Thinks It Could Fight and Win a Nuclear War," *Commentary*, July 1977.

21. See my contribution to the roundtable review of Ron Robin's biography of Albert and Roberta Wohlstetter, *The Cold War They Made*, http://issforum.org/ISSF/PDF/ISSF-Roundtable-10-17.pdf.

22. Hans Morgenthau, "The Fallacy of Thinking Conventionally About Nuclear Weapons," in *Arms Control and Technological Innovation*, ed. David Carlton and Carlo Schaerf (Wiley, 1976).

23. For my own thinking, see *The Illogic of American Nuclear Strategy* (Cornell University Press, 1984) and *The Meaning of the Nuclear Revolution* (Cornell University Press, 1989). I have updated and extended some of these ideas in "The Nuclear Age: During and After the Cold War," in *Before and After the Fall: World Politics and the End of the Cold War*, ed. N. P. Monteiro and F. Bartel (Cambridge University Press, 2021).

24. See the symposium on the thirtieth anniversary of the publication of *The Meaning of the Nuclear Revolution*: "Book Review Roundtable: The Meaning of the Nuclear Revolution

30 Years Later," *Texas National Security Review*, April 30, 2020, https://tnsr.org/roundtable /book-review-roundtable-the-meaning-of-the-nuclear-revolution-30-years-later/.

25. My own experience is far from unique; in fact, the field of nuclear strategy developed through close contact with pressing policy issues, as I have explained in "Security Studies: Ideas, Policy, and Politics," in *The Evolution of Political Knowledge*, ed. Edward D. Mansfield and Richard Sisson (Ohio State University Press, 2004).

26. I discussed this further in "International Politics and Diplomatic History."

27. Robert Jervis, *Why Intelligence Fails: Lessons from the Iranian Revolution and the Iraq War* (Cornell University Press, 2010).

28. Robert Jervis, "President Trump and IR Theory, International Security Studies Forum Policy Series, American and the World—2017 and Beyond," January 2, 2017, http://issforum .org/ISSF/PDF/Policy-Roundtable-1-5B.pdf; Jervis, "Rex Tillerson Might Be the Weakest Secretary of State Ever," *Foreign Policy*, March 10, 2017, https://foreignpolicy.com/2017 /03/10/rex-tillerson-might-be-the-weakest-secretary-of-state-ever/. Neustadt's pathbreaking and still relevant book is *Presidential Power: The Politics of Leadership* (New American Library, 1960).

29. See, for example, Michael C. Desch, *Cult of the Irrelevant: The Waning Influence of Social Science on National Security* (Princeton University Press, 2019); also see the review essay on this book by Lawrence Freedman, "Cult of the Irrelevant: The Waning Influence of Social Science on National Security," *Journal of Strategic Studies* 42 (2019): 1027–37.

30. Thomas C. Schelling, *Micromotives and Macrobehavior* (Norton, 2006).

31. Robert Jervis, "Systems Effects," in *Strategy and Choice*, ed. Richard Zeckhauser (MIT Press, 1991).

32. Robert Jervis, *System Effects: Complexity in Political and Social Life* (Princeton University Press, 1997).

33. I discussed this further in "Causation and Responsibility in a Complex World," in *Back to Basics: State Power in a Contemporary World*, ed. Martha Finnemore and Judith Goldstein (Oxford University Press, 2013).

34. John Lewis Gaddis, *The Landscape of History: How Historians Map the Past* (Oxford University Press, 2002).

CONTRIBUTORS

VOLKER R. BERGHAHN is the Seth Low Emeritus Professor of History at Columbia University.

RICHARD K. BETTS is Leo A. Shifrin Professor of War and Peace Studies at Columbia and adjunct senior fellow at the Council on Foreign Relations.

THOMAS J. CHRISTENSEN is James T. Shotwell Professor of International Relations and director of the China and the World Program at Columbia University's School of International and Public Affairs. He is also the Pritzker Chair at the Center for International and Strategic Affairs.

JAMES W. DAVIS is professor of political science and director of the Institute of Political Science at the University of St. Gallen, Switzerland.

MICHAEL DOYLE is a university professor of Columbia University with appointments in International Affairs, Law, and Political Science.

JAMES D. FEARON is the Theodore and Frances Geballe Professor in Stanford University's School of Humanities and Sciences, professor of political science, and a senior fellow at the Freeman-Spogli Institute for International Studies.

SIR LAWRENCE FREEDMAN was Professor of War Studies at King's College London from 1982 to 2014. He was the official historian of the Falklands Campaign and a member of the official UK Inquiry into the Iraq War.

CHARLES L. GLASER is a senior fellow in the Security Studies Program at MIT and a professor emeritus of political science and international affairs at George Washington University.

STACIE E. GODDARD is the Betty Freyhof Johnson '44 Professor of Political Science and faculty director of the Madeleine Korbel Albright Institute for Global Affairs at Wellesley College.

JAMES GOLDGEIER is a professor of international relations at American University, a visiting scholar at Stanford University's Center for International Security and Cooperation, and a visiting fellow at the Brookings Institution.

RICHARD H. IMMERMAN is emeritus professor and Edward Buthusiem Distinguished Faculty Fellow in History and Marvin Wachman Emeritus Director of the Center for the Study of Force and Diplomacy at Temple University.

RONALD R. KREBS is a professor of political science at the University of Minnesota and editor in chief of *Security Studies*.

DIANE N. LABROSSE is the executive and managing editor of H-Diplo and senior editor of H-Diplo/The Jervis Forum (RJISSF).

DEBORAH WELCH LARSON is a professor of political science at the University of California, Los Angeles.

MELVYN P. LEFFLER is professor emeritus at the University of Virginia.

JACK S. LEVY is the Board of Governors' Professor of Political Science at Rutgers University and a senior research scholar at the Saltzman Institute of War and Peace Studies at Columbia University.

DOUG MACDONALD is professor emeritus of political science at Colgate University

PAUL K. MACDONALD is a professor of political science at Wellesley College.

JAMES McALLISTER is the Fred Greene Third Century Professor of Political Science at Williams College.

ROSE McDERMOTT is David and Marianna Fisher University Professor of International Relations at Brown University.

JONATHAN MERCER is a professor in the Department of Political Science at the University of Washington.

DIPALI MUKHOPADHYAY is an associate professor in the School of Advanced International Studies at Johns Hopkins University.

JOSEPH M. PARENT is a professor of political science at the University of Notre Dame.

CYNTHIA ROBERTS is a professor of political science at Hunter College, City University of New York, and adjunct professor and senior research scholar at the Saltzman Institute of War and Peace Studies, Columbia University.

ELIZABETH N. SAUNDERS is a professor of political science at Columbia University and the director of the Saltzman Institute of War and Peace Studies.

RANDALL L. SCHWELLER is a professor of political science, director of the Program for the Study of Realist Foreign Policy, a Social and Behavioral Sciences Joan N. Huber Faculty Fellow at Ohio State University, and former editor in chief of *Security Studies*.

JACK SNYDER is Robert and Renée Belfer Professor of International Relations in the Department of Political Science and the Saltzman Institute of War and Peace Studies, Columbia University.

JANICE GROSS STEIN is Belzberg Professor of Conflict Management and founding director of the Munk School of Global Affairs and Public Policy at the University of Toronto.

PHILIP E. TETLOCK is the Annenberg University Professor at the University of Pennsylvania.

MARC TRACHTENBERG is a research professor of political science at the University of California, Los Angeles.

ROBERT F. TRAGER is an associate professor of political science at the University of California, Los Angeles and the strategic modeling team lead at the Centre for the Governance of Artificial Intelligence.

STEPHEN M. WALT is Robert and Renée Belfer Professor of International Affairs at the John F. Kennedy School of Government at Harvard University.

MICHAEL WARNER serves as a historian in the US Department of Defense.

KEREN YARHI-MILO is dean of Columbia University's School of International and Public Affairs and the Adlai E. Stevenson Professor of International Relations.

VLADISLAV ZUBOK is a professor of international history at the London School of Economics and Political Science.

INDEX

GPSR Authorized Representative: Easy Access System Europe, Mustamäe tee
50, 10621 Tallinn, Estonia, gpsr.requests@easproject.com